D1597006

NARRATIVE THREADS

JOE R. AND TERESA LOZANO LONG SERIES IN
LATIN AMERICAN AND LATINO ART AND CULTURE

NARRATIVE THREADS
Accounting and Recounting in Andean Khipu

EDITED BY JEFFREY QUILTER AND GARY URTON

UNIVERSITY OF TEXAS PRESS, AUSTIN

First edition, 2002

Requests for permission to reproduce material from this work should be sent to
Permissions, University of Texas Press, Box 7819, Austin, TX 78713-7819.

⊗ The paper used in this book meets the minimum requirements of ANSI/NISO
Z39.48-1992 (R1997) (Permanence of Paper).

LIBRARY OF CONGRESS CATALOGING-IN-PUBLICATION DATA
Narrative threads : accounting and recounting in Andean Khipu / edited by
Jeffrey Quilter and Gary Urton.
    p.   cm. — (Joe R. and Teresa Lozano Long series in Latin American
and Latino art and culture)
Includes bibliographical references and index.
ISBN 0-292-76903-2 (cloth : alk. paper)
1. Quipu—History—Sources.   2. Incas—Mathematics.   I. Quilter, Jeffrey,
[date]   II. Urton, Gary, [date]   III. Series.
F3429.3.Q6 N37   2002
302.2'22—dc21   2002000247

FOR SARAH AND JULIA

CONTENTS

Color illustrations follow page 204.

ACKNOWLEDGMENTS

This book is the outgrowth of a round table held at Dumbarton Oaks in 1997. We thank Angeliki Laiou, then director of Dumbarton Oaks, for supporting that round table. Janice Williams, who served as assistant to the director of Pre-Columbian Studies, was essential in organizing the myriad details that brought scholars from many different locations to Washington, D.C., for the meeting and in attending to their well-being during it.

Transforming the round table into a publication was the work of many hands. Rebecca Willson, in particular, successfully grappled with the huge tasks of standardizing the authors' manuscripts and of patiently working with editorial anxieties and demands, both far and near. Although her tenure as the assistant to the director, succeeding Ms. Williams, was brief, her role was vital and she is much thanked. Cecilia Montalvo was third in succession to the post and to the tasks associated with this book. She, too, ably lived up to many demands and is thanked most heartily. At Colgate University, Kristen Bentley ('99) and Bridget Benisch ('01) were successive research assistants to Gary Urton and likewise provided meritorious service in the creation of this book. Others at Dumbarton Oaks who variously helped to advance this project were Carol Calloway, Loa Traxler, Jennifer Younger, Billie Follensbee, and Joe Mills.

We offer sincere thanks for editorial guidance and support from Theresa May, Carolyn Wylie, and their staffs at the University of Texas Press, as well as from freelance editor Nancy Warrington. And, of course, we appreciate all the efforts given by our authors to producing the studies that constitute this book.

PREFACE   *Jeffrey Quilter*

In 1922, the founder of modern Mesoamerican iconographic research, Eduard Seler, died in Berlin. Although a number of important advances in the study of Maya hieroglyphic writing had already been accomplished, the field was still in its infancy.[1] A year later, in 1923, L. Leland Locke published *The Ancient Quipu or Peruvian Knot Record*, in which he presented the basic understanding of khipu maintained to the present. Despite an early precociousness, however, the study of khipu has lagged far behind the decipherment of Maya glyphs. This seems all the more remarkable because Mayanists were handicapped for decades by Sir J. Eric Thompson, who, though he was only just entering Cambridge University in 1922, later actively discouraged acceptance of the glyphs as true writing. Though Locke did not have as much influence over Andean studies as a whole as did Thompson over Mayanist studies, he was insistent that khipu only recorded numbers. A principal goal of this book is to question that dictum.

Given that Maya hieroglyphs and Andean khipu are two of the very few elaborated record-keeping systems of the ancient New World, why have investigations in one advanced so rapidly in comparison to the other? The answer to this question is not straightforward. One simple factor is that there are far more Mesoamericanists than Andeanists. The countries of Middle America have been easier to reach from Europe and the United States than those of the distant Andes. Thus, more and a greater variety of scholars from afar have traveled to the lands of the Maya, creating a fairly large international scholarly community.

It may also be argued that initial conditions for scholarly research have kept Mesoamerican and Andean studies following early established directions. Although Seler had wide-ranging interests in all of the Americas, he specialized in Mesoamerica. His legacy, as well as those of other Mesoamericanist scholarly pioneers, engendered subsequent generations of students who continued working in the same areas and on the same problems as their predecessors while training the next generation of scholars, who did the same.

Another factor that has helped to encourage Maya studies is the attraction Maya art and architecture have had for Westerners. Even though we now know that much of the tropical forest was cut down to support Maya centers, the discovery of ruins "lost" within dark jungles appealed to nineteenth-century romantic sensibilities. When the forest was cut back, ruins exposed, and tombs opened, Maya art was found to be mysterious but not entirely unapproachable. Here were depicted human forms bedecked in elaborate costumes performing bizarre rituals, or monkey-headed figures swaggering with strange accouterments. Although debate raged as to whether these were gods or kings, the art was original, attractive, and recognizable as representational to a greater or lesser degree.

Peering at the remains of this strange ancient world, early explorers found glyphs everywhere. They were carved on buildings, painted on ceramics, incised into jades, bone, and shell. They wrapped themselves around lintels and doorways. They covered the backs of stelae and the fronts of large panels and were delicately painted in the few Maya books preserved from destruction by the Spaniards. The sheer quantity of hieroglyphs used in Maya elite life and the way texts were inextricably associated with art made them impossible to ignore. And, not least of all, the glyphs were beautiful. The labor and skill it took to carve them in limestone or jade and the ways in which the symbols themselves were ornamented or varied to produce an aesthetic statement of their own, in addition to what they may have said, left no doubt that the Maya considered these signs as important and valuable.

Maya hieroglyphics were exotic and strange, but though arguments were made as to *what* these signs said, it was rarely doubted that they said *something*. Sir Eric Thompson slowed the course of the study of Maya writing because he believed that the glyphs could not be deciphered and that they only offered information on calendrics and astronomy. They could not be deciphered, he believed, because the system on which they were based was not a logical one and the glyphs were not constructed phonetically. Information on calendrics and astronomy was of interest, but, in Thompson's opinion, studying these arcane topics would not advance the understanding of larger issues of Maya politics, economy, and other matters that could only be revealed through field archaeology.

In the Andes, the keepers of the khipu, the Inka, have not appealed to the romantic sensibilities of Westerners as have the Maya. Scholars of the Inka have too long been caught up in debates as to whether the Inka Empire was the ideal socialist state or the worst example of fascism, and in the process, the Inka have come across as a people as cold, aloof, and abstract as their chilly mountain home. If the Maya have been cast as the Greeks of the New World, delighting in the pleasures of the senses, the Inka have been given the role of the dull, stoical Romans, building a huge empire but not having much fun while doing so. These images, of course, are the conceits of Western minds, but they have contributed much to how the fields of study of these ancient peoples have fared.

There are many differences between Maya hieroglyphs and Inka khipu. Although glyphs could be carved as three-dimensional statues, they generally were inscribed in two dimensions, on flat surfaces, much as in any other writing system. Khipu, however, are expressions of linearity, made up of cords, which are at the same time three-dimensional objects. Hieroglyphs are graphic and have a strong representational component, while khipu are material and kinesthetic: the medium of the khipu is bound up with the message in a way that hieroglyphs are not. Although there are variations in how glyphs are rendered, ultimately, it is the formal characteristics of the inscribed signs that convey meaning. For khipu, knots and their placements, the twists of cords, color combinations, and likely other elements all seem to play important roles in conveying information.

Perhaps as important as the points already made, if Maya glyphs can be appreciated as art as well as a medium for communication, khipu seem to be merely an extension of folk craft. Knotted strings, perhaps too reminiscent of macramé wall hangings, do not appeal to Western artistic tastes as do the brush strokes of a Maya scribe or limestone blocks carved as if they were butter. This point could be a departure for discussion of the whole issue of the Western distinction between art and craft, but it is more worthwhile to emphasize that khipu express their own form of beauty once one is familiar with them and that such beauty is in their tactility—an aesthetic realm severely underappreciated in the visually oriented West, where "Do not touch" signs are all too prevalent. The aesthetic sensibilities of Andean peoples are still waiting to be adequately discussed in Western literature. An assumption that khipu were merely utilitarian devices—like tying a string around a finger so as not to forget to feed the neighbor's cat—may be partly to blame for lack of interest in them. That khipu were more than simple reminders, that they were sophisticated and complex systems, is another important message of this book.

These various issues have led to different perspectives on approaching khipu. Many scholars presumed early on that the Maya were conveying meanings with their hieroglyphs, and khipu scholars knew that the Inka kept accounts with knotted strings. But did they do more than record numbers with khipu? As both Robert Ascher and Marcia Ascher point out in their chapters in this book, numbers may be interpreted as magnitudes or quantities, but they can also be interpreted as labels, and these labels may have narrative properties and functions. Thus, numbers signified by knots, along with knot directionality, the colors of cords, and other elements that made up khipu, may all have been used to convey narrative information.

It is interesting that despite differences in the nature of Maya hieroglyphs and Inka khipu, issues of understanding how these systems worked have revolved around similar problems of interpretation. These interpretive problems have not been due primarily to the inherent ways khipu and glyph systems were constructed but rather to the ways in which they were explained to Spanish investigators in the sixteenth century and to subsequent assumptions about and interpretations of what the Spanish said concerning native recording systems.

Diego de Landa, bishop of Yucatán, interviewed Maya scribes and had a Spanish alphabet written with what he thought were the Maya equivalents of Spanish letters. In doing this, he created a document that has been essential in deciphering Maya script but has also produced confusion and debate. Landa made the assumption that Maya writing was alphabetic, but it is not. When Landa or an assistant spoke the sound for a letter of the Spanish alphabet, the Maya scribes heard what they took to be a word or sound in their own language. They then wrote down the glyph for the word or sound, not a letter. This issue of the relation of signs to sounds was a chief problem in accepting the Landa syllabary. Once what had happened in Landa's *scriptorium* was clarified, the Landa document became an important tool for understanding how to read Maya hieroglyphs.

We have had no single authoritative colonial record of an extended investigation of khipu but rather a number of colonial authors who discuss khipu at greater or lesser lengths. Much of what they say is unclear or contradictory, yet there are strong indications that khipu did not simply record numbers but also kept records of poems, histories, and other narratives. The earliest breakthrough in understanding Maya writing was the identification of number notation, but scholars now can read histories and other texts. For khipu, though, there has been no significant advancement beyond the ability to read numbers. In this book, however, Carlos Sempat Assadourian provides a careful discussion of the remarks by the colonial author Antonio Calancha on how to make a khipu that tells a story. The degree to which we can rely upon Calancha's account, however, is uncertain, and we may be on the same kind of uncertain ground concerning his understanding of what Andean people were telling him, as well as the accommodations those people made to allow their system to be understandable to Calancha, as was the case with Landa and his Maya scribes.

Understanding khipu thus involves not only finding and examining colonial sources about how knotted-string records were made and used but also evaluating how we should interpret those accounts, when found. Are the apparently contradictory and unclear discussions of khipu due to lack of full understanding by colonial authors of how khipu worked, or do at least some of these different accounts express variations among khipu themselves? Added to the exploration of narrativity and the demonstration of complexity in khipu, the issue of standardization versus idiosyncrasy in khipu is the third theme of this book. Although writing systems can tolerate a certain degree of deviation from some standard, such as variant spellings of words in British as opposed to American English, there must be general intercommunicability in a writing system, as was the case with Maya glyphs. For khipu to approximate a writing system, then, they had to have been able to be read by more than just their makers.

Many of the important advances in the study of Maya hieroglyphs occurred at or through the agency of Dumbarton Oaks. In this tradition, it seemed appropriate to hold a meeting here on the issue of narrativity in Andean khipu. Gary Urton and I thus organized a meeting of leading scholars on the topic at Dumbarton Oaks in April 1997. Many of the chapters in this book are revised versions of papers given during that meeting, and others are new contributions.

The book opens with two chapters intended to provide the reader with background material. In the first chapter, Gary Urton reviews the history of khipu studies, beginning with accounts from the early Spanish chronicles and documents. Rosaleen Howard's following discussion of narrativity in contemporary Quechua stories underlines the critical role language and linguistic studies hold for decipherments. The study of Coptic was crucial for the eventual decipherment of Egyptian hieroglyphs, and Maya studies languished for many years because the earliest attempts at translation disregarded the study of contemporary Mayan languages and instead worked primarily on solving the riddle of the glyphs solely as symbolic representations. Thus, emphasizing language studies in the investigations of khipu may be critical for future advances in decipherment, although alternate approaches will undoubtedly have their own contributions to make, as well.

William Conklin discusses important technical issues on his way to developing a theory for the organization of information in knotted-string records. Additional theoretical perspectives are provided in the contributions of Marcia Ascher and Robert Ascher, with the former discussing numbers as both magnitudes and labels while the latter explores how encipherment and decipherment may have been performed on khipu without depending directly on language.

Examining common features and variability in how communication systems develop and change will be important in future work, as I discuss in my contribution. Gary Urton looks at such variability in khipu themselves in his second chapter, comparing Garcilaso de la Vega's commentaries in light of a class of known non-numerical khipu. Carlos Sempat Assadourian provides insight on another colonial commentator on khipu, Antonio Calancha, as noted above. A third colonial writer, Blas Valera, is discussed in Sabine Hyland's contribution.

Following the discussions based on colonial sources' descriptions of khipu is a series of chapters on khipu use in the same era: Tristan Platt comments on one of the few eyewitness accounts of khipu in use in a public setting, and Regina Harrison focuses on rosaries and khipu in the arena of competing yet analogous religious practices.

The chapters of the next section demonstrate that khipu are still vital parts of native Andean culture. The contributions by Frank Salomon and Carol Mackey reveal the rich sources of information available on the maintenance of special places for khipu in the Andes and the continuing use of knotted-string records, respectively.

Gary Urton and I and the other authors represented in this collection hope that this book will not only establish a benchmark in khipu studies but also stimulate a wider interest in investigating these materials. Considering recent advances in mathematics, information theory, and other scholarship involved with computers, software, and communications technology, the study of khipu should appeal to many who are challenged and intrigued by puzzle solving. Perhaps this book will stimulate someone to be the Jean François Champollion of the khipu.

To call for a Champollion of the khipu implies that someone can "crack" the code of the knots in the same way that the great French Egyptologist made a breakthrough in understanding Egyptian hieroglyphics. But it remains uncertain whether we will ever be able to "read" a khipu the way we now can read an Egyptian or a Maya hieroglyphic text. Even in the case of Maya writing, its code was not so much broken—as a Gordian knot cleanly sliced through—as it was chipped away at: a little hole was gradually made bigger until, eventually, a critical mass was reached and the wall of ignorance came tumbling down.

Will we be able to unravel the mysteries of the khipu? We are at such an early stage of investigation—only beginning to tug at the knot—that it is hard to say. The archives are full of documents yet to be seen or studied, and the tradition of knotted-string records in the New World is hardly known. There is not yet even a thorough inventory and description of the known khipu in existence, a corpus of about five hundred items, which, if documented and made easily accessible for study, would serve as a fundamental reference work for all future khipu scholars. No code can be cracked, chipped at, or unraveled unless the material to be worked on is within easy reach of those who wish to solve the riddle.

Given that we barely understand even the limits of what we may know about this complex and unique system of record keeping, it is quite likely that our abilities to understand khipu at the end of the twenty-first century will be far more advanced than they are now, at its beginning. If this book inspires others to start tugging at the knots that secure the codes of Andean khipu, then it will have served scholarship very well indeed.

NOTE

1. For a thorough and fascinating discussion of the history of investigations of Maya hieroglyphic writing, see Michael D. Coe, *Breaking the Maya Code* (London and New York: Thames and Hudson, 1992).

PART ONE

BACKGROUND FOR THE STUDY OF
KHIPU AND QUECHUA NARRATIVES

An Overview of Spanish Colonial Commentary on Andean Knotted-String Records

ONE *Gary Urton*

INTRODUCTION

One of the most intriguing, yet enigmatic, topics of study pertaining to pre-Columbian civilizations of the Andes concerns the device known as the khipu (Quechua: "knot") or *chino* (Aymara: "knot record"). Khipu were bunches of (often) dyed, knotted strings that were used by the Inka and other populations throughout the empire for recording a variety of different types of information. We are aware of the contents of these records only indirectly, through Spanish chroniclers' commentary on them, or through the handful of documents containing (Spanish) transcriptions of their "reading" by native record keepers, or through modern renderings of their numerical/quantitative arrangements of knots. What we do not have are direct, native translations of their contents unmediated by Spanish hands or voices. Nor, in those cases in which we have transcriptions of khipu readings, do we have a khipu that was the source of the record keeper's account.

It is, in fact, from the recognition of the virtual absence of serious study and reflection on the narrative aspects of the khipu recording system that Jeffrey Quilter and I offer this collection of studies. The studies assembled in this book represent, we believe, the best current understandings of the narrative component, or dimension, of the khipu accounts and some of the most productive strategies for the investigation of khipu narratives in the future.

In what follows, I provide an accounting of the forms and functions of khipu as we learn about them from written documents produced during the

Spanish colonial era (1532–1820s). In addition to simply informing the reader of much (but by no means all) of what was said about khipu in the colonial era, and by whom it was said, two larger objectives have guided my efforts in producing this historical overview; the first objective is programmatic, the second is substantive. As for the former, I present a record not only of who said what about the khipu, but also of *when* they said it. It is my belief that the absence of a clear understanding of the chronological sequence—or of what, in some instances, constitutes a virtual "genealogy" of observations on and claims about khipu—has encouraged an arbitrary selection of quotations from sources from very different time periods during the colony to suit one or another interpretation of what khipu were and how they were used. This point merits further elaboration.

There are two fundamental problems with the ahistorical use of khipu commentaries alluded to above. First, although several early colonial commentators on khipu spoke from the personal experience of actually seeing and hearing (former) Inka officials consult these devices in recounting information on the past, later commentators (especially after the 1580s) generally knew of khipu either from reading the earlier sources or from their own first-hand experiences, but of a significantly transformed, late-colonial tradition of khipu use. The earlier accounts undoubtedly provide more reliable testimony on the types of khipu that were in use in pre-Columbian times and their methods of encipherment and interpretation. This is not to suggest, however, that we can discount the evidence provided by later commentators; rather it is to stress the importance of maintaining a critical perspective on which accounts were based on eyewitness testimony of the first postconquest generation of record keepers at work on their pre-Conquest records, and which accounts were based on hearsay. It will become clear as we proceed that the latter type of accounts often reflected shifts in attitudes about khipu that emerged in late colonial times (see below).

The second reason the chronology of commentaries on the khipu is significant is that whereas the Spaniards initially expressed considerable interest in and respect for the knotted-string records—to the point that these records served as the principal sources of information the Spaniards drew on for developing an understanding of the Andean past—later colonial officials expressed deep ambivalence about the khipu and a general suspicion of the native officials (called khipukamayuq: "knot makers/keepers") who kept them. One major reason for the change in attitude about the khipu on the part of the Spaniards was that the native records increasingly came into direct competition (especially in legal disputations) with the Spaniards' own written records. For both reasons noted above, then, it is important to be aware of and exercise a critical perspective on the time period during which any given commentary on the khipu was produced.

The second objective of the historical overview presented in this chapter — its substantive contribution — is to take particular note of how different sources characterized the extent to which khipu were said to encode some form(s) of information (i.e., in their "recording units") that the khipu keepers consulted, interpreted, or read in the production of historical, genealogical, and other types of narrative accounts of the past. As we will learn in the course of this book, that narrative renderings of khipu *were* produced by khipukamayuq is undoubted; however, what is fully under investigation and often in open dispute in the pages of this volume are such questions as: What was the nature of the recording units that were interpreted in a narrative, discursive manner by the khipukamayuq? Did these units consist solely of numbers read as labels? Might they also have taken the form of semantic signifiers or syntactical markers signed by way of certain arrangements of knot types; color patterning; and spinning, plying, and knotting directions? And finally, might the narrative signifiers have taken the form of woven, three-dimensional ideogram- or logogram-like representations, as suggested by some of the Spanish chroniclers?

In addition to addressing such conundrums as those raised above regarding the nature of the khipu signing units, certain of the works collected herein are concerned with such matters as the relationship, in khipu-based narrative productions, between units of information actually recorded on the khipu and information that was retained in the memory. We will encounter very different information and opinions on this crucial question in the chapters collected here. A final, important issue addressed in some of the studies concerns the degree to which the information recorded on any given khipu was mutually intelligible, or "readable," by knot keepers throughout the empire. That is, were khipu legible only by the person who made them, or was there a high level of shared signifying units, and techniques for the manipulation of threads to produce those units, on the part of record keepers throughout the empire? As the reader will find in the pages of this book, there is still no clear consensus on these and other vital matters regarding the recording of, and the retrieval of information from, the khipu.

The purpose of the present chapter is to provide some background on the colonial source materials relevant to reading the formulations and debates that follow regarding the several issues raised above.

SIXTEENTH-CENTURY ACCOUNTS

From virtually the earliest accounts written by Spaniards in the newly conquered territory of the Inka Empire, we read about encounters with knotted-
string records. For example, Hernando Pizarro, a brother of the conqueror
and first governor of Peru, Francisco Pizarro, tells us that on one occasion
in 1533, during the first year following the European invasion, he and his soldiers took certain items—firewood, "sheep" (llamas), corn, and *chicha* (corn
beer)—from an Inka storehouse along the royal Inka highway, and the native
accountants recorded the transaction on a knotted-string recording device
(H. Pizarro does not name this device for us). Pizarro notes that when he and
his men removed these goods from the storehouse, the record keepers "untied
some of the knots which they had in the deposits section [of the khipu], and
they [re-]tied them in another section [of the khipu]" (H. Pizarro 1920: 175,
178). Curiously, this is one of the few accounts we have, in the entire corpus
of colonial literature on khipu, of an actual event of "balancing the books" in
a khipu transaction.

Around the same time that Hernando Pizarro encountered khipu along the
Inka road to the highlands, another conquistador, Miguel de Estete, made an
important observation on a different type of information recorded on certain
of these devices. He noted that "although they [the Inka] don't have writing,
they recall the memory of things by means of certain cords and knots, though
the most notable things are remembered in songs, as if lacking writing, we
were to remember past deeds by songs that recall them" (cited in Pease 1990:
67). The combined observations of Pizarro and Estete provide us with the
earliest evidence that khipu (of different types?) encoded at least two different
types of information: statistical and narrative/historical.

By the 1540s, the Spaniards had begun to write down the wealth of statistical information (e.g., census data, tribute lists) that the administrators of the
(now defunct) empire had registered on their khipu from before the time of
the conquest. The principal event that precipitated this initial episode of the
systematic transcription of statistical data from khipu into Spanish written
documents was the round of *visitas* (visits), or general inspections, ordered by
Pedro de La Gasca, president of the Real Audiencia in Lima in 1549. President La Gasca sent seventy-two teams of inspectors into the countryside to
collect and evaluate census figures and statistical data on economic resources
from various regions throughout the former empire. Though we have recovered only a fraction of these inspection records from archives, scholars
have mined certain of these accounts to provide us with an increasingly clear

understanding of the basic types of data that were recorded on these important Inka bureaucratic recording devices, as well as some of the values and principles organizing the registration of information therein (see Espinoza Soriano 1971–1972; Galdós Rodríguez 1977; Murra 1982, 1987; Pärssinen 1992: 40–43; Pease 1990; Rostworowski 1993: 293–348, 349–362; and Urton 1998).

The interaction between Andean and Spanish records and record keepers resulting from the procedures outlined above was by no means always of an amicable nature. For instance, by the early to mid-1550s, accounts of the tribute paid to the new Spanish overlords were being registered *both* on khipu and in Spanish written documents. A few decades later, as the *conquistadores/encomenderos* began dying off and transferring their wealth and privileges to their heirs, *and* as native Andeans gained facility in manipulating colonial judicial procedures, there was a marked increase in the number of legal proceedings involving disputes over differences in the native and Spanish tribute records recorded earlier, during the 1550s. One case in point that has recently received considerable attention focuses on a dispute between the heirs of Alonso de Montemayor and the tributary Indians of Sacaca, Bolivia (e.g., A.G.I., *Justicia* 653, no. 2, pza. 1: f. 409r–v; Platt, Chapter 10, this book; Solórzano y Pereyra 1972: 308–309; Urton 1998).

Moving to the decade of the 1550s, the soldier/chronicler Pedro de Cieza de León (1553) compared the khipu favorably to the system of signs or "hieroglyphs" (*carastes*) used by the Mexicans. Cieza de León noted further that the Inka used their knotted-cord records to keep track of reserves and expenditures of state, as well as "other things that had occurred many years in the past." He also states that old, wise men were charged by the Inka with composing and memorizing songs commemorating the deeds of the kings of the Inka Empire (Cieza de León 1967: 34–37). Thus, as we saw in the earlier account by Miguel de Estete, narratives from the Inka past were *both* recorded on khipu and composed and memorized by the court poet-philosophers, the *amauta*. One problem that has yet to be addressed in a comprehensive and critical manner is the relationship between the memory-based narrative productions of the *amauta* and the khipu- (and memory-?) based narrations of the khipukamayuq.

From the 1550s, we move forward more than a decade before we once again encounter an appreciable number of references to khipu in the Spanish documents. These new references were at the core of a veritable explosion of documents produced as a result of a new round of inspection visits and fact-finding activities ordered by the fourth viceroy of Peru, Francisco de Toledo (1569–

1581). With his reforms of colonial administration and tribute collection, as well as the forced relocation of the formerly dispersed Andean populations into new nucleated settlements, Toledo effected what was arguably the most profound transformation of life in the Andean highlands between the time of the European invasion and the wars of independence (in the 1820s). Innumerable documents (such as *visitas, composiciones de tierras,* and *probanzas de mérito*) derived from the Toledan activities, and these are housed in archives in Spain and the various Andean nations. These documents provide an extraordinarily detailed view of the sociopolitical and economic characteristics of local populations and communities scattered throughout the Andes at this time. Many make clear the critical role played by local khipukamayuq in supplying Spanish officials with the baseline of statistical (e.g., demographic and economic) information upon which the new, reorganized colonial state began to take shape (Espinoza Soriano 1967, 1971–1972; MacCormack 1995; Murra 1991; Rostworowski and Remy 1992; Rowe 1985).

In addition to the collection and transferal into Spanish written documents of a massive amount of statistical information, the Toledan examination and inspection procedures also called for a more systematic collection of historical information than had been carried out up to this time (i.e., the 1570s). For example, in collecting information to write his *Historia de los Incas* (1942), Pedro Sarmiento de Gamboa tells us that he interviewed more than one hundred old khipukamayuq who lived at that time in and around Cusco. He later assembled a group of more than forty members of the former Inka nobility, some of whom had served as khipukamayuq, to verify the truth of the historical account contained in his chronicle.

The points to stress with respect to this phase of the postconquest history of the khipu are, first, that the (now aged) khipukamayuq were at the center of the collection of preconquest "historical" data as well as the verification of the histories of the Inka Empire that were constructed from those data by the Toledan chroniclers (e.g., Molina 1916; Polo de Ondegardo 1916; Sarmiento de Gamboa 1942); and, second, that the era of the Toledan investigations represents the initial phase of heightened tensions and conflicts between khipu and written records. That is, by the time of the Toledan reforms, the Spaniards had for some forty years maintained their own (written) accounts of Andean statistical and historical records and were thus increasingly less inclined to defer to the native record keepers when their own records came into conflict with those of the khipukamayuq.

As with several of the earlier sources, the Toledan chroniclers make it clear that the khipukamayuq recorded both statistical data as well as narrative/historical information on the khipu. As an example of the scope of historical information recorded on these devices, one of the Toledan chroniclers, Cristóbal de Molina ("el Cuzqueño"), noted that the Inka

> used a very subtle method of accounting of knotted strings of wool
> of different colors, which they call *quipos;* they can and did under-
> stand so much by this accounting device that they were able to give
> an accounting of all the things that had happened in this land for
> more than 500 years. They had Indians who were very skilled and
> knowledgeable in the *quipos* and accounts; these [Indians] passed the
> knowledge down from generation to generation; and fixing in the
> memory all that they learned, miraculously, nothing was forgotten.
>
> (1916: 17–18)

It is important to note that, with the above commentary, Molina introduced into the written record the earliest note of ambiguity with regard to the question of the relationship between information that was recorded on a khipu as opposed to that which was memorized. The early part of this quotation suggests that the information concerning what had happened in the past five hundred years was recorded on the khipu, whereas the later part of the quotation suggests that the historical information was retained in the memory of the khipukamayuq. This ambivalence, which is virtually nonexistent before the time of the Toledan chroniclers, increases from this time forward. In addition, a couple of decades later another chronicler of the (late) Toledan era, Martín de Murúa, noted that different types of khipu, each with its own logic and rationale, were utilized by different populations within the empire (1946: 124). Platt (Chapter 10, this book) has used Murúa's observation and other similar testimony to argue against the notion that there was a high degree of mutual intelligibility among record keepers throughout the empire.

From the end of the Toledan era onward, the history of khipu may be fairly characterized as a running confrontation between the khipu accounts and the documents written in Spanish. Increasingly, the native officials (i.e., the khipukamayuq) were forced into a posture of self-defense, for the Spanish colonial officials were intent on undermining the authority of the khipu accounts as well as the veracity and trustworthiness of the khipukamayuq themselves (see Platt, Chapter 10, this book; and Urton 1998). It is notable that such confrontations overwhelmingly involved conflicts over the veracity of statistical and economic (especially tribute) records. That is, to the best of my knowledge, there were no major public disputes over the veracity of khipu accounts of Inka history as opposed to the histories written in the Toledan chronicles or those from earlier times. The partial exception to this generalization involves genealogical disputes and conflicts over who had a legitimate claim to authority, via a noble pedigree, to a local "lordship" (*cacicazgo*). In both of these types of disputes, however, what was ultimately very much at issue were economic considerations, since those who could prove that they were descendants of (former) Inka nobility were excluded from the requirements to pay tribute and to perform personal service for the Spaniards.

As becomes increasingly clear in the documents of the period, the central issue with regard to khipu in the 1570s–1590s was the political-economic question: Who—natives or Spaniards?—would be in control of public records in the colony? The khipukamayuq lost out decisively in this critical confrontation. This result was formalized in the Third Council of Lima (1581–1583), when the khipu were classified as idolatrous objects and were ordered to be burned (Tercer Concilio Limense 1583, acto 3, ch. 37; see Mannheim 1991: 66–71).

SEVENTEENTH-CENTURY ACCOUNTS

At the beginning of the seventeenth century, we encounter a particularly intriguing account of the types of information that were still recorded on the khipu at that time, as well as a poignant illustration of the Spanish will to destroy these knotted-string records, in keeping with the mandate of the Third Council of Lima. The following passage comes from Diego Avalos y Figueroa's *Miscelánea austral*, from 1602:

> In the valley of Xauxa, I met on the road an old Indian carrying a bundle of *quipus*, which he tried to hide. When challenged, he explained that these *quipus* were the account he had to give to the Inca, when he [the Inca] returned from the other world, of all that had happened in the valley in his absence. In the account were included all the Spaniards who had traveled on that royal road, what they had wanted and bought, and all they had done, both the good and the bad. The *corregidor* [high civil administrator] with whom I was traveling took and burned these accounts and punished the Indian.
>
> (CITED IN MACCORMACK 1985: 458)

It is clear that such latter-day khipukamayuq, descendants of the official record keepers of Inka times, had entered a new era, one in which the precious knotted records they retained were increasingly viewed with suspicion and outright contempt.

One of the principal sources of information about khipu is an extraordinary document, written at the end of the sixteenth century through the early years of the seventeenth century, by a native chronicler, Felipe Guaman Poma de Ayala (1980; see Adorno 1986; Cummins 1992). In his work entitled *Nueva corónica y buen gobierno*, an approximately one-thousand-page "letter" to the king of Spain, Guaman Poma not only alludes to the wide range of different types of information encoded in the khipu (e.g., economic, demographic, astronomical, astrological, and bureaucratic), but he also provides something even more tantalizing and informative with respect to the role of this device in Inka daily life: drawings of various Inka officials displaying, consulting, and in other ways manipulating khipu (Brokaw 1999; Luxton 1979). Guaman Poma's drawings depict a variety of people handling these devices (e.g., accountants, messengers, and astrologers) and also juxtapose khipu with other types of cultural artifacts, such as gaming or counting boards (*yupana*), staffs of office, particular styles of dress, and even a hand-held sign reading: *carta*, "letter" (see Quilter, Chapter 9, this book).

Both the text and the drawings of Guaman Poma's so-called "letter to a king" represent valuable sources of information on the khipu and their handlers. Equally notable, though somewhat puzzling, is the degree to which Guaman Poma's drawings of khipu depict this device in schematic, virtually iconic renderings; that is, none of Guaman Poma's drawings show khipu with knots tied into their pendant strings—all the strings are shown as plain, unknotted threads dangling from primary cords. Similarly, nowhere in his text does Guaman Poma provide an explicit statement concerning the types of information retained on the khipu nor how the information was recorded. As Guaman Poma had a high regard for the khipukamayuq and *amauta*, as well as a fairly sophisticated understanding of the ways the khipu—and possibly the Inka computing board, called *yupana*—were used by the Inka for recording statistical and historical data (Radicati di Primeglio 1979: 31–46; 1990b; Wassén 1931, 1990), it is reasonable to assume that he ought to have been capable of presenting accurate depictions and precise explanations of the khipu. Perhaps for some reason as yet unclear to us Guaman Poma was hesitant to expose the khipu to close scrutiny by the reader(s) of his "letter." In other words, he may have *chosen* not to elaborate on the formal properties of the khipu and the ways of manipulating them in reading.

By analogy with other recent analyses of certain topics discussed by Guaman Poma, we could even argue that the chronicler's silence on this particular matter may, in fact, be quite informative with regard to his view on the nature of these records. For example, Rolena Adorno (1986: 27–29) and Sabine MacCormack (1985: 464–466) have shown that Guaman Poma constructed a rather elaborate set of representations to the effect that Andean peoples had known the god of Christianity before the arrival of the Europeans; in addition, I have tried to show (Urton 1997: 201–208) that Guaman Poma suggested—in image and text—that the Inka were familiar with Hindu-Arabic numerals in pre-Hispanic times. Both of these topics elicited strong rhetorical postures on Guaman Poma's part, a fact that makes his silence on the khipu all the more interesting, and curious. Since we know Guaman Poma to have been a literate man who spent years learning the European arts of reading and writing, and who understood the high regard Europeans had for literacy, we might expect (by analogy with these other rhetorical sallies) that *if* Guaman Poma *was* of the opinion that the khipu constituted a sophisticated system of recording, not to mention a form of writing, he might also have argued that the Inka actually had writing before the arrival of the Europeans. (Such an argument was, in fact, made by another native chronicler— Garcilaso de la Vega; see Urton, Chapter 8, this book.) However, Guaman Poma himself did not make such an argument. We are therefore left with the dilemma of deciding whether or not we are justified in making an argument *ex silencio* in this instance; that is, can we say that since Guaman Poma did *not* make such an argument, this must mean that he did not believe the khipu constituted a system of writing? We cannot answer this question with any certainty at the present time.

In addition to the continuing use of khipu accounts in legal proceedings, there appeared during the first half of the seventeenth century a number of more informative descriptions of the knotted records and of the variety of methods used to record on, and read information from, these devices. For example, near the beginning of the century (in 1602), we encounter an intriguing reference to a peculiar manner of registering information in, or of attaching "signs" to, the khipu. This appears in an annual report from the head of the Jesuits in Peru, P.R. de Cabredo, to General Aquaviva, the head of the Jesuit order. In this report, we read that khipu were used by native peoples to record their sins for the purpose of giving confession (for the use of khipu in confessionals, see Harrison, Chapter 11, this book). We are told that in such khipu, the faithful tied knots in the strings as an aid to the memory. Interestingly, we are also told of one confessant who, in addition to tying knots, made the khipu "from six *varas* of twisted cord with threads spaced along it as well as some signs [*señales*] of stone or bone or feathers *conforming to the material of the sin* being confessed" (Fernández 1986: 214; my translation and emphasis).

In its presupposition of a direct, natural relationship between a sign and the thing it signifies, the above account reflects a decidedly Neoplatonic "take" on the khipu. Neoplatonism was a long-lasting philosophical tradition in Europe with roots in humanist, neoclassical thinking; this interpretive tradition was especially strong in Renaissance Italian scholarship (see Yates 1966). Neoplatonists saw the physical forms of things—such as chairs, pots and pans, and hieroglyphic signs—as corrupted, worldly reflections of the true forms that existed in the ideal realm of pure abstraction. Earthly forms were merely the simulacra of these ideal forms. Furthermore, this world of abstract ideals was the realm of deep and profound truths, a realm of knowledge accessible only to the learned elite few—those who had been instructed in the secret meanings of things.

In a fascinating study of Neoplatonic influences in the study of the Egyptian hieroglyphs, Erik Iversen (1993) has shown how (especially) Italian humanist scholars of the fifteenth and sixteenth centuries, many of whom were members of the Jesuit order, constructed an approach to the hieroglyphs based on a symbolic, allegorical interpretation of the hieroglyphic signs. This tradition, which was based on a few classical sources that were significantly *un*informed on the subject of Egyptian hieroglyphic writing, introduced elements of mysticism and humanist symbolic analysis into the study of the hieroglyphic signs, thereby effectively delaying for centuries the recognition of the ideographic and phonetic bases of Egyptian hieroglyphic writing. In fact, a strikingly similar history of Neoplatonic symbolic and mystical interpretations impeded for many years the decipherment of the Maya hieroglyphs (see Coe 1992). In both cases, decipherment of these ancient scripts was impeded because researchers of the times could not countenance the notion that such elaborate and mysterious-looking ancient scripts could possibly have had any relationship to the mundane sounds of human speech. In both cases, such presumptions proved to be profoundly wrong. We will have reason later to question whether such references as that cited above—in the Jesuit communiqué regarding khipu registering the material correlates of sins—represent the appearance of Neoplatonic influences in the history of interpretations of the khipu (a similar suspicion clouds the evaluation of the so-called "Naples document"; see below and Hyland, Chapter 7, this book).

The Inca Garcilaso de la Vega, mestizo son of an Inka princess and a Spanish *conquistador*, was born in Cusco in 1539 and lived there until the age of twenty-one. Soon after his father's death, Garcilaso went to Spain to claim his inheritance, and he remained there for the rest of his life. In 1609, Garcilaso completed his *magnum opus*, a work entitled *Comentarios reales de los Incas* (1959). The *Comentarios* contains a wealth of information concerning the khipu, which Garcilaso claims to have learned how to read as a youth in Cusco. For instance, Garcilaso describes the decimal-based system of recording numerical-statistical information (1966: 331–332); he describes the relationship between the generally numerical information recorded on the khipu and the memorized poems and stories that inform and help flesh out the numerical data into narratives (1966: 332); and he provides an account, based on notes by the mestizo Jesuit Blas Valera, of the use of a type of iconography-based khipu recording system to register Inka verse (1966: 127). In general terms, Garcilaso provides us with a seemingly well informed, though occasionally problematic (because of its idiosyncrasy), account of the technological and intellectual traditions associated with Andean knotted-string records (see Assadourian, Chapter 6, and Urton, Chapter 8, this book).

On the important question of the relationship between the nature of the information registered on the khipu and the work of memory in retrieving that information, Garcilaso gives contradictory testimony. For example, he notes at one point that

> . . . as the Incas had no knowledge of writing, they had to use what devices they could, and treating their knots as letters, they chose historians and accountants, called *quipucamayus*, to write down and preserve the tradition of their deeds by means of the knots, strings, and colored threads, using their stories and poems as an aid. This was the method of writing the Incas employed in their republic.
>
> (1966: 332)

Whereas the above account suggests, with some ambiguity, that the Inka retained some manner of "writing" in the khipu, the following statement by this chronicler suggests quite the opposite:

> [T]he Indians recalled by means of the knots the things their parents and grandparents had taught them by tradition, and these they treated with the greatest care and veneration, as sacred matters relating to the idolatrous religion and laws of their Incas, which they contrived to retain in their memories because of their ignorance of writing.   (GARCILASO DE LA VEGA 1966: 333)

The Augustinian friar Antonio de la Calancha spent many years in the Andes, primarily in Lima, Potosí, and Trujillo. Calancha comments extensively on the khipu in his chronicle *Corónica moralizada . . .* (1974, 1: 201–212). Calancha had read the works of several of his predecessors (e.g., Garcilaso de la Vega, José de Acosta, and Blas Valera), and his ideas about the khipu were formed from his reading of these earlier accounts as well as from direct conversations with khipukamayuq. Calancha expresses his admiration for the khipu early in his chronicle (Bk. 1, Ch. 14: 208), noting, for instance, that these knotted records contained a wide variety of information, such as history, law, ceremonial practices, and economic transactions. What is most remarkable about the writings of Calancha on this subject, however, is that he claims to have made personal inquiries into the techniques and modes of recording information on the khipu. From his inquiries, Calancha describes a hypothetical khipu account, complete with information on color symbolism as well as indications of dating, royal succession, bureaucratic offices, and a differentiation of signifiers denoting different levels of settlements in the Inka Empire (206–207). With only a few exceptions (e.g., Garcilaso's account of the symbolism of colors used in the khipu), most of the information given by Calancha is uncorroborated by other early sources. Scholars have therefore been hesitant to pursue studies of the khipu information system(s) based on the data given by Calancha (exceptions include Pärssinen 1992: 31–43, and Assadourian, Chapter 6, this book).

It is important to take note of the unusually explicit discussion Calancha produced on both the types of information contained on the khipu and the relationship between knowledge (the ability and the requirement to actually "read" information in the strings) and memory in the practice of the khipukamayuq:

> . . . the deeds, history, or rationale [of the past] were committed to memory by the Quipo Camayos, who were like the Secretaries of these archives, in order to provide an account of them to the Inga, or to the Cacique, or whoever might ask about it, and the *Arabicus* [*Amauta?*] who were their poets, composed brief verses and compendia, in which they encapsulated the history, the events, or the messages, and these were recounted in the towns, or provinces through which they passed, the father teaching them to his son, and he to his [son]; and the Quipo Camayos, whether because of the privileges with which they honored the office, or because, if they did not give good accounting about that on which they were questioned they were

severely castigated, were continually studying the signs, ciphers and relations [in the khipu], teaching them to those who would succeed them in office, and there were many of these Secretaries, each of whom had assigned his particular class of material, having to suit the story, tale or song to the knots of which they served as the indices, and the point of site [or place] memory [*punto para memoria local*]. By the same order, they give an account of their laws, ordenances, rites and ceremonies, establishing the restitution, or punishment of the deed, or transgression. The ceremonies of each festival, which they performed to the Sun, or to the invisible God; they learned with maximum veneration the histories of the kings, or the oracles and sacrifices of their idols. The Secretary, or Quipo Camayo, was at the pain of death if at any time he lost some of the truth, or ignored something that he should know about, or if he differed [in his accounting] from some of the deeds, legacy or oracles it [the khipu record] contained.   (CALANCHA 1974, 1: 205; MY TRANSLATION)

Calancha's testimony regarding the procedures for recording and reading information on the khipu makes it clear that these practices required the combination of certain information retained in the memory of the khipukamayuq with specialized knowledge of khipu construction techniques (knowing how and where to place certain types of information on the strings). Perhaps this is how we should read the (apparently) contradictory testimony provided in the two quotations from Garcilaso de la Vega (above).

The middle of the seventeenth century saw the completion of the Jesuit priest Bernabé Cobo's *Historia del Nuevo Mundo* (1979 and 1990). Cobo's work is informed by his reading of numerous earlier chronicles, particularly the works of Polo de Ondegardo and Cristóbal de Molina ("el Cuzqueño"). Cobo includes brief but interesting, and ultimately quite controversial, commentary on the khipu. Cobo's personal experience with khipu "readings" appears to have been both limited and linked directly to the information provided by descendants of the Inka nobility in Cusco. One of his main informants was a man named Alonso Topa Atau, a grandson of Huayna Capac, the last undisputed Inca, who ruled until just before the arrival of the Spanish. Topa Atau maintained a khipu in which he had recorded, and communicated to Cobo, the official Cusco version of Inka history (Porras Barrenechea 1986: 512).

Cobo states that all manner of information was retained on these devices (e.g., statistical and historical data) but that understanding the records required the memorization of information beyond that which was actually registered on the khipu. On the basis of this memorized information, the khipu-kamayuq constructed a full narrative of the information in question. Now, as we have seen, many other chroniclers testified to the necessity of combining recorded and memorized information in the art of khipu recording and "reading." Cobo, however, goes on to state that "among the *quipo camayos* themselves, one was unable to understand the registers and recording devices of others. Each one understood the *quipos* that he made and what the others told him" (Cobo 1979: 254). Such a characterization of the khipu recording system as based on "idiosyncratic" registers and units of notation is not, in fact, expressed in such an explicit manner in any other account produced during the previous 120 years of European writing on these devices.

If Cobo was correct in his characterization of the information system of the knotted records as based not on *shared*, but rather on *secret* (individually memorized), bodies of information, then we probably will have to refrain from classifying the khipu records as a form of "writing." This is because a writing system requires a widely shared understanding of the basic recording units on the part of all those involved in communicating by means of the system in question. I have called into question Cobo's characterization of the khipu recording system on precisely this point (Urton 1998 and Chapter 8, this book), although others have argued in support of his more restricted view (see, for example, Platt, Chapter 10, this book; Rappaport 1994; and Rappaport and Cummins 1994: 100). However the matter is eventually decided, it is undoubted that Cobo himself did not believe the Inka possessed a system of writing. In fact, he was quite explicit in his views on this matter, stating at one point in his chronicle of Inka history that

[t]here is no one who is not surprised and frightened to see that these people's [i.e., the native peoples of South America] power of reason is so dull; this is not so much because they are short on reasoning power, as some have alleged, as it is because of their very limited mental activity. On the one hand this is because *they have no written literature, sciences, or fine arts*, which generally cultivate, perfect, and make the mind quicker in its operations and reasoning powers. On the other hand, since the ingrained, savage vices to which they are commonly given have nearly become innate, these vices have dulled their ingenuity and obscured the light of their powers of reason.

(COBO 1983: 21; EMPHASIS ADDED)

EIGHTEENTH- AND NINETEENTH-CENTURY ACCOUNTS

We can be brief in discussing works concerning khipu published during the eighteenth and nineteenth centuries. The arts of khipu making and reading had clearly become "dis-established"—eliminated from the practices of record keeping among native officials—by this period. Their reemergence (or rediscovery) would occur during the nineteenth and twentieth centuries, when travelers, members of the Andean intelligentsia, anthropologists, and others would encounter the use of khipu for everyday record-keeping purposes (e.g., counts of livestock), as well as for ritual display in communities in Peru, Bolivia, and Ecuador (see Holm 1968; Mackey 1970, 1990a, 1990b, and Chapter 13, this book; Mesa and Gisbert 1966; Núñez del Prado 1950; Ruiz Estrada 1981, 1990; Salomon, Chapter 12, this book; Soto Flores 1950–1951; and Uhle 1897).

Many of the references to khipu during the eighteenth and nineteenth centuries are products of a general European antiquarian interest in hieroglyphs and other ancient, "exotic" writing systems at that time, as well as a more pointed romanticizing of the supposed "lost art" of Inka writing (see Ernst 1871; Pérez 1864; and, more recently, Miranda Rivera 1958). In the latter category, we should note a couple of examples of what Radicati di Primeglio (1979: 51) refers to as "apocryphal khipus." These include the mention of khipu writing in the work of Madame F. de Grafigny, a Parisienne whose novella *Lettres d'une Péruvienne* (Letter from a Peruvian princess; 1747) was inspired by information she obtained on khipu from Raimondo di Sangro, Prince of San Severo. The latter produced a work entitled *Lettera apologetica* ... (1750) in which he diagrams some forty complex, iconography-laden khipu knots, each signifying a distinct sacred identity or object in the Inka cosmos (these knot signs are also reproduced in Rosny 1870).

The elaborate, iconographic khipu signs described by Sangro and Rosny have recently reappeared in a curious document commonly referred to as the "Naples document" (Animato, Rossi, and Miccinelli 1989; Laurencich Minelli 1996; Laurencich Minelli, Miccinelli, and Animato 1995). This document, whose authenticity is still very much in question (see Domenici and Domenici 1996), purports to describe a system of syllabic writing—based on the forty iconographic khipu knot signs mentioned above—by means of a special class of khipu that was supposedly understood only by the *amauta* (wise men) of the Inka court. The original source of the description of this supposed syllabic writing system was the sixteenth-century Jesuit priest Blas Valera (see Hyland, Chapter 7, this book). A perplexing item in regard to the information contained in this document is the fact that Garcilaso de la Vega says that he read similar information in the papers of Blas Valera (although he does not allude to the existence of a syllabic writing system). Garcilaso even reproduces a poem, called *Sumaq Ñusta* (Beautiful princess), which he claims to have read in the papers of Blas Valera; curiously, this is the same poem used to illustrate the syllabic writing system in the document from Naples. Is this only a coincidence? Could the poem have been taken from Garcilaso in the "invention" (perhaps during the seventeenth or eighteenth century?) of an Inka system of syllabic writing? The commentators on the Naples document have so far failed to address this important and perplexing coincidence.

Under the label "apocryphal khipu" we should also reference a few nineteenth-century publications characterizing khipu whose construction features seem, from the elliptical descriptions we are given of them, stylistically similar to the "iconography-laden" type of khipu described in the Naples document (for example, see Rivero y Ustáriz 1857; Strong 1827; and Wiener 1880). In spirit and theory, these works are virtually direct descendants of the Renaissance, Neoplatonic (i.e., symbolic and allegorical) interpretations of writing systems of the ancient Near Eastern and Classical worlds. Nonetheless, approached with caution, such works may deserve more attention than they have received in the past, if for no other reason than for the insight they afford into the eighteenth- and early-nineteenth-century propensity for romanticizing "the other," and for mystifying the nature and status of signs in language and particularly in ancient writing systems.

SUMMARY AND CONCLUSIONS

This overview of colonial commentaries on the khipu permits us to recognize a few essential features of these devices and of the practices associated with their reading or interpretation. In the first place, the evidence is clear that the Inka and other peoples of the pre-Columbian Andes relied on khipu for retaining records pertaining to the state of the political economy of the societies in which they lived. This included demographic, economic, political, and other types of structural information. By the term "structural," I mean information pertaining to the composition, disposition, and distribution of material goods and other resources, including political power and authority, in the Inka state. From what we read in the Spanish chronicles and documents, it seems indisputable that information of this type was registered on the khipu by patterned variations of material; by the dyeing, spinning, and plying of strings; and by the tying of different types and numbers of knots in the strings. The latter were often accorded numerical values in the decimal (and perhaps duodecimal; see Platt, Chapter 10, this book) system(s) of numeration used by the Inka and their subjects. This much we have understood for quite some time (Ascher and Ascher 1997; Locke 1923; Urton 1994, 1997).

But, in addition, the sources from early to late colonial times make it clear that Inka as well as local, non-Inka officials throughout the empire recorded certain types of information that was "consulted" by the khipukamayuq in recounting historical and other types of narrative accounts. The major problem we face today in the study of the khipu is the meaning of the seemingly innocent term used above: "consulted." What was involved in the process of "consulting" a khipu to render a narrative account? Was this process comparable to the act of reading any number of other ancient scripts, with—in the Inka case—its full complement of grammatical units (subject/object/verb) registered in three dimensions on the khipu strings? Or was it perhaps more like a registry of general signifiers (evoking classes of objects, actions, places, and times) that were given more nuanced form and substance by a khipukamayuq, who would have brought to the reading information retained in his memory, as well as a range of creative, discursive practices for producing a narrative appropriate to a given place and perhaps audience? Or were the procedures of "consultation" perhaps somewhere between the extremes of the continuum between restricted (i.e., "literal") and free-form narrative productions outlined above?

To date, we have not even attempted to formulate answers to questions like those posed above; this is the objective of the present book. The approaches to these questions found in this volume are quite diverse. They include studies of memory and narrative productions in contemporary highland Peruvian communities (Howard); the structures and hierarchies of khipu construction (Conklin); the logic of encoding narrative information in the form of numbers interpreted as labels (M. Ascher); the strategy of "encipherment" as a route to interpreting the general information-encoding system of the khipu (R. Ascher); the analysis of Spanish chroniclers' testimony on the arts of encoding narratives in khipu (Assadourian, Hyland, Urton, and Quilter); the study of khipu transcriptions retained in Spanish colonial documents (Platt); the colonial use of khipu as confessional devices (Harrison); the present-day display of khipu as emblems of *ayllu* identity and history (Salomon); and the use of khipu for recording statistical information by Andean herders today (Mackey).

It is important to stress at the beginning of this exploration of narrativity in the Andean knotted-string records that to date no one has succeeded in producing a "reading" of a narrative khipu. The positive aspect of this otherwise distressing state of affairs is that, without a paradigm directing our work, the authors of these contributions are free to explore every conceivable avenue of argumentation and interpretation. It is hoped that the contributions assembled here, all of which are still innocent of the scourge of dogmatism that often follows the establishment of a paradigm, will stimulate others to take up the study of narrativity in the khipu.

BIBLIOGRAPHY

Primary Sources

Archivo General de Indias (A.G.I.), Seville, Spain:
    Charcas 37 [1575]. "Relación del ganado . . . [Chucuito]."
    Justicia 397, no. 2, ro. 2, pieza 2 [1551].
    Justicia 653, no. 2 (in 4 piezas) [1579]. "El cacique principal e Yndios del Pueblo de Sacaca con los herederos de Dn Alonso de Montemayor, sobre demasia de Tributos del Tiempo que tubo dhos Yndios en Encomienda."
    Justicia 653, no. 2, pieza 1 [1579]. "Relación que hazen los *quipocamayos* de las chacaras de coca . . . [Repartimiento de Sacaca]."
    Justicia 651, no. 2 [1571]: 72r–77v. "Tasa del Repartimiento de Chayanta."
    Lima 205, no. 16 [1558]. "Memoria de los indios que yo don Jerónimo Guacrapaucar di al marquez don Francisco Pizarro desde que salio de Caxamarca."
Biblioteca Nacional de Madrid:
    Legajo J #133. "Declaración de los Quipucamayos" (1542/1608).

Published Sources

Acosta, José de. 1954 [1590]. *Historia natural y moral de las Indias.* In *Obras del P. José de Acosta*, edited by P. Francisco Mateos. Biblioteca de Autores Españoles, vol. 73, 3–247. Madrid: Ediciones Atlas.
Adorno, Rolena. 1986. *Guaman Poma: Writing and Resistance in Colonial Peru.* Austin: University of Texas Press.
Animato, Carlo, Paolo A. Rossi, and Clara Miccinelli. 1989. *Quipu: Il nodo parlante dei misteriosi Inkas.* Genoa: Edizioni Culturali Internazionali.
Ascher, Marcia, and Robert Ascher. 1997. *Code of the Quipu.* New York: Dover Publications.
Brokaw, Galen. 1999. "Transcultural Intertextuality and Quipu Literacy in Felipe Guaman Poma de Ayala's *Nueva corónica y buen gobierno.*" Ph.D. dissertation, Indiana University. Ann Arbor: UMI Dissertation Services.
Calancha, Antonio de la. 1974 [1638]. *Corónica moralizada del orden de San Agustín en el Perú con sucesos ejemplares en esta monarquía.* Vol. 1. Transcripción, estudio crítico, notas bibliográficas e índices de Ignacio Prado Pastor. Lima: Universidad Nacional Mayor de San Marcos.

Cieza de León, Pedro de. 1967 [1553]. *El señorío de los Inkas.* Lima: Pontificia Universidad Católica del Perú.

Cobo, Bernabé. 1983 [1653]. *History of the Inca Empire.* Translated and edited by Roland Hamilton. Austin: University of Texas Press.

———. 1990 [1653]. *Inca Religion and Customs.* Translated and edited by Roland Hamilton. Foreword by John H. Rowe. Austin: University of Texas Press.

Coe, Michael D. 1992. *Breaking the Maya Code.* London: Thames and Hudson.

Cummins, Tom. 1992. "The Uncomfortable Image: Pictures and Words in the *Nueva corónica y buen gobierno.*" In *Guaman Poma de Ayala: The Colonial Art of an Andean Author,* edited by Rolena Adorno et al. New York: Americas Society.

Dávalos y Figueroa, Diego. 1602. *Miscelánea Austral.* Lima: N.p.

Domenici, Viviano, and Davide Domenici. 1996. "Talking Knots of the Inka." *Archaeology* 49, no. 6: 50–56.

Ernst, A. 1871. *Die peruanischen Quipos.* Berlin: N.p.

Espinoza Soriano, Waldemar. 1967. "Los señoríos étnicos de Chachapoyas y la alianza hispano-chacha." *Revista Histórica* 30: 224–322.

———. 1971–1972. "Los huancas aliados de la conquista: Tres informaciones inéditas sobre la participación indígena en la conquista del Perú, 1558, 1560 y 1561." *Anales Científicos* 1: 9–407.

Fernández, Enrique, S. I., ed. 1986. *Monumenta Peruana.* Vol. 8 (1603–1604). Monumenta Historica Societatis Iesu, vol. 128. Rome: Apud "Institutum Historicum Societattis Iesu."

Galdós Rodríguez, Guillermo. 1977 [1549]. "Visita a Atico y Caravelí." *Revista del Archivo General de la Nación* (Lima) 4–5 (1975–1976): 55–80.

Garcilaso de la Vega. 1959 [1609]. *Comentarios reales de los Incas.* Lima: Librería Internacional del Perú.

———. 1966 [1609]. *Royal Commentaries of the Incas.* 2 vols. Austin: University of Texas Press.

Grafigny, F. de. 1747. *Lettres d'une Péruvienne.* Paris: N.p.

Guaman Poma de Ayala, Felipe. 1980 [1615]. *El primer nueva corónica y buen gobierno.* Critical edition by J. V. Murra and Rolena Adorno; translation and textual analysis by Jorge L. Urioste. 3 vols. Mexico City: Siglo Veintiuno.

Holm, Olaf. 1968. "Quipu o Sapan: Un recurso mnemónico en el campo ecuatoriano." *Cuadernos de Historia y Arqueología* nos. 34–35, Año XVII: 85–90. Guayaquil: La Casa de la Cultura Ecuatoriana, Núcleo del Guayas.

Iversen, Erik. 1993 [1961]. *The Myth of Egypt and Its Hieroglyphs in European Tradition.* Princeton: Princeton University Press.

Laurencich Minelli, Laura. 1996. *La scrittura dell'antico Perù.* Bologna: CLUEB.

Laurencich Minelli, Laura, Clara Miccinelli, and Carlo Animato. 1995. "Il Documento Seicentesco 'Historia et Rudimenta Linguae Piruanorum.'" *Studi e Materiali Di Storia Delle Religioni* 61, no. 2: 363–413.

Locke, L. Leland. 1923. *The Ancient Quipu or Peruvian Knot Record.* New York: American Museum of Natural History.

Luxton, Richard N. 1979. "The Inka Khipus and Guaman Poma de Ayala's 'First New Chronicle and Good Government.'" *Ibero-Amerikanisches Archiv* n.f. 5, no. 4: 315–341.

MacCormack, Sabine G. 1985. "'The Heart Has Its Reasons': Predicaments of Missionary Christianity in Early Colonial Peru." *Hispanic American Historical Review* 65, no. 3: 443–466.

———. 1995. "'En los tiempos muy antiguos. . . ': Cómo se recordaba el pasado en el Perú de la colonía temprana." In *Revista Ecuatoriana de Historia* 7: 3–33.

Mackey, Carol. 1970. "Knot Records in Ancient and Modern Perú." Ph.D. dissertation, Department of Anthropology, University of California, Berkeley.

———. 1990a. "Comparación entre quipu inca y quipus modernos." In *Quipu y yupana*, edited by C. Mackey et al., 135–156. Lima: Consejo Nacional de Ciencia y Tecnología.

———. 1990b. "Nieves Yucra Huatta y la continuidad en la tradición del uso del quipu." In *Quipu y yupana*, edited by C. Mackey et al., 157–164. Lima: Consejo Nacional de Ciencia y Tecnología.

Mackey, Carol, Hugo Pereyra, Carlos Radicati di Primeglio, Humberto Rodríguez, and Oscar Valverde, eds. 1990. *Quipu y yupana: Colección de escritos.* Lima: Consejo Nacional de Ciencia y Tecnología.

Mannheim, Bruce. 1991. *The Language of the Inka since the European Invasion.* Austin: University of Texas Press.

Mesa, José de, and Teresa Gisbert. 1966. "Los Chipayas." *Anuario de Estudios Americanos* 23: 479–506.

Miranda Rivera, Porfirio. 1958. "Quipus y jeroglíficos." *Zeitschrift für Ethnologie* 83, no. 1: 118–132.

Molina, Cristóbal de ("el Cuzqueño"). 1916 [1573]. *Relación de las fábulas y ritos de los Incas.* Edited by Horacio H. Urteaga and Carlos A. Romero. Colección de Libros y Documentos Referentes a la Historia del Perú, vol. 1, series 1. Lima: Sanmartí.

Murra, John V. 1975. "Las etno-categorías de un *khipu* estatal." In *Formaciones económicas y políticas en el mundo andino*, 243–254. Lima: Instituto de Estudios Andinos.

———. 1982. "The Mit'a Obligations of Ethnic Groups in the Inka State." In *The Inka and Aztec States, 1400–1800*, edited by G. Collier, R. Rosaldo, and J. Wirth, 237–262. New York: Academic Press.

———. 1987. "Existieron el tributo y los mercados antes de la invasión europea?" In *La participación indígena en los mercados surandinos*, edited by O. Harris, B. Larson, and E. Tandeter, 51–61. La Paz: CERES.

———. 1991 [1568–1570]. *Visita de los Valles de Sonqo.* Madrid: Instituto de Cooperación Iberamericana/Instituto de Estudios Fiscales.

Murúa, Martín de. 1946 [1590]. *Historia del origen y genealogía real de los reyes Incas del Perú.* Madrid: Biblioteca Missionalia Hispánica, Instituto Santo Toribio de Mogrovejo; Consejo Superior de Investigaciones Científicas.

Núñez del Prado, Oscar. 1950. "El 'kipu' moderno." *Tradición.* Revista Peruana de Cultura (Cusco) 1, vol. 2, nos. 3–6: 7–24.

Pärssinen, Martti. 1992. *Tawantinsuyu: The Inka State and Its Political Organization.* Studia Historica 43. Helsinki: Societas Historica Finlandiae.

Pease G. Y., Franklin. 1990. "Utilización de quipus en los primeros tiempos coloniales." In *Quipu y yupana*, edited by C. Mackey et al., 67–71. Lima: Consejo Nacional de Ciencia y Tecnología.

Pérez, J. 1864. "Sur les Qquipos." *Revue Américaine* (Paris).

Pizarro, Hernando. 1920 [1533]. *A los Señores Oydores de la Audiencia Real de Su Magestad.* In *Informaciones sobre el antiguo Perú*, edited by Horacio H. Urteaga, 16–180. Colección de Libros y Documentos Referentes a la Historia del Perú, vol. 3 (2d series). Lima: Sanmartí.

Polo de Ondegardo, Juan. 1916 [1571]. *Informaciones acerca de la religión y gobierno de los Incas.* Colección de Libros y Documentos Referentes a la Historia del Perú, vol. 3. Lima: Sanmartí.

Porras Barrenechea, Raúl. 1986. *Los cronistas del Perú (1528–1650).* Biblioteca Clásicos del Perú, no. 2. Lima: Banco de Crédito del Perú.

Radicati di Primeglio, Carlos. 1979. *El sistema contable de los Incas: Yupana y quipu.* Lima: Librería Studium.

———. 1990a. "El cromatismo de los quipus: Significado del quipu de canutos." In *Quipu y yupana*, edited by C. Mackey et al., 39–50. Lima: Consejo Nacional de Ciencia y Tecnología.

———. 1990b. "Tableros de escaques en el antiguo Perú." In *Quipu y yupana*, edited by C. Mackey et al., 219–234. Lima: Consejo Nacional de Ciencia y Tecnología.

Rappaport, Joanne. 1994. "Object and Alphabet: Andean Indians and Documents in the Colonial Period." In *Writing without Words: Alternative Literacies in Mesoamerica and the Andes*, edited by Elizabeth Hill Boone and Walter D. Mignolo, 271–292. Durham and London: Duke University Press.

Rappaport, Joanne, and Tom Cummins. 1994. "Literacy and Power in Colonial Latin America." In *Social Construction of the Past*, edited by G. C. Bond and A. Gilliam, 89–109. London and New York: Routledge.

Rivero y Ustáriz, Mariano E. de. 1857. *Colección de memorias científicas, agrícolas e industriales publicadas en distintas épocas.* Brussels: N.p.

Rosny, Leon de. 1870. *Les Ecritures figuratives et hieroglyphiques des différents peuples anciens et modernes.* Paris: Maisonneuve, Libraires-Editeurs.

Rostworowski, María. 1993. "La visita de Urcos de 1572, un *kipu* pueblerino." In *Ensayos de historias andinas: Elites, etnías, recursos*, 363–383. Lima: Instituto de Estudios Peruanos.

Rostworowski, María, and Pilar Remy, eds. 1992. *Las visitas a Cajamarca 1571–72/1578.* Preliminary studies by María Rostworowski and Pilar Remy. Lima: Instituto de Estudios Peruanos.

Rowe, John H. 1985. "Probanza de los Incas nietos de conquistadores." *Histórica* 9, no. 2: 193–245.

Ruiz Estrada, Arturo. 1981. *Los quipus de Rapaz.* Huacho: Centro de Investigación de Ciencia y Tecnología de Huacho, Universidad Nacional "José Faustino Sánchez Carrión."

———. 1990. "Notas sobre un quipu de la costa nor-central del Perú." In *Quipu y yupana*, edited by C. Mackey et al., 191–194. Lima: Consejo Nacional de Ciencia y Tecnología.

Sangro, Raimondo de. 1750. *Lettera apologetica dell'Esercitato accademico della Crusca contenente la difesa del libro intitolato "Lettere d'una peruana, per rispetto alla supposizione de' Quipu" scritta alla duchessa d'S**** e dalla medesima fatta pubblicare.* Naples: N.p.

Sarmiento de Gamboa, Pedro. 1942 [1572]. *Historia de los Incas.* Buenos Aires: Emecé Editores.
Solórzano y Pereyra, Juan de. 1972 [1736]. *Política indiana.* Vol. 2. Biblioteca de Autores Españoles. Madrid: Lope de Vega.
Soto Flores, Froilan. 1950–1951. "Los kipus modernos de la comunidad de Laramarca." *Revista del Museo Nacional* (Lima) 19–20: 299–306.
Strong, Alexander. 1827. *A Prospectos of the Quipola, or an Explanation of the Quipoes, now open for Public Opinion.* London: N.p.
Tercer Concilio Limense. 1583. "Decretos del Concilio de Lima del año 1583, y sumario del concilio de 1567, remitidos con una carta original por el Arzobispo de los Reyes, Toribio Alfonso Mogrovejo a S.M. Felipe II." In *Organización de la iglesia y órdenes religiosas en el Virreinato del Perú en el siglo XVI, Documentos del Archivo de Indias*, edited by Roberto Levillier, vol. 2 (1919), pp. 154–233. Madrid: Rivadeneyra.
Uhle, Max. 1897. "A Modern Kipu from Cutusuma, Bolivia." *Bulletin of the Museum of Science and Art of Penna* 1, no. 2. Reprinted in *Quipu y yupana*, edited by C. Mackey et al., 127–134. Lima: Consejo Nacional de Ciencia y Tecnología.
Urton, Gary. 1994. "A New Twist in an Old Yarn: Variation in Knot Directionality in the Inka *Khipu*s." *Baessler-Archiv*, Neue Folge, Band 42: 271–305.
———(with Primitivo Nina Llanos). 1997. *The Social Life of Numbers: A Quechua Ontology of Numbers and Philosophy of Arithmetic.* Austin: University of Texas Press.
———. 1998. "From Knots to Narratives: Reconstructing the Art of Historical Record-Keeping in the Andes from Spanish Transcriptions of Inka *Khipu*s." *Ethnohistory* 45, no. 3: 409–438.
Wassén, Henry. 1931. "The Ancient Peruvian Abacus." *Comparative Ethnological Studies* 9: 191–205.
———. 1990. "El antiguo ábaco peruano según el manuscrito de Guaman Poma." In *Quipu y yupana*, edited by C. Mackey et al., 205–218. Lima: Consejo Nacional de Ciencia y Tecnología.
Wiener, Charles. 1880. *Pérou et Bolivie, récit de voyage: Suivi d'études archéologiques et ethnographiques et de notes sur l'écriture et les langues de populations indiennes.* Paris: Librairie Hachette et Cie.
Yates, Frances A. 1966. *The Art of Memory.* Chicago: University of Chicago Press.

Spinning a Yarn

TWO   *Landscape, Memory, and Discourse*
Structure in Quechua Narratives

Rosaleen Howard

INTRODUCTION

Can a study of the cognitive and discursive principles at work in the telling of oral traditional stories in Quechua contribute to our insights into how the transmission of messages through the khipu might have operated? During the conference proceedings upon which this volume is based, the verbal component of the khipu-reading performance and the role of memory in activating the knowledge stored in the knots and strings were much commented on. Doubtless both cognitive and structural similarities exist between oral narratives that have no ostensible origin in the khipu and khipu-generated oral discourses. If a khipu's message was indeed transposable from its abstract level of representation to the medium of natural language, some of the similarities may be explained by the way the Quechua and Aymara languages are structured at word, sentence, and discourse levels. Furthermore, in line with an observation by Frank Salomon during the round-table discussions, just as we need to get away from thinking of khipu as linear texts, based on their three-dimensional, visual, and tactile nature, so also do we need to rethink conventional notions of "text" with regard to Quechua oral narratives, analysis of which reveals them to be nonlinear in their discourse structure.[1] Some cross-comparison between techniques of knotting and reading khipu and strategies of telling and understanding oral stories may therefore prove fertile ground for research.

The discussion to follow is largely based on a collection of oral narratives of mythic-historical type recorded in the Huamalíes variety of Quechua I among members of the peasant community of San Pedro de Pariarca, District of Tantamayo, Province of Huamalíes, Department of Huánuco, in the early 1980s.[2] Other results of the fieldwork have been published elsewhere (Howard-Malverde 1984, 1988, 1989, 1990). The present chapter takes a look at some of the previously published texts from the perspective of discourse structure and the operation of memory, aspects not hitherto examined.[3]

Insofar as the stories I recorded had been heard or told before by their narrators, they are evidence of the operation of memory in the oral tradition. What concerns me here is how the individual memory is exercised in the reproduction of such material. A number of interconnecting factors appear to be at work; no single factor alone can be held to assist the recollection of oral traditional material. Tom Cummins (1997) talks about the Western art of memory as it was practiced in the ancient world and as it continued to influence European thinking at the time of the Spanish Conquest. In the first part of this chapter, I also take up this topic, contrasting aspects of the theory of memory in Western philosophical tradition with Andean ideas about memory. I then consider text-internal (structural) and text-external (sociocultural) factors that may influence the recollection and ordering of ideas in oral traditional narrative.

CROSS-CULTURAL THEORIES OF MEMORY

In the view of Aristotle (1972) and the sophists, "remembering" should be distinguished from "recollection," though both involve the operation of memory. Memory results from the imprint on the brain of the perceptions arising during experience that are channeled through the different senses—auditory, visual, tactile, olfactory. Remembering is the process whereby these perceptions persist from the past into the present, remaining with us as part of our individual psyches and contributing to the formation of our identities. The durability of such perceptions in memory is of varied length, and eventually forgetting may set in; it is at this point that we seek to recollect, through the exercise of active and deliberate intellectual endeavor (by means of associative strategies of cognition), the perceptions of past experience and to reactivate them in memory. Recollection is thus a more conscious intellectual activity than remembering (Aristotle 1972; Yates 1966).

Within the field of psychology, the experiments of Frederick C. Bartlett (1995) in the 1930s showed that the process of recollection of stories involves what he termed their rationalization, which is particularly evident when the stories being reactivated in memory come from a cultural setting other than that of the subject of his psychological experiments. Such rationalization particularly involves making familiar all that is strange in the original version, as he describes: "Rationalization is to render material acceptable, understandable, comfortable, straightforward; to rob it of all puzzling elements; . . . as such it is a powerful factor in all perceptual and in all reproductive processes . . . the forms it takes are often directly social in significance" (Bartlett 1995: 89). This process is comparable to the process of "understanding" a text, in the way that Paul Ricoeur uses the term to describe the hermeneutic process: a strategy of "making familiar that which was initially alien" (1981: 159).

However, theory of memory as expounded in Western philosophy and psychology only partly helps us to understand what is going on when people tell stories in Quechua-speaking cultures of the Andes. First of all, the Aristotelian model—whereby memory is "of the past," perception is "of the present," and conception is "of the future" and an emphasis is placed on the lapse of time necessary in order to be able to define thought processes as "memory" (Aristotle 1972: 47–48)—is not wholly applicable to the case of Quechua oral narrative practice. Here, mythic-historical and personal consciousness intertwine when storytellers talk about the past as a way of making sense of the present and as a projection toward the future. In this way, indigenous Andean constructs of history dwell less upon what actually happened in the past in a historicist sense than they do upon "what should have been" (see Howard-Malverde 1990; Rappaport 1990); and, equally idealistically, the future that "could come to be" is created in narrative form out of the symbolic material provided by a past that never was. Stories of the Inka buried gold that lies tantalizingly out of reach but ever potentially available to the living are evocative examples of this idealization. In the Andean way of thinking, Quechua narratives suggest, the past is ever present and is ever being remade, in the here and now; memory is a continuous process of reactivation and reformulation of the past relative to present circumstances.

In addition to the distinction between memory and recollection in the classical tradition, the distinction between both of these and imagination needs to be borne in mind. Although both memory and imagination involve mental images, the images of memory are by definition born of the perception of things past, not present (Yates 1966: 33); imagination is a wider-ranging concept and can include the things of pure invention and conception, and is therefore not necessarily tied to the perceptions arising just from experience. Imagination is the essence of all mental life, although it might be best for our purposes to restrict the notion to what is created or invented in the moment, as opposed to what is recollected and can be traced back to past experiences or indeed past imaginings. Thus, one point to explore is how much the stories of Quechua oral tradition are based on recollection and how much on imagination, the latter taken as creativity and innovation arising in the situation of performance. With this aim in mind, Western-derived theories of memory are useful but not sufficient for present purposes. As I have shown elsewhere (Howard-Malverde 1989, 1990), a performative approach to the study of narratives (cf. Bauman 1984; Hymes 1981) is also indispensable.

Although some elements in the stories remain relatively unchanged from one telling to the next, the oral medium nonetheless allows for the adaptation of narrative messages within certain culturally sanctioned parameters and in response to the creative interests of some individuals more than others. The issue of relative degrees of fixity and adaptation in the making of oral stories is also relevant for our consideration of the khipu notations: insofar as these were statistical, and as long as the same principles of coding were applied at the moment of their creation as at the moment of their reading back, one might suppose that the khipu knots recorded an objectively perceived state of things in the past which was relatively closed to reinterpretation at a later date. By contrast, when the notations were used as mnemonic devices for the recording of discursive information, one can suppose that there was more latitude. In this case, the branches, knots, and nodes could be seen as the structural equivalents of the constant motifs in narratives, while the extratextual circumstances of each khipu-reading performance, not least the imagination of the individual khipukamayuq, would be brought to bear in the decoding process.

I have so far avoided the term "mnemonic" to characterize the techniques of recollection and remembering that storytellers use in the exercise of their art. This word implies conscious effort to commit information to memory for later retrieval; to some extent it suggests a mechanical relationship between the visual sign, verbal formula, or khipu knot used to trigger recollection, and the matter that is thus remembered. I believe that the concept of mnemonics cannot fully account for the processes that enable Quechua stories to be reproduced in oral performances from one teller to the next, or by the same teller at points separated over time. Remembering in the Andes is about more than calling to mind set pieces of data by way of verbatim repetition. The latter is not a cultural ideal in the Andean art of storytelling. Remembering in the Andes (*yarpariy* in Quechua I; *yuyariy* in Quechua II) is a culturally vital activity involving not only the telling of stories but also the performance of rituals and participation in fiestas. Forgetting (*qunqay*), by contrast, is the way that neglect of social and ritual obligations is described, and it is punishable in the form of sickness, crop failure, even death. Remembering—through ritual, song, music, as well as storytelling—is about keeping the culture, and thus human and animal society, alive and in harmonious interaction with the world of the saints, the souls of the dead, and the powers of the landscape. Remembering ensures regeneration; forgetting is likely to bring degeneration in its wake. The etymology of the words *yarpay* and *yuyay* is suggestive here, both being morphologically related to *yaya* (creator god, progenitor) and *yachay* (knowledge), terms associated with creation and the generative powers of knowledge.[4]

THE LANDSCAPE AND NARRATIVE PERFORMANCES IN THE ANDES

Belief in the powers of the landscape is a pivotal feature of Andean cosmological systems, as various Quechua testimonies (e.g., Condori Mamani 1982; Gow and Condori 1982) and ethnographies (e.g., Allen 1988) show. My study of Quechua storytelling performances in relation to their context of production has led me to conclude that the single most powerful factor in the operation of memory in the oral tradition is the association that narrators make between the local landscape (context of their own lives) and the events of the stories they tell (see Howard-Malverde 1989). This association reveals itself not only in elements of narrative content but also in grammatical features of the discourse. Analysis of these texts thus suggests a cognitive relationship between land and language that I believe holds the key to the way the oral tradition is continually regenerated in human memory, and a study of which can reinforce our appreciation of the significance of the landscape in all aspects of Andean thought.[5]

As the extracts reproduced here will show, narrative information is plotted onto landscape in such a way that knowledge of the one reinforces knowledge of the other. In light of the importance of landscape as a cognitive paradigm for the shaping of narrative, and vice versa, it does not seem foolhardy to speculate that a similar two-way relationship might have operated between perceptual models of local topography and the spatialization of information distributed along the strings of the khipu. The role of the *ceque* as a mediating channel between landscape and khipu-embodied knowledge, as proposed by R. T. Zuidema in his paper to the 1997 Dumbarton Oaks meeting, provides support for such a speculation.

The conceptualized relationship between land, memory, and oral tradition is illustrated by the opening words of a storytelling performance by doña Jacinta of Pariarca in which she describes how the story she is about to tell was transmitted through the different generations of her family until it reached her own ears and her own memory. A connection between the story, the land, and her family's residence on that land is central to her preoccupations:

EXTRACT I
Kanan leyendakunata qurinaykaptiyki willapaashayki kushishmi yachayashllataq leyendakunata markaakunapita apanaykipa, musyanaykipa, imanuu leyendakuna cada sitiopa kashqantapis. Escuchaykamanki shumaq kay markaakuna imanuu kashqansi. Kanan Carpa Qucha lagunata nuqa musyaa. Say Carpa kan frenten Kiswar. Kiswarchuumi nuqakuna taayashqaa. Mamitaapis kasaraskir hipash kar kasaraskir taayash Kiswar dueñoyuq señorapa wawanwan, don Cirilo Lastra doña Cecilia Guibarrawan. Entonces paykunapis saychuu. Wambra kaptin willapaayash kash saychuu unaypita tatara abuelookuna, tatara abuelaakuna tar, mushuq nueranta willapaayash kash. Saytanami mamaa nuqatapis willapaamarqa. Mamaa willapaamashqanta willapaashayki kanan. Carpa unayshi kanaa marka. . .

Now that you are going to collect legends I shall be pleased to tell you what legends we know about our territory so that you can take them with you, so that you can find out about them, how the legends go for each of the places. Now I know the story of Carpa Lake. Carpa is opposite Kiswar. We used to live at Kiswar. When my mother was a lass, she got married and lived with the son of the owners of Kiswar, don Cirilo Lastra and doña Cecilia Guibarra. So there they were. When they were young, my great-grandparents told their new daughter-in-law the story. Then my mother told it to me. And now I shall tell to you what my mother told me. In the old days they say Carpa was once a town . . . [she goes on to tell a story about the flooding of the town and the formation of the lake in its place . . .]   (INTERVIEW WITH JACINTA L, PARIARCA, JULY 1982)

This statement suggests that a crucial function of oral tradition is to reinforce attachment both to territory and to genealogical roots.[6] The story is said to have been told to her mother by the speaker's great-grandparents in the context of the new in-law taking up virilocal residence on the family land. Its survival in the present narrator's memory has to do with the fact that the

estate at Kiswar was expropriated under agrarian reform and turned over to
the control of the peasant community, a traumatic event for her family and
a theme she returns to again and again in conversation and stories. By will-
ingly communicating her rich repertoire of oral historical knowledge to an
outsider, as she did in the recording sessions we conducted together, doña
Jacinta effectively claims ancestral ties to the territory, even if under the law
and in practice she and her family no longer have ownership of it. This function of oral tradition as a medium for vindicating territorial rights is exercised
repeatedly in many Pariarquino narrators' particular handlings of the stories
they tell, as other extracts will show.

Rural-dwelling Quechua speakers develop a detailed knowledge of the
most intricate topographical features of their local environment from an early
age (see Allen 1988). Pariarquinos verbally articulate this knowledge through
the use of toponyms that acknowledge every feature—from the more prominent mountains, rivers, and streams to the lesser gullies, rocks, clumps of
trees, hillocks, and bends in the road. Discourse about the landscape exhibits
grammatical structures that provide further insights into the way that spatial relations are conceptualized. We can take, for example, the use of the
possessive marker to describe the spatial relationship between two topological points. In the following extract from a videotaped interview, the speaker
was looking out over the mountainous scenery, gesturing with his hands as
he pointed out the different sites visible from where we were standing and
described their locations relative to each other:

EXTRACT 2

Kay chhiqan kashan Sikuya i? Haqay chimpantaqmi kashan Hatun
Hila. Kay ura laduqta Huch'uy Hila sutin. Chaymanta pata laduntaqri Qayarani. Y haqay chhiqantaq kashan Sirqiy. Chaymanta uran
kashan Chakuma. Ura ladun kashan Phanakachi. Astawan ura . . . ,
haqay wichhu wichhu chay kashan, Phiyiphiyini.

This its place is Sikuya, right? And that its opposite place is Hatun
Hila. Its name of this side below is Huch'uy Hila. And then its
side above is Qayarani. And that its place next to it is Sirqiy. Then
its place below is Chakuma. Its place below is Phanakachi. Lower
down . . . , where the bunch grass grows, that's Phiyiphiyini.

(VIDEO INTERVIEW WITH DON VITALIO,
NORTHERN POTOSÍ, BOLIVIA, AUGUST 1991)[7]

The third-person singular possessive suffix -n (its) indicates the relationship between two points in space as one of "belonging" rather than simply

being "above" (*pata*), "below" (*ura*), or "across the valley" (*chimpa*) from each other. A phrase like "pata laduntaqri Qayarani" can literally be glossed as "and then its side above is Qayarani," with the possessive adjective referring back to the previously mentioned location (Huch'uy Hila) in order to express the relative whereabouts of Qayarani. In this way, the different points on the landscape are linked together in a network of interdependency; conceptually, it is as if the landscape were being constructed as a human-like system of relationships, produced through human discourse in the very act of speaking about it.[8]

The Pariarca corpus of oral narratives also provides examples of this use of possessive markers on terms referring to points on the landscape. In storytelling, these markers combine with deictic features, indicating the ego-oriented nature of the narrative performance. In the following extract, don Eduardo describes the approach of the Inka across the local landscape in the direction of his own community, the place where he is situated as he speaks. Although these events ostensibly took place in the mythic-historical past, the narrator actualizes them in his mind's eye by use of the contrasting deictics *kay* (proximal "this") and *say* (distal "that") as he relates the different points in space one to the other:

EXTRACT 3: THE STORY OF THE CACIQUE AMBRAY, I
Say pedazo Vichachaakami saypa hutin.
Saypa kaylaaninchuunami kan Inka Wayin, posaadakuyashqa
    inkakuna.
Say posaadakuyashqanpitanami, kaylaanin, más kaylaachuunami,
    hutin Shuntur.

The name of that spot is Vichachaaka.
Over in this direction from there is Inka Wayin, where the Inkas took
    lodgings.
After that place where they took lodgings, over in this direction from
    there, more over this way, the name of the place is Shuntur.

(HOWARD-MALVERDE 1990: 74–75)

The spatial orientation of the events described in this extract is defined by reference to *kaylaa* ("this direction"; *-laa* would appear to derive from the Spanish *lado*). In the second line, this term is used in a construction that combines the genitive *-pa* with the third-person singular possessive *-n: say-pa kay-laa-ni-n* ("that of this direction" + connective + possessive; literally glossed as "of that its direction here"). The *say* (that) refers back to Vichachaaka, whereas *kay* (this) refers forward to the place of the speaker. The use of the double possessive to link the two helps to construct the landscape as a network of points in a relationship of interdependent "belonging" (cf. Extract 2). The conceptual role played by Quechua deictics and possessive markers in such narrative contexts (see also note 8) invites speculation as to how these grammatical resources might have been drawn upon in khipu-reading performances as a possible means of expressing the interdependency among the knots and between the knots and strings, and thus of structuring the information these held.

In don Eduardo's narrative, furthermore, the juxtaposing of *say* and *kay* enables the events of the mythic-historical past to be brought into the personal present: not only is "there" related to "here," but "then" relates to "now," and the persona of the story's protagonists contrasts (and at times conflates) with don Eduardo's own persona in telling the story. The contrast between *say* and *kay* thus creates a bridge between past and present, and between the actor narrated and the actor narrating (cf. Howard-Malverde 1990). This point leads me to discuss the performative features of Quechua oral narration in order better to appreciate the way the resultant discourses are constructed.

ORGANIZATIONAL PRINCIPLES OF QUECHUA NARRATIVE PERFORMANCE

In the Pariarca corpus of mythic-historical narratives, an interconnection between the three basic organizational principles of time, space, and person can be seen at work. When the narrated events occurred, where they occurred, who participated in them, and whether or not the narrators include themselves as participants are key organizational features. Mediating these three dimensions is a fourth, that of the epistemological status attributed to the information being imparted: the nature of the speaker's source of knowledge and the truth value the speakers attach to the facts being recounted.

In oral narrative performance, an important distinction emerges in light of which the interconnections between time, space, person, and epistemological value can be better discerned. This is the distinction between the events of the story told (involving events that unfold in a temporal and spatial framework not necessarily coinciding with that of the narrator's own life) and the event of the storytelling (the situation of performance, a communicative event during which a narrator puts the story into words before an audience; cf. Bakhtin 1981; Howard-Malverde 1989).[9] The face-to-face interaction that characterizes oral performance makes lack of subjective involvement in the events of the story told, on the storyteller's part, improbable in theory and rare in practice. An analysis of the Pariarca stories from this performance-oriented perspective reveals how storytellers play with the spatial and temporal frameworks of the stories in such a way as to make mythic-historical events less removed from the circumstances of their own lives. We see how so-called traditional narratives are transformed and reactualized in living practice, and how the boundaries that separate the storytelling from the story told come to blur (Howard-Malverde 1989). In seeking to ascertain how memory and imagination operate in the structuring of Quechua narrative discourse, it is useful to bear these performative principles in mind.

STRUCTURING FEATURES OF QUECHUA NARRATIVES

The structuring of the narratives can be examined from the point of view of (1) internal features of the texts themselves (grammatical devices that assist the memory and thus the flow of the story, and elements of content that have key associations for the narrator and the audience), and (2) external factors to do with the situation of performance. I discuss each of these in turn and then consider the extent to which features of narrative structure may both elucidate and be explained by the relationship between landscape, memory, and oral tradition.

Text-Internal Features

Text-internal features having to do with the structuring of the narrative are both morphological and syntactical. Elements of content (e.g., reference to features of the natural environment) also help in plotting the story's events, as does the chaining of the protagonists' actions through sequences of cause and effect.

The most typical devices at the grammatical level are (1) the use of verbal subordination or switch referencing on the verb, enabling parallelism in the sequencing of events; (2) the use of directional suffixes indicating centrifugal or centripetal movement, or movement in, out, up, and down, locating actions in space and relating protagonists to each other and the world around them; (3) use of deictic markers that connect the event of the story told with the event of the storytelling; (4) use of the possessive construction to relate spatial coordinates one to the other; (5) sequencers such as *saypita* ("after that"; equivalent to the *chaymanta* of Quechua II); (6) the use of reported speech. By the latter means, the narrative frequently shifts from monologue to dialogue (albeit through the single authorial voice of the narrator); in most cases, such dialogue is encased in a citative frame ("so saying," "when he said," etc.), but in certain instances, this frame is suppressed and the narration loses its strictly narrative qualities, taking on dramatized dialogue form. With the exception of items 3 and 4, already illustrated, all of these text-internal features are exemplified in Extract 4, each sentence of which is numbered to assist the analysis.

EXTRACT 4: THE STORY OF ACHKAY; PURSUIT SEQUENCE I

1. . . . entonces machaychuu ishkan wambrakunaq warkaraykaayaanaa
2. warkaraykaayaptinqa paasaskinaa allqay
3. allqay paasaskiptinqa wambrakuna qayakunaa "tiyuy allqay hipiykallaamay!" nir
4. nir qayakuptinqa munanaasu allqayqa
5. "imapaataa 'aqish baaraq' nimarqayki?" nir paasakunaa
6. hikpanman atuqqa paasanaa. . . .

1. . . . so in the cave the two children were hanging
2. as they were hanging there the dominico bird passed by
3. when the dominico bird passed by, the children called out: "Uncle Dominico, get us out of here!" saying
4. when they called out saying thus, the dominico didn't want to
5. "why did you call me 'worm eater' [literally, 'worm measurer']," saying he passed on by
6. behind him a fox came along. . . .   (HOWARD-MALVERDE 1984: 16)

This extract is taken from a story about Achkay, an anthropophagous female ancestress of mythic times about whom many tales are told in central highland Peru. This sequence is one of several in which a series of birds and animals pass by the place where two children have been confined to a basket and suspended from a rock by their parents, in an attempt by the latter to get rid of their hungry offspring during a time of famine. It opens with a typical narrative sequencer (in this case a Hispanism, *entonces*, which alternates with *saypita*, "after that" in this dialect), and when it closes, a spatial adverb (*hikpanman*, "behind him") moves the action on to the next sequence. Within the bounds of the sequence itself, there are no adverbial conjunctions or sequencers of any sort; the narrative is constructed entirely through the use of direct speech and verbal subordination: when a change of actor is indicated, switch reference comes into play as a means of leading on to the next action; the *-pti-* suffix achieves a seesaw effect whereby the same verb is used twice, first as main verb and then as subordinated verb, anticipating the switch to a new actor as subject of a new main verb—a form of grammatical parallelism.

The pattern is represented diagrammatically below. The letters in the diagram refer to the protagonists in the narrated event: the children hanging on the rock = A, the dominico bird = B, and the fox = C. The sequence is introduced by a conjunction (triple >>>); the tense is the indirect-knowledge narrative past marked by -naa; within the sequence, the action moves on by means of verbal subordination (same actor -r; single >) and switch reference (change of actor -pti-; double >>); when the sequence involving protagonists A and B comes to an end, an adverbial sequencer is introduced (triple >>>), and the new protagonist C comes onto the scene.

1.	entonces	>>>	so	
1.	warkaraykaayaanaa		they were hanging	A
2.	warkaraykaayaptinqa	>>	as they were hanging	A
2.	paasaskinaa		he passed by	B
3.	paasaskiptinqa	>>	when he passed by	B
3.	qayakunaa nir	>	they called out saying	A
4.	nir qayakuptinqa	>>	as they called out saying	A
4.	munanaasu		he didn't want	B
5.	nir paasakunaa	>	saying he passed by	B
6.	hikpanman	>>>	behind him	
6.	paasanaa		came by	C

This type of narrative structuring is common in those cases where the story line bears no reference to the spatial context of the performance; the structuring of the story is organized entirely within the text itself, and there is no use of deictic markers, present tenses, personal-witness validation, toponyms, or other devices that situate the action outside the imagined space of the narrated events (in this case, an unnamed rock). To put it another way, no features of this narrative create a link between the event of the storytelling and the event of the story told.

Another way story lines are structured is by attaching the action to a named territory through the use of toponyms; by this means, the shape of the land and the shape of the story iconically represent each other: as the itineraries followed by the narrated protagonists are traced over the landscape, so the story's plot unfolds. This is a striking feature of another type of story in the Achkay cycle in which the anthropophagous old woman is believed to have been a dual figure, one of whom comes onto Pariarca territory, while the other remains on the mountaintop on the other side of the valley. On arriving on local land, the old woman threatens a member of the population. The potential victim takes flight uphill toward the village, and Achkay follows in hot pursuit.[10] In so doing, Achkay's view of the path taken by her prey is made difficult by the sharp incline. She calls out to the other Achkay, who, from her distant vantage point, can see the full lay of the land. A dialogue ensues back and forth across the valley as the Achkay on the mountain opposite guides the Achkay on community territory as to the right way to follow her victim up the hill. In this dialogue, several local toponyms are mentioned, and the narrative takes shape just as the landscape is traced out in the narrator's mind's eye and portrayed for the benefit of the listener. What is noticeable in Extract 5 is the way the citative framing (*nin* "she says") is suppressed and the narrative form cedes to dramatized dialogue as the narration gathers pace:

EXTRACT 5: THE STORY OF ACHKAY; PURSUIT SEQUENCE 2

Sayman chaskir, achkay chaskirqa "¿Maytanam maytanam aywan
    tui— —y?"[11] nin.
"Wayraqtanam aywaykan tui— —y," ninmi.
"¿Maytanam maytanam?" say Wayraqman chaskir, "¿Maytanam
    maytanam aywan tui— —y?"
"Achkay Wayi iskinantanam tumarkun tui— —y."
"¿Maytanam maytanam aywan tui— —y?" Saki Warawyaman chaskir
    tapun yapayqa qayakun.
"Qiqra Krustanam wisaykan tui— —y."
"¿Maytanam maytanam aywan tui— —y?"
"Haka Qaranantanam wisaykan tui— —y."
"¿Maytanam maytanam aywan tui— —y?"
"Trensa Machaytanam wisaykan tui— —y."
"¿Maytanam maytanam aywan tui— —y?"
"Qantu Hirkawantanam aywaykan tui— —y."
Saypa pipis rikashnataaku.
¿Kay ruripita manaku?
Ruripita rikashqa.
Shamuptin rikashnataaku.
Nuqansipis kananqa taqay hirka sapaamash rikansinasu mas puntataqa
    ari, saynuu.
Sayshi aska runaman chaanaa Kanchashman niyanchaa.
Saychuuna wanurqanku imanuura pi, saychuushi pamparan say
    washalaa qallan rurinchuu.

Howard: ¿Imanuu wanusirqa?
Doña Paula: Aska runa imachir pi wanusirqa, ¿imanuuraa? Mana fijota
   sayta musyaasu.

Arriving there, Achkay said, "Which way now? Which way is she
   going now, my frie— —nd?"
"She's going past Wayraq now, my frie— —nd!" she said.
"Which way now? Which way now?" she said, arriving at Wayraq,
   "Which way now? Which way is she going now, my frie— —nd?"
"She's going up around the bend at Achkay Wayi now, my frie— —
   nd!"
"Which way now? Which way is she going now, my frie— —nd," she
   called out again on arriving at Saki Warawya.
"She's going up by Qiqra Krus now, my frie— —nd!"
"Which way now? Which way is she going now, my frie— —nd?"
"She's going up by Haka Qaranan now, my frie— —nd!"
"Which way now? Which way is she going now, my frie— —nd?"
"She's going up by Trensa Machay now, my frie— —nd!"
"Which way now? Which way is she going now, my frie— —nd?"
"She's going up by Qantu Hirka now, my frie— —nd!"
But then she couldn't see any further.
From down below you know?
She was looking from down below.
As the girl came on (in this direction) she couldn't see any more.
And we too today, we can't see any further than that because the hill
   blocks our view in that way.
And so she arrived where there were a lot of people at Kanchash they
   say.
And they killed her, I wonder how? They say they buried her over
   there under a boulder.
Howard: How did they kill her?
Doña Paula: A lot of people must have killed her, I wonder how? I
   haven't heard that part very well.   (HOWARD-MALVERDE 1989: 32)

The use of verbs of movement and verb suffixes that indicate direction of
movement over the landscape is prevalent in narratives such as this, where the
action unfolds on local territory. The structuring of the discourse amounts
to a verbal enactment of local topographical knowledge, as linguistic features
indicate. For example, in Extract 5, the verb *wisay* (to go uphill) is used to
describe direction of action. In Extract 6 below, by contrast, the verb suf-

fixes -*rku*- ("movement upwards"; -*rka*- before -*mu*-) and -*mu*- (centripetal movement) map the direction of the victim's flight onto the local territory, imagined by the narrator as he speaks:

EXTRACT 6: THE STORY OF ACHKAY; PURSUIT SEQUENCE 3

Qiqra Krusmanna hiqarkamushtami rikaskamush simpapita Martinaq.
Say oras niskinshi "Qiqra Krusmannami hiqarkun tui— —y" ninshi.
Niptin yapay sayman tro— —ti charkush pishipar aa.
"Martina— —a! Maytanam tui— —y?" niptinqa "Maqra
  Hirkamannami hiqarku— —n" nish.
Sayman charkupis "Martina— —a! Maytanam tui— —y?"
Niptinqa "Anyaymannami hiqarku— —n", nish, "Anyaychuunam
  tui— —y" nimush aa.

Martina could see across from the other side of the valley that he had
  reached up as far as Qiqra Krus.
Then they say she said, "He's reached up as far as Qiqra Krus now, my
  frie— —nd."
When the other said that, again [Achkay] hastened upward, growing
  very tired.
When she said, "Martina— —a! Which way now, my frie— —nd?"
  [the other Achkay] said, "Now he's getting up to Maqra Hirka."
When she got up there and when she called, "Martina— —a! Which
  way now, my frie— —nd?"
"He's getting up to Anyay," said [the other], "He's at Anyay now," she
  said from over there.   (HOWARD-MALVERDE 1989: 28)

Once Achkay turns the brow of the hill, her view back to the place where her counterpart (a daughter named Martina in this version) is located is obstructed, and she can no longer call out to her for guidance. The dialogue ceases, and it is not long before Achkay is captured and put to death by the local population, as described in Extract 7:

EXTRACT 7: THE STORY OF ACHKAY; PURSUIT SEQUENCE 4

Entonces Runa Hirkaman chaskirqa "Qayakuskishaa" ninampaaqa
  manana rikashqanasu wawantapis Martiinantapis.
Entonces upallana aywash.

So when she reached Runa Hirka and said to herself "I'll just call out,"
  she found she could no longer see her daughter, her Martina.
So she went on her way in silence.   (HOWARD-MALVERDE 1989: 28)

Text-External Factors

In Extracts 6 and 7, the relationship between knowledge of local topography, visibility, and knowledge of oral tradition is further exemplified. Where the lay of the land impedes vision in the real world, in the world of the narrative protagonists the story line takes a definitive turn or is curtailed altogether. This relationship can only be fully appreciated by taking the personal identities of the storytellers and their situations of performance into account. We see here the influence of text-external factors, to which I now turn, on the shaping of the narrative.

The narrator of Extract 5, for example, resided on the territory that she maps out in her account, and she was looking out over this named and familiar landscape as she told the story. We have the impression that she is placing herself, in her mind's eye, in the physical location of the Achkay sentinel figure as she comments: "And we too today, we can't see any further than that because the hill blocks our view in that way." Other narrators, resident in other localities, told the same story but traced different topographical contours in their versions. On the one hand, this variation suggests differing territorial interests on their part. The naming of local landmarks in oral narration is not an arbitrary exercise, but is tied up with issues of rights and access to particular stretches of land.[12] On the other hand, we realize that the toponyms listed as the narrative unfolds are not objective facts learned by rote and reproduced from one narrator or from one performance to the next, but that they emerge in the moment, in accordance with the particular perspectives of individual storytellers. This narrative thus provides evidence of the exercise of the imagination in the storytelling art, which does not depend solely on recollection, in the terms outlined at the beginning of this chapter. Furthermore, a relationship between "that which is seen" and "that which is known" is suggested by the fact that the narrator provides only sparse details of the story from this point on; no further toponyms on her local terrain are cited, and the description of Achkay's end is vague: "A lot of people must have killed her, I wonder how? I haven't heard that part very well." It is as if doña Paula were hampered in her knowledge of the oral tradition by the hill that blocks her view. Again the link between knowledge of landscape, memory, and cultural knowledge suggests itself.

HISTORY, MEMORY, AND DATA-SOURCE MARKING

Constructs of history and familiarity with place are mutually bound up with the operation of epistemological categories in Quechua oral cultural expres-

TABLE 2.1.   Epistemic Modality Markers in Quechua I and II

	Quechua II (Cusco)	Quechua I (Huamalíes)
Verbal Suffixes		
past tense direct knowledge	*-rqa-*	*-rqa-*
past tense indirect knowledge	*-sqa-*	*-naa*
perfect tense ("past in the present")	—	*-shqa-/-sh*
Evidential Suffixes		
direct knowledge	*-mi/-n*	*-mi*
indirect knowledge	*-si/-s*	*-shi*

sion. It is relevant here to remind ourselves of the grammatical means by which these categories are expressed in the language. Quechua, Aymara, and other Amerindian languages grammatically mark what can best be described as "epistemic modality" in a number of ways. In Quechua, this category reveals itself in the tense/aspect system and in the use of evidential suffixes. These two classes of morpheme serve to indicate either direct witness of the events described in a given utterance, or indirect knowledge of the facts reported, respectively. The tense/aspect suffixes and the evidential suffixes occur correlatively as a means for the speaker to indicate the epistemological status of the information being imparted (source of knowledge and the truth value attributed to such information). This feature of Quechua grammar has been much commented on by Andeanist researchers (e.g., Dedenbach Salazar 1997; Howard-Malverde 1988; Mannheim and Van Vleet 1998). It is here necessary to contextualize the system as it works in the Quechua I dialect spoken in Pariarca in order fully to appreciate Extracts 8 and 9 below, which appear to deviate from the norm (see Table 2.1).

According to this system, narrative discourse portraying events not witnessed by the speaker, such as stories about the community's "mythic history" of the distant past, is characterized by the use of the *-naa/-shi* combination of suffixes in Huamalíes Quechua. The equivalent combination in modern-day Cusco varieties of Quechua II is *-sqa/-si*. Validation of information based on the speaker's personal witness is achieved through the use of the *-rqa-/-mi* combination in Quechua II. In Huamalíes, this formula occurs in alternation with the perfect tense, thus the combination *-shqa-/-mi* is also found. Whereas *-rqa-* is clearly a preterite, referring to events no longer immediately relevant in the present, *-shqa-* is described by local speakers as a "tiempo casi presente" (almost present tense) used for referring to events of continuing relevance to the present, making it of a similar conceptual order to the English present perfect tense in this respect. In narrative discourse of the mythic-historical type, of which the Achkay stories are an example, the typical narrative suffix is -*naa*. The nonpersonal witness suffix -*shi* occurs in these stories in the opening scene-setting utterances, but is then dropped.

In the cycle of stories regarding a local cacique and his interaction with the Inka Pachakuti, which make up the other main theme of Pariarca oral tradition, the -*naa* suffix is also used in the majority of the versions I recorded. One particular version, however, that of don Eduardo, makes untypical use of the -*shqa*- "past in the present" tense and uses personal-witness validation to affirm as direct knowledge not only events concerning his own personal past and that of his addressee, but also those in which the cacique and the Inka participated. Extract 8 gives us an example of this:

EXTRACT 8: THE STORY OF THE CACIQUE AMBRAY, 2

1. Qallari-mu-shaa parla-r-na aa.
2. Fernando Ambray cacique Lloclla kwintu-n-ta kanan-mi yapay willa-paa-shayki qunqa-shqa-yki-pita.
3. Primero ka-shqa estabilidaa-ni-n-qa Apu Raqaa-mi.
4. Qanyantin toma-ykaa. . . . fotografía toma-ykaa-mu-shqa-yki, say-chuu-mi ta-shqa Fernando Ambray cacique Lloclla.
5. Say-pita-na-mi say inka-kuna shamu-r conquista-ta rura-r "Huk marka Lima chika-ta palacio-ta rura-shun" ni-r kay Pariarca-pa shamu-r kacha-mu-shqa enviado-n-ta, Felipe-ta.

1. I'll begin speaking now.
2. I'll tell you the story of Fernando Ambray cacique Lloclla again, as you have forgotten it.
3. His first place of residence was Apu Raqaa.
4. The other day you were taking photos over there, that's where Fernando Ambray cacique Lloclla lived.
5. Then the Inkas came to conquer, saying "Let's build a town like Lima and a palace," and they sent their envoy Felipe here.

(HOWARD-MALVERDE 1990: 18)

This use of the -*shqa*-/-*mi* combination is sustained throughout don Eduardo's performance wherever he describes the alleged past deeds on local community territory of these particular mythic-historical personages. In Extract 9, there is variation on this pattern, however:

EXTRACT 9: THE STORY OF THE CACIQUE AMBRAY, 3

1. Say Qipa Cara punta kay-laa-nin-n hunaq-na-mi, say Qipa Cara punta-chuu-na-mi kacha-ri-ya-sh ka-shqa ornamento-n-kuna-ta inka-kuna.
2. Say castillo-chuu tari-sh ka-shqa kay postrero-raa-chaa veintinueve de junio-chuu-shi tari-naa.
3. Huk primoo-mi ka-rqa-n Pablo Martel Villanueva huti-n ka-rqa-n say primoo-pa, aha.
4. Say-mi willa-ma-rqa-n say-ta-q "Tari-rqa-a inka-pa ornamento-n-ta y nuqa-qa 'Pi-ta negociante-kuna-chir kay-chuu-qa hama-pa-yka-n' ni-rqa-a-mi, say-ta rika-chaku-shqa-a-yaq tikra-ska-ku-naa-paa mana ka-naa-su say ornamento-kuna."
5. "Maha-raa-naa" ni-r-mi willa-paa-ma-rqa.
6. Say-ta-na-mi nuqa yarpa-ra-yka-a.
7. Say-chuu say-raa-shi lindo ornamento-kuna-qa.
8. Say-nuu-chaa willa-ma-rqa-n say-ta.
9. Say-na-mi pasa-shqa Qipa Cara-pa.

1. There above Qipa Cara, over in this direction, on the ridge above Qipa Cara, the Inkas had left behind their ornaments.
2. Later on in recent times, one 29th of June, they say that someone had found them.
3. He was a cousin of mine, Pablo Martel Villanueva his name was, that cousin of mine.
4. This is what he told me: "I found the Inka's ornaments and then I said to myself, 'What traveling merchant must be taking a rest around here?' whilst I was taking a look around; by the time I turned back, the ornaments weren't there anymore."
5. "They were all still spread out on the ground," so saying he told me.
6. I am just remembering that now.
7. The beautiful ornaments were still there, so they say.
8. That is the story as he told it to me.
9. So then they passed by Qipa Cara. (HOWARD-MALVERDE 1990: 34)

In this extract the switch from the narrator's habitual -shqa-/-mi combination for talking about the deeds of the Inka (line 1) to use of the nonpersonal witness -naa/-shi combination in line 2 suggests a shift in the perceived epistemological status of the information being imparted. In line 3, the story about how the Inka ornaments were seen lying about on the ground, then only to disappear, is attributed to hearsay evidence from a third party, the narrator's cousin. In the utterances where he recalls the exchange of words he had with the cousin, the speaker uses the personal-witness *-mi* suffix combined with the preterite tense *-rqa-* (lines 4 and 5). As soon as the anecdote about what the cousin had to say is concluded (line 8 rounds it off), the narrator reverts to the use of personal-witness *-shqa-/-mi* for the main story line, talking about the passage of the Inka through the place called Qipa Cara.

To explain what prompts the narrator of Extracts 8 and 9 to use personal-witness validation for talking about mythic-historical events in which he did not personally participate, we must look to text-external factors. Don Eduardo was a vociferous critic of the conduct of certain members of the Community Administrative Council at the time of his performance. On many occasions in conversation he elaborated on this, and in his interpretation of local history he also lays the blame for socioeconomic hardships in the present at the door of the recalcitrant cacique of the past. Conceptually, he appears to conflate the attitudes and behavior of past political authorities with the power struggles and factionalisms he sees in force today. At a number of levels, his story rationalizes present ills in terms of a past that should have been but never was. As if to reinforce the message, the arrival of the Inka is actualized in performance by use of proximal demonstrative phrases ("here they come"; "they went this way") and the directional suffix *-mu-* on verbs of movement, as if describing the arrival of the Inka coming toward the speaker as he speaks (cf. discussion of Extract 3 above). What enables him to build this bridge between past and present, and to assert the deeds of the cacique and the Inka as being of his own direct knowledge, is the extratextual fact that the events are associated with the known topography of his personal experience, localities that are named throughout his narrative.[13]

Through pragmatic use of the grammatical resources of his language, don Eduardo brings the past into the present. The Inka, conceptually at least, enter the spatiotemporal bounds of his own life experience. Wherever there are allusions to named places on the local territory this is so. Places thus act as direct-witness validation. What is of interest is that when he invokes word-of-mouth as a source of information (the cousin's anecdote), he reverts to indirect-knowledge marking. This pragmatic use of language suggests that for Quechua speakers, within the framework of a certain world view and in certain contexts of utterance, places speak truer than people.

CONCLUDING REMARKS

I began this chapter with some observations about memory, recollection, and imagination from the point of view of Western classical tradition. I noted that, for a number of reasons, Western theory of memory has limited application to the operation and cultural function of memory in Andean practice. In the Andes, a theory of remembering that relegates the past to a preterite time has little conceptual relevance. The cultural function of remembering in Andean ways of thinking is a regenerative one, whereby the past provides the symbolic resources for making sense of the present and projecting toward the future, in a way that allows at once for continuity and change. In storytelling, this regenerative principle activates a close relationship between the discursive construction of the landscape, the knowledge so produced, and the performance of oral traditional narratives. The storyteller cited in Extract 5 sums up the essence of this relationship when she claims to know no more details of the story "because of the hill that blocks her view."

In analyzing the different grammatical devices used in the structuring of narrative discourse, features of structure have been seen both to elucidate and to be explicable in terms of the relationship between landscape, memory, and narration. Only by adopting a context-dependent approach to the study of the storytelling event and its resultant text can this relationship be drawn out. Certain features of grammar in particular have been seen to aid the process, for example, using text-internal changes (e.g., -pti- switch reference); invoking the external setting of the performance (e.g., centripetal -mu- and the use of possessive marking in chaining place-names); and building a bridge between storytelling and story told (e.g., through use of evidential suffixes).

To return to my opening question, I can only speculate as to the insights we might gain from the above findings for our understanding of the khipu as a communicative medium. The importance of topographical knowledge for the activation of memory and the regeneration of oral tradition in performance may provide a clue. Landscape in Andean culture can be seen as the ordered product of both verbal discourse and ritual practice, which reached its most systematized form of expression in the *ceque* lines of Inka times. My speculation is that, at the very least, the discursively constructed landscape, the *ceque* lines, and the khipu may be homologous forms: visible, tactile, and emotive, they each embody knowledge, produce history, and harness the memory. At the most, we might suppose that some of the grammatical features of language that assist the structuring of context-dependent narrative, as discussed here, reveal habits of thought that might also have been applied to the process of coding and decoding the syntax of the khipu's knots and strings. More specifically, insofar as the branches, nodes, and knots were hierarchically ordered, we can speculate as to how that hierarchy might have provided a framework for the spoken discourses generated in khipu readings (helping to identify and formulate discourse segments of varying degrees of inclusivity within the narrative whole, for example). Furthermore, just as points on the landscape are discursively plotted and interconnected in both narrative and *ceque*-related ritual, so it may be fruitful to consider the khipu as a topographically structured network of meaning-bearing knots and strings. To put these hypotheses to the test, a study of the structure of early-colonial narrative accounts known to have originated directly in the performances of the khipukamayuq would be a necessary avenue for further research.

NOTES

1. Indeed, and as Bruce Mannheim also observed in the course of the discussions, the nonlinear nature of the mythic narratives recorded by some of the early-colonial Spanish chroniclers (those of Juan de Betanzos and Guaman Poma de Ayala, for example) may be due to the fact that they derive from khipu-based recitations by their Quechua-speaking informants.

2. Similar varieties of Quechua (as spoken in the Department of Ancash and in other provinces of the Department of Huánuco) have been described by authors such as Parker (1976) and Torero (1974); however, a specific description of Huamalíes Quechua remains to be published.

3. Bruce Mannheim and Krista Van Vleet (1998) make an important methodological contribution to Quechua narrative studies by demonstrating the way stories most naturally arise in the course of conversation, rather than treating them as isolable units or distinctive "genres" in performance; thus, stories should be treated as dialogical discursive phenomena rather than as monological texts. Howard-Malverde (1988, 1989, 1990) also highlights the permeability of myth, history, and personal biography in Quechua narrative practice.

4. The conceptual links between ideas about knowledge and creativity as suggested by the word *yachay* and its cognates in different contexts are further discussed in Howard n.d.; see also Itier 1993.

5. These remarks are also relevant to the debates sparked by the May 1998 international meeting of Andeanists at the University of Wales at Lampeter: "Kay Pacha: International Symposium on Earth, Land, Water, and Culture in the Andes."

6. Another example in the ethnographical literature is Allen 1988.

7. This text is taken from a corpus of interviews conducted among Bolivian (Quechua II) speakers in Northern Potosí; the grammatical feature in question (use of the possessive adjective in describing spatial relationships) is also found in the Quechua spoken in Pariarca, as will be seen.

8. It should be noted that possessive markers are frequently used to mark intrinsic relationships between "inanimate" objects or substances in Quechua (to characterize

the connection between the different parts of a woven item, or that between condiments and cooked food, for example). As is also the case with other Amerindian languages, such a feature gives us insight into the culturally relative nature of animacy and humanness.

9. This distinction can be related to that made by Roman Jakobson between "narrated event" and "speech event" (1990: 390).

10. Versions vary as to the gender of the victim and the specific route taken during the pursuit sequence.

11. The use of the formulaic "tui— —y" address term is a "key to performance," in Richard Bauman's terms (1984), in that it is a term used only in the stories about Achkay and is said to be typical of the way she speaks, with the long, drawn-out vowel and a falsetto, slightly cross tone of voice.

12. For other notable instances, see Salomon 1991 and Urton 1990.

13. The didactic tone that the *-shqa-/-mi* combination brings to his narrative may also be partly explained by the fact that don Eduardo was telling the story to an outsider to the culture, someone unfamiliar with the local topography and its nomenclature. We can only wonder whether he would have made the same choice of suffixes had he been telling the story in a more naturally occurring situation of performance.

REFERENCES

Allen, Catherine J. 1988. *The Hold Life Has: Coca and Cultural Identity in an Andean Community*. Washington, D.C.: Smithsonian Press.

Aristotle. 1972. "De memoria et reminiscentia." In *Aristotle on Memory*, edited and translated by Richard Sorabji, 47–60. London: Duckworth.

Bakhtin, Mikhail. 1981. "Forms of Time and the Chronotope in the Novel." In *The Dialogic Imagination*, edited by Michael Holquist; translated by Caryl Emerson and Michael Holquist, 84–258. Austin: University of Texas Press.

Bartlett, Frederick C. 1995. *Remembering: A Study in Experimental and Social Psychology*. Introduction by Walter Kintsch. Cambridge: Cambridge University Press.

Bauman, Richard. 1984. *Verbal Art as Performance*. Prospect Heights, Ill.: Waveland Press.

Condori Mamani, Gregorio. 1982. *Autobiografía*. Edited by Ricardo Valderrama and Carmen Escalante. Cusco: Centro Bartolomé de Las Casas.

Cummins, Tom. 1997. "Spanish Memory Devices in the Early Colonial Andes." Paper delivered to the round table on the Andean Khipu, Dumbarton Oaks, Washington, D.C. Manuscript.

Dedenbach Salazar, Sabine. 1997. "Point of View and Evidentiality in the Huarochirí Texts (Peru, Seventeenth Century)." In *Creating Context in Andean Cultures*, edited by R. Howard-Malverde, 149–167. New York: Oxford University Press.

Gow, Rosalind, and Bernabé Condori. 1982. *Kay pacha*. Cusco: Centro Bartolomé de Las Casas.

Howard, Rosaleen. N.d. "*Yachay*: The *Tragedia del fin de Atahuallpa* (Lara 1989) as evidence of the colonisation of knowledge in the Andes." In *Knowledge and Learning in the Andes: Ethnographic Perspectives*, edited by Henry Stobart and Rosaleen Howard. Liverpool: Liverpool University Press. In press.

Howard-Malverde, Rosaleen. 1984. "Achkay: Una tradición quechua del Alto Mara-ñón." *Amerindia* 9. Chantiers Amerindia Supplement 5. Paris: Association d'Ethno-linguistique Amérindienne.

―――. 1988. "Talking about the Past: Tense and Testimonials in Quechua Narrative Discourse." *Amerindia* 13: 125–155.

―――. 1989. "Storytelling Strategies in Quechua Narrative Performance." *Journal of Latin American Lore* 15, no. 2: 3–71.

―――. 1990. "The Speaking of History 'Willapaakushayki' or Quechua Ways of Tell-ing the Past." *Research Papers* 21. London: Institute of Latin American Studies, Uni-versity of London.

Hymes, Dell. 1981. "Breakthrough into Performance." In *"In Vain I Tried to Tell You": Essays in Native American Ethnopoetics,* edited by Dell Hymes, 79–141. Philadelphia: University of Pennsylvania Press.

Itier, César. 1993. "Estudio y comentario lingüístico." In *Joan de Santa Cruz Pachacuti Yamqui Salcamaygua: Relación de Antigüedades deste reyno del Piru,* edited by Pierre Duviols and César Itier, 127–178. Cusco: Institut Français d'Etudes Andines/Cen-tro Bartolomé de Las Casas.

Jakobson, Roman. 1990. "Shifters and Verbal Categories." In *On Language,* edited by Linda R. Waugh and Monique Monville-Burston, 386–392. Cambridge: Harvard University Press.

Mannheim, Bruce, and Krista Van Vleet. 1998. "The Dialogics of Southern Quechua Narrative." *American Anthropologist* 100, no. 2: 326–346.

Parker, Gary. 1976. *Gramática quechua Ancash-Huailas.* Lima: Instituto de Estudios Peruanos.

Rappaport, Joanne. 1990. *Cumbe Reborn: An Andean Ethnography of History.* Chicago: University of Chicago Press.

Ricoeur, Paul. 1981. "What Is a Text?" In *Hermeneutics and the Human Sciences,* edited by John B. Thompson, 145–164. Cambridge: Cambridge University Press.

Salomon, Frank. 1991. "Introductory Essay." In *The Huarochirí Manuscript: A Testa-ment of Ancient and Colonial Andean Religion,* 1–38. Austin: University of Texas Press.

Torero, Alfredo. 1974. *El quechua y la historia social andina.* Lima: Universidad Ricardo Palma.

Urton, Gary. 1990. *The History of a Myth: Paqariqtambo and the Origin of the Inkas.* Austin: University of Texas Press.

Yates, Frances. 1966. *The Art of Memory.* London: Routledge Kegan Paul.

PART TWO

STRUCTURE AND INFORMATION IN THE KHIPU

A Khipu Information String Theory

THREE   *William J Conklin*

INTRODUCTION

The chroniclers of the Spanish Conquest of Peru provided both eyewitness and word-of-mouth reports on the many uses of the plied and knotted-string information devices called khipu that the Inka used. Although these reports have varying degrees of credibility, the discovery, in the centuries since the conquest, of actual khipu from the Inka Empire provides material substance to those reports. In addition to these reports on the uses of khipu, Felipe Guaman Poma de Ayala, the ardent native chronicler of the woes of the conquest, provided many drawn images of khipu. A comparison of his depictions of khipu[1] with recovered khipu indicates that he indeed had a very accurate knowledge of their look and feel. Most of his drawings show khipu being held with two hands and spread out, seemingly for display to the reader, and many of his khipu images are associated with accounting tasks of Inka bureaucrats. One of his drawings (see Figure 3.1), however, shows a khipu rolled up, labeled as a letter, and being carried. Some of the khipu still in existence today (see Figure 3.2) have exactly the same rolled-up spiral form as the khipu being carried in Guaman Poma's drawing. This technical detail makes us take seriously his labeling of the khipu as a *letter*, a word that has far-reaching implications for a khipu information theory.

Discussions on the nature of khipu tend to focus on the word *mnemonic*. Those who doubt the modern readability of the Inka khipu argue that the real message resided in the mind of the person holding the khipu and that the khipu itself was used only to jog that person's occasionally forgetful mem-

FIGURE 3.1 Drawing by Guaman Poma of a runner carrying
a message in the form of a khipu, labeled *carta* (letter).

ory. This condition of the recorder also being the reader does fit many of the
described uses of khipu (see Mackey, Chapter 13, this book). Consider the
following colonial reports of the uses of khipu: the reciting of census data by
the census taker, the reciting of evidence by a witness at a trial, and the reciting of history by a historian/recorder. All of these uses of khipu and many
more could be considered examples of memory jogging and not full information conveyances. This minimalist view of the role of the khipu holds it to
be a kind of prompter, a mnemonic device not unlike the beads of a rosary.
The argument is made that with the forgetful khipu creator/reader now long
gone, there is now no hope of ever reading khipu. However, I take a more
optimistic view.

Guaman Poma's identification of the use of a khipu as a letter clearly implies a distinct difference between the person who was the creator of the khipu and the person who is to receive and read the khipu. The reader/receiver of the khipu/letter will rely upon an understanding of the nature and structure of khipu that he shares with the sender of the letter, just as a reader shares knowledge of language with a writer. However, the reader/receiver of the khipu/letter will not know the message itself in advance, and so at least when khipu were used as letters, they must truly have involved what we call language. One of the most impressive uses of khipu as letters was their role in empire-wide communication, with the Inka runners carrying khipu in relay fashion for thousands of miles. With the multiple person-to-person transfers made necessary by such lengthy travel, even the transference of associated verbal information seems improbable. So here I take the view that although khipu were indeed mnemonic devices, they relied upon a shared set of meanings and not a private idiosyncratic set of meanings. We must consider some khipu, at least, to have been letters.

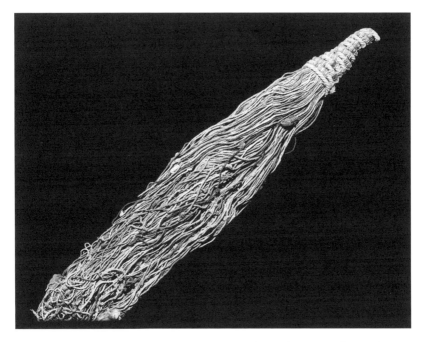

FIGURE 3.2 This khipu, never unrolled, remains in the spiral condition illustrated by Guaman Poma (6824/P.C.).

Much of the colonial evidence regarding the use of khipu in postconquest times is indeed essentially concerned with the use of khipu as prompts, not as letters. The explanation may well lie in the probability that all use of khipu for long-distance communication ceased completely at the conquest, so that the use of khipu as letters, though remembered, no longer actually occurred during colonial times.

All forms of recorded information are actually mnemonic. The letters and words on this page are not themselves information but are mere squiggles that jog the memory of the reader to recall sounds, associations, and structures that combine to provide what we commonly refer to as "the meaning." The clues to that meaning include the totality and ordering of all the visual information provided, such as:

- the style of the type font and the placement of capitals, punctuation, underlining, and boldfacing,
- the layout and graphic form of the information, including the color of the ink,
- the sequence of letters that form the words,
- the sequence and groupings of words that form phrases and sentences, etc.

The sounds (phonology), associations (semantics), and structures (grammar) provoked by the graphics are selected by the mind of the reader from those broadly held in common by reader and writer in a kind of program that we call language. The first requirement for a reader's understanding of that data is a clear comprehension of the ordering of all the visual aspects of the data. Quite obviously, a would-be reader of a khipu needs an exact and detailed understanding of all the technical construction evidence in a khipu—an understanding comparable to our detailed, easy, and immediate graphic comprehension of a page of text.

The second requirement for comprehension is an understanding of the program or language used in encoding the khipu. The nature of that khipu program is still a matter of wild speculation. The lingua franca of the Inka Empire was Southern Peruvian Quechua,[2] and khipu seem to have had somewhat the same geographic distribution as that form of Quechua. It thus seems likely that as the far-away receiver of the khipu/letter fingered the khipu, he may have mumbled to himself in a private khipu language, but he would certainly have told his cohorts the message of the khipu in verbal Quechua. Although Quechua is a language with free word order, a recitation of the data in the order of embedment would seem to be an appropriate way of beginning comprehension. The visual prompts for the khipu reader's verbal expression could not lie in the textile representation of an alphabet, as in writing, because Quechua at that time was not a written language. Quechua consisted only of orality, of syllabic sounds and utterances and their associated structures. So one possibility is that the sounds and structures of spoken Quechua are some-how embedded in the khipu. However, lest we think that it is only a matter of finding one-to-one equivalents, consider Michel Foucault's eloquent remarks on the nature of languages at the time of the Inka khipu:

> In the sixteenth century, real language is not a totality of indepen-dent signs, a uniform and unbroken entity to which things could be reflected one by one, as in a mirror, and so express their particular truths. It is rather an opaque, mysterious thing, closed in upon itself, a fragmented mass, its enigma renewed in every interval, which com-bines here and there with the forms of the world and becomes inter-woven with them: so much so that all these elements, taken together, form a network of marks in which each of them may play, and does in fact play, in relation to all of the others, the role of content or of sign, that of secret or of indicator.[3]

The first purpose of this chapter, then, is to describe fully and in detail the nature of the information and the sequence of its ordering in khipu. How-ever, even when we do understand the ordering of the data, we will still not be entering Inka kindergarten. But the work has two additional purposes: the second is an attempt to quantify the information contained in khipu—to be able to answer the question as to whether or not there is enough information capacity in a khipu for it to conceivably contain a letter. The final purpose is to suggest the nature of what we can learn about the structure of Inka thought from studying the organization and structure of khipu, even if their full mes-sages are not deciphered.

Guaman Poma's drawings of khipu (see Figure 3.3), when compared with surviving Inka khipu, seem accurate and imply his extensive visual familiarity with khipu. Curiously, though, he provides images of khipu being displayed to the reader and being carried, but he provides no images of khipu actually being read or constructed. He describes many uses of khipu, as do the chroni-clers, but he says nothing about their technical creation. However, a postu-late of my theory of khipu information is that the sequence of construction of a khipu is the major clue to the development of its information sequence.

FIGURE 3.3 Drawing by Guaman Poma of a native official
carrying a khipu in his right hand and a book in his left hand.

Knowing the linear order of creation of a line of a Western language is the
necessary first step toward understanding the message. Attempts at reading
khipu to date have begun with reading the knots, but knots were the *last*, not
the *first*, chronological element in the khipu information string.

So, in launching an investigation into the process of the creation of a
khipu, as no known information on the subject exists, we are more or less on
our own. We can consider two methodologies: one is to find comparables in
other Inka fabric or textile structures and argue by analogy, but we will find
few relevant comparables.

COMPARISON WITH INKA FABRIC CONSTRUCTION

Although khipu are often thought of as a form of textile, technically they are fabrics and not textiles, and in this case, the distinction is important. The construction of khipu does not involve a loom or a ball of yarn, nor is any interlacing or other form of interworking of elements involved. Although both textiles and khipu are forms of fabrics, the basic elements of their constructions and the processes of their constructions are distinctly different. In weaving, long threads are created and stockpiled in hanks or balls for use in the warping of the loom and in the continuous back-and-forth action of the weft. However, in khipu construction, there was no ball of twine or hank of yarn from which the individual strings were harvested. Each cord was created as a unique fabric structure by a process of selecting its proposed materials, its colors, its directionality, its spinning, doubling, plying, and lastly its knotting.

ANALYSIS OF KHIPU CONSTRUCTION

The second method is to examine khipu structure (see Figure 3.4) and then, using construction logic and real-world simulations, develop a probable construction methodology.

Posture

We can begin our analysis of the probable construction procedure by considering posture. Part of the khipu construction process can be accomplished in either a seated or a standing position, but the special actions of attaching cords and of knotting cords require two hands, with the primary cord kept in an orderly and taut condition. Reading a khipu has similar requirements. One position that seems to satisfy these needs, and in practice works quite well, is to hold one end of the primary cord between the toes, thereby using the toes as the necessary third hand (see Figure 3.5). The absence of such images in Guaman Poma's *Nueva corónica* may have been because he never witnessed such an event, or it may have been because he was embarrassed to present to the intended reader of his letter, the king of Spain, images of his ancestors sitting on the ground. However, this posture, positioning the toes to function as a third hand for the creation of a textile, *is* used by present-day fishermen on the north coast of Peru in the construction of their cotton fishnets.[4]

In order to develop a comprehensive "theory of the ordering of the khipu information system," in addition to overall posture, five aspects of khipu con-

FIGURE 3.4 An Inka khipu made entirely of natural colors of cotton. The word for "khipu creator" was *khipukamayuq*, meaning not only "khipu maker" but also "giver of life" to the strings and knots (7308/P.C.).

struction must be considered: materials, colors, construction elements, spinning and plying, and, finally, knotting.

Materials

The material used in the construction of standard Inka khipu was cotton, defining "standard" simply as those khipu that look like the depictions in Guaman Poma's document. Probably more than half of all existing khipu fit into that rough definition. In such khipu, at least eight separate natural colors of cotton are used (white, beige, light brown, medium brown, dark brown, chocolate, reddish-orange brown, and mauve), with coding seemingly utterly dependent on these cotton color distinctions. Dyed cotton is also occasionally used, particularly blue cotton.

Some khipu that remain in more-or-less untouched condition have embedded within their strings cotton bolls and cotton seeds, implying on-site spinning during khipu construction. Yet, since cotton is not grown in areas above two thousand meters in altitude, and since Cusco and the Inka heartland lie at nearly three thousand meters, cotton was definitely not a local product for the Inka. Multicolored cotton especially is distinctly coastal.[5] Today such multicolored cotton is grown and used only in the north coast of Peru. Nevertheless, cotton was used for the warp in Inka garment construction, and many brown and white cotton double-cloth textiles with seemingly Inka designs exist in museum collections. Therefore, the highland Inka must have had control of lower-level cotton fields and access to cotton know-how.

We have Spanish records as well as archaeological confirmation of Inka importation of other foreign fabric materials such as exotic feathers, as well as their associated feather workers. Even so, khipu presumably carried the deepest secrets of the empire, and it is difficult to reconcile their creation being dependent upon foreign materials or their secret messages being recorded by the associated alien workers.

Although camelid fiber was the standard material for Inka garments (with cotton used only as an invisible warp, as Anne Rowe[6] has recently noted), only one of the hundred or so khipu in the American Museum of Natural History (AMNH) collection is all alpaca[7] (see Figure 3.6). One of the khipu brought back by Max Uhle from Ica is entirely of camelid fiber.[8] In standard cotton khipu, alpaca is used only rarely as a short, brightly colored thread appearing for a few centimeters somewhere along the length of a cord. Such short threads, properly called accessory threads, were introduced apparently as special encoding elements (see Figure 3.7). Alpaca was apparently used in such instances because it can be dyed to create much brighter colors than cotton can, and thus it stands out from the naturally colored materials. In the construction sequence, these accessory threads would have been incorporated during plying, but before knotting, and thus were representative of the primary information of the cord that is then later "acted upon" by the knotting process.

FIGURE 3.5 Constructed image of possible posture used during both the creating and the reading of a khipu.

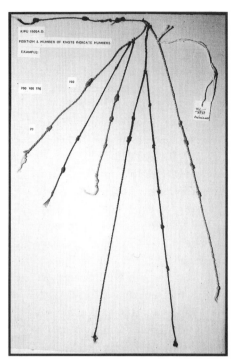

FIGURE 3.6 Khipu constructed of alpaca but technically like those constructed of cotton (AMNH 41.2/8737).

FIGURE 3.7 During the plying of this cotton khipu, short threads of brightly dyed alpaca were introduced (6824/P.C.).

In addition to the basic cotton khipu and the rare alpaca khipu, other anomalous types of archaeological khipu exist. One such type is the vegetable-fiber khipu (sometimes referred to as bast) described by the khipu scholar Carlos Radicati di Primeglio[9] and called by him a "*quipu de canutos*," but as yet no overall typology of khipu has been developed. An impressionistic review, though, of the nonstandard khipu in the khipu collection of the AMNH seems to reveal the existence of regional styles of khipu. Such apparent regional groupings imply the existence of local, non-official khipu. The Inka claimed as exclusively their own their vast highway system, but archaeologists believe that the Inka actually often utilized existing roads but connected and rebuilt them to form the network that became one of their most famous creations. The evolution of the Inka khipu may well be similar. This evolutionary development seems to be suggested by the chronicler Cristóbal de Molina when he reported that "the system [of recording information in khipu] became more complete under the Ynka Yupanqui, who first began to conquer this land, for before his time the Ynkas had not advanced beyond the vicinity of Cuzco . . ."[10]

Colors

Inka khipu fundamentally use the natural colors of the materials. This policy differs radically from the policy used in the creation of their official garments, which rely heavily on the patterned use of brilliant dyes. Natural colors do occur in Inka garments, together with the dominant greens, reds, yellows, and blacks, but they tend to appear as backgrounds for the colored designs. The chroniclers' references to the meaning of colors in khipu, such as red meaning soldiers, yellow meaning gold, and so on, implying that khipu were brightly colored, is not suggested by the surviving evidence. The fundamental color coding of Inka khipu seems to reside in the fine gradations of their natural browns, tans, and whites.

There is no clear answer as to why the Inka used cotton for their khipu rather than alpaca. Vuka Roussakis, the khipukamayuq of the American Museum of Natural History's large collection of khipu, feels that cotton khipu last better and "feel" better than alpaca. Given the intimate association that khipu had to have with the hands and fingers, perhaps cotton was preferred for the same sensory reasons that modern underwear is made of cotton and not of wool. Nevertheless, from a graphic communication point of view, the Inka were highly skilled at dying alpaca and at creating richly patterned symbol-full textiles with those dyed colors. Also, the range of possible colors in dyed alpaca far exceeds the limited range of naturally colored cotton. So the Inka selection of naturally colored cotton for their khipu may have been for historical reasons rather than functional ones. Khipu from earlier times, specifically from the Huari culture of the Middle Horizon Period,[11] were constructed entirely of cotton, so in making their khipu of cotton, the Inka were probably simply following precedents. But in addition to the precedence of Middle Horizon khipu, cotton itself, which is a coastal product, had vast ancient pre-Inka religious associations connected to its spinning, plying, and construction—a coastal tradition that the Inka may have co-opted.

The Primary Cord

Unlike textiles, khipu are not woven nor are they networks. Khipu are fabrics that have a single line for their basic structure. The Inka created many types of tensile, linear fabric structures that have a broad structural commonality with khipu, such as suspension bridges, women's necklaces, and the Inka headband, or *borla*. So the general form of the khipu—a suspension line with pendants—has several other expressions in Inka fabrics. Also, there is evidence of the great symbolic importance of fabric cords or cables, such as the following amazing report by one of the chroniclers, Cristóbal de Molina:

> In the morning the priests brought out the huacas of the Creator, the Sun, the Moon, and the Thunder, and the dead bodies, and placed them in the square. The Ynka also came forth, and took his place near the Sun. The rest of the people had gone to a house called *Moro-urco*, near the houses of the Sun, to take out a very long cable which was kept there, woven in four colours, black, white, red, and yellow, at the end of which there was a stout ball of red wool. Every one took hold of it, the men on one side, and the women on the other, performing the *taqui* [ritual dance?] called *yaqauyra*. When they came to the square, after making reverences to the huacas and the Ynka, they kept going round and round until they were the shape of a spiral shell. Then they dropped the *huascar* on the ground, and left it coiled up like a snake. They called this cable *Moro-urco*. The people returned to their places, and those who had charge of the cable took it back to its house. When they celebrated this feast, they were dressed in clothes called *pucay-urco*: a black shirt with a white band, and white fringes at the edges. They also wore white plumes from a bird called *tocto*. Presently, they brought a lamb to be sacrificed for the cable, etc.[12]

This story, loaded as it is with suggestions of meaning, we could well call "*Moro-urco*: the mother-myth of the khipu." Its ball end (like some khipu), its male and female sides, its apparent ranking with mummies and with the statues of the gods, the animal sacrifice made to it, and the fact of its having its own stone house—all speak broadly of the ritual importance of cords for the Inka and of their acceptance of the cable called Moro-urco as a highly animated entity living in the midst of their community.

The bridges of the Inka (see Figure 3.9), probably their ultimate structural achievement, usually used four multiple-ply grass cords in suspension to cross valleys. The crisscrossing cords in the photo probably perform no structural function, so, though larger, the bridges were not structurally much more complex than khipu.

On an entirely different scale than bridges, but closer in concept to a khipu, was a special part of an Inka woman's costume. An elaborately constructed

FIGURE 3.8 Constructed representation of part of
Cristóbal de Molina's story of the Inka ritual cord called
Moro-urco.

cord with pendants was hung across her chest, and the ends of the cord near-
est her shoulders were fastened to the two *tupu* (pins) that were used to hold
up her *aksu* (dress). It is thus not literally a necklace but, like the bridges, it is
a two-point suspended line. Female Inka mummies and miniature votive Inka
female figurines wear such suspended cords (see Figure 3.10).

Khipu use that Inka suspension line as a tension structure but also as an
organizing and communicating device. Using a terminology that reflects the
rigid hierarchical ordering of khipu cords, we can call this main suspension
line the *primary cord*. The two ends of this primary cord characteristically differ in that one end, the closed end, has only loops formed by the doublings of
the cord; the other, the open end, has free ends of threads and may be knotted
and wrapped to form a ball, recalling Molina's description of the cable (see
Figure 3.8). This suspension line, or primary cord, had to have been the first

FIGURE 3.9 Inka suspension bridge across the Colca Valley (1929 Shippee-Johnson Expedition). Photo courtesy of Department of Library Services, AMNH, Neg. No. 337404; photo by G. R. Johnson.

element of a khipu to be constructed and *must* therefore be the beginning of our reconstructed khipu information string. It is the primary cord from a structural point of view, but it is also primary within the chronology of construction (see Figures 3.11 and 3.12).[13] This primary cord usually seems to announce the nature of the khipu by its materials, colors, and ply directionality. Thus the primary cord, using linguistic terms, could well be called the *title* cord. An example of this "announcement" quality of a primary cord is seen in AMNH B/8705, a khipu that was initially recorded by the khipu scholar L. Leland Locke (see Figure 3.13).[14]

Secondary Cords

The secondary cords are then prepared and attached in a sequence that begins most practically near the closed or finished end of the primary cord,[15] thus establishing the order in which that information was stored. The secondary cords also have one looped or closed end that is used for attachment, leaving the open ends hanging free. The secondary cords are often grouped in sets of five, six, or ten tightly spaced together. Such groupings are then followed by a space of open primary cord before the next group begins. This spacing seems comparable to the spacing between utterances in spoken language. The sequence of successive secondary cord placement moves from the closed end to the open end. The sequence of cord groups, one following another, then also moves from the closed end to the open end.

Top Cords

Top cords are special secondary cords[16] that are attached in a manner that indicates a special relationship to a group of associated secondary cords. Often these cords contain a summary of the knot numbers on their associated cords. Several forms of these cords exist: those that are simply adjacent to their group, those that arise from the center of their group, and those that literally encompass their group. Locke believed that this encompassing form for the top cord represented the most fully developed form of the Inka khipu. Because they sometimes represent the sum of the numbers represented on their associated cords, the top cords must logically have been recorded and installed after the group itself was completed. Evidence of this sequencing

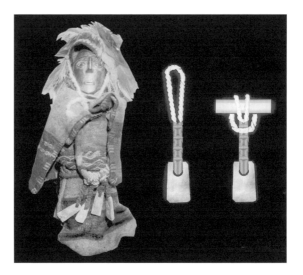

FIGURE 3.10 Spondylus shell fragments suspended by khipu-like loop hitch knots on Inka figurine from sacrificial burial on Mt. Ampato, southern Peru (author photo and reconstruction drawing).

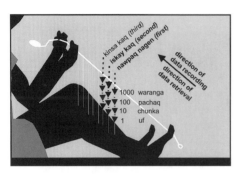

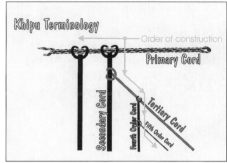

F I G U R E 3 . 1 1 In a khipu, the attachment of secondary cords begins at the closed end of the primary cord and proceeds to the open end. The secondary cords are attached by their closed end, and knotting proceeds toward their open end.

F I G U R E 3 . 1 2 A khipu is a hierarchical tension structure. The secondary and tertiary cords are thus named to respect their rank order in the construction process.

is found in the top cords that occur in the middle of their group. These top cords appear to have been literally squeezed in with no pre-thought-out allotment of space, evidence that coincides with their final summary nature.

Tertiary Cords

Tertiary cords are attached to secondary cords by their closed or looped end. The knotting of the secondary cords, as a practical matter, must have been accomplished before tertiary cords were attached. If the knotting of secondary cords were attempted *after* the attachment of tertiary cords, then the bulk of the tertiary cords, together with their knots and fourth-order cords, would have been carried through each secondary knot—a seemingly impossible task. This construction sequence thus establishes another chronological ordering in the information sequence.

Plying

After the selection of the material to be used in the creation of a cord for the khipu, fibers were spun into single-ply elements in one of two possible directions that produce a visible Z or S (see Figure 3.15). The dominant direction for spun cotton in Inka khipu is Z. Spinning is then followed by doubling and plying the two parts of the spun thread together in the opposite, or S, direction.

FIGURE 3.13 The reverse plying and long knots of the primary cord announce the dominant characteristics of this particular khipu. The long knots on the primary cord are like those found in abundance on the secondary cords (AMNH B/8705; author photo).

FIGURE 3.14 Khipu with secondary cords tied above and below the primary cord; the tertiary cords are here mounted at oblique angles to the secondary cords (7604/P.C.).

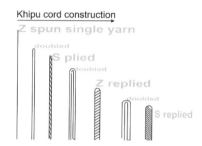

FIGURE 3.15 S- and Z-plied cords.

FIGURE 3.16 Khipu cord spinning and plying construction sequence.

The two-ply yarns thus created are then normally themselves doubled and replied in a Z direction to form a cord that is then doubled and replied again to produce S when installed in the khipu (see Figure 3.16). Although a wide variety of plying and doubling programs were used, all normally produce a final visible S—the same final appearance as that found in Inka textiles, but one produced by a much more complex process.

Though S is the common appearance of khipu cords, some cords are just the opposite. Rarely, as in the khipu illustrated in Figure 3.17, Z is the common appearance, with S being exceptional. This reversal of directions was obviously intentional and undoubtedly a way of embedding information.[17] In earlier Andean textiles, spinning and plying direction was a conveyor of place, of cultural groupings, and of religious and magical values.[18] In khipu, spinning and plying occur before knotting and therefore encode earlier information than that embedded in knotting in the information sequence being created by the khipukamayuq.

Many basic plying programs exist, such as the two described in Figure 3.18, but no khipu-plying typology exists as yet. When two yarn colors are plied and doubled together, the yarns can shift positions as they are wound around, producing what is broadly called a variegated yarn. However, in such yarns the random appearance is probably misleading. Although the position of the colors does change, the color ratio of the yarn colors stays constant. However, when two colors are interlocked and then doubled and plied, the relative position of the colors is constant and produces a color spiral like a barber pole. The variety of plying types seems almost limitless (see Figure 3.19).

Even the most visually complex appearance is not random, but rather is precisely determined construction. Color selection and plying format are the most fundamental level of the khipu information string. See, for example,

FIGURE 3.17 Detail of cords on 7604/P.C. showing variations in the directions of spinning and plying (author photo).

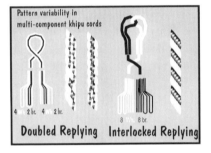

FIGURE 3.18 Construction of khipu cords by doubled and interlocked replying.

FIGURE 3.19 Primary cord (left) consisting of two-ply, two-color S-plied cords joined by Z spiraling single-colored simple cord (AMNH 41.2/6715).

Figure 3.20, wherein a group of six multicolored secondary cords is lassoed together with a summary cord. The Aschers have noted that pendant groups of six often have "top cords."[19] However, the knots on the top cord in Figure 3.20 add up to 431—close, but not quite the 429 total registered on the six associated secondary cords. Since these six cords have been called "variegated," it seemed important to examine them in detail. This examination revealed their carefully constructed individuality that the term "variegated" only disguises. Each was made separately to its own program to perform its own special purpose and to convey its unique information. As illustration, the third cord from the left of the group of six (see Figure 3.21) has three brown and two white threads, each two-ply, that form the constituent basic units of recorded information for one half of this single cord (see Figure 3.22).

This preliminary identification of plying variety in the primary, secondary, and other cords of khipu indicates a thread construction technology far more complex than anything encountered in Inka textiles (see Figure 3.23). The complexity of khipu plying was certainly intended to convey information. The selection of colors and general makeup of the cord constitutes the basic information of the cord—information that was then "acted upon" by the process of knotting the cord. The information storage capacity of a khipu, previously measured only by its knots, is thus multiplied many times.

Knots

In the practical world, knots are mostly used for joining strings together, and knots in the middle of a thread are bad news—to be removed if possible to make the cord useful. Many of the khipu knots that carry the numbers, however, are special knots, not found in everyday use. Inspired by the chroniclers, Locke[20] noted in 1923 that the knot types used on khipu could be found to stand for numbers in the decimal system, as is graphically shown in his drawing (see Figure 3.24). In Locke's drawing, however, the knot types were shown cut away from their context and then analyzed as independent topological configurations.

In actuality, however, every knot in a khipu has a deep relationship to its context: each knot has one fixed end, its root in the khipu, and one free end, providing it with an organic and directional relationship with the rest of the fabric structure. And each khipu knot actually has not one but a variety of topological configurations. For example, the simple overhand knot has two different forms (see Figure 3.25). Locke's theory stated that the overhand knot stood for the numeral one. Johann Jakob von Tschudi,[21] based appar-

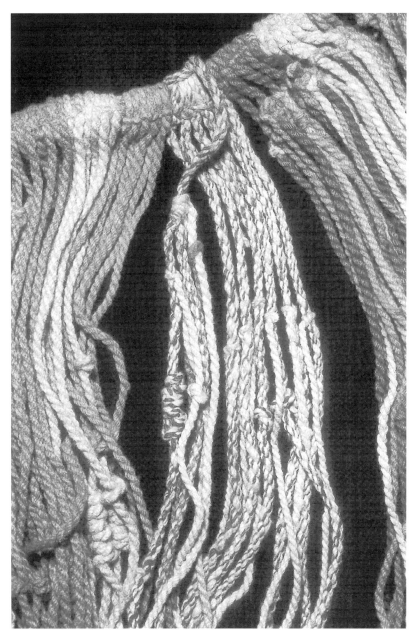

FIGURE 3.20 Group of six variegated secondary cords linked together by a top cord (left of center; see Figure 3.4 for complete khipu; 7308/P.C.).

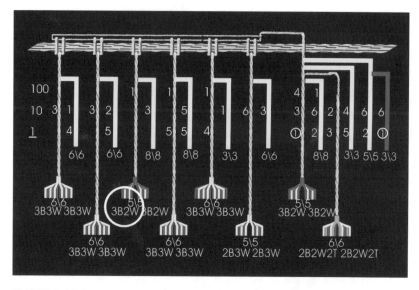

FIGURE 3.21 Diagram of the construction of the six secondary cords, together with their top cord, shown in Figure 3.20. 3B2W = 3 brown and 2 white elements. Knot values, in their relative decimal positions, are shown adjacent to the cords.

FIGURE 3.22 Microphotograph of one-half of cord circled in Figure 3.21 (labeled 3B2W).

ently on information picked up from his travels in Peru, stated that this knot stood for the numeral ten. All of Locke's calculations would actually work equally well multiplied by ten. Since the Inka told the Spaniards that everything in the empire was counted by tens, Tschudi's interpretation is tempting.

In the matter of knot directionality, Locke's analysis from 1923 does not do justice to the sophistication of actual khipu. We can examine several examples with this new understanding of khipu knot topology, summarizing an analysis this author presented at the 1983 Dumbarton Oaks conference on khipu with Gary Urton. (See Urton 1994[22] for a later, thorough presentation of the subject.)

The loop hitch[23] (see Figure 3.26), for example, has a front and back face. Having its front face on the right of the main cord is its normal condition, but the obverse face sometimes is used, as in AMNH B/8705 (see Figure 3.27).

Although apparently not a recorder of numbers, the loop hitch, from a structural and energy-flow point of view, is the most ingenious knot in a khipu. When a single-ply yarn was initially spun by the khipukamayuq, it was undoubtedly overspun, embedding energy in it as when a spring is coiled. When that yarn was doubled, plying occurred automatically, releasing a portion of the stored energy. The loop of that doubled cord was then opened and the loop hitch was formed around the primary cord. At this point, remarkably, the knot tightens by itself and grasps the primary cord using still another portion of the stored-up energy imparted to it by its initial spinning. The firm grasp of the loop hitch (formed from its stored energy) keeps every cord in place. Khipu cords, unlike yarns used in textiles, are extremely tightly

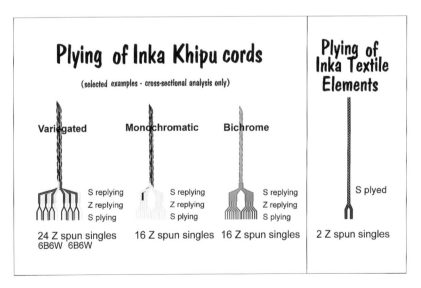

FIGURE 3.23 Schematic comparison of plying of a variety of khipu cords compared to plying of Inka textile thread.

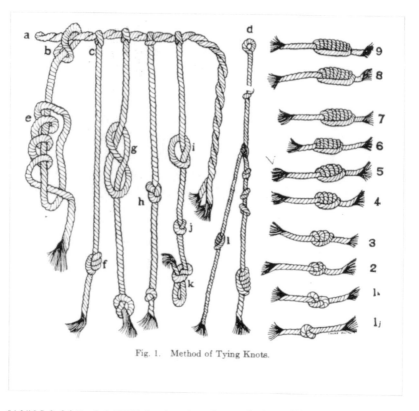

Fig. 1.   Method of Tying Knots.

FIGURE 3.24 Locke's (1923) drawing of typology and values of khipu knots.

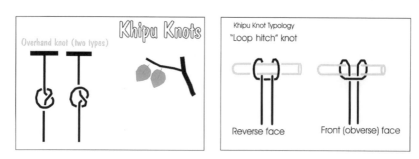

FIGURE 3.25 Two versions of overhand knots; like leaves, each knot has an attached end and a free end.

FIGURE 3.26 The loop hitch knot—for example, as used to attach secondary cords to the primary cord—has two procedures of construction, producing two distinct faces.

FIGURE 3.27 The loop hitch knot on the two-color cord shows the reverse face; the adjacent cords (to the left) show the front (obverse) face (AMNH B/8705; author photo).

plied and retain their stored energy amazingly well, even after five hundred years. Understanding this stored energy in cords helps us to understand the Inka obeisance toward the vitality of their Moro-urco.

Locke's long knot, in which the number of wrappings from two to nine indicates the represented number, has the most complex set of possible variations, but only two of the four have as yet been identified in use in khipu (see Figure 3.28). The figure-eight knot has two possible variations: the figure eight "under" and the figure eight "over" (see Figure 3.29); a figure eight "over" is shown in Figure 3.30. This understanding of the multiple forms of the knots in a khipu again greatly enlarges the definition of the quantity of information that was potentially encoded.

Knot Placement

Locke found that the position of the knot on a secondary cord represented its position in the decimal hierarchy of 1,000, 100, 10, or 1, with the highest number being closest to the loop or closed end of the cord that is fastened to the primary cord. Knot placement in khipu, though generally readable, seems a little casual compared to the decimal scale of the possible errors created by a misreading of that placement.

Numbers are read in Quechua as in English, as Urton reports,[24] with the highest order first. For example, four hundred thirty-two is read aloud in the same sequence as the placement of numbers in "432." Thus, the prob-

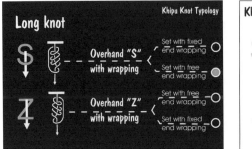

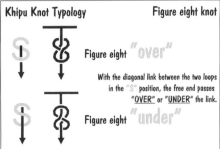

F I G U R E 3.28 Drawing illustrating variations in the form of the long knot (filled-in circle to the right indicates the most commonly found variation).

F I G U R E 3.29 Drawing showing the two variations—"over" and "under"—of the figure-eight knot.

F I G U R E 3.30 Photo of a figure-eight knot in "over" configuration (see Figure 3.29).

able chronological order of placement of the knots on a secondary cord (and therefore, according to the theory, their order of reading) proceeds from the closed end to the open end of the cord: exactly the same directionality as the proposed placement and reading sequence of the secondary cords. This understanding of the sequence of knot placement, then, completes the construction sequencing of the khipu information string theory (see Figure 3.31). A khipu is like a plant whose root is in the soil, with the root of the khipu being the closed end of the primary cord. Branches must exist before sub-branches can occur, and every twist and every knot has its physical and chronological place in a complete organic structure.

FIGURE 3.31 Drawing by Guaman Poma of an accountant-treasurer holding a khipu, with "head" to the accountant's right and "tail" to his left. Following the theory developed herein, khipu recording and reading would proceed from tail to head, or in this example, from this khipu maker's left hand toward his right hand.

Knot Erasures

Many khipu show clear evidence of the untying of some of their knots—the seeming equivalent of erasures in writing. The cord deformations remaining from the former knots seem remarkably durable considering the five hundred years that have elapsed since their probable untying. The apparent permanence of these deformations suggests that the knots were originally tied under somewhat humid conditions, as in a domestic household, and then later stored in a drier environment before the untying occurred. In some instances where secondary cords have been de-knotted, their corresponding summary cords have also been partially erased. Such de-knotting would therefore seem to have occurred after the khipu was completed and had been stored, making erasures the very last element in our information string.

KHIPU INFORMATION CAPACITY

In 1948, a mathematician at Bell Labs, Claude Shannon, wrote a paper on a mathematical theory of communication that since that time has defined modern thought on the subject of information.[25] Shannon's concept of information, now used throughout the digital world, applies not to the individual message (as the concept of meaning would), but rather to the situation as a whole. If one is confronted with an *elementary* situation with one of two conditions possible, for example, the off/on of a light switch, then the information associated with those two possibilities is one of the two conditions. This unit of information is called a "bit," a word that is a condensation of "binary digit." Mathematically, then, the amount of information conveyed (1 bit) is the logarithm of the number of available choices,[26] 1 being the log (to the base 2 as opposed to the more familiar base 10) of two choices. So in the measurement of information quantity in the modern digital world, it is the log of the number of choices that defines the number of bits of information.

To permit comparisons between khipu and the modern world of information storage, it is of interest to attempt to measure khipu information digitally. However, most of the information we commonly live by—vision, sound, smell, touch—is not received by us digitally nor is it, in its natural state, stored digitally. Khipu are part of that natural world that was created by, and is normally read by, vision and touch.

But an additional problem may lie in the interactive nature of much Andean thought—seemingly a profound limitation on a comparison of khipu and computers. The Quechua word *ayni* refers to the principle of reciprocity that governs Andean social relations, but *ayni* is also an ontological premise about how the world is organized. Such Andean dualism seems to be curiously interactive (for a thorough analysis of the subject, see Urton n.d.[27]): the two parts of an Andean duality seem to exist only in relation to each other, as if they were two interactive parts of a whole. Consider one example: the Z and S spinning and plying of threads. When the plying of a thread occurs, the direction of the prior spinning actually predicts the direction of the plying. S spinning predicts Z plying and vice versa. Also, plying does not occur in the absence of spinning. So plying and spinning directions, being two in number and therefore suggesting the presence of a binary situation, are actually a complex, inter-reactive dualism; whereas the dualism of the modern digital world consists of two clean, separate, independent conditions.

Nevertheless, we might attempt to establish a theoretical basic information unit for khipu so that we could compare khipu information capacity with that of computers. We could distinguish that khipu information unit from the bits and bytes (1,000 bits, more or less) of computers by using a special term. A possible term could be "infon," proposed by Keith Devlin[28] to designate an incremental unit of information: "The aim in choosing the name *infon* is to emphasize by analogy with physics the fundamental role these abstract objects play in our theory as items of information." He later says that "the representation has some form of physical realization—an ink pattern on paper, an electrochemical configuration in the brain, an optical or magnetic pattern on a disk, a sound wave in the air, a sequence of electrical pulses in a wire, or more generally any configuration of objects in the world." Although Devlin is probably unaware of the existence of the information system of khipu, asking his term "infon" to apply to the twist of a thread, the turn of a knot, or the color of a fiber would seem to be a coherent extension of his use of the term.

Although the deep nature of the information in a khipu remains unknown, the theoretical information capacity of a khipu can be considered. If, for example, we were to multiply the knot representational capacity of a single secondary cord, *say 10,000*, by the knot alter egos, *say 2*, by the possible colors, *say 8*, by the plying types, *say 12*,[29] by the possible plying directions, *2*, by incidental variables such as accessory threads and basic materials, *say 2*, then each such secondary cord could theoretically hold a grand possibility of some 8 million differing combinations or states. If we then define a khipu infon as a unit of khipu information, then such a secondary cord could hold 8 million infons. Attaching a tertiary cord of the same capacity to that secondary cord (the tertiary cord then being a modifier of all the information in the secondary cord) would theoretically square that information capacity. Fourth-order cords attached to and used as modifiers of tertiary cords could, each time they occur, square even that number. But certainly only a tiny portion of that vast theoretical information capacity of a khipu was ever in use at one time.

To compare the information capacity of a khipu with the bit capacity of a computer, one must take the logarithm to the base 2 of the number of khipu infons. In the example, 8,000,000 is the estimated possible number of infons in a single secondary cord, whose log produces some 23 bits,[30] comparable to the number of bits in a single word written in the ASCII alphanumeric code used to store information in computers. A single encoded ASCII character of 7 bits covers numbers, capitals, lower case, and a few dozen other characters. But since there was no written language or alphabet in use when khipu were created, this attempt at the measurement of khipu in bits and as ASCII code is perhaps only a curiosity.

Adam Price has suggested as an alternate analytic method the following: "If in attempting to develop the information capacity of a khipu, one were to assume that the range of expression was a pre-understood vocabulary, then each word would require only a fraction of the information required in using ASCII to represent a word."[31] However, estimating the size of such a base vocabulary is highly problematic for Quechua because Quechua is an agglutinating language: "If one counts only 'root' words, say *apay*, meaning 'to carry,' one would find a relatively small number, yet the operative lexicon is no smaller than other languages because suffixes are used to refine and extend meanings. The derivatives of *apay* with suffixes include verbs like 'to load,' 'to bring,' 'to take,' 'to let somebody else carry one's own objects,' plus a large number of derivatives meaning things like 'bearable,' 'carrier,' and so on and so forth. The point is that the 'word' is not a member of a finite set, but the nucleus of an indefinitely productive chain of combinations."[32]

If instead of attempting to estimate information capacity as if khipu were a record of separate countable words, we might consider the form of the information in a khipu as if it were in the form of the Quechua language itself, then the makeup of the string, the core structure of the information, could stand for a "root" word, with the other characteristics of the khipu information string standing for the agglutinations and derivative meanings that give specificity to the root meaning. It would then seem possible to build up ideas with complex associations using secondary and tertiary cords. A full khipu could then seemingly hold information equivalent to numerous sentences.

Because computers are so deeply related to the nature of language, and we really do not know how khipu actually relate to language, the analysis of the information capacity of khipu remains highly problematic. What does seem certain, though, by any analysis, is that the khipu had enough information capacity to have carried the "letter" that Guaman Poma shows in the hand of the messenger (see Figure 3.1).

Do the characteristics of khipu have any obvious resonance with Quechua language structures? "Perhaps" is the only possible answer, considering the following suggestions.

Salomon[33] has pointed out that Quechua utterances begin with one of two statements of authentication, which we can paraphrase as either "I saw it" or "it is said that." This might relate to the two-part nature of spin and ply directionality that seems to give context or flavor to the information contained in the plies. Spin directionality, and its related ply directionality, does not actually change the embedded information, but just gives it a special "slant." If we can relate the primary cord of a khipu to the Moro-urco, then the two faces of the loop hitch connections to that primary cord, insofar as they agree or disagree with the male or female side of the main cord, might themselves represent male and female.

Extensive work has recently been accomplished in studying Quechua numbers[34] and their associations and in studying the sound symbolism of Quechua,[35] but only a small portion of human communication actually concerns sounds and numbers. Most of the information in khipu is embedded long before the knots are tied, so these non-knot information sets probably contain most of the information about "things," as the "things" of the world are more frequent referents in language than are sounds and numbers. Studies of the structures of the "thingness" and of "actions" in khipu in comparison with the semantic structures of Quechua must eventually be accomplished.

CONCLUSIONS

1. The khipu information string theory presented in this chapter states that information was embedded into khipu in an orderly sequence involving materials, colors, cord construction, and cord placement, followed by knotting and the attachment of supplemental cords. Reading khipu information must replicate that sequence.

2. Statistical analysis of the full information residing in khipu, if recorded in a form capable of computer-assisted statistical analysis, could be compared with a statistical analysis of the Quechua language itself, searching for clues to comparable densities of usage

to enable the identification of recording of roots and of the various forms of agglutinations.

3. Although exact measurement does not yet seem possible, it is apparent that the information storage capacity of khipu is large. Khipu could easily contain the amount of information claimed for them by the chroniclers.

One of the reasons we have not yet deciphered khipu is that we have not yet observed and recorded their information nearly carefully enough. In order to believe that the Andeans could actually read information from the complex khipu graphic fabric, it is necessary to remind ourselves of the amazement the Andeans expressed (at that moment of contact in Cajamarca) upon hearing the Spaniards miraculously verbalize language as they moved a forefinger along a line of our own subtle graphic code in the text of the Bible.

ACKNOWLEDGMENT

I would like to express my appreciation for the far-reaching efforts that Gary Urton has made toward the goal of eventual comprehension of these elusive messages that have come down to us from the Inka. His efforts have included not only his own scholarly analysis of khipu but, equally important, the organizing of conferences on the subject, his extensive fieldwork, and his many publications. All, in one way or another, bear on the subject of his fascination with the possibility of understanding.

NOTES

1. Felipe Guaman Poma de Ayala, *Nueva corónica y buen gobierno* (Paris: Institut d'Ethnologie, 1936).

2. Bruce Mannheim, *The Language of the Inka since the European Invasion* (Austin: University of Texas Press, 1991).

3. Michel Foucault, *The Order of Things* (New York: Vintage Books, 1994), 34.

4. Personal communication from James M. Vreeland, Jr., 1997.

5. See James M. Vreeland, Jr., "Cotton Spinning and Processing on the Peruvian North Coast," *The Junius B. Bird Conference on Andean Textiles*, edited by Ann Pollard Rowe (Washington, D.C.: Textile Museum, 1984), 363–383.

6. Ann Pollard Rowe, "Inca Weaving and Costume," in *The Textile Museum Journal* (Washington, D.C.) 34–35 (1995–1996): 5–53.

7. See Frank Salomon, Chapter 12, this book, for information on postconquest camelid-fiber khipu.

8. Phoebe Hearst Museum, Berkeley, Calif., Quipu 4/5446 from Ica, Site T, Grave M, of brown and tan "wool" with some zebra-striped strands of black and white.

9. Carlos Radicati di Primeglio, "El cromatismo de los quipus: Significado del quipu de canutos," in *Quipu y yupana: Colección de escritos*, edited by Carol Mackey et al. (Lima: Consejo Nacional de Ciencia y Tecnología [CONCYTEC], 1990), 39–50.

10. Christoval de Molina, "An Account of the Fables and Rites of the Yncas," in *The Rites and Laws of the Yncas*, translated by Clements R. Markham (London: Hakluyt Society, 1873), 10.

11. William J Conklin, "The Information System of Middle Horizon Khipus," in *Ethnoastronomy and Archaeoastronomy in the American Tropics*, edited by Anthony F. Aveni and Gary Urton (New York: New York Academy of Sciences, 1982), 262–281.

12. See Molina 1873: 48–49.

13. See Conklin 1982.

14. L. Leland Locke, "Supplementary Notes on the Quipus in the American Museum of Natural History," *Anthropological Papers of the AMNH* 30, pt. 2 (1928): 47–52.

15. This sequence has been developed in part from a khipu (7604/P.C.) whose primary cord was extended to accommodate additional secondary cords and thus provides us with the direction of their placement.

16. Marcia Ascher and Robert Ascher, *Mathematics of the Incas: Code of the Quipu* (New York: Dover, 1997), 31.

17. See Tschudi and Rivero 1936, as quoted in Locke 1928, on the importance of plying directions.

18. William J Conklin, "Structure as Meaning in Ancient Andean Textiles," in *Andean Art at Dumbarton Oaks*, edited by Elizabeth H. Boone (Washington, D.C.: Dumbarton Oaks, 1996), 2, 321–328.

19. See Ascher and Ascher 1997: 89.

20. L. Leland Locke, *The Ancient Quipu or Peruvian Knot Record* (New York: American Museum of Natural History, 1923), 13.

21. See Mariano Eduardo Rivero y Ustáriz and Johann Jakob von Tschudi, *Peruvian Antiquities*, translated into English by Francis L. Haws (New York: A. S. Barnes, 1855), 110.

22. Gary Urton, "A New Twist in an Old Yarn: Variation in Knot Directionality in the Inka *Khipu*s," *Baessler-Archiv*, Neue Folge, Band 42 (1994): 271–305.

23. The knot under discussion has been variously called a cow hitch or a lark's head knot. Both terms seem remarkably inappropriate within a pre-Columbian context, hence a new, but descriptive structural term, "loop hitch knot," is used in this chapter as the name for this very important khipu knot.

24. Gary Urton, *The Social Life of Numbers* (Austin: University of Texas Press, 1997), 46.

25. Claude E. Shannon and Warren Weaver, *The Mathematical Theory of Communication* (Urbana and Chicago: University of Illinois Press, 1963).

26. Personal communication from Justin Denney (Tell Me, Palo Alto, Calif.).

27. Gary Urton, "Binary Coding in the Inka Khipu," for publication in *First Writing*, edited by Stephen Houston (Cambridge: Cambridge University Press, n.d.), in press.

28. Keith Devlin, *Logic and Information* (Cambridge: Cambridge University Press, 1996), 38–39.

29. Possible one-, two-, or three-color plying combinations such as: 1+5, 2+4, 3+3,

1+2+3, 2+2+2, 1+1+4, or 6. "Incidental variables" include allowances for the presence or absence of such items as placement of short, colored accessory threads along the cord, the alternate forms of attachment, and alternate materials for the khipu as a whole.

30. Personal communication from Adam Price, 1997.

31. This mathematical analysis reflects the insights of the mathematician Adam Price, shared with the author in August 2001.

32. Personal communication from Frank Salomon, 2001.

33. Frank Salomon and George L. Urioste, *The Huarochirí Manuscript* (Austin: University of Texas Press, 1991).

34. See Urton 1997.

35. Janis B. Nuckolls, *Sounds like Life: Sound-symbolic Grammar, Performance, and Cognition in Pastaza Quechua*, Oxford Studies in Anthropological Linguistics (New York: Oxford University Press, 1996).

Reading Khipu

FOUR   *Labels, Structure, and Format*

Marcia Ascher

Beginning some thirty years ago, my collaborator (an anthropologist) and I (a mathematician) began an extensive investigation of Inka khipu. Our work included firsthand study of over 215 khipu spread throughout thirteen countries, in thirty-four museums and private collections. Recognizing the fragility and importance of the artifacts, we recorded and published detailed descriptions, including knot types and placement, cord and space measurements, and colors, for each khipu we studied (Ascher and Ascher 1978, 1988). We analyzed the khipu as a corpus, as well as analyzing them individually. Building on previous studies of khipu and on our own findings, we came to see the khipu as richer and more significant than previously realized.

In our numerous writings (e.g., Ascher 1983, 1986; Ascher and Ascher 1975, 1997), and particularly in our book *Code of the Quipu* (Ascher and Ascher 1981), we have characterized the khipu contents as a logical-numerical system and have also emphasized that, as such, it is a general recording system. We have placed emphasis on the significance of numbers used as labels combined with numbers used as magnitudes, and on the importance of format and structure in the encoding of information on the khipu. Still, however, in regard to khipu, many equate numerical with statistical and, what is more, overlook the importance and power of symbolic systems that do other than encode speech sounds. Here I elaborate further on numbers as labels, and on structure and format.

First, a preliminary comment: as a mathematician, I have come to realize that a special clarification is needed about symbolic systems. The clarification is that with any recorded symbolic system there is a difference between (1) what is recorded; (2) how we say it; and (3) what it means. For example, for the squiggles *twenty-two*, we say "twenty-two" when we read it aloud; for the squiggles 22, we say "twenty-two" when we read it aloud; and for XXII, we say the same thing. Similarly, when we see the configuration $\sqrt{x}$, we say "square root of ex," or for $_3\int^6 x^2 dx$, we say "the integral of ex squared dee ex from three to six." And, of course, how squiggles are said depends not just on the individual items but on the others around them and how they are juxtaposed. For example, if I see 22.14, I say "twenty-two point one four," but when it is preceded by \$, that is, \$22.14, I say "twenty-two dollars and fourteen cents": and, for 22′14″ I say "twenty-two feet fourteen inches," but for 10°22′14″ I say "ten degrees twenty-two minutes and fourteen seconds."

In none of these examples have I mentioned meaning. I am not distinguishing between the signifier and the signified—I am distinguishing only between what is seen and what is said. The crucial point is that were I to say "he read 'the square root of twenty-two' from the blackboard," you have no reason to assume that what was written was encoded speech sounds. In fact, because of the context, you probably would assume otherwise, but there is no justification for that either.

The next crucial point is: What does twenty-two or any other number mean? For one thing, it can be a magnitude or a quantity, as in the cases just used. In these cases, one could, for example, double the number and add four and the result would be another magnitude. But a number can also be used as a label. Look, for example, at the following:

065-62-1803
14850
607-257-1011
3/24/35
0-472-06325-1

The first item, 065-62-1803, is my social security number. To the U.S. government and many other institutions, it stands for Marcia Ascher. These institutions could, if they chose, use letters encoding the sound of my name, but that would not be a unique identifier.

The next item, 14850, is the zip code identifying where I live—namely, in the town of Ithaca in New York State. Many of us still write the letters encoding speech sounds for addresses (such as writing out Ithaca, New York), but we know it isn't necessary. In fact, post offices disregard them. And, recognition of these number labels has spread well beyond the postal service. When I see, for example, 14851, I know that is downtown Ithaca, not on our hill; 14853 is the Cornell campus; and 04675 is Seal Harbor in Maine, whereas 04609 is Bar Harbor. And, of course, 90210 is Beverly Hills.

Next is my phone number, 607-257-1011, another label. The first number grouping, 607, represents a geographic region below Syracuse and above Binghamton in New York State; 257 is a locale within that region; and 1011 is a particular phone in that locale. In contrast to numbers that are magnitudes, for this label as well as for the others, doubling it and adding four would have no meaning.

The next label, 3/24/35, is my birth date. I say it aloud as "three twenty-four thirty-five" or, more likely, as "March twenty-fourth nineteen thirty-five." And then the final item is another ubiquitous number label, 0-472-06325-1. The first digit stands for a major grouping (generally a country or geographic area); the next set of digits stands for a specific publisher in that group; the next set for a specific book by that publisher; and the last digit is a check digit. The process of creation of the label is hierarchical. An international association assigns the first digit, the group designated by that digit assigns the next grouping to a publisher, and the publisher assigns the next grouping. Then the check digit is created, which introduces a particularly important wrinkle because it is derived algebraically from the previous digits in the label, thus causing the preceding digits to be treated, on the one hand, as labels and, on the other, to be manipulated as if they were magnitudes.[1]

But, taken together, this collection of labels constitutes a narrative. The story it tells is that Marcia Ascher lives in Ithaca, New York; she can be contacted by phone by pushing a particular sequence of buttons; she was born on March 24, 1935; and she is an author of a book published in the United States by the University of Michigan Press entitled *Code of the Quipu*. If I were to append to this the sale price of the book, say $12.95, that would be a magnitude but, nonetheless, it would be part of the narrative.

A most significant aspect of these number labels is that each has its own arrangement. That is one of the ways that we recognize them. You probably would have thought it incorrect or laughed had I said that I was born on 065-62-1803, or that my phone number was 3/24/35. The important point is that, in part, we recognize them for what they are because of their specific arrangements. Various arrangements have become part of our visual lexicons and, hence, of our shared culture. They are not abbreviations or mnemonic devices to trigger memory. They are units of meaning constructed with numbers.

If, instead of twenty-first-century Americans, we were Inka khipu makers,

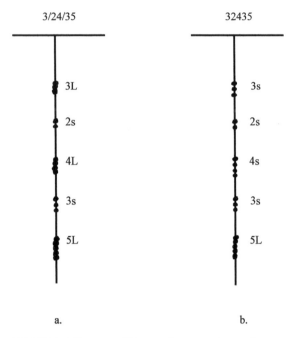

FIGURE 4.1 Knots on a khipu cord representing numbers (L = long knot, s = single knot): a) the number label 3/24/35; b) the magnitude 32435.

we would have been taught to know and recognize many arrangements encoded using khipu indicators. For example, our label 3/24/35 looks different from our magnitude 32435. Were I to put these on khipu cords, I would use Figure 4.1a for 3/24/35 but Figure 4.1b for 32435. The fact that there is a special type knot for a units positions (L) is a key element in reading khipu.

On a khipu, the numbers represented by knots on cords, whether they be magnitudes or labels, are the data that are placed into the cord array. The logical structure of the cord array is the framework for the interpretation of the data. That is, both the structure, and the data within it, carry information. Each array is defined by how the cords are placed, how they are spaced, and by their colors. Cords can be directed upward or downward; the spacing between cords can serve to group or separate cords; there can be subsidiaries on cords, and subsidiaries on subsidiaries, and so on, so that cords can be at different levels; and cords can be distinguished or related by colors. It is these features and their interrelationships that define the logical structure of an array—they shape the format into which the specific data are placed.

On a daily basis we rely so heavily on formats that we often overlook how crucial they are and how many of them we know. If, for example, you had all the information in a telephone book, but written every which way, it would be meaningless. For example, look at Figure 4.2, top.

The same information is presented in Figure 4.2, bottom, but it is more meaningful because someone created a format made up of consecutive lines of similar print, all filled in a particular order, and with columns created by spacing between letter and number groupings. The consecutive order is determined by the first letter in the last name. And, generally, most telephone books have the same format. When we see a white-paged telephone book, we first recognize it as a telephone book from its format. We even note the color because yellow pages contain a different, more complex arrangement. Only after it is recognized can we look within the book for specific information. But the fact that it has been recognized as a telephone book already conveys to us what information we expect to find.

The many various formats we encounter are related to our work, homes, cars, health, food shopping, and increasingly more and more areas of our lives. Each context calls forth its own system of meaning, and tailored to that system is a set of formats we learn to recognize. For example, only if one is knowledgeable about the academic world does a student grade slip, with its student identifier, course labels, grade labels, course credits, instructor labels, and so on, convey meaning. For people in, say, health care, shipping, or government agencies, other, different formats are daily occurrences.

Let us consider a grade slip because it, indeed, contains a narrative (see Figure 4.3, top). Before reading the data on it, we observe its layout and quite quickly note several familiar visual cues. There are vertical dividing lines, horizontal dividing lines, horizontal blocks of print grouped and separated by space, lines of dots connecting horizontal print groups, and print groups one directly below the other. These are what I term *structural indicators*, and together they form a logical structure that organizes the data and provides a framework for reading them. Going further, looking at the types of data within the structure, we identify the format as consisting of a heading, a summary section, columns with different arrangements of data, and rows repeating data of the same arrangements. And, because I said it was a grade slip, our knowledge of the context enables us to identify that the heading relates all the information to a particular student, and the consecutive columns contain courses, instructors, credits, and grades.

But instead of continuing with the facsimile grade slip, I have converted it, as shown in Figure 4.3, bottom, into a khipu, retaining only its number label

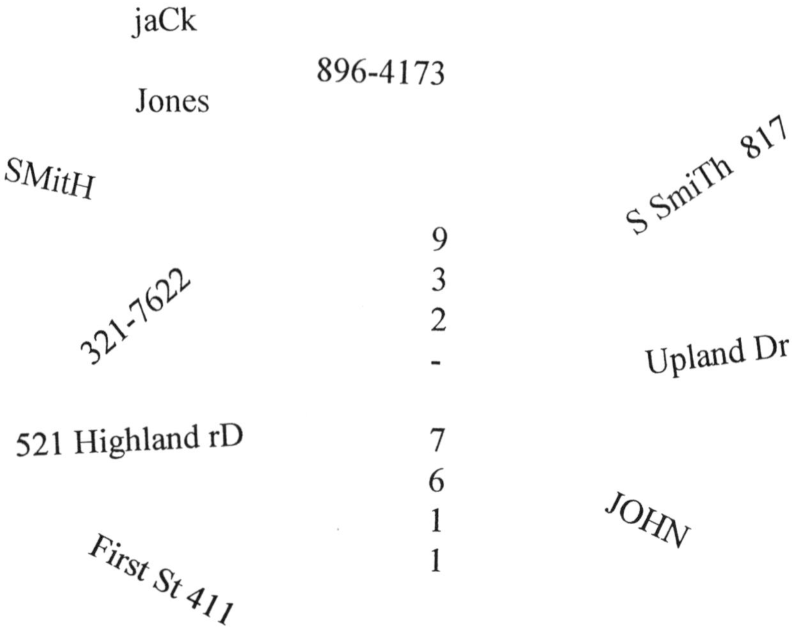

jaCk

Jones

896-4173

SMitH

S SmiTh 817

9
3
2
-

321-7622

Upland Dr

521 Highland rD

7
6
1
1

JOHN

First St 411

Jones   Jack
    521 Upland Dr.............321-7622
Smith John
    817 Highland Rd......... 932-7611
Smith S
    411 First St.................. 896-4173

FIGURE 4.2 Data in a phone book: unformatted (top) and formatted (bottom).

Jane Blank.....Id No 27-4123....3-L.So.			
			Jan. 1996
Calc I 13-201	Adams-185	4	B
Lin Alg 13-243	Owen-231	4	A
West Civ 32-103	Smith-312	4	C
Spanish 24-311	Anton-193	3	B
Sem. Credits......15		Sem. GPA........3.0	

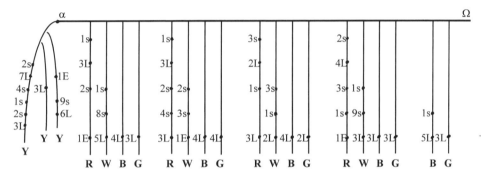

FIGURE 4.3 A facsimile grade slip (top) and its representation on a khipu (bottom).

data—the words on it are actually redundant. There are many different ways that the logic of the grade slip could be expressed on a khipu but Figure 4.3 uses one group of pendants per course. There are four pendants per group: the first is red for the course number, the next is white for the instructor identifier, then blue for the number of credits, and green for the grade. Notice that the last group has just two pendants, but we know they are the ones associated with the credits and the grade because of their colors. In addition, there is a dangle-end cord summarizing the khipu by identifying the student, semester, and class standing.

From the khipu, we read that, during her 3rd semester, student 27-4123 took course 13-201 from instructor 185, for which she received 4 credits and a grade of 3. She took course 13-243 from instructor 231, for which she received 4 credits and a grade of 4, and so on until, overall, she received 15 credits with an average grade of 3. Those course labels, incidentally, are actually made up of a department identifier and a course identifier in which the first digit is course level (1,2,3, or 4), and the last digit is odd or even depending on whether the course is normally given in fall or spring. Also, we do, in fact, replace letter grades with so-called quality points. It is this conversion from letters to magnitudes that enables us to *average* the grades, that is, to manipulate them arithmetically, which would not be possible otherwise.

Before leaving this example, notice the verbal patterning that is frequently associated with formatted material. Here we read that course such and such, taken from instructor so and so, received so many credits, and a grade of something. Then, course such and such, taken from another instructor, received so many credits, and a grade of something. And so on, four times. On a 1549 tribute list discussed by John Murra (1985) as having been read from a khipu, we find consecutive repetitively patterned statements such as:

> And they gave so and so many men to do such and such;
> And they gave so and so many men to do something else;
> And they gave 500 men to go . . . ;
> And they gave 500 men to plant. . . .

Or, in another part of it,

> And each 15 days they gave 12 jars of honey and from now on they
>   would give 10;
> And they gave each 15 days 150 breads of wax and from now on
>   only 40;
> And they gave each 15 days 40 pairs of sandals and from now on 30

This clearly is formatted information in which the format provides the narrative frame.

To recognize a format requires matching cultural knowledge with logical structures. To read a grade slip, one combines familiarity with school organization with commonly used formatting practices in our culture. To read a khipu, Inka cultural knowledge has to be integrated with khipu formatting. This, of course, was much easier for the Inka khipu makers than it is for us. But it can be done. We have provided a beginning by identifying many khipu structural indicators and analyzing, in whole or part, some two hundred khipu for their logical structures. These analyses are available in the *Code of the Quipu: Databook* (Ascher and Ascher 1978) and *Code of the Quipu: Databook II* (Ascher and Ascher 1988) and await examination by those with detailed expertise about different contexts within Inka culture. The point is that experts on Inka culture have to examine and contemplate the logical structures

of khipu, and work with them and within them to move toward further interpretation of individual khipu.

Below I briefly summarize some of the khipu structural indicators and
their usages.

1. There are usually two different end finishings on the main cord. From
this, it can be known whether the khipu is whole or broken, and, more important, all khipu being examined can be oriented the same way (see Figure
4.4.1).

2. There are cords suspended from the main cord (pendant cords) and
cords oppositely directed (top cords). There are three different means of attaching top cords (see Figure 4.4.2) Top cords serve to group pendant cords
and generally sum their values, and change in the means of top-cord attachment sets off some groups of pendants from others. Top cords are important
in that they provide internal corroboration of base-10 interpretation of knot
readings and, where used, they imply that the related data are quantitative.
Top cords, however, appear on only about 10 percent of khipu.

3. A single cord dangling from the end of a main cord generally contains
some summary of the khipu's information (see Figure 4.4.3).

4. Pendant cords are grouped and distinguished by cord spacing, and cord
groups are grouped and distinguished by larger spacing. In Figure 4.4.4, as a
result of the groupings, each cord has three distinct associations. Each is associated with part I of the khipu or part II of the khipu, as well as with group
1, 2, or 3 within each part, and with a position within the groups.

5. Pendant cords are further associated or distinguished by color. Some
examples are shown in Figure 4.5. The third example from the top, color
patterning, is particularly significant, as it enables the distinction between
a cord with a zero value and one that is intentionally omitted in a particular group. Its logical structure is three groups, each referring to four categories, but in the third group the second category (W) has deliberately been
omitted.

In the khipu corpus, numerous other uses of color occur. For example,
there is a khipu[2] containing three different types of color usages. One usage
was a specially colored cord to separate groups; another was different colors
threaded through a short portion of the pendants; and the third was using
one color part way down a pendant and then, by splicing, continuing with
another color. Together these conveyed a logical structure made up of nine
sets of twenty-seven groups of seven cord positions each, and, what is more,
highlighted different aspects of the structure depending on whether the khipu
was observed from the top or from the front.

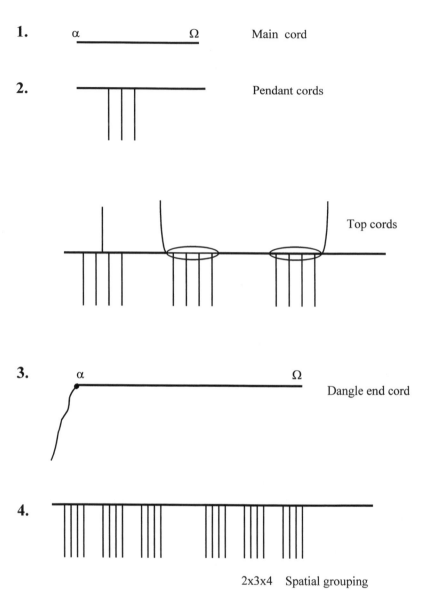

1.   α ⎯⎯⎯⎯⎯⎯⎯⎯⎯ Ω   Main cord

2.   Pendant cords

    Top cords

3.   α ⎯⎯⎯⎯⎯⎯⎯⎯⎯ Ω   Dangle end cord

4.

2x3x4   Spatial grouping

FIGURE 4.4 Khipu structural indicators: (1) main cord and end finishings; (2) cords suspended from main cord; (3) cord dangling from end of main cord; (4) spatial grouping of cords.

5.

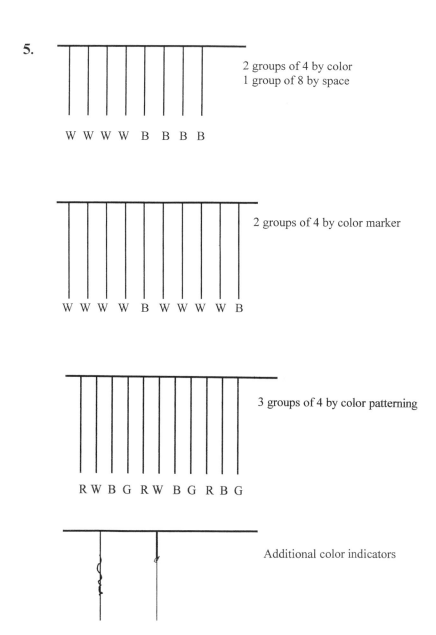

2 groups of 4 by color
1 group of 8 by space

W W W W B B B B

2 groups of 4 by color marker

W W W W B W W W W B

3 groups of 4 by color patterning

R W B G R W B G R B G

Additional color indicators

FIGURE 4.5 Khipu structural indicators continued: (5) color—color grouping; color markers; color patterning; color threading and color splicing.

6.   Subsidiaries

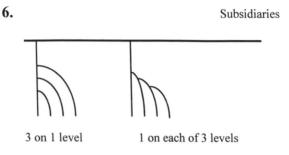

3 on 1 level   1 on each of 3 levels

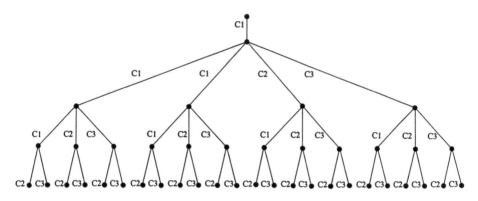

FIGURE 4.6 Khipu structural indicators continued: (6) subsidiaries—positions; levels; color and position on successive levels (from AS70).

Of course, most of the khipu are not this regular in their logical organization. The regular ones are emphasized here because they are easier to describe and because the resulting regularity can be used as internal corroboration of our reading of the structural indicators. Mixed groupings are just as common, such as two groups of two cords each followed by ten groups of three cords each, or a group of two followed by a group of twenty-two followed by a group of fifteen. It may well be the case that the less regular ones can lead to more definitive matching with cultural categories.

6. Subsidiaries attached to pendant or top cords and to other subsidiaries create different levels of cords and, on each level, position, color, and spacing again operate (see Figure 4.6, top). For example, one khipu[3] was structured as eight groups of ten pendants each. The groups were set off from each other by colored markers, with the eighth group set off from the other seven by a

marker of a different color, and this distinction was supported by differing subsidiary layouts. For the first seven of the eight groups, the ninth and tenth pendants in each group had three levels of subsidiaries; their overall structure is shown as a tree in Figure 4.6, bottom. Notice the color pattern on the first level: C1, C1, C2, C3. Then each subsequent level has one fewer subsidiary position, and each time it is another C1 that is absent. On the same khipu, again only for the first seven of the eight groups, the seventh and eighth pendants have similar but extended subsidiary logic. For them the level I subsidiaries begin similarly with C1, C1, C2, C3, but then a C4 and a C5 occur as well. Again, consistently, each level has one fewer subsidiary position and, again, it is the C1's that are reduced.

Selections from the foregoing structural indicators are combined and cascade into particular logical structures that range from the simple to the very complex. For each, cultural contexts or situations must be found that share or reflect the same logic. These contexts could be, for example, astronomy, calendrics, textiles, gold fabrication, construction, organization and administration, myths, rituals, music, dance, warfare, politics, or anything else that is believed to have been of concern to the Inka bureaucracy. There are, of course, data on each of these khipu. That is, the cords are knotted so that they contain numbers that are either magnitudes or labels. The data and the information they contain have their own interrelationships and patterning as well as particular values. But the data can only be reasonably dealt with within the overall structure of a khipu.

So, again, the point is that to relate khipu to meaning in the Inka world, one must first recognize and establish their individual logical structures. Each structure is particular to some situation. One must work from knowledge of the culture to reconstruct what this situation might be. To pursue only a model of writing that encodes speech sounds is to disregard the power of structured, formatted communication. This type of communication is not lesser than encoded speech. In fact, I cannot visualize how music could be better conveyed by words than by musical notation or mathematics by words than by its formalism. Today, most job advertisements are not seeking people who speak, say, French or German. They are directed to people who can communicate in particular structured formatted ways referred to as, for example, C+, Pascal, Word, COBOL, Lisp, etc. The power of these software systems is that each of them is limited to some information domain in order to be optimally efficient in that domain and to capture its particular complexities and nuances.

Finally, let me close with a khipu example[4] combining logical structure

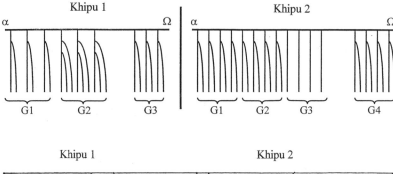

Khipu 1

Pends in G1	LB or W	Pends in G1	LB or W
Subs in G1	G0	Subs in G1	G0, GY, or LB:W
Pends in G2	W	Pends in G2	W
Subs in G2-pos 1	KB	Subs in G2	KB
-pos 2	LB:W	Pends in G3	LB:W
Pends in G3	DB or DB:LB	Pends in G4	DB or DB:LB
Subs in G3	DB:LB	Subs in G4	DB:LB

Khipu 1 — Khipu 2

Pends in G1	1-6, 1-8, 1-6	Pends in G1	3, 3, 7, 3
Subs in G1	8, 1-4, 8	Subs in G1	2, 2, 5, 2
Pends in G2	3, 4, 3	Pends in G2	7, 7, 9, 7
Subs in G2 - pos 1	3, 4, 3	Subs in G2	3, 3, 4, 3
- pos 2	1-6, 1-8, 1-6	Pends in G3	3, 3, 7, 3
Pends in G3	3, 4, 3	Pends in G4	6, 6, 1-2, 6
Subs in G3	1-6, 1-8, 1-6	Subs in G4	4, 4, 6, 4

ABA   AABA

FIGURE 4.7 Khipu pair (AS101): schematic showing structural indicators (top); chart form based on structural indicators (middle); data displayed in same chart form (bottom).

with data and, in particular, with data I believe to contain number labels, and, what is more, the data, in and of themselves, are patterned. To me, this khipu—in fact it is a pair of khipu—represents the richness of the khipu that is yet to be fully explored and that must not be passed over because it does not conform to writing in some other culture. As always, the example is of khipu small in size and relatively simple in logic, because the others are too complex to convey succinctly.

These two small khipu are linked—linked by being physically tied together but also by much more than that. First of all, using the two different end finishings, we orient them in the same direction (see Figure 4.7, top). Next, we observe that, by spacing, Khipu 1 is a set of six pendants followed by a set of three pendants, and Khipu 2 is a set of twelve pendants followed by a set of four pendants. However, by color, it is further grouped within that so that Khipu 1 is three groups of three and Khipu 2 is four groups of four. While Khipu 1 has a subsidiary on every cord, but has two subsidiaries on the same level in its second group, Khipu 2 has a subsidiary on every cord except those in its third group.

From here on, these two khipu are easier to discuss if they are converted into chart form, as has been done in Figure 4.7, middle. That is, I have converted them into *our* structural indicators.

Notice that in each khipu, spacing, color, and cord levels reinforce each other. But also notice the color and spacing consistencies from Khipu 1 to Khipu 2, as well as the fact that the anomalous second subsidiary level of Khipu 1 matches the anomalous subsidiary-free pendant group on Khipu 2.

Turning to the data, all of the knot clusters are made up of single knots—that is, no long knots or figure-eight knots are used. As such, we interpret them as number labels and display them, as shown in Figure 4.7, bottom, within the layout that was just established. Notice, most importantly, that Khipu 1 has an ABA pattern repeated on every line, while Khipu 2 has a consistent AABA pattern. Further, for both, the same data repeat on the first line and just before the spatial break. The specific data on them are different. That is, they are different specific instances of the same general story. But what that story is still remains an open question.

In this chapter, I have elaborated on some ideas that are crucial to understanding the logical-numerical system of the khipu. The concept of numbers as labels is pivotal. The concepts of structure and format are as important for decoding the khipu containing magnitudes as they are for decoding khipu that contain labels. Each khipu is a specific statement that was created by the selection and combination of structural and data elements from the overall, general system. With these ideas in mind, further progress can be made toward reading khipu.

NOTES

1. Representing the digits in the ISBN number by $a_1, a_2 \ldots, a_9, a_{10}$, the check digit a_{10} is calculated from: $10a_1 + 9a_2 + 8a_3 + 7a_4 + 6a_5 + 5a_6 + 4a_7 + 3a_8 + 2a_9 + a_{10} = 0 \pmod{11}$ where $1 \le a_{10} \le 10$. If $a_{10} = 10$, use $a_{10} = x$.

2. The khipu is AS69 as identified using the tag system established in Ascher and

Ascher 1978. A detailed description of the khipu is in Ascher and Ascher 1978, and it is also discussed in Ascher and Ascher 1981: 118.

3. The khipu is AS70. A detailed description of the khipu is in Ascher and Ascher 1978, and it is also discussed in Ascher and Ascher 1981: 120.

4. The khipu is AS101. A detailed description of the khipu is in Ascher and Ascher 1978, and it is also discussed in Ascher and Ascher 1981: 123-125.

REFERENCES

Ascher, Marcia. 1983. "The Logical-Numerical System of Inca Quipus." *Annals of the History of Computing* 5: 268–278.

———. 1986. "Mathematical Ideas of the Incas." In *Native American Mathematics*, edited by Michael Closs, 261–289. Austin: University of Texas Press.

Ascher, Marcia, and Robert Ascher. 1975. "The Quipu as a Visible Language." *Visible Language* 9: 329–356.

———. 1978. *Code of the Quipu: Databook*. Ann Arbor: University of Michigan Press. Now available at the web site http://instruct1.cit.cornell.edu/research/quipu-ascher/ and on microfiche from Cornell University Archives, Ithaca, N.Y.

———. 1981. *Code of the Quipu: A Study in Media, Mathematics, and Culture*. Ann Arbor: University of Michigan Press. Reprinted as *Mathematics of the Incas: Code of the Quipu*. New York: Dover Publications, 1997.

———. 1988. *Code of the Quipu: Databook II*. Ithaca: Ascher. Now available at the web site http://instruct1.cit.cornell.edu/research/quipu-ascher/ and on microfiche from Cornell University Archives, Ithaca, N.Y.

———. 1997. "Inca Quipus." In *Encyclopedia of the History of Science, Technology, and Medicine in Non-Western Cultures*, edited by Helene Selin, 839–841. Dordecht, The Netherlands: Kluwer Academic Publishers.

Murra, John. 1985. "Mita Obligations of the Chupaychu—an Ethnic Group in the Pillkumayu (Haullaga Valley, 1549)." Andean Ethnology course notes, Cornell University.

Inka Writing

FIVE   *Robert Ascher*

Within the company of civilizations, the Inka have, for too long, been set apart as the one civilization without writing. Here I show that the Inka did indeed have a writing system. To begin, I retell the story of the first major confrontation between Spaniards and the Inka—an encounter in which a book played a key role.

WRITING SYSTEMS

If one had to choose a place and a time to mark the start of the downfall of the Inka state, it would surely be the plaza in the town of Cajamarca on November 16, 1532. Let us follow Prescott's (1900: 378–412) version of what happened there on that day. Early in the morning, Atahuallpa, the head of the Inka state, and his entourage were on the outskirts of town. The Spaniards, led by Francisco Pizarro, were in the town's triangular plaza. Through a messenger, Atahuallpa informed Pizarro that he would meet him in the plaza. Having already decided the previous day to take Atahuallpa prisoner, Pizarro stationed his army, with its guns and horses, in the large wide-doored hallways of the plaza's buildings. Late in the afternoon, Atahuallpa, elevated on a litter and surrounded by his supporters, entered the plaza.

With the stage thus set, Vicente de Valverde, a Dominican friar, stepped forward with a Bible in his hand and addressed Atahuallpa. He talked about the death and resurrection of Jesus, the authority of the pope over all earthly powers, the Spanish monarch whom the pope had commissioned to convert native peoples, and Francisco Pizarro who was here now to execute that mission. Atahuallpa replied that he was the subject of no man, that the pope must be insane to think that he could give away the land of others, and pointing toward the west, Atahuallpa exclaimed that his God, the Sun, was still alive. Atahuallpa then demanded to know by what authority the Dominican spoke. Atahuallpa was handed the Bible, and after turning some pages, he threw it to the ground. Pizarro then waved a white scarf, the prearranged signal to attack. A massacre followed: within an hour, Atahuallpa was taken prisoner and hundreds of his followers were everywhere dying on the plaza's ground.

In watching Atahuallpa throw the Bible to the ground, the Spaniards witnessed what they took to be an insult to their religion. In fact, Vicente de Valverde said as much while Pizarro was preparing to wave his scarf. Beyond the presumed insult, the Spaniards saw the act of a person of the highest rank within his own community who, in their eyes, could not read or write. Then and now, literacy together with differences in technology and biology has been the wedge used to separate the "them" from the "us," with the clear connotation that the "them" are inferior (Pattanayak 1991). The literacy section of the wedge swelled in prominence during the waning years of the twentieth century.

It is likely that the Cajamarca Bible was a Gutenberg type-printed book. Just seventy-five years prior to the confrontation, the so-called Latin Bible, the first book printed in Europe with movable type, was issued in Mainz, Germany. By 1474, this way to make books in large numbers had reached Spain (Jennett 1967: 24–25), where it was put to good use (McLuhan 1962: 225–227). It seems that the plaza confrontation took place at a moment in history—and with a prime symbol of that moment in hand—that, according to some (Eisenstein 1979; Havelock 1986; McLuhan 1962; Ong 1982), would signal a division in the world's cultures. In this newly divided world, people who used alphabetic print would be placed to one side; everybody else would be on the far side. The alphabetic-print people are supposed to think differently, and presumably better, than other people.

The notion that human cognition changes with the introduction of writing, and then changes even more dramatically after the advent of alphabetic-print media, at first reinforced entrenched views of a nonliterate/literate divide. But recently, and for the first time, ideas based on the presumed divide were put to the test. Evidence gathered from anthropological, linguistic, and psychological perspectives, and accumulated from around the world, now suggests that the differences that separate oral and literate peoples are sometimes trivial, often mistaken, and usually exaggerated (Besmier 1995; Bloch 1989; Denny 1991; Narasimhan 1991; Parry 1989; Pattison 1982; Scribner and Cole 1981; Street 1988). For example, it has been shown that interpretation and reflection, presumed to become possible only after the introduction of written texts, are equally possible when only oral genres are present (Feldman 1991). Of particular importance here is the questioning and reexamination of the basics of writing systems that has resulted from the renewed attention to this issue.

The orthodox view of writing had been based on an evolutionary scheme (Gelb 1952) culminating, not surprisingly, in the Roman alphabet. Evidence for this scheme has been drawn largely from the Near East and Europe; much less attention was given to the history of writing in Asia, and even less to that in the Americas. Some texts still restrict writing to marks that represent utterances (e.g., Daniels and Bright 1996), but others admit a wider range of phenomena into the framework of writing (Harris 1995). The evolutionary, multilayered classifications of writing systems have been reduced in some cases to two or even to one class (McCarthy 1995). There is still no single, generally accepted definition of writing, but most tend toward being inclusive and catholic (e.g., Gaur 1992).

I think of writing as a way to represent information, and I accept a dual classification of writing systems. One group can be called thought or concept writing and the second, sound writing (Gaur 1992, 1995). Although other terms may be used, these best reflect the idea that the systems in the first group are connected to units of meaning, while those in the second are related to units of speech sound. Examples of systems in the first group include choreographics and mathematics (Harris 1995). The second group includes our alphabetic system. There are systems, for example Japanese, that have elements of both groups.

Some classification schemes (e.g., Hill 1967) add a third group, but additional groups often turn out to be further breakdowns into subgroups of either or both speech-sound or concept writing (e.g., Sampson 1985). Although concept writing is not based on sound units, it can be sounded, as in the case, for example, of a dancer talking out the steps she learned from reading choreographics while she is dancing.

The Inka khipu fits into the concept writing group. Moreover, it is likely the most general-purpose example of it. This is so because instead of being about limited phenomena such as dance or chemistry, it can be used for a wide range of phenomena (Ascher and Ascher 1981). It is easy to understand how the Spaniards, knowing only their own alphabetic sound system, believed that

Atahuallpa and the Inka were illiterate even after becoming familiar with Inka khipu. It is harder to explain why recent general studies of writing mention khipu only in passing (e.g., Coulmas 1990) or not at all (e.g., Martin 1994). A continuing neglect of writing throughout the Americas may be partly responsible. Another explanation is that we are closer to the colonial Spaniards than we like to think. With the exception of the Inka, the Spaniards found correspondences between their own mode of representation and representations in the cultures they encountered. Inka abstractions and structures, as evidenced in some of their art and in khipu, were apparently too remote from their experience (Cummins 1994). In like manner, the sophistication and unusual characteristics of khipu writing place it at a distance from our usual conceptions of writing systems.

DECIPHERMENT

To decipher unknown writing based wholly or mostly on units of sound, one must, in every case, refer back to an already known sound-based writing system (Segert 1983). For example, the multiscript Rosetta Stone made it possible to decipher Egyptian writing by reference to Greek writing and language (Gelb 1952: 72). By contrast, to decipher a concept-based system, one must ultimately grasp a number of the meaning systems of the culture using the writing. A concept-based system as general as khipu writing does not have a single encompassing resolution. Decipherment of khipu writing can only mean a solution to a khipu or a set of related khipu. This is so because khipu writing is adaptable to many different systems of meaning, and for each such system a different khipu or set of khipu comes into being. Khipu makers and others who knew these systems of meanings and their representations could read and write.

In both concept- and sound-based systems, the essential groundwork for decipherment has to be prepared through close analysis of the internal structure of the writing itself. We call this internal structure the code of the writing. In the case of the khipu, the first breakthrough in the code happened when it was shown that the top cords at the heads of groups on some khipu contained numbers that, when read in the base ten, were the sum of numbers on the pendants in the groups (Locke 1923). Further close attention to the internal structure of khipu writing, using a large database, revealed the logic of the system and the importance in it of format, category, pattern, hierarchy, and numbers used as labels. Because numerical concerns in addition to base ten are built into khipu writing, the arithmetical ideas of the Inka were also found without having to go outside the workings of the system itself (Ascher and Ascher 1981).

Access to Inka meaning systems, so necessary for deciphering khipu writing, is through artifacts and colonial documents. Archaeological artifacts are highly variable in their usefulness due to differential preservation, and they are notoriously difficult to interpret, as indeed are all material remains. The writings of the Spanish conquerors also present problems. Even under the best circumstances, the accounts are distorted as they pass from one culture (Inka) to another (Spanish colonial), where they are interpreted, and then to a third (contemporary Euro-American), where they are reinterpreted 465 years after the fact. Making do with what we have, it is still possible to find a method for khipu decipherment. The examination of a successful attempt, outlined below, suggests such a method.

Wherever writing first appeared, it was used to record information deemed important to the state. States are very much concerned with forecast and control, so the discovery that calendrics is a subject for khipu is no surprise. In general, a calendar is an agreed-upon schedule for a culture (Hockett 1962). In itself, it is a system of meaning. It is also an organizer for other systems of meaning; for example, it sets the timing of rituals. In the Inka case, colonial documents imply that a giant representation of a calendar was superimposed on Cusco, the Inka capital (Zuidema 1964). It consisted of forty-one imaginary lines in four quadrants that emanated outward from the Temple of the Sun near the capital's center and reached out to the ends of the known world. Points along the imaginary lines were marked by 328 sacred sites, including natural landmarks such as hills, piles of stones, houses, and fountains. The colonial documents are backed up by archaeological evidence, including the remains of sacred sites (Rowe 1979), and there is an excavated representation of the calendar woven into cloth (Zuidema 1977). A search of the khipu corpus led to the decipherment of four khipu that are calendric. My collaborator and I were able to associate two of these with one calendric interpretation and the third with an alternate interpretation (Ascher and Ascher 1989). The fourth and most complex khipu was tied to the alternate interpretation (Zuidema 1989).

I suggest that khipu decipherment should follow a procedure something like that used in the calendric example. First, a colonial document that is specific and reflects, as far as is possible, an Inka system of meaning is located. Supporting evidence, drawn from artifacts in particular, is then sought. In the next step, a search is undertaken in the corpus for a matching khipu or one that comes close to a match. Alternatively, it is possible to start with a promising khipu from the corpus and then search documents and artifacts for a solution. There is nothing necessary in the order of procedure. In practice, the route to decipherment is nonlinear. One might proceed, say, from khipu to document and then from document back to the same khipu or to a different one. With a khipu corpus as small as the four hundred that have survived and can be studied, the chance of success is rather low. Failing on all the above routes to decipherment, one might reroute the course and move toward *encipherment.*

ENCIPHERMENT: AN EXAMPLE

Knowing the internal structure of the khipu—that is, knowing how khipu writing works, knowing its code—opens the way to encipherment. In encipherment, information is written into khipu. For example, some colonial document makers write that the information they record was obtained from a khipu maker who read from a khipu containing the information given in the document. Information from such documents can be written back into one or more hypothetical khipu (Ascher and Ascher 1972). In other words, in encipherment, the order of things is reversed. Encipherments are kin to *thought experiments:* they allow us to explore and think about Inka representations of information.

To choose an example for encipherment, I have in mind a group of khipu that are characteristically highly patterned, almost rhythmic in nature. They make up at least 15 percent of the khipu corpus and, strikingly, are set apart from those that seem to be primarily concerned with magnitudes. They call to mind musical scores, spatial layouts, textile patterns, and formulas rather than, say, tribute and census data. Such khipu may be plans to do something rather than recordings of something collected or accomplished. An idealized, highly patterned khipu might show, for example, three groups of four cords with cord colors ABAB in the first and third groups, the colors ABBA in the second group, and with the numbers, group by group, 2, 5, 2, 5, followed by 2, 5, 5, 2, and then followed by a repeat of the first 2, 5, 2, 5. None of these highly patterned khipu have been deciphered. Below, I take a colonial documented textile and, via encipherment, explore the notion that some of the highly patterned khipu are recordings of, or plans for, textile designs.

A single page in an early Spanish document attributed to Martín de Murúa (1946) details either the plan for making a cloth belt or the description of a belt already made. At the top of the page is a preface, followed by a set of specifications. In part, the translation (Desrosiers 1986: 219) of the pref-

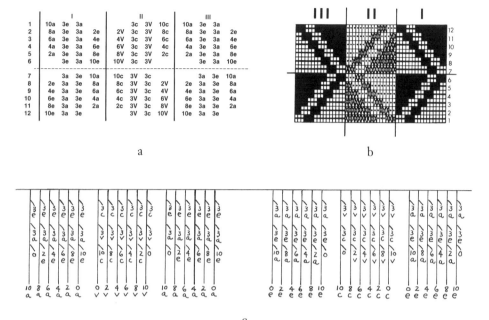

FIGURE 5.1 Cumbi belt: *a* chart, from Desrosiers 1986; *b* graphic design, from Desrosiers 1986; *c* khipu encipherment.

ace reads: "specification of a famous *lipi* or *cumbi* belt which the Coyas used to wear during the great Corn Festivals. . . ." The specifications following the preface consist of twelve lines, Yillaba 1 to Yillaba 12, interspersed with twelve lines of alternating pairs, with each pair consisting of a number and an alphabetic letter.

In a model of analysis and interpretation, Desrosiers (1986) points out several errors in the specifications and traces most of them to copying mistakes. Her resolution is detailed in Figure 5.1a, where the belt is shown composed in three bands (I, II, III) and four colors (a, e, c, V). The number-color pairs recall for Desrosiers the way she observed beginning weavers being taught in the Andes. Band I, Line 1, for example, can be read: 10 of Color a, followed by 3 of Color e, followed by 3 of Color a. The pattern that results is shown in Figure 5.1b, drawn in the graphic mode customarily used for textile pattern representation. In Figure 5.1b, a dash is used for Color a, a black rectangle for e, a cross is used for c, and a spot for V. Continuing with the example, 10a, 3e, 3a is laid out from right to left along Band I, Line 1, at the bottom, extreme right. All of Figure 5.1b is derived from Figure 5.1a in the same way, line by line, band by band. A diamond divided into four quarters is the belt's basic design motif, as can be seen in Figure 5.1b.

Desrosiers's analysis went far beyond graph-paper construction. She wove experimental textiles, studied Inka belts in museums in Europe and the United States, and examined different looms, including ones known to have been used in Inka times. She suggests the most likely colors for each of a, e, c, and V, and discusses alternative weavings that could have been used to make the belt. Her combined ethnological, linguistic, historical, artifactual, and experimental approaches are convincing.

Now, by encipherment, I add the third representation—the hypothetical khipu shown in Figure 5.1c—to the chart and the graphic representations. There are thirty-six pendants on the khipu. All the pendants show three subsidiaries. There are six groups. Three of the groups are in one part, the remaining three are in a second part. Part 1—the first three groups—corresponds to Lines 1 through 6 on both the graphic and the chart, and Part 2 corresponds to Lines 7 through 12. To read the khipu in a way that corresponds to the chart and the graphic, do as follows: read the first pendant and its subsidiaries in the first group (10a, 3e, 3a, 0); then read the first pendant and its subsidiaries in the second group (0, 3c, 3V, 10c); next, read the first pendant and its subsidiaries in the third group (10a, 3e, 3a, 0). This khipu reading corresponds to Line 1 on both the chart and the graphic. Stay in Part 1 of the khipu, and Lines 2 through 6 can be read in the same manner. To read Lines 7 through 12, move to Part 2 and proceed in the same manner.

Clearly, there is more than one way to construct a hypothetical khipu. Taking this one as an example, consider how it might help in thinking about khipu representation. The constructed khipu shows some symmetry. Numerically, Parts 1 and 2 are vertical reflections of each other. There is also redundancy. The first and third groups of Part 1 are identical, as are the first and third groups of Part 2. Redundancy is common in the khipu corpus, and the combination of redundancy with symmetry is also common, in particular, in the highly patterned, rhythmic khipu. The constructed khipu is probably adequate in leading toward the design motif, but it is less valuable in giving weaving instructions. To have accomplished that, it probably should have been laid out in groups of three, so that each group in itself corresponded to one line of weaving. But doing it that way would double the number of groups. A question of parsimony appears more seriously in the number of subsidiaries. Although subsidiaries are common enough, the number of them seems excessive. A second-generation hypothetical khipu representation of the belt might aim at reducing the number of subsidiaries and combining design with weaving instructions. A belt is a relatively small item, yet its encipherment, as envisioned here, results in an average-size khipu. Does this mean that if much larger, more complex textiles were represented in khipu, they would have likely been abbreviated versions of plans rather than full descriptions?

NARRATION AND THE NEXT FIRST STEP

One solution at a time is perhaps the best approach to khipu writing. For some, this may be unsatisfactory. Accustomed to systems based on speech sounds, where the resolution can be more general, some wonder if khipu can be made, so to speak, to talk. This notion is driven by assertions in sixteenth-century Spanish documents that khipu were used for narratives, including histories and myths. Assuming that there is truth in these assertions, it is argued that the khipu code likely included ways to directly represent speech sounds (e.g., Pärssinen 1992). It would be foolhardy to deny this possibility. But before unduly multiplying hypotheses, we need to ask if a system based on units of meaning can be used for recording and telling stories.

Everywhere, narratives have formulaic, traditional frameworks. Take, for example, a story about a diviner and a king who want to overthrow another king. The story is from Burundi, a native African state (Vansina 1965). The story can be seen unfolding in ten episodes, A–J. The initial episode (A) is followed by three episodes (B, C, D). The starting phrases of D repeat, with only slight variation, the start of C; the start of C repeats, again with slight variation, the starting phrases of B. The narrative continues with a middle episode E. Then there is another set of episodes (F, G, H, I), with repeats. The story ends with episode J. It is easy to schematically represent the framework of the narrative:

It would be easy to encipher the framework of the story on a khipu using only a small part of only one of the elements of the khipu code. Different colors, for example, might be used for each of the episodes A–J without exhausting the color repertoire. Other colors and color combinations, along with still other elements of the code, might be used for incidents within the episodes, and so on to units in the story smaller than incidents. A narrative recorded this way would look like a number of the highly patterned, rhythmic khipu in the corpus. I believe that this satisfies the uniformly nonspecific colonial Spanish assertions concerning the telling of narrative with khipu. A system based only on units of meaning is enough to tell a story.

To say that the Inka could record a narrative without recourse to direct representation of speech sounds does not diminish them in regard to writing. Writing systems are no more hierarchical than are, say, kinship systems or religious beliefs. Khipu texts could be profitably compared with late medieval European Latin alphabetic manuscripts, which lacked meaningful punctuation and were filled with abbreviations. One had to know the special vocabulary of a text and its subject matter, in addition to Latin paleography, in order to make any sense of it. Medieval readers of texts said them out loud; Greek and Roman texts had to be read out loud to be understood, largely because the words were not separated (Sirat 1994: 416).

Going further, let us speculate on the relationship between the khipu as an artifact and the actual telling of a narrative. Imagine a khipu held in the hands of a performer. We see the performer looking at the khipu from time to time as the story unfolds. All during the telling, we also watch the performer move his or her hands over, in, below, and through the soft, pliable, ever mobile, nonlinear khipu. This touching recalls Serbo-Croatian singers of tales who found it difficult, if not impossible, to tell their stories without fingering their one-stringed bowed instruments (Lord 1974: 127; 1987: 475; Parry 1987: 442).

The performer we hear and watch has developed special skills. In all non-khipu writing and reading, with the exception of Braille, touch is important only in writing; in the case of the khipu, touch comes into play and is elaborate in both writing and reading. Tactile sensitivity begins in the rhythmic, pulsating environment of the unborn child, far in advance of the development of the other senses. Still, it was difficult for us to learn the tactile control necessary in writing; as adults, we forget just how difficult. The term "scribal tract" (Watt 1994) has been used to gloss the biophysical means we use in producing writing. Watching the performer, we think that "tactile tract" is a better term to cover both the writing—assuming that he or she made the khipu in use—and the reading necessary for the performance. In fact, the performer simultaneously engages at least four tracts: tactile, visual, vocal, and auditory; and all four were wired to the brain via a complex circuitry about which we know almost nothing.

In his intriguingly entitled article "If Wittgenstein Had Been an Eskimo," Edmund Carpenter (1980) dwells on how differently Euro-Americans and native peoples interpret experience. He contends that we transfer most sense experience into the visual, often excluding other senses, as in, for example, the expression "Let us see what we can hear." For others, there is a continuing interplay of several senses at once. Applying these notions here, we say: if Wittgenstein and we were Eskimos, he and we might understand khipu writing as simultaneously tactile and visual, and probably more. Being that we are who we are, it is difficult to internalize this notion so that it becomes a part of us, but I think that it is the next step that must be taken in the study of Inka writing.

Those interested in trying their skills at decipherment, encipherment, or narrative interpretation should visit the web site http://instruct1.cit.cornell. edu/research/quipu-ascher/ to find detailed descriptions of 206 khipu studied and recorded by me and my collaborator, Marcia Ascher.

BIBLIOGRAPHY

Ascher, Marcia, and Robert Ascher. 1972. "Numbers and Relations from Ancient Andean Quipus." *Archive for History of Exact Sciences* 8: 288–320.
———. 1981. *Code of the Quipu: A Study in Media, Mathematics, and Culture.* Ann Arbor: University of Michigan Press. Reprinted as *Mathematics of the Incas: Code of the Quipu.* New York: Dover Publications, 1997.
———. 1989. "Are There Numbers in the Sky?" In *Time and Calendars in the Inca Empire*, edited by Mariusz S. Ziólkowski and Robert M. Sadowski, 35–48. Oxford: BAR International Series.
Besmier, Niko. 1995. *Literacy, Emotion and Authority.* Cambridge: Cambridge University Press.
Bloch, Maurice. 1989. "Literacy and Enlightenment." In *Literacy and Society*, edited by Karen Schousboe and Mogens Trolle Larsen, 15–38. Copenhagen: Akatemisk Forlag.
Carpenter, Edmund. 1980. "If Wittgenstein Had Been an Eskimo." *Natural History* 89, no. 2: 72–77.
Coulmas, Florian. 1990. *The Writing Systems of the World.* London: Basil Blackwell.
Cummins, Tom. 1994. "Representation in the Sixteenth Century and the Colonial Image of the Inca." In *Writing without Words: Alternative Literacies in Mesoamerica and the Andes*, edited by Elizabeth H. Boone and Walter Mignolo, 188–219. Durham: Duke University Press.
Daniels, Peter T., and William Bright. 1996. *The World's Writing Systems.* Oxford: Oxford University Press.
Denny, J. Peter. 1991. "Rational Thought in Oral Culture and Literate Decontextualization." In *Literacy and Orality*, edited by David R. Olson and Nancy Torrance, 66–89. Cambridge: Cambridge University Press.
Desrosiers, Sophie. 1986. "An Interpretation of Technical Weaving Data Found in an Early Seventeenth-Century Chronicle." In *The Junius B. Bird Conference on Andean Textiles*, edited by Anne P. Rowe, 219–241. Washington, D.C.: The Textile Museum.

Eisenstein, Elizabeth A. 1979. *The Printing Press as an Agent of Change.* Cambridge: Cambridge University Press.

Feldman, Carol Fleisher. 1991. "Oral Metalanguage." In *Literacy and Orality,* edited by David R. Olson and Nancy Torrance, 47–65. Cambridge: Cambridge University Press.

Gaur, Albertine. 1992. *A History of Writing.* New York: Abbeville Press.

———. 1995. "Scripts and Writing Systems: A Historical Perspective." In *Scripts and Literacy: Reading and Learning to Read Alphabets, Syllabaries, and Characters,* edited by Insup Taylor and David R. Olson, 19–29. Dordrecht: Kluwer Academic Publishers.

Gelb, Ignace J. 1952. *A Study of Writing.* Chicago: University of Chicago Press.

Harris, Roy. 1995. *Signs of Writing.* New York: Routledge.

Havelock, Eric A. 1986. *The Muse Learns to Write.* New Haven: Yale University Press.

Hill, Archibald A. 1967. "Typology of Writing Systems." In *Papers in Linguistics in Honor of Leon Dostert,* edited by William A. Austin, 92–99. The Hague: Mouton.

Hockett, Charles F. 1962. "Scheduling." In *Cross-Cultural Understanding: Epistemology in Anthropology,* edited by F. S. C. Northrop and H. H. Livingston, 125–144. New York: Harper and Row.

Jennett, Sean. 1967. *The Making of Books.* London: Faber and Faber.

Locke, L. Leland. 1923. *The Ancient Quipu or Peruvian Knot Record.* New York: American Museum of Natural History.

Lord, Albert B. 1974. *The Singer of Tales.* New York: Atheneum.

———. 1987. "Homer, Parry, and Huso." In *The Making of Homeric Verse: The Collected Papers of Milman Parry,* edited by Adam Parry, 465–478. Oxford: Oxford University Press.

Martin, Henri-Jean. 1994. *The History and Power of Writing.* Chicago: University of Chicago Press.

McCarthy, Suzanne. 1995. "The Cree Syllabary and the Writing System Riddle: A Paradigm in Crisis." In *Scripts and Literacy: Reading and Learning to Read Alphabets, Syllabaries, and Characters,* edited by Insup Taylor and David R. Olson, 59–75. Dordrecht: Kluwer Academic Publishers.

McLuhan, Marshall. 1962. *The Gutenberg Galaxy.* Toronto: University of Toronto Press.

Murra, John. 1962. "Cloth and Its Function in the Inca State." *American Anthropologist* 64, no. 4: 710–727.

Murúa, Martín de. 1946 [ca. 1590]. *Historia de origen y genealogía de los reyes incas del Perú,* edited by Constantino Bayle. Biblioteca Missionalia Hispánica. Madrid: Instituto Santo Toribo de Mogrovejo.

Narasimhan, R. 1991. "Literacy: Its Characterization and Implications." In *Literacy and Orality,* edited by David R. Olson and Nancy Torrance, 177–197. Cambridge: Cambridge University Press.

Ong, Walter J. 1982. *Orality and Literacy: The Technologizing of the World.* London: Routledge.

Parry, J. P. 1989. "The Brahamical Tradition and the Technology of the Intellect." In *Literacy and Society,* edited by Karen Schousboe and Mogens Trolle Larsen, 39–71. Copenhagen: Akademisk Forlag.

Parry, Milman. 1987. "Cor Huso: A Study of Southslavic Song." In *The Making of*

Homeric Verse: The Collected Papers of Milman Parry, edited by Adam Parry, 437–464. Oxford: Oxford University Press.

Pärssinen, Martti. 1992. *Tawantinsuyu: The Inca State and Its Political Organization*. Helsinki: Finnish Historical Society.

Pattanayak, D. P. 1991. "Literacy: An Instrument of Oppression." In *Literacy and Orality*, edited by David R. Olson and Nancy Torrance, 105–108. Cambridge: Cambridge University Press.

Pattison, Robert. 1982. *On Literacy: The Politics of the Word from Homer to the Age of Rock*. Oxford: Oxford University Press.

Prescott, William H. 1900. *History of the Conquest of Peru*. Philadelphia: J. B. Lippincott.

Rowe, John H. 1979. "An Account of the Shrines of Ancient Cuzco." *Nawpa Pacha* 17: 1–80.

Sampson, Geoffrey. 1985. *Writing Systems: A Linguistic Approach*. Stanford: Stanford University Press.

Scribner, Sylvia, and Michael Cole. 1981. *The Psychology of Literacy*. Cambridge: Harvard University Press.

Segert, Stanislaw. 1983. "Decipherment of Forgotten Writing Systems: Two Different Approaches." In *Writing in Focus*, edited by Florian Coulmas and Konrad Ehlich, 131–156. Berlin: Mouton Publishers.

Sirat, Colette. 1994. "Handwriting and the Writing Hand." In *Writing Systems and Cognition*, edited by W. C. Watt, 375–460. Dordrecht: Kluwer Academic Publishers.

Street, Brian V. 1988. "Literacy Practices and Literacy Myths." In *The Written Word: Studies in Literate Thought and Action*, edited by Roger Saljo, 59–72. Berlin: Springer-Verlag.

Vansina, Jan. 1965. *Oral Tradition: A Study of Historical Methodology*. Chicago: Aldine.

Watt, W. C. 1994. "The Scribal Text." In *Writing Systems and Cognition*, edited by W. C. Watt, 337–345. Dordrecht: Kluwer Academic Publishers.

Zuidema, R. Tom. 1964. *The Ceque System of Cuzco: The Social Organization of the Capital of the Inca*. Leiden: E. J. Brill.

———. 1977. "The Inca Calendar." In *Native American Astronomy*, edited by Anthony A. Aveni, 219–259. Austin: University of Texas Press.

———. 1989. "A Quipu Calendar from Inca Peru with a Comparison to the Ceque Calendar from Cuzco." In *World Astronomy*, edited by Anthony A. Aveni, 341–351. Cambridge: Cambridge University Press.

PART THREE

INTERPRETING CHRONICLERS' ACCOUNTS OF KHIPU

String Registries

SIX   *Native Accounting and Memory*
According to the Colonial Sources

Carlos Sempat Assadourian

The present chapter,[1] based on the Spanish chronicles and other colonial documents, represents an introduction to the types of accounting registers devised by Andean societies, as well as to the new uses to which they were put at the time of the European conquest of the New World. The analysis is very straightforward in the case of the khipu used for accounting purposes, but it is more complex and daring in relation to those khipu that served to register historical and literary narratives.

It is both important and feasible to investigate more thoroughly the disappearance of the memory khipu following the European invasion (as well as the disappearance of that part of what was remembered that was inculcated by means of the songs). Within this secular process there appears the question of the Jesuits, who were particularly concerned with khipu. In addition to looking for new discoveries in the archives, we can accomplish a series of reevaluations in relation to certain published sources, which all, I think, come from the same origin: the research of Blas Valera. An analysis of the works of the anonymous Jesuit (almost certainly Blas Valera), Garcilaso de la Vega, Juan Anello Oliva, and Fernando de Montesinos will give us valuable knowledge about the continuity, or reconstruction, of Andean memory through its ancient recording techniques. This approach will also permit us to compare and contrast this form of record keeping with the strictly oral memory incorporated in judicial investigations and judgments and with the colonial memory represented by Guaman Poma, both for its conceptual nature as well as for its significance with respect to alphabetic writing, whether in Spanish or in Quechua.

Published in Amberes in 1555, the book written by the accountant Agustín de Zárate informed Europe of the accounting instrument employed by the Indian nations ruled by the Inka:[2]

> One must presuppose the difficulty that exists in the investigation because the natives don't use any kind of letters or writing, nor do they even use pictures such as those that serve as books in New Spain; they only use memory which they pass on from one to another. And important matters are preserved with the help of some cotton strings that the Indians call *quipos*, denoting the numbers by differently tied knots, going up along the space of the string from the units to the tens and higher, and using strings of different colors according to what they want to show. And in each province there are people that are in charge of remembering by these strings general things, whom they call *Quipucamayos*. And so there can be found public houses full of these strings, which are easily interpreted by the person in charge of them, even though they are many ages older than he is.[3]

Zárate was mistaken in restricting the material from which the khipu were fashioned to cotton, perhaps because his direct observations were limited to the coast, where this material was commonly used; he was also ambiguous in reference to the preservation of the past by means of oral memory. As his descriptions are limited to only one type of khipu, the rest of the details in his account are correct: the khipu was a registry of accounts made of string with meaning partially signaled by color; it was an object in which numbers were represented by means of distinctive types of knots and the knots of higher value were placed toward the top; and it was an object whose control and storage were the responsibility of a specialized administrative bureaucracy.

In that early colonial decade of the 1550s, an early death kept Cieza de León from publishing the second part of his *Crónica del Perú*, which included his notes on khipu.[4] Cieza distinguished between the way the historical memory of the government of each Inka was maintained in its oral reproduction and the support for that memory derived from accounting techniques: "and the expenditures and contributions of the provinces were recorded in the khipu, in order that they should know what they gave and contributed when the ruler was dead and his successor reigned."[5] Cieza emphasized in particular the use of khipu to keep track of tribute accounts and population censuses, and the ways in which both related to centralized government. Concerning tribute, in addition to the indication that in each valley the "bookkeepers . . .

as many as there were lords in each . . . balanced their accounts every four months,"[6] Cieza remembered how in Jauja the lord (*curaca*) of Lurinhuanca gave him, from a khipu, an account of all the contributions made to the Spaniards since 1533.[7] This reference received singular and resounding confirmation when Waldemar Espinoza Soriano published a document in 1560–1561 in which the *curacas* of the Guancas detailed for a scribe the quantitative entries tied in their khipu of everything given to the Spanish (in addition to what was looted) from 1533 until 1554.[8]

With respect to population censuses, Cieza noted that the ethnic groups, each through their own group of khipukamayuq, counted all of the births and deaths that occurred during the year, and that upon completing this count, the information was taken to Cusco. But, by adding at once that in this way both the Inka and the ethnic lords knew how many men could go to war, how many Indians were poor, or how many women were widows, Cieza seems to insinuate that these khipu constituted not only a registry of vital statistics but also an annual census of the population—or at least segments of it— according to their life cycles.[9] Like Zárate, Cieza also alluded to the Mexican hieroglyphs, but he added a comparative value judgment of the *accounting* skills of the two forms of recording: the khipu "surpasses in cleverness the *carastes* [hieroglyphs] that the Mexicans used for their accounting and their contracts."[10]

In 1590, *Historia natural y moral de las Indias*, by Father José de Acosta, was published in Seville, and in 1609, the *Comentarios reales de los Incas*, by the Cusco-born mestizo Garcilaso de la Vega, was published in Lisbon. The wide diffusion of these great works gave Europe a balanced view of the empire of Tawantinsuyu. Both works considered the khipu among the achievements of Andean society, and the account by Garcilaso was recognized as the "classic" version. Son of an *encomendero*, Garcilaso learned during his youth to read the tributary khipu to the point of understanding them "as well as the Indians did."[11] And in his book, he raised a question—which is still unresolved— about the capacity of the khipu as historical "writing."

> In short, they may be said to have recorded on those knots every-
> thing that could be counted, even mentioning battles and fights, all
> the embassies that had come to visit the Inca, and all the speeches and
> arguments the king had uttered. But the purpose of the embassies or
> the contents of the speeches, or any other narrative matter, could not
> be recorded on the knots, consisting as it did of continuous spoken
> or written prose, which cannot be expressed by means of knots, since

these can give only numbers and not words. To compensate this lack they used *signs* that indicated historical events or deeds, or the existence of any embassy, argument, or discussion held in time of peace or war. Such speeches were preserved by the *quipucamayus* in memory in a summarized form of a few words; they were committed to memory and taught by tradition to their successors and descendants from father to *son*.

(GARCILASO DE LA VEGA 1966: 331–332; EMPHASES ADDED)[12]

Based on these and other chronicles and additional documents, the current interpretation distinguishes two kinds of khipu for Tawantinsuyu, or the Inka Empire:[13]

1. *Accounting Khipu.* On this type of khipu, knots on pendant strings register only numbers. Nonetheless, these khipu are endowed with "signs," which appear in the form of subsidiary strings attached to either the primary cord or the pendant strings, that modify circumstances linked to the items and numbers registered. These signs would, for example, have permitted the Guancas to transcribe what was given at different times to the Spanish, and what was looted by them from 1533 to 1554. The complexity of these khipu—the number of strings, the value of the numbers, the combination of multiple khipu—is determined by their respective "statistical collections." One can imagine a series of mega-khipu in the central accounting office in Cusco entrusted to lineages of *apu* (lords of the four quarters) officials specializing in this most important function.

Among the subject nations, as is demonstrated by the exceptional *visita* to Huánuco made in 1562 by Iñigo Ortiz de Zúñiga, all of the towns, whatever their size, had their khipukamayuq for the recording of demographic and tributary entries. All of these multiple sources of information were regularly passed on to central khipu.[14] According to the statistical collections, there were khipukamayuq *curacas*, or chiefs,[15] and lesser chiefs and other levels of authority down to those of the "common Indians." To this model of the administrative apparatus, in which the accounting khipu were used to fulfill accounting functions from Cusco down to the smallest groups in a lordship, we may integrate Guaman Poma's data concerning the female khipukamayuq in the *aqlla wasi*, the house of the chosen virgins (*aqllakuna*);[16] the khipukamayuq from the second and fourth age grades—that is, old people who could not contribute to the labor draft and the sick and the crippled[17]—and the accountants of the herds.

2. *Historical, Memory, or Rhetorical Khipu.* These khipu also had "signs" in

the strings, but beyond that, the European sources emphasized the "technical memory" of the select team trained to reproduce their "reading." A large
part of the Spanish knowledge about Tawantinsuyu—pertaining to the royal
ayllu and the succession of the Inka; the duration of the conquests; the institutions of each reign, the gods, rites, and ceremonies; and the calendar—
was learned from these khipu and their khipukamayuq.[18] Garcilaso certifies
for us the existence of other similar large "archives," to which the Spanish
paid little attention, when he comments that each province (kingdom) "has
its accounts and knots with their histories and annals and their traditions, and
for this reason, it is better remembered what happened in their kingdom than
what happened in that of their neighbor."[19]

Given the distinction between the two types of khipu, I believe that Garcilaso only learned to read the accounting type. Completing the information
given by Zárate to the effect that the knots or ciphers were arranged on the
pendant strings in values that increased up to the primary (or "mother") cord,
Garcilaso emphasized that there were nine types of knots ("because the units,
tens, etc., did not go above nine") and, concerning their placement, that "the
knots of each number on each string were aligned with each other, just like
the placements of a good accountant in making a large sum."[20]

For the demographic khipu, Garcilaso's exposition is limited to the annual
census that the ethnic lords presented to the Inka government: an account for
each town, with totals, differentiating between men and women, and signifying by the first string the elders aged sixty or more, followed by the strings
for the other age grades in ten-year grades down to the suckling infants. I
think that, in giving this explanation, Garcilaso retains the image of an annual census of all the population according to their age grades ("streets"),
but that, upon presenting this to a European public, he decided to reflect the
Andean classification by a more comprehensive decimal calendar.[21] In order
to compensate for this fallacy, it was in this part of his account that Garcilaso mentioned another valuable detail concerning the accounting khipu: the
subsidiary threads of the pendant strings.

Some of these strings had finer little threads of the same color attached, serving as offshoots or exceptions from the general rules. For
instance, the finer threads on the string referring to men or women of
a certain age, who were assumed to be married, would mean the number of widows or widowers of that age in a given year. For all their
records were annual, and they never referred to more than a single
year.   (GARCILASO DE LA VEGA 1966: 330)[22]

Garcilaso revealed other very interesting details about the tributary khipu. The pendant strings could be of one color, or of two or three or more, "because the simple and mixed colors had their own meanings"; but he only gave a few examples of those meanings: yellow = gold, white = silver, red = warriors. In any case, he clarified something else by revealing "that the things without colors were placed according to their order, starting with that of the highest quality, and proceeding to the items of least value, each thing according to its type." Here, he appealed to the example of Spanish agriculture in order to provide a way of understanding this ordering by value: the first pendant string would represent wheat, and after that, consecutively, cereals and legumes, which followed after wheat in prestige; then, barley, chick peas, peas, millet, etc.[23]

Commenting on the Andean knowledge of geometry, Garcilaso noted that they did not have "any other type of account other than the strings and little stones."[24] And, in relation to the tributary accounts, he stated that they "added, subtracted and multiplied by means of those knots, and in order to know what belonged to each village, they made piles with maize kernels and pebbles."[25] He does not enter into the details of Andean arithmetic calculations ("so as I fear not being understood, I will not say what I have learned about those details"), but as no other source has covered this omission, it has gravely limited our understanding of this important topic. I do not know, for example, if, in his eagerness to investigate Andean matters, Polo de Ondegardo also worried about the form of Andean calculation; although he does allude to this complex of "corn and pebbles" for the manipulation of entries in the khipu, he only writes that this procedure was used to divide the tribute owed to the Inka between the ayllu and the towns of each province.[26]

Hence, the details provided by Guaman Poma and Father Acosta are particularly important. One of Guaman Poma's famous drawings represents the principal accountant of Tawantinsuyu: the figure holds in his hands a large khipu, but the intriguing detail that catches our attention is the panel in a corner of the picture that is composed of four columns, each with five subdivisions, making a total of twenty squares; from left to right, in the first column there are five grains in each of the five squares, then three, two, and one grain in the second, third, and fourth columns, respectively.[27] In the text that accompanies the drawing, Guaman Poma alludes to the panel, using the expression "table of accounting," and he restricts the use of the accounting table—with its conventional structure of four successive columns with twenty squares in total—to the high officials who were responsible for the centralized accounting in the Inka state.[28] Apart from this formal apparatus, the data indicate that this table drawn by Guaman Poma, instead of being an object constructed *ex profeso*, was actually traced on the ground; perhaps such calculating devices with numbers of columns and squares, in accordance with the complexity that was needed, could be made freely at any moment.

It is certain that the calculator drawn by Guaman Poma would provide for the rapid manipulation of the calculating grains[29] observed by Father Acosta, who explained that in order to calculate how much contribution was owed by each village, "taking some from over there and adding so much from here, with hundreds of other movements, these Indians would take their grains and would place one here, three over there, eight I don't know where, and indeed, they arrived at their result with great precision, and without a single error."[30] In conclusion, the calculating device drawn by Guaman Poma and the manipulation of the grains described by Acosta lead one to suppose that the Andeans had some sort of "instrumental algebra,"[31] although it is perhaps worth waiting for additional discoveries from the archives that might shed light on this topic.

The European sources relating to the memory khipu and their khipu-kamayuq appear to have already been sufficiently examined, and the results are clearly less than satisfactory. I will reiterate this information, because it contains various clues that serve to focus better the knowledge transmitted through these sources and the problems still to be resolved.

The early chronicle attributed to Miguel de Estete estimated a mere ninety years for the duration of Inka dominion, indicating—perhaps on the basis of this calculation—that in the absence of imperial written records, the Inka recall things past "by means of certain memory strings and knots, although the principal method of remembering is through the songs they have, like we have here [in Spain] concerning ancient events and battles, and if we lacked writing, we would know by those songs the deeds performed by our ancestors."[32] Estete at least recognized the existence of the memory khipu, perceiving them as independent sources of information, although he thought the songs more outstanding. On the other hand, someone as close to Andean realities as Betanzos, for whom the accounting khipu were prominent features, seems to concentrate Inka historical memory in the songs (without the support of the khipu).[33] We should consider, however, that on one occasion, in mentioning the statutes dictated by Inka Yupanqui, Betanzos referred to the recording of these laws onto a mnemonic device that he described as "some long strings of calculation"—in other words, a group of threads or strings on which each of the notational units (pebbles or grains?) represented one of the laws that was "understood" (and retained together), "as if said in words."[34]

The investigations made by Cieza and Polo de Ondegardo in the 1550s allow us to raise many questions. In addition to the example of the accounting khipu of the Guancas, Cieza obtained information in Cusco about imperial accounting and about another group of "grand" khipukamayuq, "more rhetorical and wordy," who were charged with composing and registering in their khipu the *official version* of the deeds of each Inka. Estete was mistaken when he separated the historical songs from the khipu, and it is Cieza who restores this relationship. These more rhetorical khipukamayuq composed the official history in the form of romances, songs, or carols, "and they took great care in teaching them to their children and to the wisest and most knowledgeable men they could find in the provinces, and thus, from the mouths of some, others learned . . ."[35]

In Cusco, too, in 1559, Polo de Ondegardo made direct inquiries of some old Inka khipukamayuq "concerning both religion and government." He commented later that he "would not have believed it, had he not seen it, that by means of strings and knots one could configure laws and statutes as much for one as for the other [i.e., religion and government]," in addition to the succession and life span of each Inka, along with the dispositions promulgated in their respective reigns, as well as the rules of marriage.[36] But Polo was imprecise when he failed to mention khipu in connection with the lunar calendar, saying only that "there were people who kept this count, and what the Indians had to do in each lunar month of the year, and that they had names for the months, and that by them they regulated the sacrifices and festivals."[37] His omission is disclosed by one of the seven drawings in which Guaman Poma included khipu: that of "the astrologer-poet who knows the cycle of the sun and the moon and of eclipses and of stars and comets, of time, of the week and the month and the year and of the four winds of the world used for planting crops since ancient times."[38]

On the other hand, according to Father Cobo, Polo's investigations in Cusco among the old Inka khipukamayuq were "made on the basis of the registers of the khipu and the *paintings* that still stand."[39] The phrase "still stand" is suggestive of the paintings in the Temple of the Sun, on the hill of Puquín,[40] but Polo only mentions to us his access to another singular painting, "the chart of the *huacas* of Cuzco," which "they painted in each village, no matter how small, in the same way to show the *ceques* and *huacas* and the fixed shrines . . ."[41] Polo did not connect the chart of the *ceques* and shrines to khipu, but this has been done by John Rowe, who in 1946 had already noted that the system of *ceques* and *huacas* "is admirably adapted for recording by means of the khipus,"[42] and by R. T. Zuidema, whose analysis of the combination of astronomical dates and of rites and myths seeks to establish the relation between the *ceque* system and the calendar through a study that includes the exposition of a khipu calendar.[43]

Regarding the question of the relation between khipu and painting, no more can be said than is summarized in Father Acosta's testimony, which stated that until the arrival of the Spanish conquistadores, the Peruvian Indians compensated for the lack of writing "partially with paintings like those in Mexico, although those from Peru were very crude and rough, and more importantly, with khipus."[44] Since they were of secondary importance, then, the Europeans gave less attention to the paintings than to khipu. These few data suggest that the combination of paintings and memory revealed myths, histories, and statutes, which were also represented in the combination of khipu and memory, and that these narratives could be reproduced from the khipu to the paintings, or the reverse.[45] This dualistic transformation—in which, though the meanings were the same, the symbols represented in the paintings must have been different from the "signs" used in the khipu—perhaps would have been of some significance in understanding the form of the entries in the historical or rhetorical khipu, but the poor quality of our information makes it impossible to develop this analysis any further.

Blas Valera's investigations and writings, which we know only partly through Garcilaso de la Vega's *Comentarios reales de los Incas*, the Anonymous Jesuit's "Relación de las costumbres antiguas de los naturales del Pirú,"[46] and the work of Anello Oliva (as well as that of Montesinos?), together cover some fifty years (ca. 1570–1580 to 1620–1630), suggesting the existence among the Jesuits of a group devoted to investigating Andean antiquity among the rhetorical or historical khipukamayuq who survived in certain areas of the former Inka Empire. The known writings from this presumed Jesuit "school" of rhetorical khipu scholars amplify the diversity of the khipu registers, since, in addition to confirming the uses already established in previous sources— such as for calendrics ["those who compute the year, who go to the heights to observe the shadows of the sun and the stars," as the Anonymous Jesuit says], myths and rituals, historical annals, and religious and governmental statutes—they add other levels of khipu-related practice, such as "laws concerning the family, government, pastureland, woodlands, fishing, hunting, mining; laws regarding the postal (messenger) service, ambassadors, communities, warehouses, health and medicine; laws regarding the militia and warfare; the governing of the Republic, magistrates and the mode of hearing judicial cases."[47] On the other hand, there is a notable entry reputedly in khipu form of a complex process of intellectual reasoning in the form of a "long argument that Amaro Toco, an *amauta* [priest], developed in Cuzco, in the time of the Incas, in which he proves that no man born of man and woman can be a god, because, if one man could be this [i.e., a god], then so could all other men, and thus, there would arise a confusion of gods . . ."[48] It is impressive as well that Blas Valera collected from a khipukamayuq ("from some old annals that were in threads of diverse colors") the famous lines of the *ñusta* poem,[49] even though Cristóbal de Molina had earlier collected various "prayers" or "songs" from among the old Indian khipukamayuq or, in any case, from those faithful to the practice of khipu.[50]

We have yet to evaluate the information concerning the "signs" that were used in this type of khipu. Until the decade of the 1590s, the known sources only specified as mnemotechnic "rules" the different *colors* of the pendant strings and the knots, without being precise about whether or not these were the same as for the accounting khipu, or if they were of a different type, or even a possible combination of the two. It is Father Acosta, then, who first gives us a clear illustration of the mnemotechnic system. He says that, in the pendant strings of these khipu, there were

> so many knots, little knots and attached threads, some red, some green, others blue, others white, indeed so many differences, that just as we arrange twenty-four letters in different ways in order to obtain a virtual infinity of *words*, so they with their knots and colors derived innumerable *significations of things*.[51]

To this reference, Garcilaso added the "things" meant by the colors yellow, white, and red, and in accordance with Acosta and all the other earlier sources, he reiterated the relation between the signs—made up of colors and knots— and the things referred to—augmented by the memory work of the khipuka- mayuq. Thus, as we have already pointed out, the signs denoted "the notable historical deeds" of an Inka, or "the coming of an ambassador" in peace or in war; but as for the latter's conversations and reasonings, "since they con- sisted of spoken sentences," which could not be referred to by the signs, the khipukamayuq "memorized them in short words and entrusted them to their memory, and by tradition they taught them to their successors" (Garcilaso 1966: 331–332). On the other hand, Garcilaso sketched out, as an example, a khipu that registered a report to the Inka of the penalties to be applied by the lower judges. The manner of sending these decisions was by knots tied into cords of different colors, which they understood as a code, because the knots of such and such colors indicated which crimes had been punished. And certain small threads of different colors, which were attached to thicker strings, said what penalty had been given and the law that had been used (Garcilaso 1966: 98).[52]

But it is the Augustinian Antonio de la Calancha, around 1630, who claimed to offer the most detailed illustration of the system of recording information. Equipped with some knowledge of the system ("I have worked somewhat to understand this style of khipus"), Calancha composed for his demonstration the following historical example: "Suppose that before Manco Capac, who was the first Inka king, there were no kings in this land, nor headmen, nor religious cults or adoration. And in the fourth year of his reign, he [Manco Capac] conquered ten provinces, and he won some with the death of his enemies, and in the same war, three thousand of his own troops died. And in this campaign, he won one thousand pounds of gold and thirty thousand of silver, and in giving thanks for the victory, he held a festival for the Sun" (Calancha 1974: 206).

According to Calancha, the Inka's khipukamayuq-secretary would tie onto a black string (which signified time) many "straw-colored" threads and little knots without different colors, and in the middle of the string there was a large knot crossed by a very fine thread of crimson color, which signified the Inka, as no vassal was allowed to use this color, crimson always signifying the person of the Inka king.

Once the crimson thread was tied onto the string, the khipukamayuq would make four small knots, which would signify that the event occurred in the fourth year of his reign; and to say that he conquered ten provinces, another grayish-brown string with ten little knots would be attached to this knot, and in each one there was tied a green string, for the thousands of Indians, with their ages, that died from the opposing side. And, in order to denote the provinces they came from, they would add cords (strings made from twisted fibers) of different colors by which was signified this or that province, because each province had a different mixture of colors. Then, they would add another red string with as many knots as the number of the king's soldiers that died in the war.

Each village that was the head of a province was numbered in order of conquest; the first that they defeated had one large knot; the second, two; and so on for the rest. But Cusco, head of the empire, had three or four knots, one above the other; and adding the color green to the side of those that were conquered meant that the Inka had defeated them.

In order to indicate that he had taken as booty one thousand pounds of gold and thirty thousand pounds of silver, the khipukamayuq would put on the substring signifying the enemy (respectively) a yellow string with one thousand knots and on a white string he would tie thirty thousand knots (see below). In order to say that he made a festival to the Sun, he would add a plied string made of white, blue, and yellow threads, which served to say, "the god that lives in the blue sky and created gold and silver, for him they made the first festival," and he would make a knot in the string; and if it was the third or the fourth festival of the year, he would put three or four knots.

Now, those who saw this cord, on the bottom half of which were the strings of so many colors, knots, and little knots and on the upper half of which were only "straw-colored" strings and thousands of knots devoid of color, would say: "the people that existed before Mancocapac did not have a king because there is no crimson string, nor did they have a chief nor a head that ruled them because there is no purple string; they had no 'order' because there is no grayish-brown string, nor provinces because there are no different-colored, twisted strings, nor did they have wars for the lack of a red string, nor did they receive gold nor silver because of the lack of yellow and white strings, nor do they have cults, rites, nor sacrifices because there are no threads plied of blue, yellow and white threads; these were barbarians who lived before they had kings. . . . So by means of the absences they could tell what did not exist, and by means of the khipus [they could tell] what had happened" (Calancha 1974: 206–208).[53]

In developing this example, Calancha omits the memory work of the khipukamayuq; however, in a previous paragraph, he does recognize the existence and character of such a function.[54] Calancha's illustration seems to be an indisputable contribution to the problem of color symbolism. To the three color correspondences annotated by Garcilaso (i.e., yellow = gold, white = silver, red = warriors), Calancha added the following: black = time, crimson = Inka, purple = chiefs and *curacas*, and a three-plied fiber of a mixture of the colors yellow, blue, and white symbolized gods (only the Sun?); other plied color mixes referred to the provinces, and the grayish-brown strings indicated the presence of "order," leaving us in doubt as to the exact meaning of the color green (Did it refer to the "dead enemies" or to Cusco, in code?).

The structure of the historical khipu formulated by Calancha is disconcerting. The data from historical sources, in addition to the collections of khipu that still exist—although almost all of them are of the accounting variety—leave the impression that there is one primary cord with a variable number (as many as hundreds) of pendant strings, but here Calancha appears to register a relatively complex historical account on only one string ("cord"), to be read *vertically*. However, we could also suppose that there was a primary cord that in itself had significance (e.g., black cord), with various colored/signifying strings or subsidiaries in which they "wove" signs along with many "straw-colored" strings. In addition, Calancha's example about the knots and the little knots that were placed on the branches (*ramales*) that come off the "cord," and the subsidiary threads coming off these branches, presents a problem of interpretation. In fact, he cites with approval Garcilaso's long commentary about the khipu, including the initial paragraph in which Garcilaso notes that "khipu means 'to knot' and 'knot.' And it also means 'accounts,' for the knots could enumerate virtually anything." Calancha modifies this comment in this way: "khipu means to knot and knot (which serves among these Indians as the word both for a verb and a noun), they were strings made of varying colors of wool . . ."[55] At the very least, the literal manner in which Calancha places on the "cord" or on the branches ten, one thousand, or thirty thousand knots (whether they be knots or little threads) as the way of signing numeric codes[56] seems inappropriate, and, unfortunately, it was an even more inappropriate and poorly developed example he used to the effect that the khipukamayuq, "by means of the absences [i.e., many knots *without* colors] . . . learned what did not exist . . ." This further confuses both the indications regarding the plied cords "of different colors, which mean this or that (conquered) province, because each one had different [color] mixtures," and the point that "each head village of a province had its own code, the first that was conquered had one big knot, the second, two, and so on." Nonetheless, Calancha's text constitutes the most concrete reference we know of to date about this type of khipu.

Finally, I will pose some more theoretical questions. Regarding contemporary discussion about whether the Chinese or the Peruvian or the Mexican Indians had or had not achieved writing, Father Acosta explained his own conception that letters are used in order "to refer and to signify words directly," that is, the sounds; hence, logically, he emphasized their difference from figures or "signs that are not ordered to signify words, but things" (e.g., paintings) and from "other signs which are not similar to the thing, but instead only serve for memory, because he who invented them did not order them to mean words, but only to mean that thing."[57] In this last case, the signs, called by Acosta "codes or reminders [cues]," would be composed in the khipu by the colors of the strings, the knots, the little knots, and the little threads.

In specifying alphabetic-phonetic sounds, Father Acosta is defining writing as a system where *all* the words are represented and integrated in a complete manner. In accordance with this strict definition, the signs of the rhetorical or memory khipu are *not* a form of "writing."

But neither are these khipu simple *aide-mémoire* with any kind of semiotic mark. The analogy that Father Acosta refers to is that, just as we use twenty-six letters to represent an infinite number of words, so too the khipukamayuq use knots and colors to bring out innumerable meanings of things. This suggests a code of abstract signs (as Acosta says, of signs without "similarity to the thing" they denote) whose system and capacity would be barely suggested by the illustrations sketched out by Garcilaso and Calancha. And, as I understand his meaning, Father Acosta says that the knots and the colors do not mean words but things; this is due to his conception of writing as indicating alphabetic and phonetic sounds. This conception would correspond to our contemporary view, or it may perhaps lead us to question whether or not these abstract khipu signs represent ideas or words[58] and consequently to extend the view of Acosta regarding signs or symbols from things to signs of things, that is, words.

A visible, coded system of word signs suggests some form of graphics (e.g., logograms, rebus), and this possibility would suggest that, through an established code of relations between colors and shapes of strings, knots, and threads, the khipu were able to represent select words that fixed and governed the entire narrative. In other words, to this code the khipukamayuq would attach the faithful memory of brief phrases dependent upon the words "woven" into the strings of the khipu.

Garcilaso and Calancha appear to confirm this scheme. I have already cited Garcilaso's observations that these khipu "had signs that showed the historical events, the existence of an embassy, reasoning or addresses given in peace or in war. These addresses [i.e., "speaking done in live voice," which Garcilaso pointed out earlier] were memorized by the Indian khipukamayuq in substance, in short, words which they committed to memory, and according to tradition they taught them to their successors . . ." Calancha said the same thing when he indicated that the khipukamayuq lived continually studying the signs or codes and the total narrative, "having to relate the story, the account or the song to the knots, which served as an index and point of departure for local memory."[59]

Now, these two quotes upon which I have founded my speculative scheme also contribute to the conclusion that the presumed Andean "writing," or the "woven signs," in the khipu would consist of a *limited code* of signs/words for logograms, or rebuses. In other words, this limited development makes us appreciate the Andean signary as a code of mnemonic symbols/words, thus construed as a system of memory cues, and the European sources emphasized instead of the artifact the "mnemotechnic" of the khipukamayuq who are in charge of reproducing their "reading."[60] Regrettably, in the face of all of these questions raised by the analysis of the colonial sources, and in the absence of more convincing proof of the presumed "woven" graphic system in the khipu, there persists the opinion of Locke, written in 1923, regarding the archaeological findings: that the many khipu examined by the modern investigators "are of a *numeric nature*. It might be the case, ironically, that none of the specimens of genuine historical khipus, if they existed, have been conserved."[61]

Another problem relates to the lack of written sources. There are abundant data demonstrating that devotion to the permanent study of these khipu was directed at the exact word-for-word repetition of their content, with "universities" where this sacred obligation was learned by instruction. Another consistent series of data establishes that the institutional or religious memory of the khipukamayuq of Cusco was set up for retention, and that this information was transmitted in an exact way to the citizenry through the repetition of "songs" or through ritual language. But, although we know the verses of the *ñusta* poem that Blas Valera got directly from a khipukamayuq—whose nature I have attributed to the orations and songs collected by Cristóbal de Molina and which perhaps had a similar origin to the Quechua orations of Santa Cruz Pachacuti[62]—and we have the songs that Guaman Poma offers in his "first chapter about the festivals,"[63] I am uncertain if these examples constitute a demonstration of sufficient quality[64] to evaluate how adaptable the propositions of Milman Parry might be—particularly those concerning the construction and conservation of *memory* in oral cultures (e.g., the formulaic patterns of thought; the dependence on the selection of words; and the forms of words based on poetic meter)—to the "songs" or compositions of the khipukamayuq in ritual language.

In reviewing the continued use of the historical and accounting khipu after the Spanish Conquest, I would note, with respect to the former, that I limit myself here to the institutional or religious *memory* of Tawantinsuyu, the Inka Empire, which was fixed and retained exactly word for word in the khipu of the khipukamayuq, and that I am not considering the perpetuation of the "songs," that is, that part of this *same memory* inculcated in the populace in ritual language during collective ceremonies.[65]

In this restricted sense, then, there was a first loss that coincided with the European invasion (in the war of succession to the Inka crown, the captains of Atahuallpa "killed all of the *quipucamayos* they could get their hands on and they burnt the *khipus* . . ."),[66] the extent of which it is impossible to evaluate. Then, the new colonial dominion resulted in two contradictory perspectives on and responses to the khipu. On the one hand, it needed to retain the

accounting for a certain period of time in order to colonize the newly sub-
jugated people. Thus, in addition to the individual investigations—of which
Friar Domingo de Santo Tomás's was the earliest and perhaps the most profound—we also have channels of inquiry pursued by the colonial government
itself. Of these, the best known[67] to us are the meeting of khipukamayuq con-
vened by Vaca de Castro in 1542;[68] the meeting ordered by Polo de Ondegardo in Cusco in 1559; and the gatherings in Yucay and Cusco in 1571 and
1572, ordered by Viceroy Toledo in order to legitimize his great oppressive
"retransformation" of Andean space.[69]

However, the colonial order was also obliged to suppress the dangerous
historical-ideological "official records" (i.e., memory khipu).[70] Whether or
not they were formally prohibited, we may deduce the termination of those
"schools" in Cusco and in the other lordships that prepared the reproducers
of this harmful knowledge (perhaps occasioning a clandestine formation?).
No doubt the repression of witches, diviners, dogmatizers, and other Inka
culture bearers affected many of the cueing/memory khipukamayuq. Thus,
in 1561, Polo de Ondegardo alluded to the force of this process of "disappearance" by emphasizing that "if these inquiries [concerning Andean religion,
law codes, and customs] were delayed any further, there would be nothing to
be found out if the elders of advanced age to be found in Cuzco died and if
the registers were lost . . ."[71] Nonetheless, in 1571 and 1572 Viceroy Toledo
could still gather groups of khipukamayuq in Yucay and in Cusco, and in 1583
the Third Council of Lima decreed the following in Chapter 37 of the third
section:

> And since among the Indians, who are ignorant of letters, there were
> instead of books certain signs made of different strings, which they
> called *khipus*, and from these come many testimonies of ancient
> superstitions in which they keep the secrets of their rituals, cere-
> monies and iniquitous laws, let the Bishops completely destroy all
> these pernicious instruments.[72]

We could reconcile these data if we take Polo's information of 1561 in the
sense of a generalized tendency, and the advice of the Third Council of Lima
of 1583 as a call for the extermination of the remaining cueing/memory khipukamayuq. But in this possible "solution," one must consider that around the
time of the Third Council, there existed an important source, the "Relación
de las costumbres antiguas de los naturales del Pirú," written by the Anonymous Jesuit, which indicates the widespread persistence of this class of khipu-

kamayuq, contrary to the notion of their imminent disappearance announced by Polo de Ondegardo. If the author of this *relación* was Father Blas Valera,[73] the investigation into native sources that it discloses was undertaken near the end of the 1570s and into the decade of the 1580s. Without entering into the complex of meanings in this document, I will limit myself to mentioning the list of memory khipu-khipukamayuq incorporated by this great Jesuit investigation: Francisco Yutu, Juan Guallpa and Diego Roca, "ingas" (Inka); Don Sebastián Nina Villca, the lord of Guarochirí; Don Juan Collque, lord of the Quillacas; plus the khipu from Cusco, Sacsahuana, and Pacari Tampu; the khipu from Contisuyo, Collasuyo, Cassamarca, Huamachuco, Chincha, Pachacama, Tarama, and Quito.[74]

This continuation of the cueing/memory khipu, much greater than imagined by Polo de Ondegardo, went on until the first decades of the seventeenth century. Guaman Poma noted the great effort his historical composition signified because it had to be taken from khipu and from accounts in different languages from aged Indians[75]—a believable statement, since it seems possible to detect those parts of the *Nueva corónica y buen gobierno* of Guaman Poma that came from the memory khipukamayuq. Moreover, we have the example—once again provided by a Jesuit!—from the work of Father Anello Oliva, whose chapter dedicated to the origin and history of the Inka comes from, among other sources, the reading of the khipu (*Inka khipu*) of Don Catari, a *curaca* from Cochabamba from a royal lineage of Inka "chronicles."[76] Guaman Poma and Anello Oliva—could they be the last written reports of research using this kind of source? The Huarochirí Manuscript, for instance, which was compiled close to the end of Guaman Poma's time, already proceeds from popular oral memory (which we certainly should imagine was derived in part from the cueing/memory khipu);[77] and in the *relaciones* and treatises of the extirpators of idolatries from the first decades of the seventeenth century, we encounter no allusions to the continuity of these khipukamayuq.[78] But around 1630–1640, two authors as competent as Fathers Calancha and Cobo agreed on the continuity of these memory khipukamayuq. Calancha noted that "until today, the principal Indians use this kind of khipu [but] they are not as skillful as the ancients"; and according to Cobo, if one still investigated among the Indians that "understand them [the khipu], they tell many things from antiquity that are contained in them."[79]

Continuity in the use of *accounting khipu* was perfectly compatible with the new European domination.[80] Their conservation assured (as it did under the Inka) the existence inside a subordinated society of an efficient apparatus of "statistical" control deriving from an ancient social legitimacy, which contributed to the smooth functioning of the colonial administration. We can therefore understand the comment made by Father Cobo in 1650 regarding the factor that motivated a certain discontinuity in the use of the khipu:

> They still use these *khipus* in the *tambos* to take note of what they sell to passengers, in the *mitas*, in the shepherds' keeping of the herds, and in other business, and now that many know how to read and write, they have exchanged the *khipus* for writing, which is, without comparison, a still easier and more exact kind of accounting . . .[81]

A 1725 document about idolatry from the archbishop's archive in Lima is often cited, and it refers to "the Indian who always has his khipu of strings" by which he knew all of the people from his *panaca* (royal ayllu) who owed *mita* (labor service), and the name, circumstances, herds, and wealth of each, "but it is unknown by what method he knows it." But this attention to continuity must be related to the question of discontinuity, for, as Mariano Rivero y Ustáriz noted in the middle of the nineteenth century, "today you can still find in the *punas*" (in other words, in a marginal zone) khipukamayuq who keep account of the flocks of sheep, and in some parishes of Indians, the khipu were attached to a panel with a register of the inhabitants on which were noted "their absences on the days when Christian doctrine is taught."[82]

Also looking for survivals, Max Uhle announced in 1897 the persistence of khipu for recording herds in the puna.[83] The 1907 examination of some of these khipu allows us to compare them with the older khipu as regards the number and form of the knots, although not with respect to the color of the strings, because that depended on the "individual choice" of those who constructed them.[84] Since it is logical that color meanings should be lost,[85] we can agree with Uhle that these modern khipu are "direct descendants, with some slight differences" from the old accounting khipu, if it is specified that the simplest of them, the *khipu llamas*,[86] were equally employed to keep track of the herd.[87]

Finally, I want to comment on the creation of khipu in the context of religious change. The earliest important source known to me is the "instruction and order which the Priests must keep if they occupy themselves with the doctrine and the conversion of the Indians,"[88] in which Friar Diego de Porres—sadly without indicating or commenting in any way on the system of signs used—attempts to transform the *cueing/memory khipu* into an essential resource for the evangelization. This occurs, for example, in the following ways, which concern the khipu of the ethnic lords:

(a) With all of the people of the village gathered in the church plaza, the parish priest should proceed to "read and declare to them what the holy synod demands of them, and give it in the form of a *khipu* to the *cacique* so that they cannot allege the ignorance of those who order them to serve. . . ."

(b) Also, he should leave with each village's *alguaciles* "in writing and in *khipu* the following order, which they must keep and follow. . . ." This deals with a regulation containing thirty-nine rules regarding the new religious "order" that should obtain among the Indians and the vigilance of the said order by the Indian *alguaciles*.

(c) One of the rules—that they had to leave in the church in each village the "accounts and calendar of the whole year, with the festivals that they had to celebrate, all in order, in a *khipu* and a panel which declared all of these things"—implies the creation of a khipu whose complex contents (calendar, saints' days, festivals) incorporates what we know from the chronicles of the khipu of the "astrologers."

Two other rules of Friar Diego de Porres's religious "order" are also very significant because they show the aim of diffusing among all the local Indians a *cueing/memory* type of khipu in order to obtain the fruits of evangelization. The first of these rules, which the parish priest was directed to present to the Indians in a gathering of all the villagers, pertained to

> the four prayers which they are obliged to know and commandments by *khipu*, just as they are recited with their pauses and syllables, and instructing them that no old Indian, nor young one, may go out without this said *khipu*, so that they may know the said commandments by it, and they should always carry it with them wherever they go even if they leave their lands, so that they may have the Christian rule, and may give account of the said prayers whenever they may be asked, as well as what each prayer means.

The second one directed

> that every two weeks the *alguaciles* must test all the Christians [men and women] on the prayers they teach them, whether they know them or whether they have forgotten them, and whether each of them has their *khipu* for this purpose, as has been said, and those who don't know them or don't have their *khipus* should be given three lashes.

Let us further explore what developments are suggested by data recorded later than Friar Diego de Porres's proposals for applying the cueing/memory khipu, particularly in evangelical practice. Father Acosta, in his travels between 1573 and 1580, observed the use by Indians of three different types of register. One was in the "form of paintings and characters" for confessions, "painting each one of the Ten Commandments in a certain way, and then making certain signs as codes, which were the sins they had committed against that Commandment."[89] Another device was a khipu of threads in which an Indian woman "wrote the general confession of her whole life" (Acosta adds: "as I would have written it on paper," in order to emphasize the precision of the register). It is striking that Acosta had observed some different small strings on the pendant cords of the khipu and noted down this answer to his question as to what they were for: "they were certain circumstances necessary for the sin to be confessed entirely."[90] Finally, Acosta says that "besides these string khipus, they have others made of pebbles, with which they promptly learn the words that they want to memorize," which were used to remember prayers and pious stories.[91]

At the beginning of the seventeenth century, the khipu for evangelization also interested Friar Martín de Murúa and Guaman Poma. I will first cite the references from Murúa:

> Going about, a few years ago, the Indians [men and women] had trained confessors, experienced in confessing by these strings and *khipu*, hearing their general confessions based on the Commandments, and then each time they confess, they bring out their *khipu*, and by it they recite their sins, which has certainly been a marvelous medium and most effective in ensuring they make their confessions more complete and convincing (their truth has always been suspect), and with a better memory of their sins and more relief for those giving them the sacrament . . .

And:

> I will only refer, to illustrate the curious nature of some Indians, what I saw in an old Indian *curaca* in a certain parish where I was priest, who had in cords and *khipu* the entire Roman calendar, as well as all the Saints' days and festivals according to their different months, and he told me how he knew them all, and it was because he had asked a priest of my religious order, an inquisitive man, who had been priest here, and to read them out to him and explain them, and as the Father spoke, the Indian put it all down on his *khipu*, and for the holidays that were to be kept he put a different and thicker knot, and it was

amazing how he knew them all by his *khipu*, and knew when the holi-days and the vigils were due.[92]

Let us note, first, that the confessionary khipu was generalized among all the common Indians, perhaps because it was an application of the accounting khipu (for the Ten Commandments we can imagine ten cords, each one of a different color, and with secondary strings in order to remember the par-ticulars). On the other hand, the Roman calendar khipu, with its saints' days and festivals, does not appear to have reached as many Indians as Friar Diego de Porres would have liked; according to Murúa, it is presented as a unique creation arising from the "curious nature" of one old *curaca*.

The adaptation and general use of the accounting khipu for evangelical purposes is also corroborated by Guaman Poma's allusion to the effect that the confessions were weekly, "and that the Indian may make a khipu of his sins," and "they had another one for alms, so that they may be Christians";[93] perhaps we can understand similarly his mention of how "they went to mass by khipu and account."[94]

CONCLUSIONS

The reexamination of the colonial sources undertaken above allows me to propose certain conclusions with regard to the recording units of the his-torical narrative khipu, or what I also referred to as "memory" khipu. These appear to consist of a limited group of abstract signs, represented by an estab-lished code of relationships among colors, shapes, and placements of knots, strings, and subsidiaries denoting "words," which direct and cue the entire narration. To these recording units the khipukamayuq added the faithful memorization of short phrases linked to the "woven words" on the strings. Another equally plausible conclusion suggested by the sources is that in this type of khipu, by permitting only the recording of an inevitably finite mem-ory, the selection of what to remember is determined by a bureaucratic offi-cial and can be overruled, substituted, or modified by his successors, as in the transmission of that institutional memory to the populace in ritual lan-guage—or "songs"—during collective ceremonies.

NOTES

1. This chapter constitutes the first part of an essay entitled "The Creation of the Khipu with the Strings of the Prices," written during the second semester of 1995. The

chapter was translated by Sarah Workman and Gary Urton, with the editorial assistance of Tristan Platt.

2. The first recorded information on the khipu appears in the letter written by Hernando Pizarro to the Audiencia of Santo Domingo in November 1533, in which he mentions the accounting "through knots" by the members of an Indian army, and the deposits and withdrawals from a warehouse for the warriors, accounted for by "some knots in some strings"; Pizarro observed that "when they had to bring us some wood or sheep or corn or corn beer, they untied knots from where they had been and tied them in other places, so that they keep very careful stock of everything" (in Porras Barrenechea 1959: 82–83).

3. Zárate 1995: 28.

4. In the first part, the only one he was able to publish (Seville, 1553), Cieza alludes to these accounts "as a type of knots which they call *khipu*, . . . and certainly, although to us it seems incomprehensible and obscure, it is a fine way of accounting, which I will explain in the second part" (Cieza de León 1967: 238).

5. Cieza de León 1967: 30–38.

6. The context in which these words are inserted suggests the balancing of the accounts by the khipukamayuq, who recorded what entered and left the state's depositories. It corresponds with another statement: Inka Yupanqui ordered that the kingdoms he ruled "should be careful from then on to serve and give tribute to the city of Cuzco with everything they had in their land, and that every four months they should take special care to bring all sorts of food to the city . . ." (Betanzos 1987: 96–97). This is confirmed by another testimony: "as the tribute was in the form of labor, this was measured by the time taken, for example, in carrying out different agricultural tasks, and what was produced during the year was taken to Cuzco on three occasions, of which the most important was the first," in February, which was the Festival of the Rayme (Polo de Ondegardo 1940: 147). Is this an error of transcription? "The first month, January/Capac Raymi (the biggest festival), *camay quilla* (the month of rest)" (Guaman Poma 1980: 210). In his information from 1559 about the Indian ceremonies and rituals, Polo places December as the first month of the Rayme Festival and therefore agrees with Betanzos (1987: 71). A vivid description of the warehouses in Cusco is found in Pizarro 1978: 99–100.

7. Well informed by Cieza, or by Friar Domingo de Santo Tomás, Bartolomé de Las Casas could then eulogize the Andean creation of khipu: "and what we most admire is that they are so skillful and resolute in these accounts, although these may be several years old, so that if you ask them now to account for the payments made when the warriors of King Guainacapa came through (who died more than 35 years ago), they could give you the count with not even a grain of corn missing" (Las Casas 1958: 414).

8. Espinoza Soriano 1972; this Guanca information was the basis of Murra's innovative (1973) analysis of the accounting khipu. It also was used to represent the demographic destruction caused by the Spanish invasion (Assadourian 1994).

9. Cieza 1967: 62–63.

10. Ibid.: 35. Polo de Ondegardo (1940: 128) gave another comparative judgment with respect to the historical registers, commenting that in Peru, "because they lacked writing, as we have, and the paintings that the Indians in Mexico have, through which

they still know their customs and dominions with more certainty than in this kingdom, in which almost everything is in the memory of men, and what they heard from
their fathers and grandfathers . . ." But in the next pages, Polo transmits a rather different image of the Andean registers upon examining the memory-khipu khipukamayuq.
Another shrewd comparative judgment is found in Acosta 1979: 290.

    11. Garcilaso 1991, 1:348.

    12. Garcilaso 1991, 1:346; emphasis added.

    13. In early times, information was gathered that the lordships conquered by Inca
Yupanqui kept on their khipu the accounts of their population production (Betanzos 1987: 56, 96–97). For Calancha "this use of *khipus* was common in the time of
the Incas, it began before anyone can remember in villages, in families and in reduc-
tions" (1974: 208). There has recently been a flowering of studies of pre-Inkan khipu
of "tubes [*canutos*]," of "sheaths [*cartuches*]," or of "wrapped strings"; see Conklin 1990
and Radicati di Primeglio 1990.

    14. Owing to his privileged access to information, Las Casas was able to mention
this point that in each village there was a kind of lieutenant and minor accountant,
"whom they called Llactacamáyoc," who gave their accounts to the principal accountant, "who lived in the principal settlement" and who "placed" those accounts on his
khipu (Las Casas 1967, 2:605).

    15. "These administrators from the provinces were sons of the great lords of these
realms. They were given these jobs so that they could learn a profession, and to keep
accounts, and to command so that, when their fathers died, they could enter office and
would know how to govern the land" (Guaman Poma 1980: 321; emphasis added).

    16. Guaman Poma 1980: 192.

    17. Ibid.: 173, 177.

    18. "Because these, like scribes and like historians, kept the registers, which were
annals on *khipus*, of the events deserving of being remembered, and, as though obliged
by their profession, they were perpetually studying the signs and cyphers that were in
the knots so as to preserve in memory their tradition of famous events, because like
historians, they had to give an account of them when someone asked for it . . . And thus
they gave an account of everything else, memorizing it by tradition, so that each thread
and knot brought to their memory what it contained . . ." (Garcilaso 1991, 1:347).

    19. Ibid., 1:49. Garcilaso adds that, on deciding to write the history of the Inka
while living in Spain, he asked for help from his fellow students of "school and grammar" in Peru (mestizos whose mothers came from noble lineages), who managed to
get their "mother and relatives" to take out "from their archives the accounts they had
of their histories, and send them to him." Perhaps, but it may be that here Garcilaso
has self-attributed and elaborated a reference from Blas Valera about the "archives" of
the lordships. For testimonies before Valera about the research in the "archives" of the
lordships (old Indians, khipukamayuq), see Molina 1989.

    20. Garcilaso 1991, 1:345.

    21. For more about the Inka census, considering Garcilaso and the other sources,
see Rowe 1958.

    22. Garcilaso 1991, 1:344. These subsidiary little threads have been found on al-
most all the khipu still extant (Locke 1978: 711).

    23. Garcilaso 1991, 1:344. His is a generic explanation, in contrast with this one:

"each province, as it had its own native language, also had its own kind of *khipu* and a unique logic in it" (Murúa 1987: 374).

24. Platt (1987: 81, 86–87) has recorded from the Aymara vocabulary of Bertonio the way of accounting, besides the khipu, that was done with black and white pebbles: "counting stone, to count what it owed: *cchaara*. For what has been paid: *hanko* . . . ," which seems to have been limited to exchanges and loans between households.

25. Garcilaso 1991, 1:128. This contradicts the version in Locke (1978), for whom the khipu was only a register of numbers and not a tool for calculation, which was done with the use of pebbles and kernels of corn; see more recently Marcia Ascher and Robert Ascher 1978.

26. Polo de Ondegardo 1940: 148–149, 177; 1571: 151, 154. He adds nothing to the conception already common in Spain in the 1540s: "they count with stones and by means of knots in colored strings, and it is so exact and regulated that we marvel at it" (López de Gomara 1852: 278).

27. Guaman Poma's picture gave rise to Henry Wassen's classic (1940) essay about the Peruvian abacus, which was so decisive for the reinterpretation of Andean arithmetic operations. Wassen's following opinion should be rejected: "It is improbable that the use of such divisions was commonly propagated in ancient Peru."

28. According to the translation from the Quechua made by J. Urioste, the *senior accountant and treasurer* is he who takes count of the people of Tawantinsuyu, he who receives the revenues of the Inka; the *senior accountant* is he who keeps track of the major defaults; and the *junior accountant* is he who keeps track of the minor defaults (Guaman Poma 1980: 332–333).

29. This movement represents the "voices" of the chiefs and the khipukamayuq of the kingdom meeting in order to divide proportionally the tribute among themselves (Polo de Ondegardo 1990: 151).

30. Acosta 1979: 291–292.

31. A summary of all the conjectures concerning the calculating tablets and their interpretation is given in Radicati di Primeglio 1979: 9–46.

32. Similarly, Estete wrote concerning the *chasqui* that they ran from one post to the other where they said the message they had been given, and who it was for, carrying "certain knots to help them remember, with which they understood each other concerning many things, and in this way . . . they spoke their message until it came to the attention of the one to whom they were sent" (Salas, Guerin, and Moure 1987: 311, 314).

33. Betanzos 1987: 86, 182–183.

34. I interpret this from a very confusing explanation; see Betanzos 1987: 119.

35. Cieza de León 1967: 30–31, 34–35.

36. Polo de Ondegardo 1940: 130.

37. Ibid.: 131.

38. Guaman Poma 1980: 829, 830–831. Earlier, Molina (1989: 58) makes the same observation. Points of departure for disentangling the links between the khipu and the combination of cosmology-time-calendar-cycle with agricultural rituals, which Polo de Ondegardo's brief allusion and Guaman Poma's drawing establishes, are in Zuidema 1964, Urton 1981, and these authors' later essays on the above subjects.

39. Cobo 1964: 59.

40. "[T]hey had in a house of the Sun called Poquen Cancha, which is next to Cuzco, the life of each of the Incas and of the lands that he conquered, painted by their figures in panels, and what their origin was, and among these paintings they also had painted the following fable . . . ," which only offers a brief summary of little interest to our topic (Molina 1989: 49–52). For another, later, example of paintings/texts in the Temple of the Sun in which are highlighted the images of the Creator, the Sun, and the Moon, see Pachacuti Yamqui Salcamaygua 1995: 35–41.

41. Polo de Ondegardo 1990: 47.

42. Rowe 1981: 211.

43. See Zuidema 1989.

44. "[T]hey had no type of writing, nor letters, nor characters nor figures or codes, like those from China or Mexico . . . " (Acosta 1979: 290). Almost all of the information that we have about the paintings and the meaning of *quilca* ["writing"] is derived from Friar Domingo de Santo Tomás's vocabulary and is presented in Porras Barrenechea 1986 in his lesson "*Quipu* and *Quilca*." Another proposition concerning *quilca*, with some organizational disorder in the facts, is in Radicati di Primeglio 1984.

45. According to one of Guaman Poma's textual drawings, central to the structure of the Inka government was a special class of distinguished khipukamayuq, from the lineages of great lords; these "honored secretaries, who had *khipus* of dyed colors, were called *quilca camayoc* [in charge of the iconography] or *quilla uata quipoc* [he that keeps account of the months and years]" (Guaman Poma 1980: 330–331).

46. The writing of this text was attributed to Blas Valera by M. González de la Rosa in 1907; that attribution was disputed in 1908 by José de la Riva Aguero and by José Durand in 1961, but it received the influential approval of Porras Barrenechea in 1944 and 1948 (Porras Barrenechea 1986: 462–467, 468–475). An examination of the problem appears in Urbano 1992. Still, even supposing that this "Relación" was written by another member of the Jesuit "school" of khipu, this does not conflict with the possible use of several of Father Valera's manuscripts.

47. Anonymous Jesuit 1992: 105. It seems to me that this paragraph summarizes a manuscript in which Valera points out that these diverse laws "were written and distinctly entrusted to the knots of the threads of diverse colors that they had for their accounts," and that in his conquests, the Inca ordered some lords "to set down in their knots and accounts [information on] pasturelands (*dehesas*), high and low mountains, the cultivable fields, the metal mines, the salt mines . . ." (see Valera's texts in Garcilaso 1991, 1:273–276, 281–282).

48. "And this disputation was pleasing to the Inca, who was still living, and because of it he made a law that no man should adore a mortal being on Earth, neither while living nor when dead . . ." (Anonymous Jesuit 1992: 64). He cites as sources the "*khipus* of Cuzco and of Sacsahuana."

49. Garcilaso 1991, 1:132–133.

50. Molina 1989.

51. Acosta 1979: 291; emphasis added.

52. Garcilaso 1991, 1:100.

53. Calancha 1974: 206–208.

54. "In order to remedy this absence of not having such things, or words for colors, or a code, there were the *amautas*, who were their philosophers or writers, to make up

stories in which they officially referred to the event, history or reasoning; they took them from the memory of the *quipucamayos*, who were like secretaries of those archives," and who were "continually studying the signs, codes and relations, teaching them to those who would succeed them in the office"; each khipukamayuq-secretary "had his specific topical material, having to make a correlation between the story, relation or song to the knots, which served as an index and point for local memory" (Calancha 1974: 204–205).

55. Garcilaso 1991, 1:344, and Calancha 1974: 204.

56. A confusion perhaps correctable by Garcilaso, since this seems to indicate that the codes in these cueing khipu were annotated by employing the system of knots from the accounting khipu ("we say that they wrote everything concerning numbers in the system of knots . . . because the knot means the number, but not the word"); see Garcilaso 1991, 1:346, already cited in this work.

57. Acosta 1979: 284–290. See also note 58 citing the work of the Dominican Gregorio García, published in Valencia in 1607.

58. In light of Acosta's arguments, it is fitting to remember some of the divergences of Gregorio García, one of his contemporaries, who writes that, for the old ones, "it was easier to invent signs that were similar to letters, with which they were able to make syllables, words, and sentences." They were called signs correctly, "because their meaning was hidden in what they manifested, and they didn't teach anything to anyone with what they said, but with what they hid"; or, in other words, to understand them it is not necessary that the figure be "an animal, an instrument, etc., it only matters that everyone agree on its meaning," so, in a way, the signs "including the meaning of words, or sentences, did not mean anything to those who were unaware of the purpose for which they were formed, although it might be supposed of all of the languages and all of the alphabets." Earlier in his work García mentions that these figures or signs were a medium "to fix the voices, . . . because the figure supplements the written voice," and from these they were later able to derive the invention of letters. See García 1981: 223, 201.

59. Calancha 1974: 205.

60. Because of the importance of this proposition, let me reiterate and combine what is certain according to our two sources, Garcilaso and Calancha: (1) the key facts (nouns) are conveyed in the memory khipu through "signs"; (2) the total narration, "because it consists of sentences in live voice," depends on the memory (Garcilaso); and (3) "in order to remedy the lack of such facts, or words, color or codes," khipuka-mayuq construct and memorize the total narration (Calancha).

61. Locke 1978: 731; see also Radicati di Primeglio 1984 and 1990 regarding the "tube" (*canuto*) khipu. Of course, I do not share Locke's doubt regarding the real existence of rhetorical and historical khipu.

62. Concerning these sentences, see the paleographic transcriptions and translations done by Jan Szemiński and César Itier in Itier 1988. I do not include the two poems in Quechua by Friar Martín de Murúa in the group, not because of their late creation—in the decade of the 1570s—but because Murúa adjusted his version to the Hispanic octosyllabic meter; see Beyersdorff 1986 and Itier 1987.

63. Guaman Poma 1980: 288–302.

64. I have still been unable to consult the John H. Rowe article "Once oraciones inca del ritual del *zithuwa*," published in Cusco in 1970.

65. There is information about the trustworthy reproduction of these ritual songs at least through the four first decades of colonial dominion. Of course, I cannot know if during the time of the Inka these hymns and sacred pledges, whose verbal fidelity should be rigorous, exact, were sung outside of the collective ritual meeting, allowing for the possibility, in consequence, that they might have acquired other, nonfaithful forms. On the other hand, although it may be difficult to determine, one should try to see how this sacred Cusco memory was encrusted, corrupted, or modified by the more recent events of European domination.

66. Quipocamayos 1920: 4.

67. It seems to have been forgotten that when Francisco Pizarro entered Cusco, he asked Manco Inca to list for him, "by accounts or by memory, all of the landed societies (*repartimientos*) that there were in the country" (i.e., the lordships [*señoríos*], with their population and "tributary" obligations to the central power); and "Manco Inca had the *llactacamayos* (the heads of the villages) called and also those in Cuzco who were in charge of keeping track of what they were asked for." With this information, Pizarro began to divide the land among his men (Betanzos 1987: 289). One can deduce from this case that the quantitative basis for the division of the country into *encomiendas* by the conquistadores proceeded from the centralized and regional administrative apparatus of the khipukamayuq-accountants.

68. Quipocamayos 1920. On the text of this consultation, see Porras Barrenechea 1986: 747–751, and Duviols 1979.

69. Miguel Cabello Valboa (1951: 240) characterizes these last two assemblies as "a scrutiny and consultations carried out with old Indians knowledgeable in the art and ability of the *quipus*"; see also Sarmiento de Gamboa 1988. Concerning indications about the "political" character of these meetings, see Assadourian 1982.

70. In 1582, three authoritative Andean informants remembered one of the earliest and most significant destructions: "at present, there is no memory of khipus nor of the panels which recorded laws and memories for the Inca, because when the Spanish conquered the city and kingdom they destroyed them. . . ." The mestizo Bartolomé de Porras and two elders of *hurin* and *hanancuzco* declared this before the *corregidor* Córdova Mejía, the interpreter being Felipe Sayre; see Levillier 1925, 9:287.

71. Polo de Ondegardo 1940: 130.

72. Lisi 1990: 191.

73. If Blas Valera *was* the author, it seems to me very important to remember that the Third Council of Lima elected Valera and two monks to prepare the Quechua and Aymara versions of the catechisms for the Indians. This commission would lie behind the harsh criticisms, made in the "Relación de las costumbres antiguas . . . ," of Polo de Ondegardo's knowledge of Andean religion and of his "treatise and research about the errors and the superstitions of the Indians," which was so highly esteemed by the Council that it was included in the *Confesionario para curas de indios con la instrucción contra ritos y exhortaciones . . .* , printed in Lima in 1585. At this conjectural level, we can raise such questions as how themes and facts were selected from Polo's information for the abridged version published by the Council, and why Father Acosta expressly recognized Polo's report while the Jesuit Father Valera categorically rejected it, and so on.

74. Anonymous Jesuit 1992. The Inka histories by Fernando Montesinos raise a crucial problem regarding this and successive investigations. As an expert in mining

technology, or as a historian of Spanish actions, Montesinos is a serious author. From this, we can conclude that he did not "invent" an Inkan history, but rather he exposes it, based on the sources that he believed to be authoritative. And if he consulted the *"amautas,"* or had access to Valera's papers or those of other Jesuits, it seems, then, that at a certain time during the colonial period, the memory khipukamayuq were reformulating "the Inkan historical memory" under the influence of certain values presented by European culture. See Montesinos 1882.

75. Guaman Poma 1980: 5, 9.

76. With respect to Anello Oliva's original remarks on the history of Quito, Porras Barrenechea warned that they "cannot come from the Cochabamban Cacique tradition, but rather from northern sources"; from which one can deduce that "[Anello] Oliva was in Quito for a few years, before arriving in Lima." Francisco Esteve Barba (1968) reiterates the same hypothesis. Instead of supposing direct data collection among khipukamayuq from Quito, it seems to me more probable that Anello Oliva had earlier sources: for example, the Anonymous Jesuit cites "the *khipus* from Quito" three times. The same could be true for parts of the Cusco history by Anello Oliva or for other allusions of his, such as that "there are also traditions among the Indian *Quipucamayo . . ."* (1895).

77. See Urioste 1983: xxiv–xxv; I have already mentioned that sometime during the decade of 1570–1580 the Anonymous Jesuit (almost certainly Blas Valera) in Huarochirí could still ask the lord Sebastián Nina Villca for a direct reading of a *memory khipu* on Andean rituals.

78. In this connection, it is very eloquent that in the Synodal Constitutions of Lima (1614), unlike the Third Council of Lima, the chapter on the extermination of the idolatries eliminated any reference to their possible conservation in khipu-khipukamayuq; see Duviols 1986: 511–514.

79. Calancha 1974: 208; Cobo 1964, 2:143.

80. But the use of the khipu-khipukamayuq of the *huacas* was not, of course. Viceroy Toledo's government is full of information (persecutions) concerning this genre.

81. Cobo 1964, 2:143.

82. Rivero y Ustáriz 1857, 2:84.

83. Uhle 1949.

84. Guimaraes 1978.

85. The herds of the Inka were divided according to their colors, and they were accounted for "according to their knots, because the strings were the same colors as the herd"; Garcilaso 1991, 1:272.

86. Guaman Poma 1980: 841.

87. Besides Uhle, it is also worth noting Rafael Larco Hoyle's insistence on showing the continuity of the khipu and other kinds of Andean accounting; see also Núñez del Prado 1950, Soto Flores 1950–1951, and Carol J. Mackey's current research.

88. My quotes come from AGI Patronato 231, no. 7, r. 8; they have been published in *Revista del Archivo Histórico del Cuzco* 3 (1952).

89. Acosta 1979: 290.

90. Ibid.: 291.

91. Ibid.: 291.

92. Murúa 1987: 375–376.

93. Guaman Poma 1980: 585, 605.
94. Ibid.: 827. I know of no earlier description of this type of khipu. I have already stated that, around the middle of the nineteenth century, M. Rivero could still
note, in some Indian parishes, the "use of these strings [as khipu] attached to a panel"
for controlling the attendance at mass; perhaps this is related to what Rivero observed, and called an alphabetic khipu, found in the church of Mangas, or a panel
containing a community register of the townspeople, on which each one of the 316
names was associated with woolen strings, "each different from the others, in length,
in knotting and in color"; see R. Robles Mendoza's description in Mackey et al. 1990:
198–202.

BIBLIOGRAPHY

Acosta, José de. 1979 [1590]. *Historia natural y moral de las Indias.* Edited by E. O'Gor-
man. Mexico City: Fondo de Cultura Económica.
Anello Oliva, Juan. 1895 [1630]. *Historia del reino y provincias del Perú y varones insignes
en santidad de la Compañía de Jesús.* Edited by J. F. Pazos Varela and L. Varela y
Orbegoso. Lima: N.p.
Anonymous Jesuit. 1992. "Relación de las costumbres antiguas de los naturales del
Pirú." In *Antigüedades del Perú,* edited by H. Urbano and A. Sánchez. Lima: Historia 16.
Ascher, Marcia, and Robert Ascher. 1978. "Números y relaciones de los antiguos quipus
andinos." In Ravines 1978: 733–772.
———. 1981. "El quipu como lenguaje visible." In Lechtman and Soldi 1981: 407–432.
Assadourian, Carlos Sempat. 1982. "Dominio colonial y señores étnicos en el espacio
andino." *Diálogos* (El Colegio de México), no. 108.
———. 1994. "La gran vejación y destrucción de la tierra: Las guerras de sucesión y de
conquista en el derrumbe de la población indígena del Perú." In *Transiciones hacia
el sistema colonial andino.* Lima: Instituto de Estudios Peruanos.
Betanzos, Juan de. 1987 [1551]. *Suma y narración de los Incas.* Edited by M. C. Martín
Rubio. Lima: Ediciones Atlas.
Beyersdorff, Margot. 1986. "Fray Martín de Murúa y el 'Cantar' histórico inka." *Re-
vista Andina* 4, no. 2: 501–521.
Cabello Valboa, Miguel. 1951 [1586]. *Miscelánea antártica: Una historia del Perú antiguo.*
Lima: Instituto de Etnología, Universidad Nacional Mayor de San Marcos.
Calancha, Antonio de la. 1974 [1638]. *Crónica moralizada del orden de San Agustín en
el Peru con sucesos ejemplares en esta monarquía.* Vol. 1. Lima: Universidad Nacional
Mayor de San Marcos.
Cieza de León, Pedro de. 1967 [1553]. *El señorío de los Incas.* Edited by C. Araníbar.
Lima: Instituto de Estudios Peruanos.
———. 1984 [1553]. *Crónica del Perú (Primera parte).* Edited by F. Pease and M. Mati-
corena. Lima: Pontificia Universidad Católica del Perú.
Cobo, Bernabé. 1964 [1653]. *Obras.* 2d ed. Madrid: Biblioteca de Autores Españoles,
vols. 91–92.
Conklin, William J. 1990. "El sistema informativo de los quipus del horizonte medio."
In Mackey et al. 1990: 21–38.

Duviols, Pierre. 1979. "Datation, paternité et ideologie de la 'Declaración de los Qui-pucamayos a Vaca de Castro.'" In *Les Cultures ibériques en devenir: Essais publiés en homenage à la mémoire de Marcel Bataillon (1895–1977)*, 583–591. Paris: La Fonda-tion Singer-Polignac.

———. 1986. *Cultura andina y represión: Procesos y visitas de idolatrías y hechicerías, Caja-tambo, siglo XVII.* Cusco: Centro de Estudios Rurales Andinos "Bartolomé de las Casas."

Espinoza Soriano, Waldemar. 1972. "Los huancas, aliados de la conquista: Tres infor-maciones inéditas sobre la participación indígena en la conquista del Peru." *Anales Científicos de la Universidad del Centro del Perú* 1: 9–407.

Esteve Barba, Francisco. 1968. *Crónicas peruanas de interés indígena.* Madrid: Ediciones Atlas.

García, Gregorio. 1981 [1607]. *Orígen de los indios del nuevo mundo.* Preliminary study by F. Pease. Mexico City: Fondo de Cultura Económica.

Garcilaso de la Vega. 1991 [1609]. *Comentarios reales de los Incas.* Edited by C. Araníbar. Mexico City: Fondo de Cultura Económica.

———. 1966 [1609]. *Royal Commentaries of the Incas.* 2 vols. Translated by H. V. Liver-more. Austin: University of Texas Press.

Guaman Poma de Ayala, Felipe. 1980 [1585–1613]. *El primer nueva corónica y buen go-bierno.* Edited by J. V. Murra, R. Adorno, and J. L. Urioste. Mexico City: Siglo Veintiuno.

Guimaraes, Enrique de. 1978. "Algo sobre el quipu." In Ravines 1978: 773–780.

Itier, César. 1987. "A propósito de los dos poemas en quechua de la crónica de fray Martín de Murúa." *Revista Andina* 5, no. 1.

———. 1988. "Las oraciones en quechua de la *Relación* de Joan de Santa Cruz Pachacuti Yamqui Salcamaygua." *Revista Andina* 6, no. 2: 555–580.

Las Casas, Bartolomé de. 1958. *Opúsculos, cartas y memoriales.* Edited by J. Pérez de Tudela Bueso. Madrid: Biblioteca de Autores Españoles.

———. 1967. *Apologetica historia sumaria.* Edited by E. O'Gorman. Lima: Instituto de Estudios Peruanos.

Lechtman, Heather, and Ana María Soldi, eds. 1981. *Runakunap kawsayninkupaq ruras-qankunaqa: La tecnología en el mundo andino.* Mexico City: Universidad Nacional Autónoma de México.

Levillier, Roberto. 1925. *Gobernantes del Perú: Cartas y papeles. Siglo XVI.* Vol. 9. Ma-drid: Biblioteca del Congreso Argentino.

Lisi, Francesco Leonardo. 1990. *El Tercer Concilio Limense: La aculturación de los indí-genas sudamericanos.* Salamanca, Spain: Universidad de Salamanca.

Locke, L. Leland. 1978 [1923]. "El quipu antiguo o registro peruano de nudos." In Ravines 1978.

López de Gomara, Francisco. 1852. *Hispania Victorix.* Vol. 12. Madrid: Biblioteca de Autores Españoles.

Mackey, Carol, Hugo Pereyra, Carlos Radicati, Humberto Rodríguez, and Oscar Val-verde, eds. 1990. *Quipu y yupana: Colección de escritos.* Lima: Consejo Nacional de Ciencia y Tecnología.

Molina, Cristóbal de. 1989 [1574]. *Relación de las fábulas i ritos de los Ingas. . . .* Edited by H. Urbano. Madrid: Historia 16.

Montesinos, Fernando. 1882. *Memorias antiguas historiales y políticas del Perú.* Edited by M. Jiménez de la Espada. Madrid: N.p.

Murra, John V. 1975. "Las etno-categorías de un *khipu* estatal." In *Formaciones económicas y políticas del mundo andino*, 243–254. Lima: Instituto de Estudios Peruanos.

Murúa, Martín de. 1987 [1590]. *Historia general del Perú.* Edited by M. Ballesteros Gaibrois. Madrid: Historia 16.

Ortiz de Zúñiga, Iñigo. 1967 [1562]. *Visita de la provincia de León de Huánuco en 1562.* Edited by J. V. Murra. Huánuco: Universidad Nacional Hermilio Valdizan.

Pachacuti Yamqui Salcamaygua, Juan de Santa Cruz. 1995 [ca. 1613]. *Relación de antigüedades de este reino del Perú.* Edited by C. Aranibar. Mexico City: Fondo de Cultura Económica.

Pizarro, Pedro. 1978 [1613]. *Relación del descubrimiento y conquista de los reinos del Perú.* Edited by G. Lohmann Villena and P. Duviols. Lima: Pontificia Universidad Católica del Perú.

Platt, Tristan. 1987. "Entre *ch'axwa* y *muxsa:* Para una historia del pensamiento político aymara." In *Tres reflexiones sobre el pensamiento andino*, edited by T. Bouysse-Casagne, O. Harris, T. Platt, and V. Cereceda, 61–132. La Paz: HISBOL.

Polo de Ondegardo, Juan. 1940 [1561]. "Informe . . . al licenciado Briviesca de Muñatones." *Revista Histórica* 12: 125–196.

———. 1990 [1571]. "Relación de los fundamentos acerca del notable daño que resulta de no guardar a los indios sus fueros." In *Polo de Ondegardo: El mundo de los Incas*, edited by L. González and A. Alonso. Madrid: Historia 16.

Porras Barrenechea, Raúl. 1954. *Fuentes históricas peruanas.* Lima: J. Mejía Baca and P. L. Villanueva.

———. 1959. *Cartas del Perú (1524–1543).* Lima: La Sociedad de Bibliófilos Peruanos.

———. 1986. *Los cronistas del Perú (1528–1650).* Biblioteca Clásicos del Perú, no. 2. Lima: Banco de Crédito del Perú.

Quipocamayos. 1920 [1542/1608]. *Declaración de los quipocamayos a Vaca de Castro, discurso sobre la descendencia y gobierno de los Incas.* Lima: Colección de Libros y Documentos Referentes a la Historia del Perú. Second Series, Vol. 3.

Radicati di Primeglio, Carlos. 1979. *El sistema contable de los Incas: Yupana y quipu.* Lima: Librería Studium.

———. 1984. "El secreto de la quilca." *Revista de Indias* 173.

———. 1990. "El cromatismo en los quipus: Significado del quipu de canutos." In Mackey et al. 1990: 39–52.

Ravines, Rogger, ed. 1978. *Tecnología andina.* Lima: Instituto de Estudios Peruanos.

Rivero y Ustariz, Mariano Eduardo de. 1857. "Quipus." In *Colección de memorias científicas, agrícolas e industriales*, vol. 2. Brussels: N.p.

Robles Mendoza, Román. 1990. "El kipu alfabético de Mangas." In Mackey et al. 1990: 195–202.

Rowe, John H. 1958. "The Age-grades of the Inca Census." In *Miscellanea Paul Rivet, octogenario dicata.* International Congress of Americanists. Serie Antropológica 5. Mexico City: Universidad Nacional Autónoma de México.

———. 1981. "Una relación de los adoratorios del antiguo Cuzco." *Histórica* 5, no. 2.

Salas, A. M., M. A. Guerin, and J. L. Moure. 1987. *Crónicas iniciales de la conquista del Perú.* Buenos Aires: Plus Ultra.

Sarmiento de Gamboa, Pedro. 1988 [1572]. *Historia de los Incas.* Madrid: Biblioteca de Viajeros Hispánicos.

Uhle, Max. 1949 [1897]. "Un kipu moderno procedente de Cutusuma, Bolivia." *Revista del Museo Nacional* 9.

Urbano, Henrique. 1992. "Introducción a la Relación de las costumbres antiguas de los naturales del Pirú." *Antigüedades del Perú.* Madrid: Historia 16.

Urioste, George L. 1983. *Hijos de Pariya Qaqa: La tradición oral de Waru Chiri.* Syracuse, N.Y.: Foreign and Comparative Studies Program, Syracuse University.

Urton, Gary. 1981. "La orientación en la astronomía quechua e inca." In Lechtman and Soldi: 475–490.

Wassen, Henry. 1940. "El antiguo ábaco peruano según el manuscrito de Guaman Poma." *Etnologisca Studies,* no. 11.

Zárate, Agustín de. 1995 [1555]. *Historia del descubrimiento y conquista del Perú.* Edited by F. Pease and T. Hampe Martínez. Lima: Pontificia Universidad Católica del Peru.

Zuidema, R. Tom. 1964. *The Ceque System of Cuzco: The Social Organization of the Capital of the Inca.* Leiden: International Archives of Ethnography.

———. 1983. "Towards a General Andean Star Calendar in Ancient Peru." In *Calendars in Mesoamerica and Peru: Native American Computations of Time,* edited by Anthony F. Aveni and Gordon Brotherston. Oxford: BAR International Series 174.

———. 1989. "A quipu calendar from Ica, Peru, with a comparison to the ceque calendar from Cuzco." In *World Archaeoastronomy,* edited by A. F. Aveni. Cambridge: Cambridge University Press.

Woven Words

SEVEN   *The Royal Khipu of Blas Valera*

Sabine P. Hyland

INTRODUCTION

In 1750, Raimondo di Sangro, prince of Sansevero, published a curious book entitled *Lettera apologetica*. In this work, di Sangro reflected on the history of writing and, in particular, on the relationship between the mark of Cain described in the Bible (Genesis 4:50) and early textile-based writing methods. Among the more unusual passages in this book is the description of a secret writing system once used, di Sangro claimed, by ancient Peruvian bards (*amauta*) in the Inka Empire. According to the prince, this writing system was depicted in a seventeenth-century manuscript he had purchased from a Jesuit priest, Father Pedro de Illanes (di Sangro 1750: 241–245); in fact, a record of this purchase, dated to 1744, still exists in the Naples city archives (Domenici and Domenici 1996: 54). The Inka were known to have communicated through the use of *khipu*, or knotted-string records. However, unlike the common khipu, which apparently served only as memory aides or to record numbers, di Sangro's "royal" khipu consisted of woven images representing the syllables of Quechua. In other words, the royal khipu formed a phonetic writing system, capable of denoting any utterance in spoken Quechua. According to the text, the entire system was based on a Quechua syllabary represented by forty symbols. The prince emphasized that the existence of these royal khipu had been a closely guarded secret of the *amauta*, the most learned historians of the Inka Empire. Furthermore, in his description of the manuscript purchased from Illanes, the prince associated the knowledge of this system with the Jesuit Blas Valera, a sixteenth-century chronicler of the Inka whose writings have been lost almost entirely (di Sangro 1750: 232–261).

Di Sangro's work on Inka writing received little attention from the academic community until the nineteenth century. In 1870, León de Rosny, the noted Mayanist, published a facsimile of di Sangro's set of forty khipu symbols in *Les Ecritures figuratives et hiéroglyphiques des différents peuples anciens et modernes* (de Rosny 1870: 20–21).[1] Yet it was not until the 1990s that scholarly attention focused on this syllabic method of writing with khipu. In 1989, Carlo Animato, Paolo Rossi, and Clara Miccinelli published part of a manuscript purporting to be the original document purchased by di Sangro from Father Illanes (Animato, Rossi, and Miccinelli 1989; see also Laurencich Minelli, Miccinelli, and Animato 1995). This manuscript, known as the *Historia et Rudimenta Linguae Piruanorum*, was found in the family archives of Riccardo Cera. (The *Exsul immeritus*, the other principal document discovered in these archives, has not been published and cannot be cited, so it will not be discussed here.) According to the dedication on the last page of the manuscript, Cera had received the document in 1927 from Duke Amedeo de Savoia-Aosta, a member of Italy's royal family. In 1951, the *Historia et Rudimenta* was shown to both Lidio Cipriani, former director of Florence's anthropology museum, and Paul Rivet, of the Museum of Man in Paris, but was not more generally known until its partial publication in 1989 (Domenici and Domenici 1996: 54). The document consists primarily of three short texts purportedly by the following authors: one allegedly by the Jesuit Juan Antonio Cumis, written in Latin in 1610 (7 pages); one supposedly by the Jesuit Juan Anello Oliva, written in 1637[2] (8 pages); and a final text allegedly by Anello Oliva, written in 1638. In the first text, Cumis explains how the Jesuit chronicler Blas Valera had been falsely charged by the Jesuits of fornication, when, in fact, he had been imprisoned for idolatry. Cumis then presents information told to him by Mayachac Azuay, a former disciple of Valera's, concerning the latter's description of a syllabic khipu writing system. This system, he states, was a secret known only to the wise men and priests of the Inka Empire. Anello Oliva, in his two accounts, discusses a variety of issues, including Valera's persecution by the Society of Jesus and his use of khipu for recording history. Anello Oliva explains how to read the secret "royal" khipu and encloses a woven fragment of one of these khipu with the text, along with a Quechua vocabulary of Ecuadorian origin (Domenici and Domenici 1996: 55). He also illustrates how to transfer the information from the syllabic royal khipu onto a system of colored stones arranged within a rectangular grid (Laurencich Minelli, Miccinelli, and Animato 1995: 382–405).

The discovery of *Historia et Rudimenta* has raised a storm of controversy in the world of Andean studies. Did the Inka really possess a secret syllabic writing system? Or is the entire manuscript a modern forgery? Anello Oliva's final section of the manuscript makes extraordinary claims about Valera—that he was imprisoned by the Jesuits for idolatry; that he faked his death in Spain; and that he returned covertly to Peru to pen the chronicle *Nueva corónica y buen gobierno*, attributed to the native writer Felipe Guaman Poma de Ayala. These claims have led some scholars to doubt the authenticity of the document (Domenici and Domenici 1996: 50–58; Estenssoro 1997). However, recently discovered archival evidence has revealed that the Jesuits secretly *did* incarcerate Valera for the crime of heresy, while stating publicly that Valera was imprisoned by the Inquisition for fornication (Hyland 1998). This chapter will examine the issues concerning khipu and history raised by the *Historia et Rudimenta* in light of a virtually unknown manuscript based on Valera's lost writings. In this text, Book 1 of the *Memorias historiales I politicas del Piru*, the author, Fernando de Montesinos, confirms the existence of a secret khipu writing tradition and links this writing system to the era of Atahuallpa. Here I consider Valera's system of syllabic khipu writing, as described by di Sangro, to explore whether the iconography of this system could be pre-Columbian or whether it reflects Valera's own polemics about religion and writing in the Inka Empire.

BLAS VALERA (1544–1597)

Blas Valera was born in Chachapoyas in 1544, the natural son of the conquistador Luis Valera and a native woman named Francisca Pérez. Because of Valera's intimate knowledge of the life of the emperor Atahuallpa, toward whom the chronicler was deeply partisan, it is often assumed that Francisca had been a member of Atahuallpa's court (see González de la Rosa 1907 and Santisteban Ochoa 1946). As a youth, Valera was educated in theology and the liberal arts in Trujillo, joining the Society of Jesus in Lima in 1568. Between 1570 and 1583, Valera worked as a missionary among the native peoples of Huarochirí, Lima, Cusco, Juli, and Potosí. During these years, he arduously collected the myths and legends of the native peoples with whom he worked. He also attended the Third Lima Council (1582–1583), where he was among those chosen to translate the catechism into Quechua and Aymara. However, in 1583, Valera was imprisoned and would remain in custody for the rest of his life. Documents from the archives of the Spanish Inquisition have revealed that the Jesuits in Peru claimed, falsely, that Valera had been charged by the

Holy Office for seduction; in fact, the Jesuits had jailed Valera themselves because of heretical tendencies in his teaching (Hyland 1998). After three years
of imprisonment and eight years of house arrest, Valera was sent by the Jesuits
into exile in Spain. Soon after his arrival in Spain, he was severely injured
in the English raid on Cádiz in 1596. Most of his papers were burned in the
attack, and Valera died of his injuries on April 2, 1597 (Durand 1987).

Although Valera wrote copiously about the Inka, most of his writings have
been lost. Except for the controversial *Relación de las costumbres antiguas*,[3] the
remnants of Valera's works survive only in citations by later authors. The
most famous of these writers is Garcilaso de la Vega, who claimed to possess
the charred remains of Valera's *Historia Occidentalis*, saved from the ashes of
Cádiz. Garcilaso, in his *Comentarios reales*, provides the best-known and most
extensive quotations from the Jesuit chronicler. However, the seventeenth-
century writer Juan Anello Oliva also had access to Valera's lost *Vocabulario*,
which explained native terms and provided biographies of pre-Inka and Inka
rulers. Likewise, Fernando de Montesinos also used texts either written by
Valera or derived from his historical tradition; Montesinos's work, in particular, can shed light on some of the claims made in the *Historia et Rudimenta*
concerning khipu, Andean history, and Blas Valera.

MONTESINOS, ATAHUALLPA, AND KHIPU

Fernando de Montesinos was a Spanish priest and canon lawyer who lived in
Peru from 1628 to 1653. While in Peru, he held a variety of posts, including
secretary to the bishop of Trujillo, parish priest in Potosí, and chaplain to the
church of Nuestra Señora de la Cabeza in Lima, a benefice proffered by the
Holy Office of that city. He possessed an abiding interest in mining and metallurgy, and collected information on mining in his travels throughout the
Peruvian colony. In 1637 he organized an *entrada* into the jungle near Tarma
to search for new sources of mineral wealth. Although the journey failed to
find the hoped-for riches, the venture increased his reputation as an expert
on Peruvian natural history. His reputation in the colonies was further en-
hanced by the publication, in 1640, of his description of the auto-da-fé held
in Lima on January 23, 1639. This work, recording the bloodiest auto-da-fé
ever celebrated in Peru, provides detailed biographies of all of the condemned
(Hiltunen 1999: 166–181).

Yet Montesinos's interests were not confined to metallurgy and "followers
of the law of Moses." Deeply concerned with Andean history, he conducted
interviews and collected historical texts to serve as the basis of his magnum

opus, the *Memorias historiales*. This work, divided into four books, remained in manuscript in Montesinos's lifetime and still has never been published fully.[4] Book 2, which narrates Andean history beginning from the reign of Pirua Pacaric Manco and continuing through ninety-two subsequent pre-Inka rulers, is the best-known section of the work. Books 1 and 3, however, were dismissed as worthless early in this century, and have attracted virtually no scholarly attention. In 1920, Philip Ainsworth Means wrote that "[Book] One is mainly made up of Biblical and astrological matter of no value. Whatever good material it has seems to have been duplicated in [Book] Two" (Means 1920: xi). Not only is Book 1 concerned with placing the discovery of Peru in an Old Testament biblical framework, but it also expresses opinions that are offensive to modern sensibilities. For example, Montesinos lashes out against Las Casas's attempts at peaceful conversion of the Indians to Christianity, arguing instead that the only valid means of converting the natives is through military force (Montesinos [post-1644]: ch. 7). Yet despite its shortcomings, Book 1 provides valuable ethnohistorical information that has been overlooked until now.

In particular, Chapter 4 of Book 1 explains one of the central mysteries of the entire text: the native source of the Andean history recounted in Book 2. The source of this book has long puzzled scholars. Although its mythology contains many Andean elements, its unbroken line of some ninety-three pre-Inka rulers, eight of whom bear the honorific title "Pachacutec," is unique (the so-called Pirua and Amauta pre-Inka dynasties are not distinguished in the original manuscripts). Marcos Jiménez de la Espada, the primary editor of Book 2, was uncertain as to the place of this material in Andean lore, and he and other scholars have published only inconclusive speculations about its origins (e.g., Jiménez de la Espada 1882). Yet Book 1 states clearly from where this long history of Peruvian kings is derived. According to Montesinos, this history comes from the historians of the emperor Atahuallpa, the victor in the Inka civil war whose power was based near Quito and whose mother (or foster mother) was a native of Quito (see Haro Alvear 1965). Atahuallpa's historians, Montesinos contends, had actually been interviewed about this material by an earlier colonial historian whose writings Montesinos possessed. The explanation for the name of the first king of this line, Pirua Pacaric Manco, a name that occurs only in this chronology, was provided by "asking the *amautas*, or Historians, who belonged to the era of Atahuallpa, last Peruvian king . . ." (Montesinos [post-1644]: ch. 4).[5] In keeping with this observation, Montesinos's narrative is extremely pro-Atahuallpa, referring to the latter as a "natural lord," instead of the more common title of "usurper," and not even including Huascar in the list of Inka emperors (Montesinos 1644: Book 3, ch. 4; also chs. 5–8).

Atahuallpa's activities in Cusco at the close of the Inka civil war between Atahuallpa and his half-brother Huascar suggest that Atahuallpa was, in fact, preparing a new version of Andean history. One of his first acts after taking Cusco was to find all of the historians associated with Huascar's reign; these men were then murdered by being forced to eat fatal quantities of hot chili peppers (Quipucamayos 1922: 3–5). Atahuallpa's subsequent violence in the capital also suggests that the new emperor may have been planning a radical revisioning of Inka history: he organized the destruction of the Inka nobility in Cusco on a massive scale (Garcilaso 1987: 613–624); and he also ordered his generals in Cusco to burn the mummy of his grandfather, the emperor Topa Inka Yupanqui (Murúa 1987: 202–203).

Whatever Atahuallpa's motivations or final plans, if Montesinos's history represents the version told by Atahuallpa's historians, as Montesinos claims, it certainly does break from earlier Inka traditions. According to Montesinos, for example, the royal *panacas* were not each descended from a previous Inka, with all of the ritual and symbolic connotations this carried in the Inka Empire. Instead, Montesinos's legends narrate that the fifth Peruvian ruler, Inti Capac Yupanqui, instituted the *panacas* as a means of imposing imperial control over the citizens of Cusco (Montesinos 1930: 33–34). If this history is linked to Atahuallpa, one can perhaps glimpse the emperor's future plans for the royal houses of Cusco in this explanation of their existence. Incidentally, the author of the controversial *Historia et Rudimenta* states that Atahuallpa destroyed previous histories because "he wanted to create a new race of Incas of which he himself would have become the Fountainhead, and to make forgotten the original traditions."[6]

Although Montesinos does not reveal the identity of the early colonial chronicler upon whose writings (Manuscript A) this list of kings is based, most scholars believe Valera to have been closely associated with Montesinos's source (e.g., Markham 1920; Vásquez 1930: 132–135). Valera, in the fragments that remain from his writings, is the *only* other chronicler to mention any of the same rulers that occur in Montesinos's pre-Inka chronology. For example, Valera's *Vocabulario*, "an old handwritten vocabulary by Padre Blas Valera," describes at least three of the pre-Inka rulers—Capac Raymi Amauta, Capac Yupanqui, and Cuiz Manco—found only in these two texts (Anello Oliva 1998: 95–96). Not only are the names provided, but both texts recount identical stories about Capac Raymi Amauta. Likewise, the name given by Montesinos to the first Andean king, Pirua Pacaric Manco, occurs only in Valera; similarly, the explanation of this name is unique to these two authors (Montesinos [post-1644]: ch. 4; Valera 1968: 153–154). In addition, Montesinos's chronology includes eight pre-Inka kings known as Pachacutec; Valera is the only other chronicler to name these same Pachacutis and to describe Pachacutec VII in a manner corresponding to Montesinos's version (Valera 1968: 167–170). Furthermore, Montesinos dates his king list by using a native method of reckoning time by thousand-year intervals called "Suns" (Intip-huata), described elsewhere *only* by Valera (Garcilaso 1987: 33, 83; Montesinos 1930: 38–39); moreover, the two chroniclers agree that the last complete "year of the Sun" ended in A.D. 1043 (see Montesinos 1930: 38–39, 62, 70–71).

Additionally, Montesinos tells us that the earlier chronicler whom he cites was from the city of Quito: "he who composed it was a loquacious man from Quito, a long-time resident of the city." Montesinos adds that the author of this earlier chronicle had participated in Bishop Luis López de Solís's examination of natives within his diocese of Quito and had at least partially based his "history of Peruvian kings" on Solís's "examination of the Indians" ([post-1644]: ch. 4). On his voyage to exile in Spain, Valera was delayed in Quito for over a year, from 1594 to 1595, the same year that Solís conducted a visitation and rigorous examination of the natives within his diocese (Egaña 1966: 431–432); furthermore, Solís's primary assistant and translator during his visitation was Valera's friend and fellow Chachapoyan, the Jesuit Onofre Esteban (Egaña 1974: 301–302). It is likely that Solís knew Valera personally from the Third Lima Council, where the future bishop was an official theologian. A radical supporter of native rights who worked tirelessly to end the abuse of the native peoples, the bishop had much in common with Valera. When Solís entered his diocese of Quito for the first time in 1594, he immediately established very close ties with the Jesuits there, much to the outrage of the diocesan clergy and the other religious communities in Quito (see Carmona Moreno 1993). The bishop justified his favoritism of the Jesuits—ordering, for example, that the diocesan seminary be run by Jesuits rather than by diocesan clergy—by testifying that "[the Jesuits] are such faithful and useful assistants to the prelates in this diocese . . . as is seen in particular in the great fruit that they bear among the Indians of this diocese . . ." ("Testimony of Don Fray Luis López de Solís," vol. 21, folder 3, 1.89b).[7]

Valera, like Montesinos's textual source, did interview Atahuallpa's historians; Garcilaso tells us that Valera learned Inka history from the "vassals of Atahuallpa" (Garcilaso 1987: 593). Certainly, Valera was emphatically partisan in favor of Atahuallpa, arguing, for instance, that Atahuallpa's life was so holy that the emperor's soul was received in heaven as a saint immediately after his execution. Valera also recorded details from Atahuallpa's life that are not available elsewhere, such as information about Diego Titu Atauchi, Atahuallpa's full brother ("hermano de padre y madre de Atahuallpa" [Anello Oliva 1998: 142–143]).[8] Though it is not certain whose hand actually wrote the "history of Peruvian kings" that was Montesinos's source, it is clear that Valera was part of the milieu that helped to produce this chronicle (Manuscript A) in Quito.

Montesinos's assertions in Book 1 about the source of Book 2 of the *Memorias historiales* raise a host of daunting textual problems, made more complicated because there is no definitive edition of the text.[9] It is worth turning our attention now, however, to a passage in Book 1 in which Montesinos associates this history of over ninety Andean kings with a special kind of khipu that did not rely upon human memory to be "read." Although there has been debate concerning the manner in which khipu encoded information, it generally has been believed that khipu functioned primarily as memory aides in the recording of myths and histories (e.g., Ascher and Ascher 1991). Garcilaso, one of the most influential chroniclers of the Inka, makes this point very strongly in the *Comentarios reales*. He tells us that khipu only assisted the recollection of already memorized histories; they were only "perishable expedients . . . , [for they could not serve] as letters that perpetuate the memory of events" beyond the lives of their authors (Garcilaso 1987: 332).

However, the *Historia et Rudimenta* accuses Garcilaso of lying about the khipu. According to Anello Oliva, one of the alleged authors of *Historia et Rudimenta*, Garcilaso "distorted and censored" Valera's work, and "particularly sullied the things that Father Valera had widely written about the royal *quipus*" (Laurencich Minelli, Miccinelli, and Animato 1995: 398). This text claims that Blas Valera had described a secret kind of khipu, known only to the kings, historians, and wise men of the empire, that functioned as an actual writing system. In other words, these royal khipu—many of which had actually been sent to Garcilaso—could be read on their own as texts, without reference to narratives memorized by their creators. In Book 1 of the *Memorias historiales*, Montesinos likewise accuses Garcilaso of seriously misrepresenting Valera ([post-1644]: ch. 4), and he repeats the claim that Garcilaso was mistaken about khipu because he did not know about the different khipu used by the historians and wise men of the empire. Montesinos writes:

> But because Garcilaso Ynga did not have knowledge of . . . the Quipus that the Amautas, or Indian Historians, used, and of the [khipu's]

difference for the tradition and knowledge of the Peruvian Kings, thus it was necessary to send him some of these Quipus, whose information was contained in themselves; he created a false account of these Quipus that they used in place of letters . . . there were a great number [of these khipu] in Peru and especially in Quito.[10]

In this passage, the chronicler informs us of several things. Among these are: (1) that a different type of khipu, distinct from the mnemonic ones described by Garcilaso, was used by the Inka historians "for the tradition and knowledge of the Peruvian Kings," and (2) that the information in these khipu "was contained in themselves." Garcilaso, the text states, was ignorant about the khipu used by the *amauta* for recording history. These khipu could be sent to someone and read without the assistance of their creators; apparently, therefore, these special khipu were self-contained bodies of knowledge that functioned as writing, rather than as mere memory aids.

In another draft of *Memorias historiales* that Montesinos wrote, he specifies that Garcilaso had been sent many of these special khipu:

> . . . and because Garcilaso did not have news of this, says the author of the manuscript [Manuscript A] in Discourse 2, chapter 1 dealing with the *Amautas* and Indian historians and with the difference in the *quipus* that they used for the tradition of the events and deeds of the Peruvian kings . . . , he knows that many of those *quipus* had been sent in that year [1594–1595?] so that Garcilaso would see them. There were many of these *quipus* in Peru, and in the city of Quito.
>
> (MONTESINOS 1644: CH. 4, F. 9).[11]

Yet this passage from Chapter 4 does more than confirm the existence of special historical khipu that functioned as writing. Montesinos also informs us about the specific cultural context of these khipu, associating them with the distinctive historical traditions of Quito. Montesinos specifies that the use of these khipu was centered in Quito, the seat of Atahuallpa's power. He also tells us that these khipu were used "for the tradition and knowledge of the Peruvian Kings"; by the phrase "Peruvian Kings" he is referring specifically to the legends of over ninety pre-Inka kings, beginning with Pirua, derived from the historians of Atahuallpa. It is certainly possible that the historians from Quito could have developed a method of using khipu as a phonetic writing system. There is evidence that the native peoples of the Quito region had developed at least one other type of khipu (similar perhaps to the grid method discussed in the *Historia et Rudimenta* and the *Exsul immeritus*) described by the Jesuit Juan de Velasco in the eighteenth century:

> They used a type of writing, more imperfect than the Peruvian Quipos. They reduced [writing] to certain archives, or deposits, made of wood, of stone, or of clay, with diverse separations, in which they arranged little stones of different sizes, colors, and angular figures worked to perfection, because they were excellent lapidaries. With the different combinations of these that can be called characters, they perpetuated their deeds, kept an exact note of each one of the provinces, and formed their counts of all.   (VELASCO 1977: 91)[12]

According to the chronicler Martín de Murúa, an enormous amount of local variation existed in the Andes in the creation and use of khipu; as a Mercedarian friar, Murúa would have known about khipu usages, because the Mercedarians had employed khipu extensively in evangelization since the 1580s.[13] The Mercedarians in Peru routinely encoded on khipu sections of the canonical legislation concerning Indians, as well as lengthy discourses on Christian behavior (Porras 1953: 174–177).

Interestingly, in the *Historia et Rudimenta*, Anello Oliva summarizes a historical narrative read to him from one of these special royal khipu. This narrative, which describes the historical events leading to the development of the khipu, closely matches the story found in Montesinos's text—an account found only in these two works.[14]

THE ROYAL KHIPU OF BLAS VALERA

The question then remains: was Valera's system of khipu writing used in pre-Spanish Quito, and was it a system whose development was cut short by the arrival of Pizarro? To answer that, we have to look at the actual system. The most reliable depiction of Valera's khipu writing can be found in di Sangro's 1750 *Lettera apologetica*. The system depended on a basic syllabary of forty "Master Words," as they were called, representing the full range of syllables in spoken Quechua (see Figure 7.1; di Sangro 1750, plate 2).

The khipu in the *Historia et Rudimenta* use these same symbols, with only very slight modifications. In this syllabary, each pendant symbol corresponds to a multisyllabic Master Word in Quechua. The Master Words are subdivided into four groups: (1) celestial objects or events; (2) human figures (*figura humana*); (3) quadrupeds (*quadrupedi*); and (4) miscellaneous items

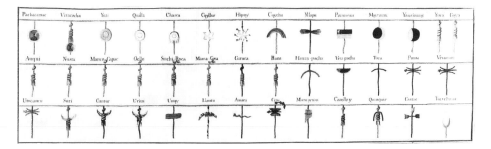

FIGURE 7.1 Khipu signs from Raimondo di Sangro's *Lettera apologetica* (1750).

such as royal vestments; this latter group also includes the two symbols depicting the gods Pachacamac and Viracocha. According to the text, the major division is between nonhuman and human symbols. The symbol for "person" (*runa*) consists of a top knot followed by three knots and a "skirt," and this symbolism is carried throughout the syllabary; for example, the symbols for "prince" (*auqui*) and "princess" (*ñusta*) follow the pattern for *runa*, but with differently colored yarn. There is also a song to go with the words to help memorize them in order. According to ethnolinguists, it is very common in syllabic writing systems such as this to use songs for memorizing the basic syllabary (Conklin 1991; di Sangro 1750, plate 3).[15]

The system itself is quite straightforward. If one wanted to represent the syllable "cha," for example, one would select the pendant symbol for Pachacamac, tie it onto a horizontal string, and then place two knots in the string hanging down from the symbol; the two knots show that the second syllable "cha" is indicated. If one wanted to represent the entire word, one would not place any knots in the string that hangs from the pendant symbol. We do not know the conventions governing the division of words into syllables. Given the redundancy of the syllabary (many syllables are repeated several times), there must have been an agreement that certain syllables could represent lone vowel or consonant sounds. With this proviso, these special, royal khipu can represent any utterance in Quechua; thus, they represent a complete syllabic writing system.

Do they, however, represent the khipu system used in Quito, perhaps by the *amauta* of Atahuallpa? One of the intriguing aspects of the syllabary is the inclusion of the word "Pinunsun" (Equinox), with this explanation, "The Equinox was carefully observed and solemnly celebrated" (di Sangro 1750: 251). According to Bauer and Dearborn (1995: 46–50; 153–154), the only textual evidence that the Inka ever celebrated the equinox occurs in the works of Montesinos and Garcilaso, two chroniclers influenced by Valera. Montesinos informs us that the observance and worship of the equinox was instituted by the Peruvian ruler Toca Corca Apucapac to divide the year into four periods. Garcilaso explains that the equinox was most highly venerated in Quito, and gives a correct discussion of the relationship between the latitude and dates of the zenith passage in Quito, "information [that] would not have been part of any Western knowledge that Garcilaso de la Vega could have casually acquired" (Bauer and Dearborn 1995: 49). Juan de Velasco, a Jesuit chronicler who lived in Quito in the eighteenth century, claims that the rulers of Quito celebrated the March equinox, which they considered the beginning of the year, as one of the most important festivals (Velasco 1977: 147–149). It is possible that the presence in the syllabary of a sign for the equinox, an event that was apparently more highly celebrated near Quito, may reflect a northern Andean origin for the system.

However, all of our sources for this system lead back to Blas Valera, who was involved in humanist polemics about the nature of Quechua; he argued, in fact, that Quechua was part of a constellation of sacred languages that included Latin and Hebrew. For his arguments to be convincing, he needed to assert that Quechua was a written tongue; in other words, he had a vested interest in demonstrating that Quechua was a written language (see Hyland 1998).

If we examine the iconography of this syllabary, along with the explanations that accompany each Master Word, we see Valera's apologetics at work. This is demonstrated by the first two words of the syllabary, "Pachacamac" and "Viracocha." Pachacamac was a local pre-Inka deity whose cult centered around an oracle and a ritual complex on the coast south of Lima. The Inka and the priests of Pachacamac had formed a powerful alliance during Inka times; the Inka helped to spread the Pachacamac cult and, in return, the Pachacamac oracle lent its support to Inka expansion. Some colonial Spanish accounts describe Pachacamac as "he who gives being to the Earth," as a Creator; other chronicles mention Pachacamac's children and document the offering of sacrifices to him (MacCormack 1991: 353). In di Sangro's text, Pachacamac is described as "God, the Creator of the Universe" (di Sangro 1750: 246). We know that Valera certainly considered Pachacamac, also called Illa Tecce, as the true God, equivalent to the supreme deity worshipped by the Hebrews and Christians (e.g., Valera 1968: 153). Pachacamac's icon, di Sangro explains, is divided into four equal parts colored to represent the four essential elements of the universe—red for Fire, blue for Air, brown for Earth, and sea-green for Water. Most Spanish thinkers of the sixteenth century, following classical Greek theories, believed that these same four elements made up the universe. Native Andean cosmography did not share a belief in the four elements; the depiction of these elements on an allegedly Inka symbol apparently stems from the Spanish colonial period.

The second pendant symbol, "Viracocha," reveals an even stronger European bias. There is considerable dispute among scholars over the exact nature of Viracocha, an Andean culture hero and deity.[16] Some colonial accounts describe Viracocha as an omnipotent high god, but other chroniclers deny his importance. Not one Inka ceremony was dedicated exclusively to Viracocha, and he lacked an endowment to support his worship. Nonetheless, the royal syllabary describes Viracocha in no uncertain terms as the true God, the Creator, "in Human figure"; in other words, as Christ, the incarnation of God as Man. The fact of the incarnation is shown in the very iconography of the symbol—we see the small symbol for God the Creator, Pachacamac, hanging from a flesh-colored thread with three knots. The text explains that the flesh color and the knots symbolize the human form of God (that is, of Pachacamac) incarnate. The Viracocha icon, therefore, is formed by combining the symbol of the true God with that of humanity; Christian beliefs about the nature of Christ are embedded in the very structure of this symbol. It is important to note that Valera is not merely providing a Christian gloss for a pagan symbol. The European bias is intrinsic to the iconography of the Viracocha icon, combining, as it does, the visual symbols for "human" and for "true God."

The text goes on to state that the true God, as Man (in other words, Christ), had appeared to the son of the Inka Yahuar Huacac, and that this apparition was given the name Viracocha; the Inka, therefore, already worshipped Christ along with God the Father. This estimation of Viracocha is in keeping with Valera's beliefs about Andean religion. In another text, Valera writes that the word "Viracocha" should be translated by the Latin word *numen*, "the will and power of God" (Garcilaso 1987: 288), an appropriate title for Christ. The Jesuit scholar also stated that Viracocha was the name used by modern Andeans for God, signifying the "immense God of Pirua" (Valera 1968: 153; also Montesinos [post-1644]: ch 4). According to Valera, Pirua, who reigned long before the time of Christ, was the first king of Peru. His god, Valera tells us, was the true God worshipped by the Hebrews in the Old Testament. It is fitting that Viracocha would have been a relatively more modern name for God, in Valera's theology, because this name could only have been applied by the Andeans to God after the incarnation of Christ.

Valera's discussion of Pachacamac and Viracocha portrays an image of

Andean paganism that, in European terms, places Peruvian religion on a high level. By arguing that the Andeans worshipped the true invisible God along with Christ, he implied that Inka religion could serve as a solid basis for Christianity. In his estimation of native religion, Valera was opposed by most of the Catholic Church leadership in Peru at the time. For example, José de Acosta, Valera's Jesuit superior, believed that the Andeans held only a "sparse and attenuated knowledge" of the true God. Furthermore, Acosta argued that native worship of the gods Viracocha, Pachacamac, and others was so profoundly compromised by blasphemous idolatries that such native cults must be rooted out in their entirety (Acosta 1670: 237–240). Valera's assertions about God in the royal khipu were thus part of his ongoing polemics with other Christian religious leaders in colonial Peru.

It is worth noting that this manner of argumentation through lexicography, that is, through providing ideologically charged definitions of Quechua words, was a central aspect of Valera's thought. In his *Vocabulario* and in other writings, he bases important polemical points on what he believes to be the proper definition of Andean terms. For example, in his *Vocabulario*, in the definition of "Atahuallpa," he includes the significant detail that the formerly pagan king was one of God's elect and was taken directly to heaven upon death (Anello Oliva 1998: 138–139); implicit within this definition is a profound statement about the relationship between the Inka Empire and divine providence. Elsewhere, Valera criticizes Polo de Ondegardo, one of the most respected Spanish chroniclers of the Inka, claiming that Polo's statements about the Inka are mistaken because the Spanish author knew nothing about native languages or the Andean love of metaphor. Valera then corrects Polo's mistaken conclusions about the Andean peoples by providing better definitions of Andean religious terms (e.g., Valera 1968: 153–155, 157, 161–173; see also Montesinos 1930, ch. 7). Although all the early linguists in Peru attempted to give accurate definitions of native words, Valera was extraordinary in the extent to which he used polemically charged definitions to make theological and political statements. Valera's syllabary in di Sangro reflects Valera's beliefs about Inka theology; it seems clear that the royal khipu, as they are presented here, pertain at least in part to colonial Peru and not to the pre-Spanish Andean past.

CONCLUSION

In conclusion, we are left with two possibilities concerning these royal khipu. The first possibility is that Valera invented the system entirely on his own, as the great Cherokee intellectual Sequoya did for his people. This in itself, of course, would have been a remarkable achievement. Sequoya's efforts to establish literacy in a native Cherokee script led to a flowering of Cherokee literature and civic discourse. Valera's dissemination of the royal khipu may even have inspired a similar outpouring of colonial Indian literature among his followers in the Cusco confraternity "el Nombre de Jesús"; Valera led the members, all Inka Christians in Cusco, in weekly spiritual discussions from 1573 to 1576. We know from Valera's writings that several Inka noblemen in this confraternity left accounts of Inka religion and history encoded on khipu; it is possible that these khipu were woven in this style of royal khipu that Valera taught. Of course, if Valera did invent this system in its entirety, then his association of it with Atahuallpa is also an invention; however, this does not necessarily imply that his account of Atahuallpa's "new history" is itself untrue. There are still many textual problems to be addressed before we can begin to evaluate the relationship between the *Memorias antiguas* and the historiography of *amauta* in colonial Quito.

Another possibility, however, is that Valera based his system on one used in Quito or elsewhere, simply creating some of his own pendant symbols to serve his ideological program. Typically, Valera based his work on actual Andean realities, which he reshaped to fit his defense of Inka religion. We know from the Mercedarians that there was great local variation in the types of khipu used in the Andes; it is certainly possible that there existed a northern style of khipu similar to that described by Valera, one that recorded the sounds of speech rather than served as a memory aid. In the American Museum of Natural History, there is a khipu on display (#41.2/7679) that exhibits the elements of these royal khipu. It has pendant symbols—in this case, abstract patterns of lines of varying widths and colors—with strings hanging from the pendant symbols; each of these strings has a varying number of knots, and, in some cases, no knots at all. Unfortunately, this particular khipu has no archaeological data associated with it, but it does demonstrate that there may have existed some type of native prototype for the kind of khipu that Valera depicted. At this point in time, it is impossible to say whether Valera invented the royal khipu on his own or based them on an indigenous khipu type; more research remains to be done before we can answer this question.

ACKNOWLEDGMENTS

An earlier version of this chapter was presented at the Northeast Andean Ethnohistory and Archaeology Conference in Orono, Maine, on October 5, 1997. The author would like to thank William P. Hyland, David Fleming,

Monica Barnes, Elayne Zorn, Gary Urton, Laura Laurencich Minelli, Craig Morris, Anahid Akasheh, and an anonymous reviewer for their comments and assistance. Any mistakes are, of course, the fault of the author.

NOTES

1. However, de Rosny did not provide any explanation of the system, and he made several minor errors in recording the sounds indicated by each symbol.

2. Juan Estenssoro has charged that the manner in which this date is given in the text, "de los Reyes 30 [*sic*] de Julio," is anachronistic; an authentic text of this period, he states, should read "'a 30 de Julio' y no 30 directamente, que es el uso actual" (1997: 572). However, dates could be and were written in sixteenth- and seventeenth-century Spanish without an "a" preceding the day. For example, in Anello Oliva's manuscript *Historia de los varones insignes de la Compañía de Jesús en el Perú*, Father Alonso Messía dates his approval for the publication of Anello Oliva's work, "de Lima, 10 de marzo de 1631"; likewise, the date on Provincial Nicolás Duran's approbation of Anello Oliva's text reads, "Lima, diez de marzo de 1631" (Anello Oliva 1998: 17, 19).

3. This anonymous Jesuit manuscript generally is ascribed to Valera, based on evidence within the text (see Urbano 1992).

4. This discussion of the titles of Montesinos's text follows that of Hiltunen (1999).

5. ". . . preguntando á los Amautas, o Historiadores, que ancanzó del tiempo de Atahualpa último Rey Peruano . . ."

6. ". . . volea creare una nuova razza Inga, della quale esso medesimo sarebbe divenuto Capostipte, e fare obliare la tradizione primigenia." The text is given in Animato, Rossi, and Miccinelli 1989: 70.

7. "los dhos padres son en este obispado tan fieles y provechosos coadjutores de los prelados como se be en particular en el gran fruto que en los yndios deste obispado [hay]" ("Testimony of Don Fray Luis López de Solís," vol. 21, folder 3, 1.89b).

8. It is worth noting that Doña Angelina Yupanqui, the widow of Atahuallpa and a major source for her husband Juan de Betanzos's *Suma y narración de los ingas . . .* , was only a child of ten in 1532 when she left her home in Cusco to marry Atahuallpa; after Atahuallpa's murder the following year, she returned to live in Cusco until her alliance with Francisco Pizarro began around 1538 (Hamilton 1996: x–xi). Despite her marriage to Atahuallpa, it is not clear that she would have been particularly well informed about the details of Atahuallpa's plans for his new empire.

9. Until a definitive edition of the text is produced, it will be difficult to assess whether Montesinos's long pre-Inka history of Peru was, in fact, related to Atahuallpa's new history. Velasco's history of the kingdom of Quito, which was derived from the Caran ethnic group, provides a pre-Inka dynasty list that is quite distinct from that in Montesinos's work. However, Velasco's history relates that the reign of the Carans was replaced by that of the Puruas, another ethnic group in the region; it is possible that the Montesinos/Valera chronology may derive from the Purua people. On the other hand, Juha Hiltunen (1999) has argued that Montesinos's history is an orally preserved history of the Wari Empire.

10. "Mas porque dello no tuvo noticia Garcilaso Ynga, ni de los Quipos, que los

Amautas, o Historiadores Yndios usaban, y su diferencia para la tradición, y noticia de los Reyes Peruanos, pues para ello fue necesario remitirle algunos, cuya inteligencia se quedó en ellos mismos; formó la falsa relación . . . destos Quipos, que usaron en lugar de letras . . . hubo gran número en el Perú, y con especialidad en Quito" (Montesinos [post-1644]: ch. 4).

11. "y porque desto no tubo noticia Garcilaso dice el autor del manuscrito en el discurso 2, cap. 1 tratando de los Amautas e istoriadores indios y de la diferencia de los quipos de que usaban para tradiccion de los sucesos y hechos de los reis Peruanos . . . , que saue se an inbiado a esse año muchos de aquellos quipos para que los viese Garcilaso. Destos quipos ai de gran numero en el Piru, y en la ciudad de Quito" (Montesinos 1644: ch. 4, f. 9).

12. "Usaban de una especie de escritura, más imperfecta que la de los Quipos peruanos. Se reducía a ciertos archivos, o depósitos, hechos de madera, de piedra, o de barro, con diversas separaciones, en las cuales colocaban piedrecillas de distintos tamaños, colores, y figuras angulares labradas a perfección, porque eran excelentes lapidarios. Con las diversas combinaciones de aquellos que pueden llamarse caracteres, perpetuaban sus hechos, tenían la exacta nota de cada una de las provincias, y formaban sus cuentas de todo" (Velasco 1977:91).

13. "Había otra maravilla, que cada provincia como tenía propio lenguaje nativo, también tenía nuevo modo de *Quipu* y nueva razon dello" (Murúa 1987: 374). Numerous scholars in recent years have argued that we must expand our concepts of communication in order to understand problems of representation in the Andes; see, for example, Cummins 1994, Hiltunen 1999, and Zuidema 1991.

14. According to the narrative in the *Historia et Rudimenta*, South America was invaded by dark-skinned people from Tartary around A.D. 650. The dark-skinned people fought with the Peruvian natives, who were light-skinned descendants of giants (although these giants are called *gente bianca* in the text, the context of the story makes it clear that this term is not meant to refer to Spaniards or Europeans). During the combat, the Peruvians were nearly exterminated. Those Peruvians who remained, mixed with the newcomers to create a "new lineage" that eventually gave rise to the Inka. In the aftermath of this war, the sacred royal khipu were first introduced to Peru (Laurencich Minelli, Miccinelli, Animato 1995). Montesinos's account, which spans several chapters, essentially agrees with the brief one-page tale of the khipukamayuq Chahuarurac in the *Historia et Rudimenta*. In the *Memorias antiguas historiales*, a race of giants came to the Andes early in Peruvian history. Although most of the giants were killed, a few survived to mix with the native Peruvians (Montesinos 1930: 43–47). Some time after the appearance of the giants, there were two successive invasions of Peru by dark-skinned peoples. The first wave of dark-skinned invaders arrived in Peru around A.D. 550. The invaders battled fiercely with the native inhabitants, resulting in the death of most of the Peruvians. Shortly after this war, khipu were first developed (Montesinos 1930: 64–65). Eventually, there was a second invasion of Peru by foreigners. During this invasion, there were virtually no native Peruvians left to fight the newcomers. The Peruvian king, Tupac Cauri Pachacuti, made peace with the foreigners, who then "mixed" with the older race of Peruvians. This combined lineage formed the basis of what would later become the Inka people (Montesinos 1930: 67–68). The date for the first invasion of dark-skinned peoples—the invasion that led

to the introduction of the khipu—varies by only a hundred years between the two accounts.

15. See, for example, Harold Conklin's (1991) discussion of the syllabic "bamboo script" used by the Ifugao in the Philippines.

16. Rowe (1960) has argued that Viracocha was an omnipotent high god invented by Pachacuti to celebrate Inka power; Pease (1973), on the other hand, has suggested that Viracocha was a pre-Inka culture hero who was later "solarized"; and Guardia Mayorga (1962) has speculated that Viracocha was a pre-Columbian culture hero who was reinvented as a high god by colonial priests wishing to stress the virtues of native Peruvian religion.

REFERENCES CITED

Acosta, José. 1670. *De Promulgando Evangelio apud Barbaros: Sive de Procuranda Indorum Salute.* Lyon: Editio novissima, L. Anisson.

Anello Oliva, Juan. 1998 [1631]. *Historia del reino y provincias del Perú.* Edited by Carlos Gálvez Peña. Lima: Pontificia Universidad Católica del Perú.

Animato, Carlo, Paolo Rossi, and Clara Miccinelli. 1989. *Quipu: Il nodo parlante dei misteriosi Incas.* Genoa: Edizioni Culturali Internazionali Genova.

Ascher, Marcia, and Robert Ascher. 1991. *Code of the Quipu: A Study in Media, Mathematics, and Culture.* Ann Arbor: University of Michigan Press.

Bauer, Brian S., and David S. P. Dearborn. 1995. *Astronomy and Empire in the Ancient Andes.* Austin: University of Texas Press.

Carmona Moreno, Félix. 1993. *Fray Luis López de Solís: Figura estelar de la evangelización de América.* Madrid: Editorial Revista Agustiniana.

Conklin, Harold. 1991. "Doctrina Christiana, en lengua española y tagala. Manila, 1593: Rosenwald Collection 1302." In *Vision of a Collector: The Lessing J. Rosenwald Collection in the Library of Congress,* edited by Kathleen Mang and Peter VanWingen, 36–40. Washington, D.C.: Library of Congress.

Cummins, Tom. 1994. "Representation in the Sixteenth Century and the Colonial Image of the Inca." In *Writing without Words,* edited by Elizabeth Hill Boone and Walter D. Mignolo, 188–219. Durham: Duke University Press.

de Rosny, León. 1870. *Les Ecritures figuratives et hiéroglyphiques des différents peuples anciens et modernes.* Paris: Maisonneuve et cie., Libraires-Editeurs.

di Sangro, Raimondo (Prince of Sansevero). 1750. *Lettera apologetica.* Naples: N.p.

Domenici, Davide, and Viviano Domenici. 1996. "Talking Knots of the Inka." *Archaeology* 49, no. 6: 50–58.

Durand, José. 1987. "Los últimos días de Blas Valera." In *Libro de homenaje a Aurelio Miro Quesada Sosa.* Lima: Talleres Gráf. P. L. Villanueva.

Egaña, Antonio de. 1974. *Monumenta peruana.* Vol. 6. Rome: Institutum Historicum Societatis Iesu.

Estenssoro F., Juan Carlos. 1997. "Historia de un fraude o fraude histórico?" *Revista de Indias* 210: 566–578.

Garcilaso de la Vega, el Inca. 1987 [1609]. *Royal Commentaries of the Incas and General History of Peru.* Translated by Harold V. Livermore. Austin: University of Texas Press.

González de la Rosa, Manuel. 1907. "El Padre Valera, primer historiador peruano." *Revista Histórica* 2 : 180–199.

Guardia Mayorga, C. A. 1962. "El enigma del Dios Wira-Qocha." In *Congreso Nacional de Historia del Perú*, vol. 2, 133–155. Lima: El Centro.

Hamilton, Roland. 1996. Introduction to *Narrative of the Incas* by Juan de Betanzos. Austin: University of Texas Press.

Haro Alvear, Silvio Luis. 1965. *Atahuallpa Duhicela*. Ibarra, Ecuador: Imprenta Municipal.

Hiltunen, Juha. 1999. *Ancient Kings of Peru: The Reliability of the Chronicle of Fernando de Montesinos*. Helsinki: Suomen Historiallinen Seura.

Hyland, Sabine. 1998. "The Imprisonment of Blas Valera: Heresy and Inca History in Colonial Peru." *Colonial Latin American Historical Review* 7, no. 1: 43–58.

Jiménez de la Espada, Marcos. 1882. "Dedicatoria." In *Memorias antiguas historiales y políticas del Perú*, Book 2, by Fernando de Montesinos, vii–xxxii. Madrid: Imprenta de Miguel Ginesta.

Laurencich Minelli, Laura, Clara Miccinelli, and Carlo Animato. 1995. "Il Documento Seicentesco 'Historia et Rudimenta Linguae Piruanorum.'" *Studi e materiale, storia delle religioni* 61, no. 2: 363–413.

MacCormack, Sabine. 1991. *Religion in the Andes: Vision and Imagination in Early Colonial Peru*. Princeton: Princeton University Press.

Markham, Sir Clements R. 1920. Introduction to *Memorias antiguas historiales del Perú*, Book 2, by Fernando de Montesinos, 3–15. Translated and edited by Philip Ainsworth Means. London: Hakluyt Society.

Means, Philip Ainsworth. 1920. Introduction to *Memorias antiguas historiales del Perú*, Book 2, by Fernando de Montesinos, xi–xxix. Translated and edited by Philip Ainsworth Means. London: Hakluyt Society.

Montesinos, Fernando de. 1930 [1644]. *Memorias antiguas historiales y políticas del Perú*. Book 2. Annotated by Horacio H. Urteaga. Lima: Librería e Imprenta Gil.

———. [post-1644]. *Memorias antiguas historiales del Perú*. Book 1. Yale ms., Latin American Manuscript Collection, Sterling Library, Yale University, New Haven, Conn.

———. 1644. *Memorias historiales I politicas del Piru*. Books 1–3. Universitaria ms. #332/35. Biblioteca de la Universidad de Seville.

Murúa, Martín de. 1987 [ca. 1613]. *Historia general del Perú*. Edited by Manuel Ballesteros. Madrid: Historia 16.

Pease, Franklin. 1973. *El Dios Creador andino*. Lima: Mosca Azul Editores.

Porras, Diego de. 1953 [ca. 1583]. "Instrucciones que escribió el P. Fr. Diego de Porras para los sacerdotes que se ocuparon en la doctrina y conversión de los indios." In *Los mercedarios en el Perú en el siglo XVI*, vol. 4, edited by Fr. Víctor M. Barriga, 174–177. Arequipa, Peru.

Quipucamayos. 1920 [1542–1544]. "Declaración de los *quipu*camayos a Vaca de Castro, discurso sobre la descendencia y gobierno de los Incas." In *Colección de libros y documentos referentes a la historia del Perú*, Series 2, Vol. 3. Lima: Sanmartí.

Rowe, John. 1960. "The Origins of Creator Worship among the Incas." In *Culture in History*, edited by Stanley Diamond, 408–429. New York: Columbia University Press.

Santisteban Ochoa, Julián. 1946. *Los cronistas del Perú*. Cusco: Imprenta D. Miranda.

Sarmiento de Gamboa, Pedro. 1999. *History of the Incas*. New York: Dover Publications.

Societatis Iesu, Rome. 1966. *Historia de la Iglesia en la América Española: Hemisferio Sur*. Madrid: Biblioteca de Autores Españoles.

"Testimony of Don Fray Luis López de Solís." July 24, 1600, Quito. Bloomington: University of Indiana, Latin American mss., vol. 21, folder 3, 1.89b.

Toribio Polo, José. 1907. "El historiador Blas Valera S.I." *Revista Histórica* 2: 544–552.

Urbano, Henrique. 1992. Introduction to *Varios: Antigüedades del Perú*, edited by Henrique Urbano, 1–23. Madrid: Historia 16.

Valera, Blas. 1594. *Relación de las costumbres antiguas de los naturales del Pirú*. Biblioteca Nacional de Madrid, Ms. #3177.

———. 1968 [1594]. *Relación de las costumbres antiguas de los naturales del Perú*. In *Crónicas peruanas de interés indígena*, edited by Francisco Esteve Barba, 153–189. Madrid: Biblioteca de Autores Españoles.

Vásquez, Guinaldo M. 1930. "Los monarcas de Montesinos." In *Memorias antiguas historiales y políticas del Perú*, Book 2, by Fernando de Montesinos; annotated by Horacio H. Urteaga, 132–172. Lima: Librería e Imprenta Gil.

Velasco, Juan de. 1977 [1789]. *Historia del reino de Quito en la América Meridional*. Quito: Casa de Cultura Ecuatoriana.

Zuidema, R. T. 1991. "Guaman Poma and the Art of Empire: Toward an Iconography of Inca Royal Dress." In *Transatlantic Encounters*, edited by K. Andrien and Rolena Adorno, 151–202. Berkeley: University of California Press.

Recording Signs in Narrative-Accounting Khipu

EIGHT   *Gary Urton*

INTRODUCTION

Writing about writing is a particularly vexed example of the general relationship, experienced by humans in all cultures, between acting, on the one hand, and commenting on that action, on the other hand. There are not, in fact, many examples of the parallelism between "doing the thing that we are commenting on" in the performance of, and commentary on, most other forms of human activities. Another such example is the closely related activity of talking; that is, we *do* (even commonly) "talk about talking." There are certainly a few other areas of social life in which action and the commentary on that action—as constituted by the performance of the act itself—are in a dialogue with each other in the manner noted above (e.g., crying about crying, or laughing about laughing). The more general and important point I want to make, however, is that when our metacommentaries on our actions take the form of performing those activities themselves, there is no reason to think that either side of such an action/reflection "equation" will be performed in a way that differs significantly from the way(s) we perform that activity spontaneously in our everyday lives. Thus, for example, we would not expect that laughing about laughing would produce, on the metacommentary side of the equation, a unique or truly distinctive form of laughter; rather, such a reflexive episode would likely only imply that the latter may represent an unusual *motivation* for a particular occurrence of this otherwise common form of activity.

The question I want to examine here with respect to the issues outlined

above concerns the act of *writing about writing* itself. In particular, I am concerned about the conceivable scope and degree of self-consciousness of such
metacommentary before the accumulation (early in the twentieth century)
of an extensive body of comparative analytical and interpretive literature on
different types of writing systems. Writing and literacy are forms of human
activities about which there now exists an abundance of *written* commentary. Thus, anyone who now sets out to write about writing, especially about
"other" nonalphabetic (e.g., syllabic, logographic, pictographic) forms of
writing, will have available numerous descriptive materials and analytical
works concerning different scripts and types of writing systems whose signs,
procedures, and levels of reference (phonemes, morphemes, ideas) may be
quite distinct from those that characterize the writing system used by the
commentator him/herself. But in what ways might the act of writing about
other systems of writing have been constrained *before* the accumulation of the
present large body of descriptive and analytical studies on different writing
systems? That is, what would (or should) we expect in terms of the nature of
the (self-)consciousness and degree of reflexivity about writing on the part of
someone commenting on another, potentially quite distinct, "alien" writing
system in a cultural and ideological context *un*conditioned by the substantial
body of literature that exists on this topic today? Addressing this question is
one of the challenges we face in this study.

More specifically, the initial topic that I take up here concerns the commentary by the famed early-seventeenth-century mestizo (that is, of mixed
Quechua and Spanish ancestry) writer Garcilaso de la Vega on Inka writing
and record keeping. Later in this chapter, I introduce the reader to a small
group of Inka khipu currently housed in museum collections in Europe and
in the United States. I argue there that Garcilaso's commentaries on Inka
record keeping and writing prompt us to ask whether this group (or class) of
khipu may actually constitute records of sufficient syntactical and semantic
complexity to regard these khipu as products of a system of writing.

GARCILASO DE LA VEGA ON INKA "WRITING"

The Inca Garcilaso de la Vega was born in Cusco, Peru, the former capital of
the Inka Empire, in 1539. He was the son of an Inka princess, Isabel Chimpu
Ocllo, and a Spanish conquistador, the captain Garcilaso de la Vega. Having
spent his adolescence playing with local youths in Cusco, Garcilaso was a
native speaker of Quechua, the "general language" of the Inka Empire; moreover, he knew the descendants of Inka nobility intimately, and he observed

firsthand the transformation of Cusco from imperial capital to colonial out-
post. In 1560, at the age of twenty-one, following the death of his father (in
1559), Garcilaso traveled to Spain, never again to return to Peru (see Anadón
1998; Porras Barrenechea 1986: 391–408).

Almost forty-two years later, in 1602, as an old man living out his life
in Andalusia, Garcilaso began writing an account of his boyhood in Cusco,
weaving his personal memories into a general history of Peru from just before the Spanish Conquest of the Inka Empire through the first few decades
of the colony. As Margarita Zamora has noted in her valuable and incisive
study *Language, Authority, and Indigenous History in the "Comentarios reales de
los Incas"* (1988: 50–58), Garcilaso wrote his account as a sustained "correc-
tive" to earlier histories that had been written for the most part by Europeans and, in particular, by people who did not know Quechua as their mother
tongue. It is also relevant to note at this point that Garcilaso included in his
account information gleaned from clerics and other commentators—such as
(the mestizo) Blas Valera and José de Acosta—who had firsthand knowledge
of Peruvian affairs, especially during the period when he (Garcilaso) had been
absent, living in Spain. Garcilaso's account, a classic work of the Golden Age
of Spanish literature and one of the first pieces of *American* literature, is titled
Royal Commentaries of the Incas (1966 [1609–1617]).[1]

Present-day scholars (especially anthropologists) of Inka civilization and
culture tend to approach Garcilaso with great reservation, principally due
to his verbose, highly rhetorical style of presentation and his insistence on
promoting his own authority and authenticity in virtually all matters having
to do with Inka history and culture. Indeed, much of the information contained in the *Commentaries* is decidedly idiosyncratic in nature. Despite such
reservations about Garcilaso and his writings on Peru, the *Commentaries* was,
nonetheless, a seminal work in the construction of Western consciousness
and understanding about the nature and attributes of Inka civilization. This
was certainly the case in terms of the influence Garcilaso's writings exerted
on European ideas about Inka "writing" (see Hernández 1993: 143–153).

We are obliged to put the word *writing* in quotation marks, particularly as
Garcilaso uses this term—*escribir* (to write)—to refer to the "species" of activity he thinks the Inka may (or may not) have been involved with in recording information on the device known as the khipu.[2] The khipu (from the
Quechua word for "knot") was a knotted-string device made of (usually)
multicolored strings of wool or cotton that were knotted in very complex patterns. The reason for this qualification or equivocation (i.e., the insistence on
putting quotation marks around the word *writing*) is that Garcilaso himself

was so deeply ambivalent about whether or not the Inka could, by means of this device, "write" *in some manner comparable to what he understood this term to mean.*

The qualification emphasized at the end of the last sentence is intended to recall the issue that was raised at the beginning of this chapter. Writing "innocently" as he did—that is, before Rousseau (1966 [1817]), de Saussure (1966 [1915]), Gelb (1963), Derrida (1976), Goody (1977), Ong (1988), Boone and Mignolo (1994), and, most recently, Harris (1995)—Garcilaso clearly did not know what to make of Inka record keeping in his writing about the khipu. A few things he was certain of, however. For instance, he knew the Inka did not "write" signs with pen and ink on paper (or parchment); he knew they kept their records on colorful, knotted strings; he knew the Inka generally used these knotted-string devices to record statistical data relating to censuses, taxation, and other matters; but he also knew that, on occasion, the old khipukamayuq (knot makers/keepers) consulted these knotted-string records in narrating events of the past. These things Garcilaso seems to have been sure of, as he confirms for the reader explicitly that he himself became quite proficient at "reading" (*leyendo*) the khipu accounts.

> I used the *quipus* and knots with my father's Indians and other *curacas* when they came to the city to pay tribute on St. John's Day or at Christmas. The *curacas* under the charge of others would ask my mother to send me to check their accounts [*cuentas*], for they were suspicious people and did not trust the Spaniards to deal honestly with them in these matters until I had reassured them by reading [*leyendo*] the documents referring to their tributes which they brought me, and *comparing them with their knots: in this way I came to understand the latter as well as the Indians themselves.*
>
> (GARCILASO DE LA VEGA 1966: 333; EMPHASIS ADDED)

His extensive knowledge of the khipu notwithstanding, a considerable amount of ambivalence and confusion entered Garcilaso's account when he tried to string together the various bits of knowledge he had about the nature of Inka record keeping, the types and levels of information signed by means of the various recording units, and, particularly, whether Inka record keeping by means of the khipu constituted what he felt comfortable classifying as a system of writing.

I want to stress the importance the (presumed) Inka ability to write had *for Garcilaso himself.* Zamora has, rightly, I think, emphasized Garcilaso's claim to authority on Inkaic matters by virtue of the fact that he was a native Quechua speaker. However, for Garcilaso himself, his authority was grounded in more than the ability *to speak* the Quechua language, for he also claimed the ability *to read* it, in the khipu, as well. Curiously, Zamora fails even to mention Garcilaso's claims to being able to read the khipu or his characterization of these knotted records as *libros anales* (history books).[3] In addition, Zamora (1988: 81) summarily dismisses the supposed narrative-recording capacities of this device, which is in direct contradiction to what Garcilaso himself had to say on the matter. It is important to bear in mind, then, that Garcilaso's claims to authority in speaking about, and for, the Inka were not just *linguistically* based; rather, they were for him *text* based, as well.

GARCILASO DE LA VEGA ON NUMBERS, PROSODY, ICONOGRAPHY, AND WRITING IN THE KHIPU

If we want to understand how Garcilaso conceived of Inka record keeping, we have to read his account very carefully. What we will find as we undertake this project is that, while Garcilaso insisted, on the one hand, that the khipu signs were composed of knots that had strictly numerical values, he also argued, on the other hand, that *since* the Inka *needed* to sign "letters" (*letras*)—that is, to engage in the activity he referred to as *escribir* (to write)—they also were able to interpret their knots as letters. In effect, he describes a signing system that sounds, oddly enough, like a kind of "knot alphabet." Our tasks here will be, first, to attempt to understand what kind(s) of system(s) of signing Garcilaso may have been referring to; second, to determine the degree to which his understanding of Inka record keeping may have been influenced by (especially) Spanish- or Latin-derived alphabetic or logocentric presuppositions about any irreducible elements of writing systems; and, finally, to investigate surviving khipu traits or organizational properties that might represent units of information in a technology of narrative record keeping that was similar to what Garcilaso described, or perhaps (mis)interpreted, as "knotted letters."

Garcilaso first states that the Inka commonly tied knots into the strings of the khipu in a decimal system of place notation. There were knots for units, tens, hundreds, thousands, and tens of thousands. These knotted records were kept by the khipukamayuq. Garcilaso then states that

> . . . they may be said to have recorded [*escrivían*] on their knots everything that could be counted, even mentioning battles and fights, all

the embassies that had come to visit the Inca, and all the speeches and arguments the king had uttered. But the purpose of the embassies or the contents of the speeches, or any other descriptive matter could not be recorded on the knots, consisting as it did of continuous spoken or written prose, which cannot be expressed by means of knots, since these can give only numbers and not words [*la palabra*].

(GARCILASO 1966: 331–332)[4]

Garcilaso goes on to state that, in supplying what we could term (following Derrida) a "mark," "trace," or record of such "event/discourse" units of signification, the Inka invented a number of "signs" (*señales*). Furthermore, he tells us that, in order to remember the notable events of the past, the Inka reduced them "in a summarized form of a few words"; that is, the Inka incorporated schematized versions of, or references to, important historical events in poems and songs (Garcilaso 1966: 332). Given the juxtaposition of his discussion of the invention of the event/discourse "signs," on the one hand, and the reduced vignettes or memory cues of notable historical events, on the other, it seems that Garcilaso intends to relate these two phenomena to each other. If so, he does not make the connection between them clear, at least not in this part of his chronicle. However, if we turn to another section of the *Commentaries*, we find what may be a reference to a (perhaps alternative) form of Inka record keeping, one that made use of such signs and memory vignettes; here, I am referring to Garcilaso's discussion of Blas Valera's notes on khipu writing.

The Jesuit priest Blas Valera was a mestizo from the region of Chachapoyas, Peru, who became—through his service in Lima, Cusco, and Potosí—a staunch defender of the native Andean peoples. As Sabine Hyland argues (Chapter 7, this book), Valera ran afoul of the Jesuit hierarchy, apparently at least partly because of his radical ideas about the status of the Quechua language, which (along with Latin) he considered to be a "sacred language," and his—what was considered by his superiors to be seditious—teaching of Quechua grammar (see also Hyland n.d.). It has generally been assumed that soon after Blas Valera was exiled to Spain by General Aquaviva (the head of the Jesuit order at the time), he died from injuries sustained in the English sack of the port city of Cádiz, in 1596. The remains of Blas Valera's papers, which were for a time lost in the destruction of Cádiz, were later recovered and turned over to Garcilaso de la Vega for safekeeping. Garcilaso quotes and paraphrases extensively from these papers in his *Royal Commentaries*. For example, in his discussion of Inka poetry, Garcilaso notes that the Inka made long and short lines of verse, "measuring the number of syllables in each [line]" (Garcilaso 1966: 126). Garcilaso continues:

> In Padre Blas Valera's papers, I found other verses which he calls spondees: they all have four syllables, while these [i.e., ones referred to earlier, in the text] are four followed by three. He [Blas Valera] sets them down in Indian [i.e., Quechua] and Latin. . . . The fables and verses, Padre Blas Valera says he found in the knots and beads of some ancient annals [*anales*] in threads of different colors: the Indian accountants in charge of the historical knots and beads [*ñudos y cuentas historiales*] told him the tradition of the verses and the fable; and, surprised that the *amautas* [priests] should have achieved so much, he copied down the verses and memorized them.
>
> (GARCILASO 1966: 127)[5]

At this point in his text, Garcilaso goes on to cite one of the verses, called "Sumac Ñusta," contained in the papers of Blas Valera; oddly enough, this is the same exemplary verse that was used, and supposedly encoded in a syllabic, knotted script, in the so-called "Naples document" (see Laurencich Minelli 1996).

Leaving for the moment the question of the woven, iconographic khipu signs of the "ancient annals" reported by Blas Valera, I return to topics addressed by Garcilaso in the later portion of his chronicle in which he describes the relationship between knot numbers and knot letters. It is after the place in his narrative where he made reference to the event/discourse "signs" (discussed above) that Garcilaso introduces the most intriguing, yet confusing, observation into an account that, up to this point, has been fairly straightforward. Garcilaso says:

> But *as experience has shown*, all these [i.e., summaries, poems, and songs] were perishable expedients, for *it is letters* [*las letras*] *that perpetuate the memory of events*. But as the Incas had no knowledge of writing, they had to use what devices they could, *and treating their knots as letters*, they chose historians and accountants, called *quipucamayus* ("those who have charge of the knots") to write down and preserve the tradition of their deeds by means of the knots, strings, and colored threads, *using their stories and poems as an aid*. This was the method of writing [*escribir*] the Incas employed in their republic.
>
> (GARCILASO 1966: 332; EMPHASIS ADDED)[6]

This passage, which will serve as the "key text" for the remainder of this chapter, is, or rather *ought* to have been, of exceptional importance in our attempts to construct a comprehensive understanding of Inka record keeping by means of the khipu. However, to the best of my knowledge, no past student of the khipu has followed up on the implications of this passage (but see Assadourian, Chapter 6, this book) in developing a line of inquiry into the possible *narrative contents* of the class of khipu similar in appearance to the knotted, generally decimal-based accounting khipu (i.e., *not* to the type of khipu bearing iconographic signs, as described by Blas Valera).

We should take a moment to reflect on the significance of the passage from Garcilaso cited above in relation to the comments made at the beginning of this chapter concerning early (i.e., premodern) acts of "writing about writing."

GARCILASO DE LA VEGA'S PRESUPPOSITIONS ABOUT THE NATURE OF INKA WRITING

Garcilaso begins the above passage by stating what was apparently, for him, a condition necessitating the Inkaic translation of knots that seemingly otherwise had numerical values into knots signifying letters; that is, he says: ". . . as *experience* has shown . . . it is letters that perpetuate the memory of events." Whose "experience" is Garcilaso referring to here? That of the Inka? Or his own? At first sight, and given that this passage immediately follows his discussion of the impossibility of signing historical events and discourse by means of numbers, it appears that the chronicler must be referring to his own experience. That is, if the passage was intended to apply to the experience of the Inka, then why, if *they* knew that it is letters that perpetuate memories, wouldn't they simply have invented knots signifying letters directly, rather than having had to resort to the expedient of "treating their knots as letters" (i.e., rather than as numbers)?

However, on closer study, there *does*, in fact, seem to be some ambiguity within this text with regard to the question of whether Garcilaso is implying (a) that the Inka used the *same* knots to sign letters that they had earlier used only to sign numbers, or (b) that the Inka may actually have invented two different systems of knot signs, one for numbers and another for letters. If the former of these two possibilities was the truth of the matter, then Garcilaso's initial, conditional statement—i.e., "as experience has shown"—*could* have been meant to refer to the *Inkaic* experience. According to this telling of the story, the Inka would have first only signed numbers with their knots;

later, however, *when they realized they needed to record speech*, they would have given letter values to the knots (which formerly would have had only numerical value). This latter interpretation, however, sounds suspiciously like that of an individual who was himself convinced that the only way to record events, discourse, and other narrative forms was to do so phonologically, that is, by recording *speech sounds* by means of letters in an alphabetic script.

Although we do not know as yet precisely how the Quechua-speaking Inka viewed this matter, we do know that Garcilaso, who (though a native speaker of Quechua) spoke and read Spanish, Latin, and Tuscan fluently, *was* a man with a deep understanding and an appreciation of written alphabetic scripts (see Porras Barrenechea 1986: 394–395, and Zamora 1988: 62–63, on Garcilaso's linguistic and philological abilities). These comments raise for us directly the problems, alluded to at the beginning of this chapter, inherent in Garcilaso's practice of "writing—i.e., *in an alphabetic script*—about writing."

My own interpretation of the quandary outlined above is that it is highly unlikely, although certainly not impossible, that in writing at the time he did, Garcilaso would have conceived of the possibility of "writing without letters." The issue here concerns the distinction between *glottographic* scripts (of which Spanish and Latin were examples), in which the script provides either phonological (syllabic, alphabetic) or morphemic or word-level (logographic) representations of spoken-language utterances, and *semasiographic* scripts, in which the recording units indicate ideas directly (see Sampson 1985: 29–32). Geoffrey Sampson, among others, argues that all true writing systems are glottographic in nature (but see Boone and Mignolo 1994 and Harris 1995), that is, they are systems that represent the "utterances of a spoken language by means of permanent, visible marks" (Sampson 1985: 26). Now, it is clear that in certain parts of his account, Garcilaso took the khipu to represent the most extreme form of a glottographic system—that is, an alphabet. In this, I argue that Garcilaso was almost certainly guilty of projecting onto the Inka his own experience of the necessity and convenience of using an alphabetic script for writing.

One of the most intriguing problems we face in simply accepting Garcilaso's presupposition on this matter, however, is the fact that there were at least two major forms of *non*alphabetic writing/recording systems used elsewhere in the Americas in the late pre-Hispanic era. These included the logo-syllabic script of Maya hieroglyphics (Fields 1990; Lounsbury 1989) and a variety of "pictographic" (i.e., semasiographic) systems used by the Aztecs of central Mexico (Boone 1994; King 1994) as well as by the Mixtecs of Oaxaca (Troike 1990).

Thus, we should not feel compelled to accept what I take to have been *Garcilaso's* presupposition about the necessity of "letters" for the practice of writing. However, if we *do* conclude that Garcilaso probably misunderstood the nature of the units signed in the khipu recording system, we are confronted by the more difficult task of explaining, first, *how wrong* he was about the nature of the khipu signing system. For example, was the khipu based on a semasiographic, rather than a glottographic, recording principle? Or was it, more narrowly, that he got the *type* of glottographic script wrong (e.g., that he mistook a logographic for an alphabetic script)? Second, how could a man who claimed to be so skilled in this particular recording system have been so mistaken about its basic characteristics? And finally, if not an alphabetic system of knots, then what kind of system for recording narratives *did* the Inka possess, if any?

I want to stress that I am not arguing that it is impossible that the Inka developed a system of signing letters by means of knots. Rather, I am arguing against the *necessary connection* that Garcilaso articulates between a phonographic system of letters and the recording of historical discourse. I will return to address this problem in a moment; before doing so, however, it will be helpful to make an observation on one other curious comment included in the passage I have called our "key text."

THE NATURE, LOCATION, AND STATUS OF "MNEMONIC UNITS" IN NARRATIVE PRODUCTIONS

The "curious" comment alluded to above concerns Garcilaso's statement that the Inka "used their stories and poems as an aid" in preserving their traditions "by means of the knots, strings, and colored threads" (see text above and note 6). In fact, this statement is quite remarkable, because it *reverses* the common presupposition about which of these two elements—the stories or the khipu—served as the "mnemonic" for the other. That is, it has generally been supposed that the khipu stored some manner of (schematic) "bits" of information, which served as mnemonic aids for remembering full narrative accounts of events of the past. The full narratives themselves, however, are generally considered to have been stored in the memories of the khipukamayuq, who performed/constructed them in their entirety during ritualized public recitations (Murúa 1946: 169, 176). Much to our surprise, however, Garcilaso states instead that the short, summarized stories and poems alluded to earlier (see above) served as memory aids for knowing how to read/interpret the full narrative traditions, *the latter of which were recorded in the knots and strings of the khipu.*

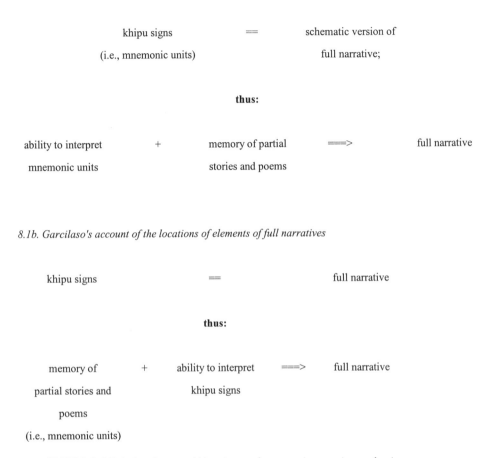

8.1a. *Traditional view of the locations of elements of full narratives*

khipu signs   ==   schematic version of

(i.e., mnemonic units)   full narrative;

thus:

ability to interpret   +   memory of partial   ===>   full narrative

mnemonic units   stories and poems

8.1b. *Garcilaso's account of the locations of elements of full narratives*

khipu signs   ==   full narrative

thus:

memory of   +   ability to interpret   ===>   full narrative

partial stories and   khipu signs

poems

(i.e., mnemonic units)

FIGURE 8.1 Relations between khipu signs and memory in narrative productions.

    The difference between these two views of the locations of the mnemonic units, schematic summaries, and complete versions of narratives is illustrated in Figures 8.1a and 8.1b. If Garcilaso's account is correct, this implies that the khipu recorded (relatively) complete versions of Inka narratives of the past.

    Perhaps we do not want to read the one sentence Garcilaso devoted to the question of the location and status of mnemonic units as concretely, or literally, as implied by Figure 8.1b. In any case, we are far from needing to reach a conclusion on such technicalities, given the decidedly crude state of our present understanding of the encoding of narrative information in the khipu.

THE RELATIONSHIP BETWEEN READING AND SPEAKING

I return now to the query (which may seem an odd one) raised earlier: How wrong was Garcilaso in his apparent belief that the Inka used knots to sign *letters*? Our answer to this question requires some background information. From the studies of the khipu that have been carried out to date, there appear to have been at least two major types, or classes, of khipu. One is the type, found in most museum collections today, employing knots and (often) colored strings; many, but not all, examples of this type of khipu have been shown to have been used as accounting devices to record numerical-statistical information (Locke 1923; Urton 1998). The other major type of khipu is that employing dyed strings, into or onto which were tied more complex, iconographic (and semasiographic?) "knot signs." Though the nature and genealogy of the latter type of khipu remain unclear, the suggestion has been made from various sources that this latter type of khipu primarily encoded narrative constructions or forms of information (see Hyland, Chapter 7, this book; Laurencich Minelli 1996).

Now, in Garcilaso's long discussion of the khipu that we have been examining here, it is quite clear that he is referring to the "knot-and-string"-type accounting khipu, not to the iconography-type khipu. We can assert this with some confidence because, as I mentioned earlier, Garcilaso refers specifically to the iconography-type khipu in his discussion of the information Blas Valera collected on the encoding of poems on khipu (Garcilaso 1966: 126). Thus, Garcilaso himself distinguished between these two classes or types of khipu. The point here is that when Garcilaso talks in our "key text" about the Inka "treating their knots as letters," he is clearly referring to the knots of accounting khipu.

I draw the following two conclusions from the above observations and lines of reasoning. First, I conclude that the Inka did not, in fact, use a phonological knot-alphabet. Given the grammatical peculiarities of the Quechua language, such a "script" would have been enormously complex, not to mention inefficient and cumbersome. That is, the basic strategy of Quechua syntactic and semantic constructions is to string multiple suffixes—indicating number, inclusivity/exclusivity, data-source marking, etc.—onto roots. As a consequence of this grammatical proclivity, a large proportion of Quechua words stretch to alarming lengths (10–15, or more, letters)! Tying one knot *per* letter in a khipu to record a Quechua narrative would have been an absurdly time- and energy-consuming enterprise.

The second conclusion I draw is that though Garcilaso may have been mistaken when he asserted that the Inka signed their historical discourses by means of a knot-alphabet, nonetheless, *for some reason* this conclusion apparently made sense to him. I suggest that the reason may have gone beyond his own familiarity with alphabetic, phonological scripts, such as Spanish and Latin. It is apparent from his writing on this subject that Garcilaso had frequently had the experience in his youth of watching and listening as *khipukamayuq "read" from their khipu.* What does this latter (italicized) phrase mean? It means, I would suggest, that on innumerable occasions, Garcilaso would have watched as khipukamayuq consulted, manipulated, or "read" their knotted-string devices *while they spoke.* From this, I argue that he reasonably concluded that—just as he looked at his own written texts, which were composed of alphabetic symbols, and then read/spoke the letters and words he saw there—he imagined that the Inka were performing essentially the same kind of operation *using the same kind of symbols* (i.e., letters). I suggest below that we may have a few museum specimens of such khipu, which I will refer to as "narrative-accounting" khipu.

We have now come to the heart of the matter insofar as our interest in understanding the types and levels of information (glottographic or semasiographic) encoded in the khipu is concerned. That is, we must now ask what follows from my conclusions (a) that the Inka did not use a knot-alphabet, but (b) that there was some kind of connection between the knots of knot-and-string-type accounting khipu and speech? What follows, I think, is that the Inka must have had a subclass of accounting khipu that was used to record units of signification employed by khipukamayuq in the construction, interpretation, or "reading" of narrative discourses stored in, or constructed from, those khipu. That is, Blas Valera's iconography-type khipu must not have been the only form used in narrative record keeping; rather, this was accomplished as well by certain accounting khipu whose knots were interpreted—in Garcilaso's phraseology—as "letters."

In concluding this portion of our inquiry, we should also recognize that Garcilaso de la Vega may, in fact, have felt himself under a powerful obligation to (*mis*)represent, at least to some degree, Inka record keeping as alphabetically based. Zamora has made a compelling case for the conclusion that Garcilaso understood his mission in writing the *Commentaries* as the need not only to convince his Spanish readership of his own authority to speak about Inka history and culture, but also to insist on the high level of civilization achieved by the Inka (1988: 3). Alphabetic writing was a central criterion of "civilization" in the sixteenth-century Spanish understanding (see Mignolo 1995). Thus, Garcilaso may have felt a powerful rhetorical and political urge to "give" alphabetic writing to the Inka. Such a move would have been entirely consistent with what has been argued elsewhere regarding claims made by another indigenous chronicler, Guaman Poma de Ayala, to the effect that the Inka knew both the God of Christianity (Adorno 1986: 27–29) and Hindu-Arabic numerals (Urton 1997: 201–208) before the arrival of the Spaniards. This having been said, it is nonetheless clear that Garcilaso and other chroniclers confirm that some manner and form of mnemonic notation or "reading and writing" was going on by means of the khipu (see Assadourian, Chapter 6, this book; Cummins 1994; MacCormack 1995).

DO WE HAVE EXAMPLES OF NARRATIVE, KNOT-AND-STRING-TYPE ACCOUNTING KHIPU?

My interest in analyzing closely Garcilaso de la Vega's extensive commentary on the khipu arose as a consequence of my search of the ethnohistorical sources for some way to explain the unusual characteristics typifying a small subset of what, on the surface at least, appear to be knot-and-string-type accounting khipu. I will describe these khipu and then return to consider if, and if so, how, Garcilaso's comments on Inka writing might help us to interpret these "narrative-accounting" khipu, as I have called them.

Over the past five years, I have conducted intensive research in the two major museum collections of khipu that are available to us for study. One collection, containing some three hundred specimens, is in the American Archaeology holdings of the Museum für Völkerkunde in Berlin (Dahlem), Germany.[7] The other, smaller collection—composed of about one hundred samples—is in the American Museum of Natural History in New York.[8] What one finds overwhelmingly in both of these collections are accounting khipu employing the standard knot-and-string-type construction.

Equally overwhelmingly, khipu in the Berlin and New York collections display knots tied into the pendant strings according to a "standard" decimal hierarchical format. That is, as noted by Garcilaso in a passage cited earlier, and then as "rediscovered" by Leland Locke in his studies of the khipu early in this century (1923), information registered on what were presumably accounting khipu utilizes a set of three types of knots, which we know by the following designations: single knots, long knots, and figure-eight knots. These knots normally signify certain units of value in the Quechua decimal-based system of numeration. Figure-eight knots signify ones (i.e., single units); long knots signify the units 2–9, depending on the number of turns of the string within the body of the knot; and finally, depending on their

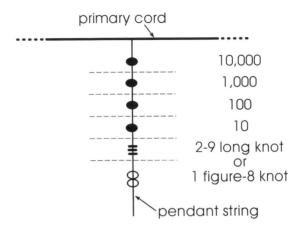

FIGURE 8.2 Decimal numeration on pendant strings of accounting khipu.

hierarchical placement along a string, single knots denote the whole decimal values 10, 100, 1,000, and 10,000 (for the best analysis to date of the logical-numerical properties of accounting khipu, see Ascher and Ascher 1997).

On the majority of khipu, the three knot types described above assume *fixed* hierarchical positions vis-à-vis each other along any given khipu pendant string (see Figure 8.2).

As viewed from the point of attachment of the khipu pendant string with the primary cord, one encounters, in moving down the body of the string, single knots tied on successively lower levels, indicating decreasing powers of 10; then, one encounters *either* (a) a long knot, signifying units from 2 to 9, followed by a space (where the figure-eight knot would otherwise stand), *or* (b) a space (where a long knot would otherwise be found) followed by a figure-eight knot. To clarify the alternative defined here, we should note that khipu numbers were registered as *completed counts,* broken down into their constituent decimal units (e.g., 100 + 10 + 5 = 115). Thus, the long knot and the figure-eight knot are normally *mutually exclusive,* and there is usually only one or the other of these knots on a pendant string. For example, the number 5 is registered in the complete form of a long knot of five turns, not in the additive form of a long knot of four turns *plus* a figure-eight knot (i.e., 4 + 1 = 5).

As I indicated earlier, the overwhelming majority of khipu follow the above "rules" in the organization of knots denoting the various units and powers of 10 of the decimal system. However, in a handful of cases, khipu display

TABLE 8.1.   Narrative-Accounting Khipu

Collection and Catalog #	AS# (Ascher Cat.#)	Provenience (if known)	Published Reference
(1) AMNH #B/8705	—	Chancay	Locke 1928: 47–52
(2) British Museum (unnumbered)	14	—	Ascher and Ascher 1978: 47–52
(3) Museum für Völk., Munich #G3319	90/N2	—	Ascher and Ascher 1978: 635–639
(4) Museum für Völk., Munich #G3299	95/N4	—	Ascher and Ascher 1978: 658–668

knotting patterns that on close inspection are rather dramatically at odds with the patterns—and therefore, presumably, with the principles and values —described above. These are the samples that I will refer to as narrative-accounting khipu. As of this writing, I have studied closely four of these khipu: the samples listed in Table 8.1 (see Table 8.1; see also Ascher and Ascher 1997: 122–124).[9]

What do the narrative-accounting khipu look like? I have illustrated a segment (String Nos. 27–30) of one of these khipu—Sample B/8705 from the AMNH—in Figure 8.3 (see also Figure 8.4).[10] In addition, I have transcribed in Table 8.2 a run of eleven representative, sequential pendant strings (String Nos. 25–35) from Khipu B/8705.[11] As will be noted, several of the pendant strings of this khipu carry "subsidiary strings"; these are indicated in Table 8.2 by the designation *s1* for each subsequent subsidiary string (for example, Pendant No. 25 bears one subsidiary [No. 25s1], which itself bears a subsidiary [No. 25s1s1]).

A few words of explanation are in order concerning the transcription system used in Table 8.2. Though I will argue below that the narrative-accounting khipu (like B/8705) were essentially narrative in function, nonetheless, since these khipu do contain various *quantities* of single knots organized in clusters, as well as long knots composed of different *numbers* of turns of the string within the bodies of the knots, I have found it most convenient and reasonable to "transcribe" these khipu using numbers. In this transcription system, however, each single knot simply is given the value "10," regardless of its hierarchical placement on a string. That is, in the transcription used in Table 8.2, there are no higher powers of 10—such as 100, 1,000, etc.—indicated. Thus, the transcription of the first pendant string (No. 25) in Table 8.2 describes a string bearing an arrangement of three clusters of single knots; beginning at the top of this string (closest to its attachment to the primary cord), there is, first, a cluster of four knots (4 × 10 = 40); followed by a cluster of three knots (3 × 10 = 30); and finally, another cluster of three single knots at the bottom of the string (3 × 10 = 30).

As for the long knots of narrative-accounting khipu, the transcription convention used in Table 8.2 is to place in parentheses the number of turns in the long knot; for example, a long knot of six turns = (6). Thus, the second entry in Table 8.2, which is a subsidiary string of Pendant No. 25 (i.e., No. 25s1), contains the following information: first, a long knot of seven turns = (7), then one of three turns = (3), and finally, a pair of single knots (2 × 10 = 20). In this case, we see that on narrative-accounting khipu, long knots can be found in the highest position on a string, *above single knots!* A further comment on the long knots contained in Khipu B/8705 is in order here. On the overwhelming majority of accounting khipu, long knots display a maximum of nine turns, after which (i.e., with the addition of 1) the long knot will

TABLE 8.2. Transcription of Segment of Khipu B/8705 (AMNH)

Pendant	Transcription			
	(from top of string)			
25	40 -	30 -	30	
25s1	(7) -	(3) -	20	
25s1s1	(8) -	(6) -	90	
26	50 -	30 -	20	
26s1	(5) -	70 -	40	
27	40 -	50 -	40	
28	(4) -	30 -	30	
29	(7) -	(13) -	30	
30	(9) -	(12) -	20	
30s1	(5) -	20 -	40 -	20
31	1 -	50 -	(13)	
32	50 -	20 -	(12)	
33	(7) -	(13) -	30	
34	(7) -	10 -	(5)	
34s1	30 -	20 -	60	
35	(4) -	(10) -	30	

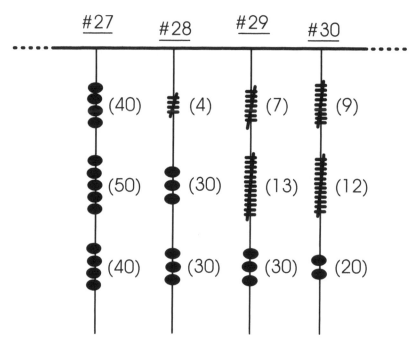

FIGURE 8.3 Selected pendant strings on Khipu B/8705 (AMNH).

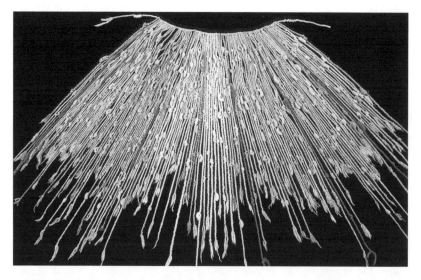

FIGURE 8.4 Khipu B/8705—AMNH. Courtesy of Division of Anthropology, American Museum of Natural History.

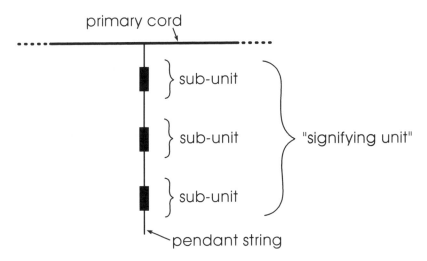

FIGURE 8.5 The subunits and signifying units of narrative-accounting khipu.

have been replaced by a single knot (= 10), but I have identified long knots on narrative-accounting khipu containing *up to sixteen turns!*[12] Therefore, the use of parentheses to enclose long-knot transcriptions will allow us, for instance, to distinguish between a long knot of ten turns = (10) and a single single knot (1 × 10 = 10). Finally, I would note that figure-eight knots are transcribed as 1 in Table 8.2.[13]

There are several structural and organizational features of narrative-accounting Khipu B/8705 that distinguish it, and others like it (Table 8.1), from the majority of standard accounting khipu. Notable among these features is the regular patterning of "informational units" on the strings. That is, a total of 153 strings compose this khipu (i.e., there are 96 pendant strings + 57 subsidiary strings = 153 strings). Now, on 133 of the 153 strings (87%), the knot patterning consists of groupings of *three* what I will call notational "sub-units." I assume that these subunits represent the different classes or bits of information that go together—in some way that we do not yet understand—to compose what I will refer to as a "signifying unit" (see Figure 8.5). Of the remaining 20 strings on Khipu B/8705 that do not carry three subunits of information, 19 have four subunits (see, for example, Pendant No. 30s1 on Table 8.2), and 1 has only two subunits of information (this occurs on String No. 70s1s1s1; i.e., the subsidiary of the subsidiary of the subsidiary of Pendant No. 70).[14]

WHAT DO THE SUBUNITS AND SIGNIFYING UNITS SIGNIFY?

The questions that we finally seek to answer concerning narrative-accounting khipu are (1) What did the subunits on one of these khipu *signify*? and (2) How did the subunits relate to and interact with each other in order to achieve the higher level signification that was (presumably) represented in the signifying units? At present, we do not know precisely where to turn in order to begin to formulate answers to these and other related questions. However, a number of possible paths of interpretation present themselves. I will briefly outline two such approaches below.

If we begin with the assumption that the multiple subunits composing the signifying unit could have been glottographic-type signifiers (modified by string color as well as by spin, ply, and knot-direction variation),[15] we could suppose that these three-subunit units might individually or collectively represent logograph-like constructions. In this interpretation, each pendant string would have constituted the glottographic (e.g., uni- or multilogographic) schematic material—a "cue"—for a sentence-level utterance. One way to test such a scheme might be to undertake a program of computer modeling, seeking correlations between the structures and patterning of narrative-accounting type khipu and printed texts in Quechua. For example, one might seek correlations (at some established level of significance) between the knot patterns (the distribution and patterning of subunits), as well as patterning in color and variations in spin, ply, and knot directionality of narrative-accounting khipu, on the one hand, and word frequencies in a Quechua document—such as the Huarochirí manuscript (see Salomon and Urioste 1991)—on the other hand. Such an analysis has never been attempted.

Another avenue of investigation, one that assumes that the subunits might represent some form of semasiographic units of signification, could begin with the premise that the *types* of number units, *as magnitudes*, as well as "classes" of magnitude types (e.g., even and odd numerical units), represented in the transcription system used to construct Table 8.2 may, in fact, have had some level of representational or symbolic (semasiographic) significance for the Inka. For example, a particular subunit—a cluster of three "Z-type" (see Urton 1994) single knots in the lowest position of an S-plied, Z-spun string of a particular color—could have identified a particular class, or "ethnocategory" (see Murra 1975), of information in Quechua/Inka ideology, state administration, material culture, or other area of activity. For example, we know from our studies of Quechua numbers (see Urton 1997) that the numerical categories of "odd" (*ch'ulla*) and "even" (*ch'ullantin*), as well as the distinction between whole decimal units (e.g., 10, 20, 100) versus "incomplete" units (e.g., 1–9, 11–19), are critical classificatory operators in Quechua numerical ontology and practice. If certain products, statuses, or tasks were to have been linked to particular categories or classes of numbers in Inka administration, then the subunits of a signifying unit might indicate a particular nexus of statuses or conditions that obtained in Inka state production/consumption, narrative-historical formulation, and so on. This approach has some affinities with the proposal for khipu decipherment put forward by Pärssinen (1992: 31–43).

The above two suggestions—the first glottographic in nature, the second semasiographic—are only intended as possible routes of analysis that we may want to consider in our future investigations of the subclass of narrative-accounting khipu. My overall suggestion concerning khipu of the type exemplified by the segment transcribed in Table 8.2 is that these may represent the type of khipu alluded to in Garcilaso de la Vega's commentary discussed earlier in this chapter. That is, these may be khipu in which the Inka utilized the standard inventory of knot types, which they regularly employed in the accounting khipu, but in which the knots were assigned some type and level of information that allowed them to be used for storing narrative, discursive information; in the alphabet-centered terms used by Garcilaso de la Vega, these would have been khipu in which the "knots were used as letters." The information recorded in these khipu would have been used by khipukamayuq to construct and recite histories and other types of narrative traditions about the Inka past.

CONCLUSIONS

As I have noted above, we do not, in fact, know what types of information or levels of meaning the Inka signed in the subunits of signifying units, like those on Khipu B/8705 in the American Museum of Natural History collection. What *does* seem clear, however, is that the organization of knots in such khipu does not follow the general patterns and principles organizing regular accounting khipu. Thus, we must seek some other set of values and principles (other than decimal valuation) upon which to ground our interpretations of these narrative-accounting khipu. I argue that we have everything to gain—especially since such an approach has never before been consistently applied—if we begin by theorizing on the basis of the syntactic, semantic, and overall grammatical properties of the Quechua and Aymara languages (see Pärssinen 1992; Platt, Chapter 10, this book; and Urton 1998), particularly as these were the languages that gave coherence and structure to the thinking, logic, and communication among local, regional, and imperial officials within the Inka Empire who constructed these devices in the first place.

The only stipulation I would place on investigative and discovery procedures in the future is that we avoid dogmatism. One is reminded at this stage in our studies of the khipu of the example of J. Eric Thompson, who ridiculed the suggestion, made most forcefully at the time by Yuri Knorosov, that the Maya hieroglyphs were at least partially phonetically based—a suggestion, of course, which turned out to be entirely correct (see Coe 1993). Simply put: no one knows, as yet, how the Inka signified narrative information by means of their khipu records. Thus, *all* possibilities should remain open for investigation.

ACKNOWLEDGMENTS

I would like to thank, first, Frank Salomon, who provided important and insightful commentary during my initial attempts to formulate the line of argument developed in this chapter. I also express my great appreciation to Marcia Ascher, Tony Aveni, Bill Conklin, Dana Lewis, Julia Meyerson, and Jeffrey Quilter for reading and commenting on an early draft of the chapter. Thanks to Bruce Mannheim for steering me back on course at one point. I alone, of course, am responsible for any errors that remain in the study. Support for my research in the Museum für Völkerkunde in Berlin was provided in 1993 by a National Endowment for the Humanities Summer Stipend and a Study Visit grant from the German Academic Exchange Service (DAAD). Research in the American Museum of Natural History in 1995 was provided by the AMNH's Study Visit program, as well as by a grant from the Research Council of Colgate University. I express my appreciation to these organizations and institutions for their support.

NOTES

1. Unless otherwise stated, all translations from Garcilaso de la Vega's *Royal Commentaries of the Incas* come from the translation made by Harold V. Livermore in the 1966 publication by the University of Texas Press. When referring to terms or passages in the original text of *Comentarios reales de los Incas*, I use the 1943 edition by Angel Rosenblat (which is based on the Madrid edition of 1723).

2. Garcilaso de la Vega employs a number of different Spanish words as glosses for what he understands to be different types of khipu records, or "annals" (*los quipus anales*), and "registers" (*registros*). When writing about the knot notations recording numerical-statistical data, he often employs the word *cifra* (cipher); the set of knotted

records composed of such "ciphers" he refers to as a *cuenta* (count, account), from *contar* (to count, to account; see Urton 1997: 96–111). When writing about "words" that are written in alphabetic script on paper or parchment, Garcilaso generally employs the term *letras* (letters; i.e., groupings of alphabetic signs composing words). When writing about the act of writing alphabet-based texts in Spanish script, he generally uses the term *escribir* (to write); however, he also occasionally uses the verb *escribir* in reference to the recording of information in the "cipher" (numerical) records themselves (e.g., ". . . dezimos que escrivían en aquellos ñudos todas las cosas que consistían en cuenta de números . . ." [1943, 2: 25]).

3. In Sebastián de Covarrubias's dictionary of the Spanish language, which was published in 1611 (two years after the publication of Garcilaso's *Commentaries*), the term *anales* is defined as follows: "Las historias escritas año por año, como centurias las de cien en cien años, efemérides las que van día por día, décadas las de diez en diez años, calendarios los que van escritos por meses" [Histories written year by year, those (written) in centuries of one hundred years by one hundred years, ephemerises composed day by day, (those) in decades of ten by ten years, (or those) calendars composed/written by months] (1943: 116).

4. ". . . dezimos que escrivían en aquellos ñudos todas las cosas que consistían en cuenta de números, hasta poner las batallas y recuentos que se davan, hasta dezir cuántas embaxadas havían traído al Inca y cuántas pláticas y razonamientos había hecho el Rey. Pero lo que contenía la embaxada, ni las palabras del razonamiento ni otro sucesso historial, no podían dezirlo por los ñudos, porque consiste en oración ordenada de viva voz o por escrito, la cual no se puede referir por ñudos, porque el ñudo dize el número, mas no la palabra" (Garcilaso de la Vega 1943, 2: 25).

5. "En los papeles del Padre Blas Valera hallé otros versos que él llama spondaicos: todos son de a cuatro sílabas, a diferencia de estotros que son de a cuatro y a tres. Escrívelos en indio y en latín. . . . La fábula y los versos, dize el Padre Blas Valera que halló en los ñudos y cuentas de unos anales antiguos, que estavan en hilos de diversas colores, y que la tradición de los versos y de la fábula se la dixeron los indios contadores, que tenían cargo de los ñudos y cuentas historiales, y que, admirado de que los amautas huviessen alcançado tanto, escrivió los versos y los tomó de memoria para dar cuenta dellos" (Garcilaso de la Vega 1943, 1: 122).

6. "Empero, como la esperiencia o muestra, todos eran remedios perescederos, porque las letras son las que perpetúan los hechos; mas como aquellos Incas no las alcançaron, valiéronse de lo que pudieron inventar, y, como si los ñudos fueran letras, eligieron historiadores y contadores que lamaron *quipucamayu*, que es el que tiene cargo de los ñudos, para que por ellos y por los hilos y por los colores de los hilos, y con el favor de los cuentos y de la poesía, escriviessen y retuviessen la tradición de sus hechos: ésta fué la manera del escrivir que los Incas tuvieron en su república" (Garcilaso de la Vega 1943, 2: 25–26).

7. I express my great appreciation to Dr. Manuela Fischer and Dr. Marie Gaida for their cooperation and collegiality in allowing me relatively unrestricted access to the collection of khipu in the Museum für Völkerkunde, in Berlin.

8. I would like to thank Dr. Craig Morris, Vuka Roussakis, and Anahid Akasheh, who made possible my two sessions of study (in the summers of 1995 and 1997) of the khipu collection in the American Museum of Natural History in New York.

9. I have also identified several examples of narrative-accounting khipu in a new collection of some thirty khipu recently discovered at the site of Laguna de los Cóndores, in the region of Chachapoyas, Peru (von Hagen and Guillén 1998). As my study of these khipu is ongoing, I do not discuss them in this chapter (see Urton 2001).

10. Khipu B/8705 was studied earlier in this century by Locke, who published a full reading of the knot values on all 153 strings and subsidiaries of this khipu (Locke 1928). Locke published his readings in a "working paper," in which he first made the information on this and several other khipu available for study. Curiously, Locke begins his recording of the values on Khipu B/8705 by reasserting his conclusion, from one of his earlier publications (1923), to the effect that the khipu record numerical values in a base-10 system of numeration. However, when one looks at Locke's transcription of Khipu B/8705, it is clear that this particular khipu violates the fundamental patterns of knot-type placement and other organizational principles that he had identified for numerical-statistical khipu.

11. I should note that the knots of Khipu B/8705 are tied very tightly and are pulled snugly together; thus, it is unusually difficult to "read" this khipu (i.e., determine the accurate number of single knots in a cluster, or the number of turns of the string within the body of any given long knot). For example, I found a relatively large number of discrepancies—one in eight readings—between Locke's transcription of knot values on this khipu (in Locke 1928) and my own. However, in no case was there greater than a difference of one unit between Locke's and my readings (e.g., Locke might have read 8 knots in a cluster, whereas I might have read 7 or 9). I will analyze these differences in a later study.

12. The construction and patterning of knots on the khipu of Tupicocha (see Salomon, Chapter 12, this book) bear some resemblances to what I have termed here narrative-accounting khipu.

13. All knots on Khipu B/8705 are tied as "Z-knots" (see Urton 1994).

14. String No. 70s1s1s1 is unusual for another reason: its ply direction. That is, the strings composing 151 of the 153 strings of Khipu B/8705 are S-spun and Z-plied; however, Pendant No. 32, as well as Subsidiary 70s1s1s1, are Z-spun and S-plied.

15. For an excellent characterization of the full richness and complexity of the information storage capacity of the Inka khipu, see Conklin, Chapter 3, this book.

BIBLIOGRAPHY

Adorno, Rolena. 1986. *Guaman Poma: Writing and Resistance in Colonial Peru.* Austin: University of Texas Press.

Anadón, José, ed. 1998. *Garcilaso Inca de la Vega: An American Humanist.* Notre Dame, Ind.: University of Notre Dame.

Ascher, Marcia, and Robert Ascher. 1978. *Code of the Quipu: Databook.* Ann Arbor: University of Michigan Microfilms (out-of-print; available from the Cornell University Archivist, Ithaca, N.Y.).

———. 1997. *Code of the Quipu: A Study in Media, Mathematics, and Culture.* New York: Dover Publications.

Boone, Elizabeth Hill. 1994. "Aztec Pictorial Histories: Records without Words." In

Writing without Words: Alternative Literacies in Mesoamerica and the Andes, edited by E. H. Boone and W. D. Mignolo, 50–76. Durham and London: Duke University Press.

Boone, Elizabeth H., and Walter D. Mignolo, eds. 1994. *Writing without Words: Alternative Literacies in Mesoamerica and the Andes.* Durham and London: Duke University Press.

Coe, Michael D. 1993. *Breaking the Maya Code.* New York: Thames and Hudson.

Covarrubias, Sebastián de. 1943 [1611]. *Tesoro de la lengua castellana o española.* Edition prepared by Martín de Riquer. From the impression of 1611, with the additions by Benito Remigio Noydens published in the edition of 1647. Barcelona: S. A. Horta, I.E.

Cummins, Tom. 1994. "Representation in the Sixteenth Century and the Colonial Image of the Inca." In *Writing without Words: Alternative Literacies in Mesoamerica and the Andes*, edited by E. H. Boone and W. D. Mignolo, 188–219. Durham and London: Duke University Press.

Derrida, Jacques. 1976. *Of Grammatology.* Translated by Gayatri Chakravorty Spivak. Baltimore and London: Johns Hopkins University Press.

de Saussure, Ferdinand. 1966 [1915]. *Course in General Linguistics.* New York: McGraw-Hill.

Fields, Virginia M. 1990. "Deciphering Maya Hieroglyphic Writing: The State of the Art." *Visible Language* 24, no. 1: 62–73.

Garcilaso de la Vega, El Inca. 1943 [1609]. *Comentarios reales de los Incas.* Edited by Angel Rosenblat; prologue by Ricardo Rojas. Buenos Aires: Emecé Editores.

———. 1966 [1609–1617]. *Royal Commentaries of the Incas.* Translated with an introduction by Harold V. Livermore. Austin: University of Texas Press.

Gelb, I. J. 1963. *A Study of Writing.* London and Chicago: University of Chicago Press.

Goody, Jack. 1977. *The Domestication of the Savage Mind.* Cambridge: Cambridge University Press.

Harris, Roy. 1995. *Signs of Writing.* London and New York: Routledge.

Hernández, Max. 1993. *Memoria del bien perdido: Conflicto, identidad, y nostalgia en el Inca Garcilaso de la Vega.* Lima: Instituto de Estudios Peruanos and Biblioteca Peruana de Psicoanálisis.

Hyland, Sabine. N.d. "The Imprisonment of Blas Valera: Heresy and Inca History in Sixteenth-Century Peru." Manuscript.

King, Mark B. 1994. "Hearing the Echoes of Verbal Art in Mixtec Writing." In *Writing without Words: Alternative Literacies in Mesoamerica and the Andes*, edited by E. H. Boone and W. D. Mignolo, 102–136. Durham and London: Duke University Press.

Laurencich Minelli, Laura. 1996. *La scrittura dell'antico Perù.* Bologna: CLUEB.

Locke, L. Leland. 1923. *The Ancient Quipu or Peruvian Knot Record.* New York: American Museum of Natural History.

———. 1928. "Supplementary Notes on the Quipus in the American Museum of Natural History." *Anthropological Papers of the American Museum of Natural History* 30, Part 2: 39–71.

Lounsbury, Floyd G. 1989. "The Ancient Writing of Middle America." In *The Origins of Writing*, edited by Wayne M. Senner, 171–202. Lincoln and London: University of Nebraska Press.

MacCormack, Sabine. 1995. "'En los tiempos muy antiguos . . .': Cómo se recordaba el pasado en el Perú de la colonía temprana." *Revista Ecuatoriana de Historia* 7: 3–33.

Mignolo, Walter D. 1995. *The Darker Side of the Renaissance: Literacy, Territoriality, and Colonization.* Ann Arbor: University of Michigan Press.

Murra, John V. 1975. "Las etno-categorías de un khipu estatal." In *Formaciones económicas y políticas en el mundo andino,* 243–254. Lima: Instituto de Estudios Andinos.

Murúa, Martín de. 1946 [1590]. *Historia del origen y genealogía real de los reyes del Perú.* Madrid: C. Bermejo.

Ong, Walter J. 1988. *Orality and Literacy: The Technologizing of the Word.* London and New York: Routledge.

Pärssinen, Martti. 1992. *Tawantinsuyu: The Inca State and Its Political Organization.* Helsinki: Societas Historica Finlandiae, Studia Historica #43.

Porras Barrenechea, Raúl. 1986. *Los cronistas del Perú (1528–1650).* Biblioteca Clásicos del Perú No. 2. Lima: Banco de Crédito del Perú.

Rousseau, Jean-Jacques. 1966 [1817]. *Essay on the Origin of Language.* Translated by John H. Moran and Alexander Gode. New York: N.p.

Salomon, Frank, and George L. Urioste. 1991. *The Huarochirí Manuscript: A Testament of Ancient and Colonial Andean Religion.* Austin: University of Texas Press.

Sampson, Geoffrey. 1985. *Writing Systems.* Stanford: Stanford University Press.

Troike, Nancy P. 1990. "Pre-Hispanic Pictorial Communication: The Codex System of the Mixtec of Oaxaca, Mexico." *Visible Language* 24, no. 1: 74–87.

Urton, Gary. 1994. "A New Twist in an Old Yarn: Variation in Knot Directionality in the Inka *Khipu*s." *Baessler-Archiv,* Neue Folge, Band 42: 271–305.

——— (with Primitivo Nina Llanos). 1997. *The Social Life of Numbers: A Quechua Ontology of Numbers and Philosophy of Arithmetic.* Austin: University of Texas Press.

———. 1998. "From Knots to Narratives: Reconstructing the Art of Historical Record-Keeping in the Andes from Spanish Transcriptions of Inka *Khipu*s." *Ethnohistory* 45, no. 3: 409–438.

———. 2001. "A Calendrical and Demographic Tomb Text from Northern Peru." *Latin American Antiquity* 12, no. 2: 127–147.

Von Hagen, Adriana, and Sonia Guillén. 1998. "Tombs with a View." *Archaeology* 51, no. 2 (March–April): 48–54.

Zamora, Margarita. 1988. *Language, Authority, and Indigenous History in the "Comentarios reales de los Incas."* Cambridge: Cambridge University Press.

Yncap Cimin Quipococ's Knots

NINE   *Jeffrey Quilter*

CONTEXT: TEXT AND TWINE INTERTWINED

The knot records that the Inka called khipu have fascinated scholars and lay-men alike for centuries. But despite such long interest, our understanding of these assemblages of strings is still quite limited. The chief questions schol-ars of the Andean past ask about them often concern issues of how they were "read" in the past and how we may or may not be able to read them today. In this chapter, I discuss some issues relating to the study of khipu. My dis-cussion will focus on two issues: the relative standardization or diversity of khipu systems, and the interrelated matter of who might have read them. As a possible aid in approaching these topics, I provide two sections of case studies on three other communication systems: the telegraph, stenography, and the development of writing in the Near East.

There are two principal means by which khipu are studied: (1) examina-tion of the physical structure and nature of khipu, and (2) reading what the Spanish chroniclers wrote about them in the years after the conquest of the Inka. Relatively few khipu have been found in archaeological excavations, and even when they are so encountered, their circumstances of recovery usually do not provide the kinds of contexts that help archaeologists determine the uses of other remains such as tools and implements. A third line of investiga-tion uses transcriptions of khipu read in colonial courtrooms and other legal venues. This field of study is relatively new but holds great promise in helping us link knots to words through the intermediary of writing.

The apparent intransigence of khipu in yielding the code(s) to their decipherment lies, in large measure, in the nature of the objects themselves. The messages of true writing have considerable independence from the means of their inscription in the sense that written messages can be placed on many different kinds of surfaces. Maya glyphs, for example, are found on jade pendants, ceramic vessels, in books (codices), and carved on monuments and buildings. These were produced by chisels, paint brushes, and other tools. But khipu are khipu: the medium and the message appear to be intertwined in a way in which writing and the surfaces on which it is placed are not. There is thus an irony in approaching khipu in comparison to the decipherment of hieroglyphs. Because writing is free to be placed almost anywhere desired, the contexts the hieroglyphs were given when inscribed in books, on monuments, and on walls have aided in interpreting them. Even John Lloyd Stephens assumed that glyphs on Maya stelae were saying something about the persons carved on those same stones. Though the breaking of the Maya hieroglyphic code was a long and difficult process, nevertheless, the links between writing and the places it was found were valuable aids in decipherment (Coe 1992). But the khipu remain mute in their independent existence. We do not have the same kinds of associations of the "writing" of khipu as occur with hieroglyphs; no system analogous to knot records was carved on walls or statues, at least none of which we are aware.

The intertwining of form and meaning in khipu does offer one line of investigation that is tied to the empirical nature of these knotted strings. The fact that khipu are textiles, with methods of construction and meanings expressed through variation in the manipulation of threads, offers the possibility of approaching an understanding of them from the perspective of textiles, as William Conklin does in Chapter 3 of this book.

Of course, khipu were not independent in the past; they were made and used by people in a complex cultural web. Who first made and used them is unclear. As Conklin (Chapter 3, this book) notes, Middle Horizon (ca. A.D. 550–900) khipu are known. But this is already considerably late in the history of Andean culture, and it is surprising that we do not have earlier examples. The stringy, portable nature of khipu suggests ancient origins in the mobile lifeways of hunters and gatherers. The use of snares, slings, and other rope work was an essential part of survival, especially in mobile hunting societies. Tying knots to keep count of game seen or baskets of food gathered would have come naturally to the earliest occupants of the New World, who have left so little evidence of their skills save, mostly, for chipped-stone tools. So, too, knots are well known in maritime cultures, and the Andes is the locus of one of the great early seagoing traditions in the world. Still, we have no evidence for early khipu use, even though a wealth of textile evidence is available for as early as 5000 B.C. in the coastal fishing villages of Peru (see Quilter 1989).

Apparently, it is in the Andean highland cultures where khipu first appeared, although, ironically, no preserved examples of the string records come from the highlands. As with other highland styles of fiber and textile objects, our best examples come from the coast. This complicates matters somewhat, since there is a lingering uncertainty as to whether what appear to be highland styles found on the coast are truly highland, rather than an amalgam of styles. As khipu were portable recording devices, the places where they were found present compounded problems concerning the significance of where they were found, where they may have been made, and their history of use and transport before their deposition into the archaeological record. It raises questions about the standardization of khipu and their uses and, in turn, about the nature of the Inka bureaucracy that utilized them. These issues will be discussed in some detail below.

It may be no accident that knotted-string records apparently were most elaborated in the region where the only native herd animals in ancient America were domesticated. As in hunting and fishing, herding South American camelids requires the use of ropes, and keeping count of male, female, young, and old llamas and alpacas is an essential part of herd management, as both Carol Mackey and Tristan Platt discuss in this book (Chapters 13 and 10, respectively). Until clear evidence of khipu precursors is found, however, their origins must remain open to question, and the fact that khipu are only in evidence at the same time as the emergence of bureaucratic expansionist states— in the Middle and Late Horizons—must be seen as a significant factor in understanding them.

In Mexico, the Spanish made the clerks of the Mexica Aztec state write down tribute lists so that revenues could be appropriated by the conquerors. This and other circumstances led to the creation of documents that preserved and transmitted, to greater or lesser degrees, the native notational system, often mixed with or annotated in Spanish. In the Viceroyalty of Peru, no such mix could occur because the Inka had no writing system. Khipu did continue in use in native hands, however, and in some cases they were transcribed in court cases and other venues in which native and Spaniard interacted (see Urton, Chapter 8; Platt, Chapter 10; and Harrison, Chapter 11, this book), as previously mentioned. But whereas we know that a particular Aztec symbol is a place-name for a specific locale or that another indicates a particular kind of tribute, we do not have the same kind of close annotation for khipu.

Though we may hope that archival research will provide more examples of specific links between khipu forms and their meanings, for now there is a gap between the meanings of khipu as known from transcriptions and how the system of recording on and "reading" from khipu actually worked. Thus, we must depend upon the writings of chroniclers, most of whom did not make or use khipu themselves, to tell us what these knotted strings were about. As in so many other areas of the early colonial and preconquest worlds, these chroniclers often do not provide straightforward and clear answers to our questions.

DIVERSITY AND STANDARDIZATION OF KHIPU IN THE INKA IMPERIAL BUREAUCRACY

The chroniclers are consistent in stating that there were various imperial officials who served as secretaries for the purposes of running the empire. According to Guaman Poma de Ayala (1980: 331), the secretary of the Inka himself was called Yncap Cimin Quipococ, and the "viceroy" also had a personal secretary. There was a secretary for the royal council and two classes of secretaries for the officials of the royal court. One of these groups is said to have been in charge of "iconography" (*encargado de la iconografía*), a rather unclear statement on Guaman Poma's part. The other group kept count of the calendars, including the months, years, and festival days. In addition to these secretaries, there was an important state official in charge of a bureau that kept track of state taxes and the census.

The evidence suggests that khipu literacy was not widespread outside of those bureaucrats charged with keeping records, for the chroniclers state that only khipukamayuq could read the knotted strings and there are repeated references to Inka monarchs sending for khipukamayuq to read their khipu. As in the case of European medieval kings, reading and recording probably were skills left to servants, so rulers did not have to master them themselves.

Guaman Poma is quite clear on the importance of the "keepers of the khipu," or the khipukamayuq. He says, "With these cords the entire realm was governed" (Guaman Poma 1980: 331). He says that there were khipu keepers in every community for judges and rulers as well as for the ubiquitous tax officials. It is because of the emphasis that Guaman Poma and other chroniclers place on the bureaucratic role of khipukamayuq that one of the chief problems in understanding the knotted strings arises. At the same time that the role of the khipu keepers as organs of state power is emphasized, claims are also made that the khipu could only be read by their makers. Bernabé Cobo, in particular, emphasizes this point:

However, not all of the Indians were capable of understanding the *quipos;* only those dedicated to this job could do it; and those who did not study *quipos* failed to understand them. Even among the *quipo camayos* themselves, one was unable to understand the registers and recording devices of others. Each one understood the *quipos* that he made and what the others told him.   (COBO 1979: 254)

But Garcilaso de la Vega claims to have learned to read khipu himself as a young man in Peru. He states that he read the khipu brought to him by the retainers of his father as they brought their goods to him on feast days to be tallied with the accounts on the khipu (see Urton, Chapter 8, this book). This means that at least some khipu were intelligible on some level by those who had not made them. Granted, the khipu makers may have been available to instruct young Garcilaso on their particular recording system, but an efficient accounting of goods brought in, especially in a short period of time as on a feast day, necessitated that one could learn such systems rapidly and that there was little variation between the recording system of one khipu and another. If we had more information on the numbers of retainers who came to the estate, the kinds of goods they brought, and the way in which they interacted with their masters, it might add much to our ability to better understand khipu. Though we may lament that this information is lacking, this case demonstrates how aspects of early colonial life seemingly unrelated to khipu might shed light on their nature and uses.

The research of L. Leland Locke (1923) presented in his *Ancient Quipu or Peruvian Knot Record* is one of the greatest advances to have occurred in understanding these records in modern times. Locke demonstrated that khipu displayed consistent decimal-place value patterns in the forms and placements of knots. A decimal system was used in which sections of pendant strings, hanging from the main, horizontal cord, were used to mark places of tens of thousands, thousands, hundreds, tens, and ones. Studies of khipu have shown that this system was widely followed, and today the numerical values of khipu are fairly easily determined. If young Garcilaso was reading these kinds of records, which stated quantities of sheep or llamas or units of grain, it suggests that Cobo's reference to khipu as not intelligible to anyone but their makers was misinformed. But perhaps Garcilaso de la Vega and Bernabé Cobo were both speaking truthfully. Perhaps they understood different aspects of the larger universe of khipu making and use in Peru. Perhaps there was not one single, master khipu system, but rather, a number of different systems in use at the same time.

As noted above, khipu are little in evidence before the Inka, but neither are they completely absent. This suggests that khipu were present and in use for probably five centuries or more, from the time of the Middle Horizon to the arrival of the Spaniards. The Middle Horizon was a period of relative unity in the Andes, with the dominance of economic and political entities centered at Tiwanaku, Bolivia, and Huari, Peru. The collapse of those systems might have curtailed the growth of large-scale bureaucracies and the need for khipu, but a number of different polities of substantial size remained in the central Andes, nonetheless. It thus seems reasonable to believe that there were local traditions of khipu making out of which developed the Inka system.

Recently, arguments have been made (Bauer 1992; D'Altroy, Lorandi, and Williams in press) that the Inka Empire developed over a much longer period than the accepted short chronology of about 150 years. Even if the amount of time it took the Inka to become an empire was doubled, however, crucial questions remain as to the origins of a khipukamayuq bureaucracy and the length of time it took for its recording system to develop. With conquest or other forms of incorporation of different ethnic groups, no matter what the pace, it is likely that the Inka would have absorbed people with different recording systems into their realm. Alternatively, the Inka could have developed the khipu system themselves as a means to control their growing empire. The varying comments on the ability of khipu to be read or not by different chroniclers suggests, however, that there were different kinds of khipu or different kinds of khipu systems in the empire.

A diversity in record-keeping systems might help explain apparent contradictions in the chronicles: why Garcilaso de la Vega could state that he learned how to read khipu while Cobo claims that only the makers of khipu could read them. If the diversity were due to the incorporation of different khipu systems as a result of imperial expansion, then Cusco, as the seat of the empire, would have been the place in all of the Andes with the greatest variety of khipu and khipukamayuq. Perhaps there were some constants in the total system and mutual intelligibility, to greater or lesser degrees, among khipu keepers from the same regional tradition. Such variability might also explain why it is said that when the Sapa Inka consulted his khipukamayuq, he called *many* of them to assemble. Redundancy in record keeping helps prevent mistakes and loss of records—each Inka community had a minimum of four khipukamayuq—but different groups using their own systems would have added another means of checking if the record of one individual or group was accurate, just as preserving modern office records in different media—"hard copy," hard drives, floppy disks, tapes, and so on in terms of hardware, and "Text Only" files and various software-program formats in terms of software—enhances both the preservation and transmission of information.

We know that some forms of redundancy were in the system by the fact that Cobo (1979: 91) states that when Inka Yupanqui defeated the Soras, he had made two of each of the khipu recording the amounts of tribute for the vanquished; one was to be kept by the defeated lord so that he would know how much to pay in tribute, and one was for the Inka records. Were the different khipu made in different "scripts," one local and one Inkaic ("Quechua"?)? Does the double recording suggest that a "foreign" style, in this case, that of the Inka, could be learned by the Soras fairly quickly? Were Inka khipu-kamayuq posted in Soras to read the khipu and keep additional accounts, of tribute, for example? One suspects that both of the khipu would have been made in the same manner to make sure that the records were identical, thus suggesting that either a common khipu notational system was shared by both Inka and Soras or that one group was able to learn the khipu system of the other quickly.

The unity brought to the central Andes under the Inka Empire was quite new. Though all the members of the imperial government had to know the general language (Damián de la Bandera [1557], cited in Rowe 1982: 96), much of the populace spoke their own local tongue. Inka Quechua is part of a language area south of the region of its original development, but it was the language of empire and was spread by it, even if the present-day distribution is more due to the promulgation of the language by the Spanish as a lingua franca (Mannheim 1991; Urton 1997: 9).

It is likely that the Inka imposed similar record-keeping systems on every group they conquered. Certainly, for those groups that had no khipu tradition, the Inka imposed their own system. For groups that had their own styles of khipu, we do not know what arrangements might have been made. This pattern does suggest, however, a possible line of future archaeological research. If enough information can eventually be gleaned on the provenience of recovered Inka-era khipu, and if assumptions can be made on the likelihood of previous or local khipu traditions, then we can begin to search for patterns in the degree of variance between khipu from conquered provinces and those from securely identified Inka contexts. For example, if the Huari state had khipu, and if this tradition lasted to the time of the Inka, then do Inka-era khipu found in the area of modern-day Ayacucho, which was the heart of the Huari state, differ in significant ways from khipu more likely the product of Inka khipukamayuq from Cusco? We are a long way from being able to address this kind of problem, but it is potentially feasible to do in the future and it may reveal significant information about how khipu worked, even if we cannot "read" what khipu may say.

A project such as this has already been done. Gary Urton (1994: 284–287) studied a set of ninety-nine khipu in the Museum für Völkerkunde, Berlin, which had provenience information dividing the collection into groups from four distinct regions of the Peruvian coast (near Lima, Pachacamac, Ica/Pisco, and Nazca). No compelling regional patterns were detected in the frequency of different knot types and their combinations among the khipu of the four provenience zones, however. Still, with continued efforts in this kind of analysis, future studies may detect discernible patterns of interest that will inform us as to the nature of khipu in the Inka realm.

COMPARATIVE STUDY: THE TELEGRAPH AND STENOGRAPHY

The fact that the Inka Empire was a fairly recent phenomenon that incorporated different ethnic units and required a useful system of record keeping and communication encourages examination of situations analogous to the development of the Inka Empire and khipu. The telegraph and stenography are apt cases in point as both were introduced into Western European culture at times of political expansion and cultural changes that called for better means of communication over great distances.

The telegraph is a device emphasizing the transmission of information, while stenography was developed to record information quickly and accurately. The telegraph is a means to transmit coded words, whereas stenography is a form of abbreviated writing. Writing only enters into telegraphy when there is a desire to preserve decoded messages, perhaps analogous to the preservation of words on a khipu. Since we are interested in the degree to which khipu could be read, these two systems of communication provide interesting cases for comparison.[1]

The concept of sending messages via electricity was first publicly suggested in an anonymous letter to the *Scots Magazine* in 1753. The system was complicated, though, involving separate electrical cables for each letter of the alphabet. Practical application did not occur until the mid-nineteenth century, after Samuel Morse's invention in 1838. A number of systems were subsequently developed very quickly, but the one most commonly represented in popular media—of the telegraph operator clicking Morse code on a handset—was not the primary one, at first. Some of the earliest systems emphasized the transmission of individual letters directly, in modified versions of the idea originally proposed in 1753. One of the most common applications

COLOR PHOTO 1 An Inka khipu made entirely of natural colors of cotton (7308/P.C.).

COLOR PHOTO 2 During the plying of this cotton khipu, short threads of brightly dyed alpaca were introduced (6824/P.C.).

COLOR PHOTO 3 Constructed representation of part of Cristóbal de Molina's story of the Inka ritual cord called Moro-urco.

COLOR PHOTO 4 The reverse plying and long knots of the primary cord announce the dominant characteristics of this particular khipu. The long knots on the primary cord are like those found in abundance in the secondary cords (AMNH B/8705; author photo).

COLOR PHOTO 5 Construction of khipu cords by doubled and interlocked replying.

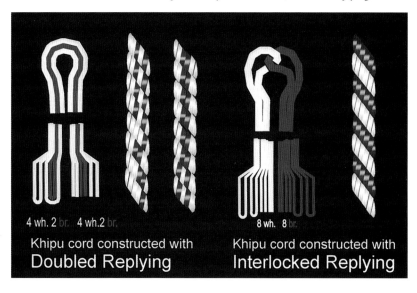

4 wh. 2 br.   4 wh.2 br.

8 wh.   8 br.

Khipu cord constructed with
Doubled Replying

Khipu cord constructed with
Interlocked Replying

COLOR PHOTO 6 Primary cord (left) consisting of two-ply, two-color S-plied cords joined by Z spiraling single-colored simple cord (AMNH 41.2/6715).

COLOR PHOTO 7 Group of six variegated secondary cords linked together by a top cord (left of center; see color photo 1 for complete khipu; 7308/P.C.).

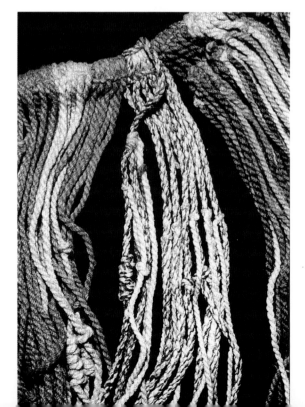

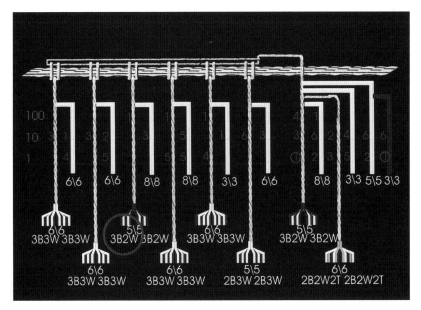

COLOR PHOTO 8   Diagram of the construction of the six secondary cords, together with their top cord, shown in color photo 7. 3B2W = 3 brown and 2 white elements. Knot values, in their relative decimal positions, are shown adjacent to the cords.

COLOR PHOTO 9   Microphotograph of one-half of cord circled in color photo 8 (labeled 3B2W).

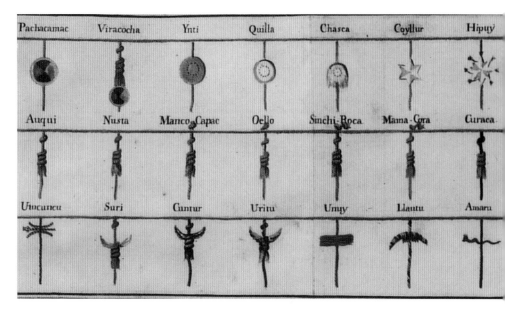

Pachacamac	Viracocha	Ynti	Quilla	Chasca	Coyllur	Hipuy
Auqui	Nusta	Manco Capac	Oello	Sinchi-Roca	Mama-Cora	Curaca
Uiucuncu	Suri	Cuntur	Uritu	Umiy	Llautu	Amaru

COLOR PHOTO 10   Khipu signs from Raimondo di Sangro's *Lettera apologetica* (1750).

COLOR PHOTO 11   *Pachacamanta*, or end ornament, of Quipocamayo 1G-01, belonging to Ayllu Primer Huangre. Note metal-wound threads making up the "Turk's head" ornamentation.

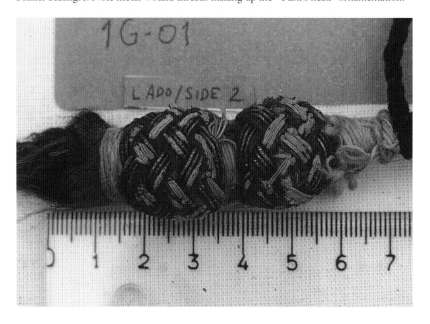

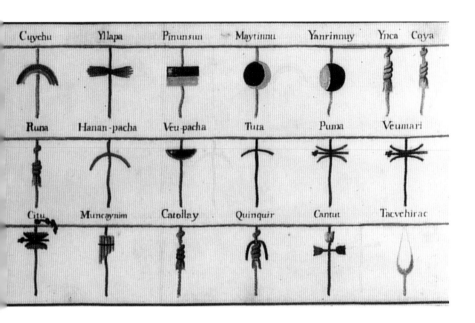

Cuychu	Yllapa	Pimunsun	Maytinnu	Yanrinnuy	Ynca	Coya

Runa	Hanan-pacha	Veu-pacha	Tuta	Puma	Veumari

Citu	Muncaynim	Catollay	Quinquir	Cantut	Tacychirac

COLOR PHOTO 12   Pendant 5 of Segunda Satafasca's Quipocamayo 2SF-01 contains a "Tupicocha" long knot.

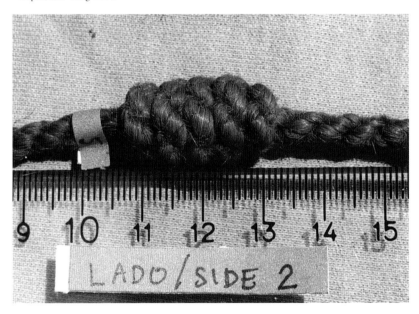

COLOR PHOTO 13 In Pendants 29–31 of Unión Chaucacolca's Quipocamayo Uch-01, *pallaris* (bicolors) of "mottled" structure vary in diameter by a ratio of 1 to 3.

COLOR PHOTO 14 Seen in radial array, Ayllu Primera Allauca's Quipocamayo 1A-01 shows unstandardized placement of knots on pendants.

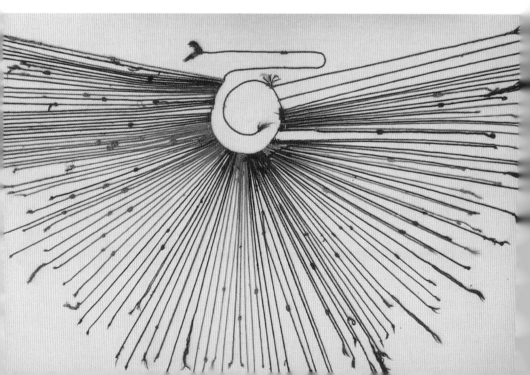

was a ratchet-wheel mechanism used to point a dial at individual letters, in sequence. This information was sent by wire to a similar device that duplicated the letter sequence on an identical receiving mechanism, and the letters were then copied to form words. The system was extremely slow, although it was used into the twentieth century when speed was not important. It was highly accurate, with little room for error, and it was *visual*, since the sender and receiver communicated by looking at letters indicated on the ratchet wheel.

The ratchet-wheel telegraph was slow and cumbersome. Furthermore, as is common in bureaucratic societies of all kinds, it was not simply the ability to send a message that was important to the state (or businesses) but also the ability to preserve the message after it was sent. So, early telegraph inventors sought ways to develop recording devices. One system was Lord Kelvin's Siphon Recorder, patented in 1867. A long strip of paper, similar to those of the more familiar (and also obsolete) ticker-tape machine, received a rapid series of ink dots. Deflection to one side or the other of the center line of the paper determined whether the message was a dot or a dash.

Despite what might appear to be the inherent advantages of the Kelvin system and others, telegraph operators found that they could hear messages being sent as fast as they were being transmitted by *listening* to the click of the recording armature against its stop. This is the "classic" Morse code transmission and receiving system commonly depicted in films and other popular media.

Listening freed the hands and eyes to read and write. Although various systems that allowed for the direct transmission of code onto paper persisted throughout the history of telegraph use, the standard use of telegraphs—when copies were not essential—was through hearing the code transmitted. It is also noteworthy that attempts to elaborate the sound system, through the use of bells, for example, failed; the simple click of the armature against its stop was preferable to attempts to make the system "better." This is an interesting case in which an aspect of the original transmission and receiving system became more important than originally intended; it could not be improved upon by the introduction of more complicated or elaborate hardware.

As far as the actual "code" used for transmitting messages by telegraph, even as late as 1911 there were two major ones in use: "Morse's International" and "Morse's American." What is particularly striking about these two systems is that they were very similar to each other, yet they had significant differences: both were composed of "dots" and "dashes," but the specific combinations that signified letters were somewhat different in each system. One would assume that closely related systems with significant differences would have led to greater confusion than widely differing systems. Only by sending an opening statement announcing the system in which the following message was encoded could confusion be avoided. Even so, operators had to learn at least two systems, and messages received in which the opening address was lost were prone to mistranslation until a pattern could be recognized to indicate one code as opposed to the other.

These issues in the development of telegraphy may have relevance for our attempts to understand khipu. Very similar systems—"dots" and "dashes" or Z and S knots—potentially can signify different code systems. At the same time, however, differences in two similar systems can be tolerated. An initial message signaled which Morse code system was to be used. Even if this opening message was lost, a good operator could determine which system was being used by looking for inconsistencies in the message as written down or even while hearing it. The confusion caused by the lack of a single standardized system was not so great as to disrupt the entire enterprise of using the telegraph as a means of communication. Presumably, a similar level of inconsistency could have existed in khipu yet still have allowed the overall system to work tolerably well.

An even better example of the struggle to work out a uniform coding system and the tolerance of diversity over long periods of time is to be found in the history of shorthand. Shorthand has considerable antiquity. Although there is debate on earlier forms, by the fourth century B.C. a system of abbreviated writing was used in Greece, and Tiro, ex-slave and secretary of the Roman orator M. Tullius Cicero (143–106 B.C.), later developed a shorthand known as "Tironian notae" (Daniels 1996a: 807). Although some forms of shorthand existed in medieval times, not until the sixteenth century do we have evidence of a variety of new systems being proposed. The impetus for revival seems to have been the emphasis on the word, written and spoken, during the Reformation and the desire to preserve sermons as accurately as possible; in Britain, the reporting of parliamentary debates (Daniels 1996a: 811) was another incentive. Dr. Timothy Bright (ca. 1551–1615) invented a system that was based on an arbitrary sign for each distinct word, making it almost impossible to learn. Other attempts, such as those by Peter Blake (1547?–1610) and John Willis (d. 1627), who coined the term "stenographie," were similarly awkward, although Willis was the first to attempt a system based on phonetics. Earlier systems tended to depend on initial letters or arbitrary signs.

In addition to exploring the use of arbitrary signs, erstwhile inventors began to focus on the problem of vowels: how to distinguish "pauper" from "paper," for example, if the vowels were omitted to produce "ppr." The efforts of these people are all the more admirable when one considers that English was not fully standardized in its written form until well into the eighteenth century.

Spurred by the considerable profits to be made from devising an efficient shorthand method that could be used by accelerating commerce and industry, inventors proposed seven different systems based on phonetics alone between 1750 and 1839, not counting numerous other attempts based on different principles. It was only with the 1837 publication of Sir Isaac Pitman's shorthand, which used a purely phonetic system, that a method was produced that attracted wide usage and greater standardization. By 1894, 95 percent of British newspaper reporters used Pitman, and it still remains the most popular system in Britain.

John Robert Gregg, adopting a more cursive script than Pitman and choosing the easiest-made shapes for the most common sounds in English, invented the other recent popular shorthand. Through self-promotion and salesmanship, his system became the principal method used in the United States (Daniels 1996a: 813–814).

Even so, considerable variation remained. After being instructed and trained in a system, professional stenographers often developed their own, usually minor, variations of the standard methods, just as those trained in penmanship develop their own handwriting styles, although variance too far from the taught system would make the notes of one person uninterpretable by another. So, too, local and regional shorthand systems with limited distributions were introduced. For example, a local man of influence invented his own stenographic system in the region around Springfield, Illinois, in the 1950s and successfully convinced judges and court officials to use it for some time (D. McAnulty, personal communication, 1999). The Springfield system would have been unreadable, or at least difficult to interpret, by those not familiar with it, even though the system itself was a form of the general category called "shorthand."

The lessons to be learned from these two examples of the development of communications and recording systems are many. First, both systems began, as do languages themselves, with a high degree of variability: competing coding systems were devised and a variety of encoding mechanisms were tried. The same is true in modern-day development of computer hardware technology and software programs: as but one example, there are well over one hundred computer languages in use today (see Bergin and Gibson 1996). Both systems, to greater and lesser degrees, also began by attempting to follow previously existing methods of communication. The telegraph sent individual letters of the alphabet in the same way that a person would orally spell out a word. The earliest stenographic systems often utilized a key set of words or an abstract symbol representing a key word, augmented by letters for the specific word in question. Both systems became much more efficient when they stopped trying to follow the "parent" system of writing and found more efficient systems: telegraph operators switched to relying on their ears, and stenography became based on phonemes, not words, and used a system of cursive lines instead of letters. For everyday use, telegraph systems went a step further by abandoning direct recording in favor of freeing the hands of operators to transcribe what they heard. But neither telegraphy nor stenography was ever completely standardized. Although there was some movement toward greater standardization in the codes used and in the technical aspects of their transmission, reception, and, in the case of telegraphy, recording, for both telegraphy and stenography a high degree of variability was maintained. Political and social factors, such as the case of unique stenographic methods promulgated in local areas, also maintained diversity, even if we might think that factors of efficiency would have encouraged greater standardization.

A final point of consideration must be raised in regard to the modern origins of stenography. The fact that it developed as a way to record sermons is of signal importance because it emphasizes the severe limitations encountered by most nonliterate societies in their abilities to keep accurate records of speeches and other oral communications. In literate societies, written versions of public addresses might have been made prior to their delivery, but in many instances the only way a record could be made of what was said by someone was through reliance on the memories of the speaker and the listeners. Of course, writing existed for many centuries prior to the development of stenography in Europe, for such things as religious worship, court records, and other important documents, but these forms of written communication could be copied or composed without the psychological pressure of recording words quickly before they faded from memory.

The chroniclers consistently note that the Inka, as did many nonliterate societies, emphasized speech making, songs, poetry, and other forms of oral performance. Without any means of rapidly recording language as it was spoken or sung, the Inka would have had to rely on memory in order to later record the texts on khipu, just as pre-stenography Europeans would have done. The first "World's Shorthand Championship" was held in London in 1908. The winner of that event recorded an average of 220 words per minute for a period of five minutes. The average rate of public speaking, in British

English, at the turn of the century was between 120 and 150 words per minute. Though the rapidity of speech may vary from culture to culture, even if we assume that the slowest world rate might be about 60 to 75 words per minute, this still is a considerable amount of verbiage to be recorded in writing by someone listening to a talk without prior knowledge of what was to be said.

The same was true for the Inka. If khipu did record speeches, they would have been created *after* an oration was made. This raises two interesting points, however. First, it reiterates the fact that the Inka, like most people in most places in the world until relatively recent times, depended on memory to a considerable degree in many of their everyday and more official dealings that required some record keeping of what had been said. The second point may actually support the notion that speeches were recorded on khipu. If the points of a speech or other oral presentation were well remembered, it would be a fairly simple matter to abstract it into a series of main points, secondary points, and so on in the same way that a public speaker today might outline a speech before it is to be given. The act of abstracting a speech into a hierarchy of "opening statement," "secondary statement," "closing statement," and so forth lends itself to the kind of formal organization observable in khipu. Thus, that khipu could have served to record narratives and prose seems to fit well with what we know knotted records are capable of recording.

READING AND NARRATIVES

Were histories, poems, and more narrative, nonactuarial prose maintained on the same kinds of khipu that served as accounting ledgers? This is another of the perennial questions regarding khipu. In Chapter 4 of this book, Marcia Ascher demonstrates how a string of numbers can serve to provide a narrative: our social security numbers, zip codes, telephone numbers, and the plethora of digits that are given to or kept by us can be strung together to say who we are, where we live, and much more. Is this how narrative khipu worked?

One compelling piece of evidence for the ability to "read" a khipu made by someone else is to be found in a discussion and illustration by Guaman Poma (1980: 178) of a boy running with a khipu in his hand (Figure 9.1). The khipu is labeled "letter" (*carta*). The discussion occurs in the context of Guaman Poma's recounting of the stages of life among the Inka. He states that boys between eight and ten years old were given in service to the state to carry messages from one town to the other and to other locations in their valleys. Could boys this age have been literate in khipu so that they could read the messages they carried? Although it is possible, one suspects that this was not

FIGURE 9.1 A messenger boy (Guaman Poma 1980: 178).

FIGURE 9.2 A *chasqui* (Guaman Poma 1980: 757).

the case, but rather that the boys were used for their legs more than their reading abilities, if any. The implication in the Guaman Poma account is that boys, in general, were used as messengers at this stage in their lives; this is not a section of his account about khipukamayuq in training. If the message could be delivered by the messenger, then why send the khipu? Perhaps for accuracy or because the message was fairly long or because the kind of information being sent on the khipu was special, such as that it was needed for future reference when the messenger would not be present. Nevertheless, it seems probable, although arguable, that if ten-year-olds were used to deliver khipu, they would not be able to read them, and, thus, the khipu they carried were communications composed by a person in one place and read by a different person in another place, albeit not too far away from the point of khipu creation, presumably within a local or regional khipu encoding system.

The little sign on the khipu in Guaman Poma's drawing is particularly intriguing. Guaman Poma consistently labeled the actors and objects in the scenes he drew, but he usually did so in a free-flowing hand near the identified image or within the drawing itself, in "blank" space. The *chasqui* and dog are so labeled in Figure 9.2. He almost never placed small labels such as this one on his objects. One of the few other examples is his labeling of the flags held by Almagro and Pizzaro (Guaman Poma 1980: 38) in the scene of the flotilla of conquest. Those labels are similar to the *carta* sign in the banner/plaque-like forms of both and, perhaps, in the fact that the objects inscribed in their picture form were themselves meant to serve as signs in actuality.

The only other example of a sign such as that shown on the messenger carrying the khipu appears in his drawing of a *chasqui* (Guaman Poma 1980: 756–757), one of the messengers who ran the Inka roads transmitting brief verbal statements of importance (Figure 9.2). The *chasqui* depicted by Guaman Poma carries a little sign in his hand, somewhat bigger than the one carried by the youth with the khipu, but of the same design. The writing on this plaque cannot be easily deciphered. Nevertheless, it seems significant that both a messenger who relied on his vocal cords and a khipu have the same object linked to them. Perhaps little signs such as the one pictured by Guaman Poma were in actual use.

It may also be valuable to reflect on the *chasqui* system itself in relation to khipu. Garcilaso recognized a connection between the two, witnessed by the fact that he discussed them together, shifting from describing *chasqui* to describing khipu. In fact, he implies that khipu were carried by *chasqui*, but in the section in question, it is not clear if he is discussing khipu and *chasqui* as two different communication methods or if he is deliberately linking *chasqui* with khipu. Although this passage is unclear, other discussions emphasize the role of spoken messages in the *chasqui* service. All the chroniclers who discuss them (and most do) emphasize that the *chasqui* transmitted short oral messages, repeated several times so that the next runner in the chain could memorize it as he began to run. Surely, if khipu were effective means of transmitting narratives, it would have been much easier to give a *chasqui* a khipu and tell him to be on his way. There would have been much less chance of messages being incorrectly transmitted if a khipu could be made at one end of the empire and easily read at the other end, rather than having to trust to even the most brief messages being repeated many times by *chasqui* after *chasqui*.

The fact that khipu were not part of a regular mail service, as it were, seems to add support to the notion that Inka khipu recording systems were heterogeneous, and that contradictory statements about them in the chronicles, such as that they were intelligible only to their makers and that they were sent as letters, are both true. One of the points made by Guaman Poma about the young messenger boys is that they only traveled relatively short distances, but we know that the *chasqui* covered many leagues in the service of the Inka. So, too, did khipukamayuq travel the empire with their records, but this suggests that the maker and the khipu needed to stay together. With planning, of course, two or more khipukamayuq who shared the same recording system could be posted at different locales in the empire to send and receive messages to one another, but this apparently was not frequently done or, at least, is not mentioned in the chronicles.

Although the ideal system may have called for a uniform khipu system, many an empire or modern-day state can be run efficiently even if its systems of record keeping are not consistent or uniform. The examples of the telegraph, stenography, and modern computers are cases in point.[2] More important than uniformity of the code is the control of the information encoded. So long as khipukamayuq were made responsible to the Inka state, diverse recording systems with less than universal intelligibility could be tolerated. The control of information and information makers was the key to power.

Bernabé Cobo states that there were many kinds of khipu to record different kinds of information: "such as for paying tribute, lands, ceremonies, and all kinds of matters pertaining to peace and war" (1979: 254). There is clear evidence that khipu had a role as accounting devices, and numeric values can easily be imagined for tribute payments and land records. But how does one keep track of ceremonies and "all kinds of matters pertaining to peace and war"? As Marcia Ascher shows in Chapter 4 of this book, an ingenious use of numbers could carry one very far in recording such information.

But does Cobo's statement about different kinds of khipu mean that there were khipu physically distinguishable from one another or that the same recording system was used to record different kinds of information? Garcilaso de la Vega (1966: 331–332) provides tantalizing but unclear language about historical and similar, presumably non-numeric, khipu. After distinctly stating that the knots can provide only numbers, not words, he writes:

> To supply this want they used signs [*señales*] that indicated historical events or facts or the existence of any embassy, speech, or discussion in time of peace or war. Such speeches were preserved by the *quipucamayus* by memory in a summarized form of a few words: they were committed to memory and taught by tradition to their successors and descendants from father to son.
>
> (GARCILASO DE LA VEGA 1966: 332
> [CF. GARCILASO DE LA VEGA 1991, 1:346])

In the sentence prior to this discussion, Garcilaso discusses khipu knots at length, but here the use of "signs" suggests some other kind of marker on the knotted-string record.

Guaman Poma's statement that there were two classes of secretaries for the royal council, one of which was in charge of "iconography," as noted above, hints at a group that would have benefited much by a khipu system suitable for holding narrative information as distinct from census records or astronomical data, both of which rely on numbers. A distinct sign in the form of a *tocapu*-like emblem, such as is carried by the messenger boy in Guaman Poma's drawing, could have helped a khipu reader to know that the knotted sequence that followed was to be interpreted differently than simply as a numeric value, although there may have been other ways to signal qualitative differences in the kind of information held on a khipu.[3]

COMPARATIVE STUDY: ARITHMETIC AND WRITING ORIGINS IN THE NEAR EAST

Although the examples of the development of the telegraph and stenography were useful in examining the processes by which new communication systems develop, they differ from khipu development in that both came into existence within cultures already literate. In the earliest creative attempts, systems were condensed forms of writing that served as a kind of baseline. But khipu are an example of a communication system that did not develop out of any earlier encoding system that we know of, or perhaps came out of systems so simple, such as keeping tallies by tying knots, that their invention might be better compared to that of writing than to stenography or the telegraph, which are outgrowths of writing.

Denise Schmandt-Besserat (1996) has spent decades studying the development of cuneiform in the Near East. Several aspects of her findings are relevant to khipu and thus worthy of discussion here. One important point she raises is that the development of writing in Mesopotamia lagged far behind socioeconomic developments. The rise of cities and the development of the temple institutions that received tribute occurred at least two centuries before the first pictographic writing. Contrary to previous evolutionary theory, she notes, writing did not enable the development of civilization, but rather came about because of the need for efficient means to keep records of increasingly complex economic transactions.

This relationship between the temple economy, record keeping, and writing in the Near East may serve as a lesson for students of the Andean khipu. We cannot extract the khipu from the larger social, cultural, and economic matrix in which they existed. In the Andes, although the data are not completely clear and although there is some debate on the matter, the evidence suggests that socioeconomic structures analogous to the temple/city complexes in the Near East did not exist for many centuries, even though other signs of "complexity" *do* exist (see Burger 1992). Only in the Early Intermediate Period (ca. 400 B.C.–A.D. 550), especially in its later part with the rise of Huari and Tiwanaku, can centers be identified that, with some certainty, seem to have combined religious, political, and economic enterprises on large scales, and it is exactly at that time that the first khipu we know of occur. The lack of khipu in earlier prehistoric eras might therefore not be as odd as it appears, even if they did grow out of some earlier system of keeping tallies and the like.

Schmandt-Besserat's work also sheds light on the question of how numerical khipu might have transmitted narrative information. The most surprising result of her investigations is that Near Eastern writing did not develop from pictographs for everyday objects (a drawing of a cow representing the animal, for example), but rather grew out of a system of clay tokens for counting and accounting goods, the earliest of which dated to the Neolithic, ca. 8000 B.C. (Schmandt-Besserat 1996: 7). Small, fire-hardened tokens formed into abstract shapes represented measures of grain, oil, and the like (a cone for a cup; a sphere for a large measure of grain; an ovoid for a jar of oil). These were sent or stored in "envelopes" made of hollow balls of clay.

The token system used a "concrete" form of counting; that is, there are no tokens that represent numbers, per se. Instead, if nine jars of oil were to be recorded, nine ovoid tokens were placed in an envelope in a one-to-one correspondence of token to the measurement it symbolized (Schmandt-Besserat 1996: 7). Tokens for groups of objects did exist, however, such as ten animals together, but numbers were always attached to a specific class of thing or creature. Because one could not see inside the sealed clay envelopes, accountants would imprint on the envelope surface the shapes of the tokens inside. Over time, it was realized that the markings on the envelope made the interior contents redundant, so solid round balls of clay with markings made directly on them replaced hollow clay balls containing tokens. These were the ancestors of clay tablets.

The same system of one-to-one correspondence for tokens was at first carried over to clay tablets. Again over time, however, numerals provided an economy in recording. Now, instead of depicting seven signs for seven measures of grain, a single numeral "7" was paired with a pictograph for the sign "measure of grain." The derivation of the pictograph was not directly from an actual measure of grain but from the already abstracted token that represented that measure (Schmandt-Besserat 1996: 83–84). Thus, the cone-shaped token was transformed into a triangular wedge symbol, which eventually evolved into true cuneiform writing.

In the evolution from tokens to writing, Schmandt-Besserat notes that the tokens were an advancement over previous forms of record keeping because they were made by humans (in contrast to pebble or grain counters) and because they were part of a system. The system made it possible to manipulate information about different kinds of items, allowing for a complexity of data processing and information storage previously impossible (Schmandt-Besserat 1996: 93–94). In addition, the system was open; new signs could be added when needed by creating new token shapes. It also seems likely that there was a rudimentary syntax for reading the tokens in a given envelope. Schmandt-Besserat (1996: 94) points out that signs on a tablet were organized in a hierarchical order, with the largest units placed on the right, and speculates that earlier accountants may have lined up their tokens in a similar arrangement.

Tokens presaged true writing in a number of their features, as shown in Table 9.1. Comparing what we know, what we can reasonably infer, and what is still uncertain about khipu (Table 9.2) with the early systems of the Near East highlights the challenges to future khipu studies. At first glance, comparison of the two systems suggests similar levels of sophistication and current knowledge. This is a hopeful sign, although, on closer inspection, many of the features are still uncertain for khipu studies, especially when questions other than those relating to numerals are raised. We likely could understand much more about these features of khipu through careful review of transcriptions of khipu readings and accounts of khipu being read during the colonial period.

One important difference between tokens and khipu is that the former could be used for calculations, whereas the latter were primarily records *of* calculations and accounts. Actual calculation of amounts before records were set in knots was likely done by the Inka using a device known as a *taptana*, still in use today in Ecuador (Figure 9.3). Though it appears to be a simple device of sets of holes made in a flat-surfaced stone or other material, it provides a sophisticated means of carrying out complex mathematical calculations. It was still in use among the Cañari of Ecuador in the early twentieth century (Arriaga 1922; Yanez Cossio 1985), and it seems highly likely that it or a very similar device was used by the Inka, as suggested by the "abacus" depicted by Guaman Poma (Figure 9.4) in one of his illustrations of a khipukamayuq.

Gary Urton's (1998) analysis of transcriptions of khipu "readings," particularly one dating to 1578 in Bolivia, is illuminating in light of these issues

TABLE 9.1.   Features of Near Eastern Token System and Writing (after Schmandt-Besserat 1996)

---

1. Semanticity: Each token was meaningful and communicated information.

2. Discreteness: The information conveyed was specific. Each token shape, as each pictograph, was bestowed a unique meaning.

3. Systematization: Each of the token shapes was systematically repeated in order to carry the same meaning.

4. Codification: The token system consisted of a multiplicity of interrelated elements (small measures, big measures, grain, oil, animals), allowing simultaneous handling of information concerning different items.

5. Openness: The repertory of tokens could be expanded by creating further shapes representing new concepts.

6. Arbitrariness: Many token forms were abstract; others were arbitrary representations (e.g., animal head with collar symbolized "dog").

7. Discontinuity: Tokens of closely related shapes could refer to unrelated concepts.

8. Independence of phonetics: Tokens were concept signs standing for units of goods. They were independent of spoken language and phonetics and thus could be understood by people speaking different tongues.

9. Syntax: Tokens were organized according to set rules, such as suggested alignment of counters of same kind, with largest units to the right of others.

10. Economic content: Tokens and earliest written texts were limited to handling information concerning real goods.

(see also Platt, Chapter 10, this book). One aspect of this transcription and discussion is the reference in the colonial document to the manipulation of stones on the ground, in combination with a khipu held in the hands. No mention is made of a *taptana* or similar device. One might assume that veteran khipukamayuq wouldn't necessarily need a *taptana*, since they could reproduce the general format of one on the ground, without having an actual board to hand.[4]

Another point of interest is that the khipu used in the transcribed court case held the record of unit prices of goods, not the grand total of all the units together, and when asked about the total number of any particular kind of item, the khipukamayuq used their calculating stones in combination with their khipu to arrive at the answer (Urton 1998: 414–417). Bearing in mind that there likely were different khipu-keeping traditions in the late prehistoric

TABLE 9.2.   Comparison of Khipu with Features of Near Eastern Token and Early Writing Systems

1. Semanticity: Present. Each knot, its place, and other characteristics of cords appear to have communicated information.

2. Discreteness: Present. Specific information was conveyed. Discrete meanings were made by type of knot and place value. Universality of discreteness cannot be determined beyond knot types and placement.

3. Systematization: Present. At least in terms of numeric values, the same knot shapes systematically carried the same meanings.

4. Codification: Present. Information concerning different items could be expressed on the same khipu.

5. Openness: Theoretically open. New colors, thread twists, etc., could expand repertory of categories on a khipu.

6. Arbitrariness: Arbitrariness in evidence. Presumably, colors, twists, and other characteristics of yarns indicated different categories of thought and things.

7. Discontinuity: Uncertain but likely, given high degree of arbitrariness.

8. Independence of phonetics: Uncertain. Naples khipu fragment and associated document claim phonetic links.

9. Syntax: Khipu were organized with set rules that included numeric place values and rank orders of classes.

10. Economic content: Khipu as a class are said to have recorded economic information, narratives, histories, and poems.

Andes, this seems an extremely important point. It suggests that, for at least these khipu, the knots themselves were indeed numerals and did not convey other kinds of information. This implies that the coding of other kinds of information, such as the kinds of goods numbered, was not in the knots but in other attributes of the khipu such as the color or twists of cords.

Schmandt-Besserat (1996: 121) notes that tokens were firmly tied to numbers. Although pictographs were derived from counting, they broke free of it, as discussed above, when the token for grain, which had to be repeated when more than one unit was meant, was changed to a symbol for the concept of a measure of grain, which could then be paired with a symbol for a number. She also notes that when pictographic tables began to be used, the field for recording provided by a tablet allowed for simple narrative, since the signs for the sponsor and the recipient of goods could be placed below signs repre-

FIGURE 9.3 A *taptana*. Reproduced with permission and courtesy of the Banco Central, Quito, Ecuador.

FIGURE 9.4 Khipukamayuq with "abacus," probably a version of the *taptana*, or stone calculating device (Guaman Poma 1980: 332).

senting goods: "In this fashion the scribe was able to transcribe information such as 'ten sheep received from Kulil' even though no particular signs were available to indicate verbs and prepositions."

Both of the points raised by Schmandt-Besserat regarding the possibilities for narrative in early forms of communication on clay also hold true for knotted-string records. Many of the knots clearly were numbers, but they may also have broken free to the point that a knot or other variable in the khipu system represented a concept, such as a unit of measure, which could then be paired with a knot signifying the number of specific items. This is one step toward narrative, and another is using relational information, such as the relation of colored cords or knots to one another or the relative positions of signs on a clay tablet.

Urton (1998) has referred to these kinds of issues in noting that the transcribed khipu required the recording of a full subject-object-verb construction in order to render the items listed on the khipu as intelligible. He suggests that the verb "to give" could have been marked in the knotted record once, perhaps on the primary cord. Marcia Ascher's discussion in Chapter 4 of this book is another example of how numbers can be used for narrative. Whatever the specific means by which verbs and their objects and subjects might have been recorded, strong arguments have been made in support of the potential for the expression of narrative in khipu.

Khipu and *taptana* may have been on their own vectors of change, and thus the path of development taken in the Andes may not necessarily have followed the same routes taken for tokens and pictographs in the Old World. However, using examples from a variety of early arithmetic and writing systems, in the time-honored tradition of cross-cultural comparison, may help to significantly advance our knowledge of the commonalties and distinct differences of khipu as recording devices and communication systems.

CONCLUDING REMARKS

Systematic study of khipu is a relatively recent phenomenon, and far fewer scholars have been attempting to unravel the secrets of the khipu than have tackled the complexities of Maya hieroglyphs. We still do not fully comprehend the variety extant among khipu. Given the fact that there is ample evidence for different khipu systems in the late prehistoric Andes, we may expect to find more varieties of khipu as research continues. The two largest collections of khipu consist of one of about 300 specimens in the Museum für Völkerkunde, Berlin, and another of 100 at the American Museum of Natural History, New York. With careful searching in other museums and smaller collections, the total number could easily be doubled. But even doubling the total number of khipu available for study would probably yield only a small fraction of the thousands of knotted-string records that must have existed throughout the Inka Empire—if the chronicles are to be believed.

In this chapter, I reviewed a number of lessons to be learned from contrasting some of the problems that face us in khipu studies with what is known about the early development of writing, the telegraph, and stenography. Three factors—diversity, redundancy, and "expendable" aspects of communication codes—were discussed for their relation to the development of communication systems. Initially, systems tend to show high degrees of diversity and then move toward increased standardization as they become more refined through time. Successful systems also reduce redundancy, although they can tolerate high degrees of it and still operate relatively well.

Similar to redundancy, expendable aspects of communication systems are commonly shed as they evolve, but they can also remain in use for some time.

As an example, Thomas Bauer (1996: 563) refers to the positive "effects of defectiveness," noting that some of the so-called defects of Arabic writing as it is commonly written today make it more readable, more widely accessible, and quicker to read and write than if, for example, all diacritical marks that could be added for absolute clarity were consistently used. So, too, Japanese *kanji* script allows multiple potential readings for each character, depending on the lexical context and sometimes even the larger textual environment (Smith 1996: 209–217). Thus, what may appear to be lack of rigor in communication systems can be used to advantage in a number of ways.

In studying khipu, then, we must not necessarily expect to find consistent systems that maximize efficiency. Instead, we are likely to find interesting systems that worked well enough for the purposes for which they were intended. It is worth considering that Morse code, even though it was based on an alphabet—not the most efficient means of communication, as stenography demonstrates—is carried out in the single dimension of time (Daniels 1996b: 887). It also uses a single variable—the presence or absence of sound, expressed in an on/off system—to communicate the complexities of language. If such a simple system can do so much, must not the khipu, with its different cords, knots, twists, colors, and more, be part of a system with a great potential for complex communication? The final lesson of our comparative study is that an absence of standardized scripts or signs is neither a sign of immaturity of a writing system nor of its inability to communicate complex messages. Lack of standardization often opens possibilities for communication while allowing for new developments in the system.

When Alexander the Great was confronted with the Gordian knot that no one could untie, he simply drew his sword and cut through it. The knotty problems tied to the great many khipu knots left by Yncap Cimin Quipococ and his legions of khipukamayuq have resisted scholarly unraveling, and we have yet to find an analytical sword that will provide a lightning-swift answer to our problems. But the field of study is still quite young, and textile work always takes time, as does decipherment.

ACKNOWLEDGMENTS

Thanks to Mrs. Dorothea McAnulty of Springfield, Illinois, for consultation on shorthand systems. Thanks to Tamara Estupiñán Viteri of the Banco Central, Ecuador, for providing me with information on *taptana*, an image of one, and permission to use it, and to Jorge Marcos for helping me get in touch with her. Gary Urton has been of very great help in offering comments on drafts of this chapter. It is he who has stimulated my interest in khipu, and I have learned much from him and the other fine scholars who investigate these issues. I thank him and them for inspiration and for their cordial collegiality as I have gradually developed some of my own ideas on these matters.

NOTES

1. Interestingly, despite an extensive bibliographic search, I found only one recent article on the history of stenography, Peter T. Daniels's (1996a) "Shorthand," and none on the history of telegraphy. Two entries in the *Encyclopaedia Britannica*, 11th edition (1911), however, discuss both stenography and telegraphy at length. Most of the ensuing discussion of these topics is from that publication: "Stenography," vol. 24: 1007–1013, and "Telegraph," vol. 26: 510–541.

2. As I write this, there is worldwide concern regarding the "2000," or Y2K, problem, when some computer programs will change their year indicators and records, kept only as units of ten, from "99" to "00." It has been noted that many large computer systems are running on programs for which there are few or no experts available. Although the problem is serious, this case emphasizes that, for many large organizations, it is the information itself that is seen as most important, whereas the means and systems to record it are given less attention than they might optimally require. It seems reasonable that in a rapidly expanding Inka Empire the same situation could have held true: that Inka officials were most concerned with having information available, whereas systematizing the means of record keeping was less important.

3. *T'oqapu* are abstract, geometric designs, usually quadrangular in shape, woven into Inka tapestry tunics. They are shown on tunics worn by Inka in the illustrations of Guaman Poma de Ayala. *T'oqapu* patterns resemble heraldic devices, and on some tunics there are complex patterns of repetition of *t'oqapu*. Some writers have suggested that the *t'oqapu* served as a form of writing. Rowe and Rowe (1996) discuss theories of *t'oqapu* in their analysis of a tunic completely covered in these designs. They conclude that, as a class, *t'oqapu* were signs of rank and nothing more.

4. Urton and Platt both note that the math done in these cases is extremely simple and may have been a validating performance rather than an actual calculation, in which case a *taptana* would be even less important than if complex math had been carried out.

REFERENCES CITED

Arriaga, Jesús. 1922. *Apuntes de arqueología del Cañar, Cuenca.* Cuenca, Ecuador: Imprenta del Cleso.

Bauer, Brian S. 1992. *The Development of the Inca State.* Austin: University of Texas Press.

Bauer, Thomas. 1996. "Arabic Writing." In *The World's Writing Systems*, edited by Peter T. Daniels and William Bright, 559–564. New York: Oxford University Press.

Bergin, Thomas J., Jr., and Richard G. Gibson, Jr., eds. 1996. *History of Programming Languages II.* Reading, Mass.: Addison-Wesley.

Burger, Richard L. 1992. *Chavín and the Origins of Andean Civilization.* London and New York: Thames and Hudson.

Cobo, Bernabe. 1979 [1653]. *History of the Inca Empire.* Translated by Roland Hamilton. Austin: University of Texas Press.

Coe, Michael D. 1992. *Breaking the Maya Code*. London and New York: Thames and Hudson.

D'Altroy, Terence, Ana María Lorandi, and Verónica Williams. In press. "The Inka Occupation of the South Andes." In *Variations in the Expression of Inka Power*, edited by R. Matos, R. Burger, and C. Morris. Symposium Volume. Washington, D.C.: Dumbarton Oaks.

Daniels, Peter T. 1996a. "Shorthand." In *The World's Writing Systems*, edited by Peter T. Daniels and William Bright, 807–820. New York: Oxford University Press.

———. 1996b. "Analog and Digital Writing." In *The World's Writing Systems*, edited by Peter T. Daniels and William Bright, 883–892. New York: Oxford University Press.

Garcilaso de la Vega, El Inca. 1966 [1609–1617]. *Royal Commentaries of the Incas and General History of Peru*. Translated by H. V. Livermore. Austin: University of Texas Press.

———. 1991. *Comentarios reales de los Incas*. 2 vols. Edición, prólogo, índice analítico y glosario de Carlos Araníbar. Lima; México; Madrid: Fondo de Cultura Económica.

Guaman Poma de Ayala, Felipe. 1980 [1612]. *El primer nueva corónica y buen gobierno*. Edited by John V. Murra and Rolena Adorno. Mexico City: Siglo Veintiuno.

Locke, L. Leland. 1923. *The Ancient Quipu or Peruvian Knot Record*. New York: American Museum of Natural History.

Mannheim, Bruce. 1991. *The Language of the Inka since the European Invasion*. Austin: University of Texas Press.

Quilter, Jeffrey. 1989. *Life and Death at Paloma: Society and Mortuary Practices in a Preceramic Peruvian Village*. Iowa City: University of Iowa Press.

Rowe, John H. 1982. "Inca Policies and Institutions Relating to the Cultural Unification of the Empire." In *The Inca and Aztec States, 1400–1800*, edited by G. A. Collier, R. I. Rosaldo, and J. D. Worth, 93–118. New York: Academic Press.

Rowe, Ann Pollard, and John Howland Rowe. 1996. "All-*T'oqapu* Tunic." In *Andean Art at Dumbarton Oaks*, vol. 2, edited by Elizabeth Hill Boone, 453–465. Washington, D.C.: Dumbarton Oaks Research Library and Collection.

Schmandt-Besserat, Denise. 1996. *How Writing Came About*. Austin: University of Texas Press.

Smith, Janet S. (Shimbamoto). 1996. "Japanese Writing." In *The World's Writing Systems*, edited by Peter T. Daniels and William Bright, 209–217. New York: Oxford University Press.

Urton, Gary. 1994. "A New Twist in an Old Yarn: Variation in Knot Directionality in the Inka *Khipu*s." *Baessler-Archiv*, Neue Folge, Band 42: 271–305.

——— (with Primitivo Nina Llanos). 1997. *The Social Life of Numbers: A Quechua Ontology of Numbers and Philosophy of Arithmetic*. Austin: University of Texas Press.

———. 1998. "From Knots to Narratives: Reconstructing the Art of Historical Record-Keeping in the Andes from Spanish Transcriptions of Inka *Khipu*s." *Ethnohistory* 45, no. 3: 409–438.

Yanez Cossio, Consuelo. 1985. "Elementos de análisis quichua en matemáticas." *Revista Cultura* (Quito: Banco Central del Ecuador) 21, no. 2: 391–420.

PART FOUR

COLONIAL USES AND TRANSFORMATIONS
OF THE KHIPU

"Without Deceit or Lies"

TEN

Variable Chinu *Readings during a Sixteenth-Century Tribute-Restitution Trial*

Tristan Platt

The quipocamayos *are the community accountants who keep reckoning and order [*cuenta y razón*] with some threads of different colours. . . . And the intelligence [*inteligencia*] of the threads is not generalized, because if in one Province yellow means the silver accounts, in another it is indicated by black, the differences lying in the colours.* LUIS DE CAPOCHE (1959)

*Each province, as it had its own native language, also had a different form and logic [*razón*] of quipo.* MARTÍN DE MURÚA (1986)

INTRODUCTION

The study of khipu has traditionally reflected the dominant role of Cusco at the center of the Tawantinsuyu, or "Four-fold Whole," which was the Quechua name used by the Inka for their empire. As a prime instrument of state administration and royal hegemony, the khipu tradition was raised by the Inka to new levels of sophistication, power, and flexibility. Yet khipu pre-dated the Inka Empire by at least a thousand years. Moreover, in the south, whence the Inka came according to their dynastic histories, the khipu tradition of Tiwanaku-Huari (Conklin 1982) had been inherited by the Aymara federations, which developed their own knot-record, or *chinu*,[1] tradition on the basis of the camelid wool of which they had become the prime producers. One aim of this chapter is to suggest that the study of regional *chinu* may offer an appropriate perspective from which to understand better the purpose and function of Inka khipu.

We do not know the origins of khipu in the southern Andes, though they may be linked with the hunting and herding societies responsible for the domestication of camelids. This hypothesis receives some support from the gentle weapon used to hunt herds of timid vicuñas. A thread was set up on stakes surrounding an open plain, with a space left open for the animals to enter. The thread was marked at intervals with red woolen tassels, which alone prevented the vicuñas from breaking the circle.[2] The practice suggests the delicacy of touch and sensibility communicated to their hunters by these bearers of the most delicate of all animal fibers. But it also suggests a significant association between the tassels, which were clearly meant to propitiate a good catch, and ideas of number. The semantic link between "counting" and "catching" can be seen in the Aymara compound *chinujasitha*, which the Jesuit lexicographer translates as "tie a shawl, or handkerchief," "knot a thread or cord," and "keep prisoner for a long time."[3] The image seems to be that of the knots "trapping" bits of information, like so many vicuñas, and thereby ensuring their steady availability.

Part of the problem with khipu has always been to know what sort of graphic system they represent. In general textbooks on writing and its relation to speaking, the khipu still tends to appear as a marginal oddity (e.g., Ong 1982). In spite of recent suggestions to the contrary, I argue here that Andean khipu were not a *phonographic* form of "writing," which could be "read" by matching sign to sound on a one-to-one basis. I say this without denying that they may be considered a form of writing in the wider sense of that word, considered more generally as an *ordered set of visual (and tactile) cues to the oral realization of meanings.* Nor do I deny that they could have contained some syllabic elements. The khipukamayuq's use of the rebus principle, for example, as proposed by Martti Pärssinen (1992), is also suggested by the Jesuit authors of the so-called Naples manuscript (Cumis, Oliva, and Valera 1611–1638), discussed by Laura Laurencich Minelli (1996). However, a rebus constructed by numbering syllables in logographic "key words" at the head of each khipu string (the system proposed by the Jesuits for "narrative khipu") is quite different from a phonographic system based on the literal representation of the sounds of well-formed Quechua or Aymara sentences.[4]

Khipu have generally been divided into two broad classes, those consisting mainly of categories of numbered units ("numerical khipu") and the so-called "narrative khipu." This contrast is replicated in the Jesuits' distinction between numerical khipu, used to count "ordinary things," and the so-called *quipu trascendente*, or "royal khipu," which dealt with the secrets of religion and history and were known only to the elite.[5] The Jesuits also refer to a third kind of khipu in which the "key words" used for constructing the rebus are replaced by numbers, perhaps to increase their esoteric and numerological power. But all needed to be "read," and have their meanings realized by the readers.

The performative realization of numerical khipu is a convenient point of departure, since it has recently been argued that even they might have contained some phonetic information, in addition to the color categories of the strings and the numerical knots, to allow "reading" of the content (Urton 1998). Following the regional emphasis I propose, it should first be questioned whether, even within the category of numerical khipu, all shared the same basic code, or formed examples of a single "script" whose structure and meaning might be decoded by formal comparison across the entire universe of such khipu. I argue from the case of the Aymara-speaking Sakaka ethnic group, in the Province of Charcas,[6] that even numerical khipu may not necessarily have shared the same code and structure in different Andean regions.

I begin by discussing the conceptual opposition sometimes adduced between khipu as "idiosyncratic" devices, and khipu as a generalized form of "writing." Arguing that administration requires transparency, Gary Urton (1994) emphasizes the requirements of the state bureaucracy as proof of the second position. I suggest, on the contrary, that the opposition itself, in any strong sense, is meaningless.

In the second part, I consider different forms of articulation between the Cusco central administration and the regional societies of the Aymara-speaking provinces, as a means of establishing the points at which Aymara traditions of *chinu* construction might have survived the standardizing thrust of imperial control. Here my point of departure is Catherine Julien's (1988) essay on Inka decimal organization. I try to qualify the single-minded Cusco-centricity of her vision by appealing to a less clear-cut situation among the sixteenth-century federation of the Charka.

In the last part, I consider different types of numerical *chinu* presented as evidence in a tribute-restitution trial heard between 1572 and 1578, in which the Charka lords and their Indians tried to recover excess tributes extorted by their Spanish *encomenderos* between 1548 and 1551. These depredations occurred before the official list of tributary obligations (the *tasa*), finalized for the Sakaka ethnic group on October 1, 1550, by President La Gasca's tribute committee in Lima,[7] had finally reached the region toward the end of 1551.

To evaluate the nature of the evidence, it is necessary to ask what procedural factors lay behind the variable readings to be found in the documentary transcripts, and to what extent the traditional accuracy of the *chinu*—"without deceit or lies," *sin fraude ni mentira*, as one witness put it—might have been modified, under the pressures of the European invasion, to take account of an alien body of legal rules and practices.

I also ask how different recording tasks were distributed and how, in the case of the *chinu* registering the coca deliveries, the information might have been structured on the cords. As for the *chinu* registering the rest of the tribute delivered during those early years, I observe certain differences between the order of the tribute categories used by the Aymara *chinukamana* and the ordering of the categories on a Wanka khipu, transcribed in 1561 and analyzed by John Murra (1975). I take this as evidence of regional variation in the cultural ordering of ethnocategories.

In seeking to reconstruct khipu whose transcriptions can be found in the Spanish documentary record, this chapter follows the route proposed by Murra. Little further progress can be expected on the "literal" deciphering of archaeological khipu beyond the important contributions on formal structure provided by Locke (1912, 1923), the Aschers (1975), and Urton (1994), unless we can find khipu, together with their transcriptions, that can also be re-embedded in the social and political context within which they were constructed and read. Meanwhile, many little-used sources exist for studying the ways in which khipu were actually interrogated and "read" in the sixteenth century. Suggestions from anthropology and linguistics on the structuring of Aymara narrative sequences, making use of metaphors that appeal directly to spinning, plying, and weaving procedures, may also offer valuable clues to the way the twisted fibers are organized. This would later have been made manifest during oral performance (Arnold, Jiménez, and Yapita 1992).

PRIVATE ''IDIOSYNCRASY'' OR UNIVERSAL ''WRITING'': A FALSE DICHOTOMY?

There is a considerable literature dealing with methods of storage of quantitative data on khipu (Ascher and Ascher 1975; Locke 1923; Radicati di Primeglio 1979). Urton (1998) has gone so far as to propose that various grammatical and syntactic elements in putative Quechua sentences—nouns, adjectives, verbs with their tenses, and evidentials—could have been represented directly

on the cords of numerical khipu. In an earlier paper (1994), Urton also questioned the idea of the khipu as an "idiosyncratic" memory aid, intelligible
only to the individual who made it, preferring to move the khipu information
system closer to "writing," understood as a "device" for storing and retrieving information "in a relatively unambiguous way." I begin by commenting
further on this thesis.[8]

The "idiosyncratic" thesis, in its strong form, is meaningless if—as seems
undeniable—we are dealing with information of an intersubjective nature.
Even if khipu were simply methods of storing private information according to an individual code, the nature of each code would necessarily involve
principles derived from a prior process of socialization that would establish
certain common cultural problems and solutions.

On the other hand, various sources state clearly that khipu did not follow any single universal code. Cobo stated that "even among the *quipocamayos*
themselves, one was unable to understand the registers and recording devices of others."[9] This may refer not so much to individual variation (though
this is also possible where the system in use left open alternative patterns of
coding and structural organization) as to a significant degree of regional and
social variation in khipu design between different Andean societies. This is
supported by Luis Capoche (1959), who referred to differences in the color-
coding systems used by different ethnic groups in Potosí (see epigraph); and
Martín de Murúa wrote, in a similar vein, that "each province, as it had its
own native language, also had a different form and logic [*razón*] of *quipo*."[10]
Such testimonies allow us, I think, to move beyond a false dichotomy between
"private mnemonic" and "universal writing," while reinstating different social
traditions of khipu making at the center of our inquiry.

The notion of "writing" as storing information that can be "retrieved" in
a "relatively unambiguous way" leaves open exactly what was stored and what
was contributed in performance by the "reader." It also implies that ambiguity
is a systemic disadvantage, which may be true for census or fiscal accounts,
but is not so evident where symbolic elements relating to religion and cos-
mology are concerned. One problem is how to distinguish those readings that
creatively exploit symbolic ambiguity from others that simply realize unambiguous bits of information encoded as such in numerical khipu.

However, Urton wishes his use of "unambiguous" to cover the precise
grammatical and syntactic forms emitted by the khipukamayuq's speech organs during the process of "reading" a knotted representation of those same
forms. Here it may be useful to emphasize that reading always involves the
spoken realization of graphic information that varies even in the case of a

phonographic system of writing (such as an alphabet), and may be far freer in the case of logographic or semasiological systems.[11] The reading of a message always involves a specific contribution by the reader, who introduces his/her personal understandings and skills with regard to a different set of rules, in particular those of speaking (rhetoric). In reading a rebus, moreover, a capacity to perceive grammatical structure behind the punning with unanalyzed "syllabic sounds" is also required.

Cieza de León helps us to envisage the difference between reading out information on the past history of specific Inka stored in khipu, and converting it into a literary and artistic text for speaking or singing at funerals and commemorations. Cieza's enthusiasm for the khipu knew few bounds, particularly after his experience with Lord Guacarapora of Maycavilca, who had shown him and read out the khipu of all the effects taken by Pizarro and his band in Jauja (this is the khipu analyzed by Murra in 1975). But he was quite clear that where "history" was concerned, the "great khipukamayuq" gave the "facts" relating to each Inka's life and deeds, while it was the expert rhetoricians— the artists in spoken and intoned language—who converted these data into poetry and song.[12]

At the same time, we should not envisage khipu as fixed "texts." Each was capable of change, in accordance with changes in the wider society to which they referred. Old knots could be unknotted, new knots and cords introduced. The result of this approach over various khipu would be the complete lack of any visible patterning that Urton (1994) reports for the coastal khipu stored in Berlin, precisely because the pattern can only emerge when the "parallel lives" of different khipu are compared, rather than their respective states at any one point in time. This suggests that khipu—long subject to formal analyses of different kinds—should be returned to the living social context in which they were created and transformed as changing social objects, even "living" beings (Cereceda 1986), continually responding to new external constraints transmitted to them more or less effectively by their keepers.

So there are at least three parameters of difference among khipu: historical (changes from Wari to Inka, for example); spatial (between different contemporary social and cultural traditions of code and structure); and individual (what we may call the "developmental cycle" in the lives of different kinds of domesticated khipu). It is unlikely, therefore, that any attempt to force all khipu into a single grid of interpretation will be successful. Urton (1994: 294) proposes a research agenda centered on the Inka Empire and its bureaucratic requirements, and invites us to seek "the shared values and meanings that linked people in positions of authority at all levels of society." How, he asks, could a society permit itself the "luxury of a recording system . . . grounded in the individual, or family, control of and access to state records, whether statistical or historical?" This implies that all khipu were transparently intelligible to all state bureaucrats, ignoring clear suggestions by Cobo, Capoche, and Murúa that many khipu, like local dialects (or perhaps—following Murúa—even languages), contained local design features that would naturally have appeared "impenetrable" to strangers from a different regional tradition of communication and khipu construction.

The assumption of transparency, efficacy, and homogeneity within a unified set of bureaucratic conventions is further questioned by the variety of forms of articulation between regional societies and Cusco. Cusco did indeed seek to unify and standardize the running of the empire with a range of sophisticated techniques—among them, the generalization of bronze artifacts (Lechtman 1980), the transformation of local lords into the liveried functionaries of the empire,[13] and the diffusion of decimally organized khipu in line with a decimally organized system of social segmentation (Julien 1988). But in 1538, when Emperor Charles V succeeded to the Inka's authority in Charcas, the process was not complete, and there is no reason to assume that all Aymara traditions of *chinu* construction had been forced to follow all the Inka's coding conventions.

Certain similarities are, of course, found across the entire range of khipu-like objects—for example, at the level of spin or ply directionality. But these indicate deep continuities rooted, as already suggested, in experimental research by Andean hunters and gatherers into the relation between twists and loops of fiber, and ideas of dual unity, plurality, and number.

FORMS OF REGIONAL ARTICULATION: HOW DECIMAL WERE THE CHARKA?

Let us now ask how far the decimal system (perhaps adopted by the Inka from Chimú coastal civilization) can in fact be detected among two powerful southern Aymara federations: the Charka and the Qaraqara. Our point of departure is Julien's demonstration of how a decimal system of social organization could be imposed by the Inka in order to facilitate the recruitment of labor services, allowing a degree of standardization that would facilitate comparisons between different regional rates of productivity. Her argument, which is strikingly convincing in spite of the tiny fragments of evidence available, is based on two well-known examples of Andean regional society: the Quechua-speaking Chupaycho (Huánuco) and the Aymara-speaking Lupaqa.

In both cases, she finds evidence that ceramic and weaving obligations were met by a standard percentage (respectively, 1% and 10%), which was applied to the labor pool of each society, regardless of population.

Julien has, I believe, shown that the decimal system not only was an imposed taxonomic system that implied regrouping populations (as Murra has argued), but could also function—at least in the cases mentioned—as a practical method of calculating labor obligations on the basis of percentages. This was the ideal form of decimal organization that the Inka tried to generalize; and we shall shortly see another example of Andean facility with percentages (see note 49 and text below). However, from this Julien concludes that "the requirement of decimal administration alone would have created a new territorial configuration" (1988: 271), and that Inka decimal administration relied on local political authority while at the same time transforming it into the structural equivalent of provincial authority elsewhere. These extrapolations are obviously more risky. Her Lupaqa case shows the use of Inka census khipu to calculate labor obligations as late as 1567, but the 100 potters and 1,000 weavers near Huancané could well be exceptional, evidence of an incipient policy (perhaps as retaliation for Lupaqa resistance to imperial rule) rather than proof of its generality even among the Lupaqa. Further south, it becomes more difficult to argue that the Inka had "transformed the territoriality" of the Charcas "nations" outside the Cochabamba Valley (Wachtel 1982).

One text does spell out a model of Inka decimal organization for the Sakaka, the dominant ethnic grouping within the Charka "nation." In 1582 the "natural lords" of the Charka and Qaraqara sent a "Memorial" to Spain claiming redress for Toledo's campaign against their hereditary privileges.[14] One argument adduced was, precisely, their traditional role as *hunu mallku* (lords of 10,000 vassals) at the head of the local system of decimal organization:

> In our Province of the Charcas, before and after the Incas, there used to be natural lords, the greater with 10,000 vassals, others with 8,000 Indians, others with 6,000 Indians and vassals. The said lords and knights were superior to the other *caciques* and lords which there were in each nation. And so there was one for the Charcas and another for the Caracaras and another for the Soras and another for the Quillacas and another for the Carangas and another for the Chuis and another for the Chichas, each of them different in their nation, habits and costume. And so each of these lords used to have 8 *segundas personas*, and 10 too, of 1,000 Indians, and 4 principals in each *ayllu* of 500

to 100 Indians, and 4 chiefs in each *ayllu*, each one in his nation of
Hanansaya and Hurinasaya.   (ESPINOZA SORIANO 1969: F. 4R)

Now, there are some oddities in this account. In the first place, we know
from other sources that the lord of Charka was said to have 10,000 vassals
and the lord of Qaraqara 20,000; but here they are said to be "one" for each
nation, in spite of the apparent division of each into two moieties ("Hanansaya and Hurinsaya"). For the Qaraqara we know that this is a gross simplification because, although Muruq'u, the lord of Hurinsaya resident in the
capital of Macha, is alone mentioned as present in the battle of Cochabamba
against the Pizarros in 1538, another lord, Wallqa, was lord of Hanansaya
at the same time and was also resident in Macha when the Spanish arrived.
Wallqa's genealogy is included in a "Probanza" presented by a descendant,
and is no less "illustrious" than that of Muruq'u except that Muruq'u's mother
was Payku Chimpu, a daughter of Wayna Qhapaq. In the *encomienda* document awarding the Qaraqara to Gonzalo Pizarro,[15] Muruq'u is said to be lord
of 20,000 Indians (i.e., of both moieties); and this is confirmed by the fact
that Wallqa took over from Muruq'u as representative of all these "20,000
Indians" when Muruq'u died in 1548.[16]
   In the case of the ethnic group of Macha, senior "capital" (*cabecera*) of the
Qaraqara nation where the two *hunu mallku* lived, both moieties have persisted since the sixteenth century, each divided into five ayllu. Here, there is
some reason to suppose the presence of the Inka decimal system, although a
"new territoriality" cannot be observed in our sources outside Cochabamba.
But other Qaraqara groups—including the Pikachuri, whose lord also received a woman and other privileges from the Inka—seem to have escaped
even the limited degree of imperial standardization visible in Macha.
   In the case of the Charka, the pretensions to sole power of the *hunu mallku*
don Fernando Ayawiri are also suspect. In a letter sent in 1575 to Viceroy
Toledo, Ayawiri protests against the nomination of three lords to three divisions (*parcialidades*) in his hometown of Sakaka, capital of the Charka, and his
own demotion to an inferior position:

   . . . My father [don Alonso Ayavire] remained as the only lord of the
   said *repartimiento* of Sakaka which is where I am from, and it seems
   that there must have been some false or malicious information given
   during the *visita* of Diego Núñez Bazán [carried out] on instructions from Your Excellence, because three *caciques* were named for
   three *parcialidades* in the said *repartimiento*, and they were assigned

salaries of principal *caciques*, when there is no other principal *cacique* but myself since over a 100 years ago till today . . .[17]

Now we know that the Ayawiris were not the only lords of Sakaka any more than Muruq'u had been of Macha. In the restitution trial of 1572, we hear of another lord, Achakata, whose division—according to one witness—was even richer than that of Ayawiri.[18] The *tasa* sent from Lima, which reached Sakaka in 1551, was directed to Montemayor and to "you, Ayavire and Achacata, caciques. . . ."[19] Moreover, in 1572 three "*caciques principales*," don Fernando Ayawiri, don Fernando Achakata, and don Diego Mamani, together named Joan de Baños as their *procurador;*[20] and there is independent evidence from Viceroy Toledo's *visita* and from the early seventeenth-century tributary lists (*padrones*) for the existence of three divisions in Sakaka. In 1572, a group of *chinu* was read out by three *chinukamana* (one of them Achakata himself), who referred to themselves as "*principales* and *quipocamayos* of the *repartimiento* of Sakaka" (though unfortunately without specifying their division).

This is also the case in Chayanta, the other large social group within the Charka "nation," dependent on Sakaka till separated by Francisco Pizarro's *encomienda* grant of the "Urinsaya" moiety of Chayanta to Hernando Pizarro in 1539.[21] Here there appear to be two moieties, sometimes called Hanansaya and Hurinsaya in Spanish documents, following Inka practice. But each seems to have included *three* ayllu, making a total of six, and the name of each "moiety" is more often (in later colonial documents and till today) the same as that of the dominant ayllu in each: Laymi and Chayantaka.[22]

In Sakaka and Chayanta, the emphasis on three and six rather than five or ten suggests a nondecimal form of organization. How can we reconcile this with the decimal vision put forward by don Fernando Ayawiri in 1582? I think we have here a case of an *ideal* form of decimal organization, put forward as "history" by a colonial lord who hopes to revindicate his special position as grandson of an Inka imperial functionary. This functionary was the Charka lord Kuysara. In 1538, Kuysara had headed both the resistance of the Charcas "nations" in Cochabamba, and the subsequent gift of obedience to His Majesty.[23] He had also shared with the lord of the neighboring Sura "nation" and with the Inka fortress commander the right to be carried by his Indians in a litter. No doubt it was through him that the Inka were trying to introduce the decimal organization among the Charka; this would also explain Wayna Qhapaq's gift of thirty-five pieces of *kumpi* cloth, which would have been designed to induce Kuysara to accept his new role as a liveried functionary of the empire (see note 13).

Thus, don Fernando's enthusiasm for the decimal system can be seen as just another way of legitimizing his own unique position as grandson of the co-opted regional governor of the Inka "province." Nevertheless, Diego Núñez Bazán's *visita* in 1571 showed that a different form of organization persisted on the ground in Sakaka, consisting of three "submerged" *parcialidades* that were ready to reenter the (colonial) state's political awareness if an appropriate opportunity presented itself.

The Inka decimal vision is all-embracing when we look at the Andes from Cusco, particularly if fortified with such a compelling argument as that presented by Julien. Yet local histories allow us to recognize considerable local variation, which should be related to the different political circumstances that accompanied the incorporation of each nation into the Tawantinsuyu. The same situation exists, I suspect, with regard to khipu and *chinu* organization: the standardizing thrust from Cusco was decimal, but regional traditions remained, at least in the Aymara-dominated south. Again, we must ask how other methods of accounting had combined with the Inka's decimal approach as a consequence of different local patterns of articulation with the Inka state.

STRUCTURE AND INTEREST IN COLONIAL AYMARA *CHINU*

Let us now consider in more detail the case of the Sakaka *chinu* presented by the lords and Indians of Sakaka during the tribute-restitution trial heard in La Plata between 1572 and 1578. Their aim was to extract compensation from the heirs of their *encomendero*, don Alonso de Montemayor, whom they declared to have taken excessive tribute from them between 1548 and 1551.[24] Before the arrival of the *tasa* toward the end of 1551, the *encomendero* of Sakaka had carried off unauthorized quantities of produce, which, it was alleged, had driven Sakaka's once-rich society to the verge of ruin. In 1572, the *chinuka-mana* of Sakaka, who had knotted down every detail of the *encomendero*'s depredations on their *chinu*, were summoned to La Plata to read out lists of all the species extorted by Montemayor. These were then compared with the amount officially demanded in the *tasa*, which substantially reduced the amount of silver demanded, reduced the supply of high Andean staples (potatoes and quinoa), and increased the supply of maize, meat, poultry, and salt for the new towns of La Plata and Potosí (Tables 10.1 and 10.2).

The Sakaka Indians presented their first questionnaire and called their first witnesses on January 11, 1572, when they were represented by their *procurador*, Joan de Baños, a lawyer we know to have defended several Andean causes.[25] The *chinukamana* gave their evidence in July 1572, but the case was

TABLE 10.1.   Sakaka's Annual Tribute Obligation According to the *Tasa* of October 1, 1550[1]

4,500 pesos	Assayed silver standard (*plata ensayada*)
750 *cestos*[2]	Coca
30 pieces[3]	Clothing (half male, half female)
6	Blankets
8	Horse Blankets
8	Aprons
600 *fanegas*	Maize
80 *fanegas*	Potatoes and *chuño*
100	Sheep
6 *arrobas* [150 pounds]	Lard
16 little jugs	Sheep's fat
20	Pigs (or sheep)
25 brace	Poultry (25 cocks, 25 hens)
200 brace	Ducks and drakes
150 brace	Partridges
1,560[4]	Eggs
1 *arroba* [25 pounds]	Honey
1 *arroba*	Beeswax
30	Pickled meat shoulders
12 loads	Salt
10	Reins, whips, halters, girths, hobbles
Product of 2 *fanegas* seed sown in *encomendero*'s fields in La Plata	Maize and wheat[5]
Product of 8 *fanegas* sown in own fields	Maize and wheat[6]
12	[Male laborers to help *encomendero* plough, sow, and irrigate]
30	[Male and female laborers to weed and harvest[7]]
15 (3 officials)	Servants in the *encomendero*'s house in La Plata[8]
8 herders or orchard minders	6 in Sakaka lands, 2 in La Plata
30 (twice yearly)	Herders for *encomendero*'s llamas when carrying food to Potosí, Porco, La Plata

[1] AGI, Justicia 653: ff. 4v–7v. Some items are requested annually, some every six months, and coca is requested at each of the three *mitas* per year. I have adjusted the figures to give annual totals. Support for the priest is not shown.

[2] 250 *cestos* for each of the three annual harvests (*mitas*). The coca tribute was calculated on the basis of an on-site inspection (*visita*) of "the Inka's coca fields," carried out on September 5, 1549 (AGI, Justicia 653: f. 4v).

TABLE 10.1.   Continued

---

³ "Dareis cada seis meses 15 vestidos de abasca [*awasqa* = woven], la mitad de hombre y otra de mujer, que se entiende un vestido [dress], manta [woman's shawl] y camiseta y anaco y liquido [*lliclla* = carrying cloth], la manta y el anaco de la india de dos varas en ancho y otras dos varas en largo [two yards square], y la camiseta de vara y ochava en largo y en el ancho del ruedo dos varas menos ochava, y la liquida de vara y tercia en largo y en el ancho de una vara, puestos en casa del encomendero en la dicha Villa."
⁴ Thirty eggs per week "and some fish if you have it." The tribute committee no doubt had their eye on the Friday fast.
⁵ Wheat seed is to be provided by the *encomendero*, maize seed by the Indians.
⁶ Ditto. The maize harvest is to be given decobbed, and the wheat harvest off the ear to be winnowed by the *encomendero* with Indian assistance. This item may be commuted for the next two.
⁷ These two items may be offered in place of the previous one.
⁸ Eight Indian men and women out of these fifteen are to form the *encomendero*'s retinue when he visits his *encomienda*.

then delayed by an attempt to get an embargo placed on the income enjoyed by the heirs of Montemayor from the treasury in Potosí, which was still being paid from Sakaka's tribute. The heirs prevaricated, only presenting their own questionnaire and witnesses in 1576; Sakaka called more witnesses in 1577. Following an appeal by the heirs against the sentence of restitution given by the two judges in La Plata, Dr. Manuel Barros de Sanmillán (whose role in defending Andean claims has been studied by John Murra) and Dr. Peralta, a final review of the Sakaka *chinukamana*'s evidence was ordered. In 1578, therefore, two of the *chinukamana* reappeared in court, and their declarations were taken all over again, together with some additional information. The accountants for both parties then calculated what each party owed the other. To counter the accountants' assignment of almost 29,000 *pesos ensayados* to Montemayor's heirs for undelivered *cestos* (baskets) of coca leaf, the Sakaka finally produced three further *chinukamana* from the coca-producing yungas (precipitous semitropical valleys) of Tiraque, whose *chinu* showed that Montemayor had in fact received 547 more *cestos* of coca leaf than was stipulated in the *tasa*. With this evidence, the heirs' case collapsed, and the sentence of restitution given in La Plata was upheld, with minor modifications, by the Royal Council of the Indies in Madrid on August 9, 1581.

TABLE 10.2. Sakaka's Tribute Payments, 1548–1551, According to the Tributary *Chinu*

Ethnocategory	Tribute	1548	1549	1550	1551
People and silver	Miners	100	80	70	60
	Marks per week	100	80	70	60
	Value in *pesos corrientes*	21,200	16,960	14,840	12,432
Maize	Maize (*pocchas*)	1,700	1,100	900	600
Chuño	Chuño (llama loads, *cargas*)	500	400	250	200
Animals and	Camelids (adults)	552	402	192	121
animal products	Camelid lambs (for the table)	53	53	31	19
	Fat (*arrobas*)	20	16	7	3
	Cloth (pieces)	120	90	35	20
	Blankets	60	35	21	11
	Camelid wool (*arrobas*)	10	7	3	1
	Aprons (*mandiles*)	50	30	11	6
Rope products	Reins, whips, halters,				
(*cosas de cabuya*)	girths, hobbles, etc.	80	45	13	11
Meat	Pickled meat shoulders (*pescuezos adobados* "*para riendas*")	40	21	6	4
Honey products	Jars (*arrobas*) of honey	20	14	7	4
	Wax (*arrobas*)	23	8	4	2
Poultry and eggs	Chickens	103	60	30	15
	Ducks	208	130	50	34
	Eggs	1,205	1,304	850	540
High Andean	Quinoa (loads)	15	10	3	1
agriculture	Potatoes (loads)	10	13	4	5
Salt	Salt (loads)	30	23	11	6

SOURCE: AGI Justicia 653: ff. 58r–77v; cf. ff. 259v–264v.
For deliveries of coca leaf, see Table 10.5.

Did the *Chinukamana* Always Speak "the Whole Truth"?

Khipu evidence has often been taken as close to flawless, and political critiques of khipu texts are rare, although in 1975 Murra had warned against too ingenuous a belief in the khipukamayuq's truthfulness, and Urton (1998: 430) cites Juan de Solórzano's more disdainful opinion (1736) of khipu and their keepers as "Indians whose honesty is shifty, so that the explanation they gave on the basis of their *quipos* will also be shifty." Solórzano's view may have reflected Martín de Murúa's warning that the good faith of khipukamayuq had been negatively affected by a common tendency in European jurisprudence to seek compromise rather than truth:[26]

> . . . in these *quipos* they tend to put down when the *corregidor* or priest or others don't pay them for all the food and other things they demand, and later they demand payment in the officials' residence or during official inspections (*visitas*), and even ask for more than what is owed them so as not to fall short, for their slyness has grown beyond what it was, and as they see that such requests always lead to compromises and deductions, they generally put down more than what they are owed, so that with the deduction they can get back everything they gave. . . .[27]

In placing bargaining above an exact regard for truth, which we shall see operating during the Sakaka restitution trial, the Andean khipukamayuq will also have been advised by their Spanish advocates and defenders.

The first clue that not everything alleged by the Sakaka Indians is to be taken at its face value emerges in connection with the date when Montemayor is said to have received Sakaka as his *encomienda*. This date coincides with the first year of the Indians' claim. In the questionnaire presented by the Sakaka lords to witnesses in 1572, we find that Montemayor is said to have received his *encomienda* in 1548, and the restitution claim is then directed at the first *three* years of Montemayor's tenure (i.e., 1548–1550). This is supported by two Potosí residents, Antonio Quixada and Francisco Lobato,[28] who said Montemayor had received the Sakaka Indians in 1548 and invoked the grant document (which does not appear in the file) as evidence. They assigned the extortion of excess tribute to the first two or three years of Montemayor's *encomienda*. Pedro de Leiceguín agreed: he had been in Sakaka and other parts of Charka territory as a collector of tithes on the tribute and had seen Montemayor in action during "the first three years."

However, Diego Núñez Bazán, who knew the land well as Corregidor of Carangas and Quillacas and in 1571 had been Toledo's inspector (*visitador*) in Sacaca,[29] stated on the basis of information gathered in the field that President La Gasca had in fact assigned the Sakaka *encomienda* to Marshal Alonso de Alvarado shortly after Gonzalo Pizarro's defeat in 1548. The Marshal then "possessed them [the Indians] for a few months." In 1549, the *encomienda* was transferred to Alonso de Montemayor, who held it in his turn for "only two years" before Lorenzo de Estupiñán brought the Lima *tasa* to

Sakaka in 1551.[30] A Florentine witness, Nicolás de Benino,[31] while accepting that Montemayor received his *encomienda* in Sakaka from La Gasca, attributed it to the president's "last distribution at the beginning of 1550 before leaving for Spain," because before he had given him "certain Indians in the Province of Quito." Benino himself had arrived in Potosí in 1550, when he saw Montemayor's steward selling "great quantities of *fanegas* of maize and *chuño* and camelids and cloth and other items" at high prices, and later witnessed the ill treatment of the Sakaka Indians at the hands of Montemayor himself.

Now, it happens that a letter sent by Montemayor on February 18, 1549, to the Viceroy of New Spain confirms that at this time he had still not received his *encomienda* in Sakaka.[32] His hopes for an "improvement" (*mejora*) of his existing *encomienda* in Quito (Tomebamba) are pinned rather on the late Gabriel de Rojas's succulent *encomienda* in the coca fields of Songo.[33] In fact, Marshal Alonso de Alvarado would shortly be assigned this precious *encomienda*, but in 1548 the Marshal had been given Sakaka briefly to keep him happy. Clearly, Diego Núñez Bazán and Nicolás de Benino were right, and Montemayor did not get Sakaka in 1548, as was claimed by the Indians and reiterated by other Spanish witnesses. Should the Indians, at least, not have known, with such an exact recording system as their *chinu* to rely on, exactly *when* Montemayor had entered into his domain?

The problem is compounded when we remember that all the *chinu* read into the file cover extortions of tribute during four years rather than three: 1548 till 1551. In the Sakaka questionnaire, it was alleged (question 10) that even after the arrival of the *tasa*, Montemayor went on exceeding the new legal limit till his death in 1556;[34] but the witnesses did not enlarge on this, and the *chinukamana* who eventually arrived in court said that the *encomendero* and his stewards had respected the *tasa* once it arrived (apart from substituting 80 loads of *chuño* for the less valuable 80 loads of potatoes).[35] However, there were other items, extorted by Montemayor before the tasa arrived, which did not appear knotted down on the *chinu* (e.g., the 35 pieces of *cumbi* cloth given to Kuysara by Wayna Qhapaq), and there was the matter of the vicious treatment he had given the Sakaka and Chayanta lords, for which no monetary compensation was requested.[36] Should we conclude that, in the end, the Indians and their legal advisors had deliberately decided to present the period of extortion as four years rather than two or three, covering up the fact that Montemayor had not been given his *encomienda* in Sakaka until at least 1549 so as to be compensated for other values not restituted and for the uncompensated ill treatment?

I can think of no other alternative. For the *chinukamana*, there was little problem: after all, both Spaniards were called Alonso, and the baptismal name of their own lord, don Alonso Ayawiri, son of Kuysara, was probably an imitation of Alvarado's own Christian name. If, as I suspect, *chinu* were classified by the lord in whose "reign" they were made, a new series begun in 1548 would have coincided with don Alonso's "rebirth" as a Christian. Meanwhile, Alvarado, no less than Montemayor, clearly took advantage of his favored position to extort what he could from his Indians. There would have been little difficulty in attributing Alvarado's extortions to Montemayor by covering up the difference under the shared name of Alonso and reading out to the court records that began with "Alonso's reign" in 1548.[37]

The surprising thing is that Montemayor's heirs did not contest the point, something that would surely have been inevitable if they had had access to the *encomienda* grant document. But they were far away in Spain, though receiving a stipend from the Royal Treasury in distant Potosí, and their own questionnaire and testimony has a triviality about it which suggests they did not think it possible to question seriously the Indian claim—one among so many others being heard in the courts at that time concerning a period notorious for its depredations. Their only recourse was prevarication, postponement, and—as Murúa saw—a search for compromise (see the Judgment on the Second Appeal given in Madrid in 1581).

But this is not the only reason for supposing that the Sakaka *chinukamana* considered their declarations as a basis for negotiation and "compromise," rather than a simple rehearsal of the "whole truth." During the revision of 1578, the accountant for Montemayor's heirs found several instances in which the Sakaka Indians had in fact given less tribute (e.g., maize, birds and eggs, salt, and labor services) than the amount approved in Lima in October 1550, something that had not been mentioned either by the Sakaka lords or by the Sakaka *chinukamana*. This meant that, before the coca tribute was taken into account—which had to wait till the *chinukamana* of the coca plantations arrived in court—the heirs could claim from Sakaka 33,447 pesos, 3 *tomines*, and 7 *granos*,[38] as against the 56,329 pesos, 6 *tomines*, and 11 *granos* claimed from the heirs by Sakaka (see Table 10.3). The Sakaka *chinukamana* had read out the contributions they had made, but not those they had not made; as Joan de Baños put it, it was not up to them to answer questions they were not asked.[39] After all, in a European system of justice no one is expected to give evidence "against themselves," an idea that may have led the Andean khipukamayuq to collude in the deterioration of their own image and practice as truth tellers.

TABLE 10.3. Balance of Debts between Sakaka and Montemayor, 1548–1551, According to the 1550 *Tasa* (in pesos, *tomines*, and *granos ensayados*)[1]

Tasa Kind	Montemayor's Debt to Sakaka	Sakaka's Debt to Montemayor
Silver	39,405 - 2 - 0	
Chuño	4,578 - 7 - 6	
Camelids	8,061 - 3 - 0	
Fat	21 - 0 - 6	
Cloth (*ropa*)	131 - 4 - 8	
Blankets	213 - 1 - 3	
Aprons (*mandiles*)	64 - 7 - 3	
Camelid wool (*arrobas*)	73 - 5 - 6	
Reins, whips, halters, girths, hobbles, etc. (*cosas de cabuya*)	385 - 7 - 9	
Jugs (*arrobas*) of honey	73 - 5 - 9	
Wax (*arrobas*)	148 - 3 - 6	
Chickens	7 - 0 - 0	
Quinoa (llama loads)	66 - 5 - 4	
Potatoes (llama loads)	28 - 0 - 6	
Transport of 700 *cestos* coca	3,070 - 1 - 6	
Maize		2,193 - 0 - 0
Pickled shoulders of meat (*pescuezos adobados*)		85 - 7 - 9
Ducks and partridges		227 - 1 - 9
Eggs		48 - 6 - 0
Salt (llama loads)		38 - 4 - 8
Coca[2]		28,947 - 3 - 0
Product of 32 *fanegas* seed sown in own fields		373 - 6 - 5 [maize] 74 - 4 - 0 [wheat]
Product of 8 *fanegas* seed sown in City fields		111 - 7 - 0
Llama drovers (*arrieros*)		842 - 1 - 0
Herders		505 - 2 - 0
TOTALs	56,329 - 6 - 11	33,447 - 3 - 7
BALANCE	22,882 - 3 - 4	

[1] AGI, Justicia 653: ff. 302r–305v; 12 *granos* (grains) = 1 *tomín*, 8 tomines = 1 peso. The figures express, in the assayed silver standard of monetary accounting, the values of what was, or was not, given to the *encomendero*, calculated by the two accountants after questioning witnesses on wages and prices during the years in question, and after discounting from the result the values considered to be just in the 1551 *tasa*. The final figure is the amount by which each party is in credit (*alcance*) with the other.

[2] The first three *chinukamana* did not declare the 3,000 *cestos* required in the *tasa*, which therefore appears to be owing to Alonso de Montemayor. Later, the three *chinukamana* of the coca clarified that they had in fact given Montemayor 3,547 *cestos* over the four years in question.

TABLE 10.4. The Value of the Tribute, 1548–1551, According to the *Chinu* of the Prices (in pesos *corrientes* per unit)

Year	1548	1549	1550	1551
Maize (*pocchas*)	5	5	5	5
Chuño (loads)	6	6	6	6
Llamas and alpacas (per head)	10 (adults)	10	10	10
	4 (lambs)	4	4	4
Fat (*arrobas*)	4	4	4	4
Cloth (pieces)	6	6	6	6
Blankets	3	3	3	3
Camelid wool (*arrobas*)	4	4	4	4
Aprons (*mandiles*)	1	1	1	1
Reins, whips, girths, halters, hobbles	4	4	4	nd
Pickled shoulders of meat	2	2	2	2
Jars (*arrobas*) of honey	4	4	4	4
Wax (*arrobas*)	5	5	5	5
Chickens	1	1	1	1
Ducks	½ peso	½ peso	½ peso	½ peso
Eggs (per hundred)	5	5	5	5
Quinoa (loads)	4	4	4	4
Potatoes (loads)	1	1	1	1
Salt (loads)	2	2	2	2

SOURCE: AGI, Justicia 653: ff. 58r–77v; cf. ff. 259–264v.

The Variable Readings of the Sakaka *Chinu*

Four types of *chinu* were referred to, or brought to the court, by the Sakaka *chinukamana* in 1572 and 1578:

1. The tributary *chinu* of species delivered by Sakaka for each year between 1548 and 1551 (see Table 10.2).
2. The *chinu* of the prices at which the species were sold in each of the four years (Table 10.4).
3. The *chinu* where the new *tasa*, brought from Lima by Lorenzo de Estupiñán in 1551, was knotted down (see Table 10.1 for the Spanish version).
4. The *chinu* of the coca leaf kept by *chinukamana* resident in the valleys and yungas where the coca was grown (Table 10.5).

Let us begin by looking in detail at the first type.

TABLE 10.5. Hypothetical Outline of a *Chinu* Constructed by *Chinukamana* of the Sakaka Coca Plantations Showing Coca Deliveries by *Mita* in Year "Alonso I" (1548)

TOP CORD (total value for three *mitas*)

COCA DELIVERED IN YEAR "ALONSO 1" (1548)

MITA 1				MITA 2	
CESTOS OF COCA 314	Indians Yungas to Totora 157	Llamas Totora to Chuquisaca 100	Indians Totora to Chuquisaca 57	CESTOS OF COCA 355	Indians Yungas to Totora 179
	Carry coca in three days @ 2 cestos each	*of Sakaka carry coca @ 2 cestos each*	*carry coca @ 2 cestos each*		*carry coca in three days @ 2 cestos each*
	with steward Antón Gomez, who was two years in the yungas	*in care of 57 Indians*	*with steward Quintero (or "Tintero")*		*[name of steward omitted]*

NOTE: Oral gloss is summarized at the bottom in italics

ALTERNATIVE STRUCTURE FOR BOTTOM LINE (*MITA* 1)

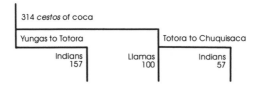

314 *cestos* of coca		
Yungas to Totora		Totora to Chuquisaca
Indians 157	Llamas 100	Indians 57

The three *chinukamana* who arrived in court from Sakaka in 1572, don Hernando Achakata, don Luis Kumba, and don Pedro Hururu, answered the same questionnaire as the previous Spanish witnesses. Only the third question, concerning the goods extorted in quantities beyond those fixed in the *tasa*, was answered in impressive detail by reference to "cords of different colors with many knots," together with the results of operations performed with "certain stones." Achakata gave his evidence in La Plata on July 9, 1572, and Kumba and Hururu gave theirs two days later.

Following protests by the heirs' lawyer, Judges Barros and Peralta then ordered the revision of the evidence "by *quipos* and witnesses," which was

		MITA 3			
Llamas Totora to Potosí 116	**Indians** Totora to Potosí 63	*CESTOS* OF COCA 377	**Indians** Yungas to Totora 189	**Llamas** Totora to Chuquisaca 126	**Indians** Totora to Chuquisaca 63
of Sakaka carry coca @ 2 cestos each	*carry coca @ 2 cestos each*		*carry coca in three days @ 2 cestos each*	*carry coca @ 2 cestos each*	*carry coca @ 2 cestos each*
	with steward Quintero		*with steward Antón Gomez*		*with steward Quintero*

not carried out till October 1578, when the 1572 transcriptions were checked against a new transcription of the same information, this time provided only by Achakata and Kumba. On close examination of the declarations, certain differences appear, both between the three versions transcribed in 1572, and between these and the two revised transcriptions made in 1578.[40]

To understand why exactly the same information was not transcribed from each reading, we must first recognize that the declarations of the *chinukamana* were themselves "readings" of coded information, and, as such, they probably included the oral "filling" necessary to transform "bits" of information into coherent statements structured by the grammatical and syntactic rules of spoken Aymara. These Aymara sentences were then translated into Spanish by interpreters, before being written down by the notaries according to the conventions of their craft. Therefore, three stages of interpretation (not to mention errors possibly introduced by later notaries) separate us from the code of the *chinu*. The last two stages moved the transcription we have before us away from an exact rendering of the *chinukamana*'s Aymara words (themselves extrapolations from the information coded in the *chinu*) by introducing renderings appropriate for a Spanish-language legal audience.

One example of Spanish-language intrusions is the use in different transcriptions of different units of measurement—*fanegas* and *cargas* (llama loads) —to quantify the same product delivered. For example, the transcription of Achakata's evidence in 1572 gives 250 *fanegas* of *chuño* for 1548, which agrees with Kumba's figure, although Hururu gives only 200 *fanegas* (answers to question 3). In the revision of 1578, however, Achakata and Kumba are transcribed as giving 500 *cargas* (f. 262v), which confirms the error in the transcription of Hururu, because two *cargas* are regularly given as equivalent to one *fanega*. We do not know whether Hururu's error is to be located in the knots he had made in his *chinu*, in his reading of the knots, in the translation made by the interpreter, or in the transcription made by the scribe writing it down. However, the use of *fanegas* rather than *cargas* is a conversion that would have been made first by the interpreter, either alone or in discussion with the notary. The absence of *fanegas* on the original *chinu* is confirmed by the single appearance of an Aymara measure of maize, the *poccha*, which turns out to be equivalent to half a *fanega*. If this measure was used for other products besides maize, the knots would have measured numbers of *poccha*, which would be the Aymara word for the *cargas*, or llama loads, appearing elsewhere in the transcriptions (see Table 10.2).

Another conflict in the units of measurement employed can be seen in the case of the deliveries of honey. Honey was one of the specialties of pre-Hispanic Charcas and was produced, not by the European honeybee (*Apis mellifera*) introduced from Spain, but by several tropical species of honey-making wasps and stingless bees. The three transcriptions of 1572 gave the measure of honey as *arrobas* in each of the four years. Only in 1578 do we find what was probably the Aymara measure for honey: jars (*cántaros*). "Jars," then, were probably read out by the *chinukamana* in 1572, but were converted into *arrobas* by the interpreters and notaries, following the Spanish measure also employed in the Lima *tasa* of 1550 (see Table 10.1).

A more problematic case is that of the number of camelids given. For 1548, Achakata gives 300 *ovejas* and *carneros* (alpacas and llamas? or females and males?) worth 10 pesos per head, plus a further 52 *carneros*, with 53 lambs (*corderos*) worth 4 pesos each "for the *encomendero*'s table." But, according to Kumba and Hururu, 300 should be 500, and in the 1578 revision, all the animals are aggregated as 605 *carneros de la tierra* (llamas), and a single price of 10 pesos per head is assigned to each animal. I take it that here there is an error in Achakata's transcription; but the 1578 assignment of a single price is more difficult to explain. Moreover, the revision of 1578 repeats the same aggregation and price unification for each of the four years 1548–1551. It may be a simplification made by a hasty notary, but could it not also be a sly move by the *chinukamana* to increase the overall value of the camelids given?

Interestingly, the same question occurred to the court. In 1578, after making their declarations, Achakata and Kumba were asked, first, "whether the quantity of camelids given to their *encomendero* during the four years included those given for his table?" They answered in the affirmative. They were then asked, "How many head were given for the *encomendero*'s table?" The two *chinukamana* replied that "the *quipos* which contained the information grouped everything together in the figure they have given, and they cannot say how many they gave specifically for the table. . ." (ff. 277v–278). There are only two possibilities: either they are lying, or the separation of adult animals from lambs in 1572 was based on an oral memory gloss. However, since the prices of each were also given apart in 1572, it seems difficult to interpret the 1578 explanation except as a cover-up for a new piece of slyness on the part of the *chinukamana*.[41]

The *Chinu*, the Stones, and Memory: When Were the Figures Added Up?

Let us now consider the place occupied by the accounting stones in the declarations read out in court. Urton has suggested, on the basis of this very document from Sakaka, that what was knotted down on the cords was only a single "share" corresponding to a single component social group. This share had therefore to be multiplied by the number of social groups involved, and the stones would have been used by the *chinukamana* to carry out this calculation (Urton 1998). Although the stones mentioned in 1572 and 1578 are left colorless (colors—"some white and others of other colors"—are emphasized rather for the *chinu* cords), we can probably assume that they were black and white, as in the famous drawing by Guaman Poma. In this context, black and white may indicate complex concepts such as subtraction/addition, debt/credit, increase/decrease, abundance/dearth, or others.[42]

However, it is not clear why such accomplished arithmeticians as the *chinu-*

kamana would need to make such simple calculations as those required by Urton's solution. Moreover, the importance given by the *chinukamana* to the role of memory and the descriptions of the operations carried out in court suggest that these operations were very rapid, to the point where, although capable of making substantive calculations, they could also have been manipulated to skim through calculations already made and knotted down, thereby acquiring an additional function as part of what we may call the *chinukamana*'s "rituals of authorization."

The importance of combining memory with *chinu* "text" is evident from a comment made by don Luis Kumba. After saying (like the rest) that he had put down everything delivered to Montemayor on his *chinu*, he began to demonstrate this "according to the *quipo* which he held in his hands, and stones placed in relation to it [*conforme a él*]"; but then he added: "*besides the fact that the declarer knew it very well and held it in his memory.*" Here the role of the *chinu* and the stones as a "cue to memory" is stated very nicely. The need to combine *chinu* with memory is further confirmed by Kumba's answer to question 10, where he affirms that "he that declares as *quipocamayo* has what the *tasa* says *in his memory and on his quipos.*" If memory was so important, then, we need not expect the *chinu* to have done more than simply record the essential numerical and categorical information, which was then elaborated on orally from the *chinukamana*'s memory.

Now, if we accept that the *chinu* themselves were not calculating devices (as the Aschers [1975] have argued), what was the role of the stones? Let us note, first, that the *chinukamana* were present at the collection of each consignment of tribute, and this occurred not once a year but "two or three times and more in each of the said years, and whenever Montemayor demanded it" (Achakata, question 5). On each occasion, the quantities were knotted down, and then the goods were taken to La Plata or Potosí, where they were delivered to Montemayor or his stewards: "and they paid and delivered it by their khipu to the said *encomendero*" (Hururu, question 4). Moreover, according to Hururu, it was the *chinukamana* and the Indians themselves who then took the goods to the marketplace, sold them, and delivered the cash proceeds to Montemayor (Hururu, question 4). Thus, each consignment was checked against the *chinu* on three or four different occasions: first, in Sakaka before transport to La Plata or Potosí; next, on delivery to the *encomendero*'s steward; and third, on being sold in the marketplace. Probably, the monetary value of each item was then knotted down as well, and the amount registered was then used to check the cash amounts subsequently delivered to the steward.

Now, each of these operations occurred several times each year: as Hururu put it, "although he has not declared the times they gave [the goods] in each of the said years, they sometimes gave them to him three times a year, at other times four times, and more. . . ." During the year, then, the *chinukamana* had to travel constantly between Sakaka and La Plata or Potosí, accompanying each delivery to the *encomendero*'s house for checking, and thence to the marketplace. It was the *chinukamana* who registered the prices at which each effect was sold and the value in money finally delivered on each occasion to Montemayor. But when were these totals added up?

Some sources say that the accounts were "*fenecidos*" (concluded, totted up) every four months (i.e., three times a year). But for the 1550s the *chinukamana* make repeated reference to the year as the unit of accountancy. What needed to be added up, then, were the units of each species that were delivered several times in each year, and their corresponding monetary values. Let us assume that in 1572 and 1578 each *chinukamana* made his declarations from four different tributary *chinu*, one for each of the four years under scrutiny. In that case, the annual monetary totals could have been (k)no(t)ted down on the top string of the *chinu* for the year in question, if we assume here a practice similar to that discovered for archaeological khipu by Locke and the Aschers. I suggest, therefore, that the annual "summations" (in Aymara, *haccuthapitha*; in Spanish, "*sumar las partidas, resumirlo todo*" [Bertonio 1956]) were made with the stones (however these worked), and that they had been carried out many years before the 1572 court case, probably at the moment the accounts were balanced at the end of each of the four years 1548–1551. The totals were therefore already in place on the *chinu*'s top string when the *chinukamana* arrived in court in 1572.

If we consider this prior summation, together with the role of memory, as factors no less important than the *chinu* and the stones themselves in producing the declarations of the *chinukamana*, we can distinguish two different functions for the stones. First, they were used to make substantive calculations, such as the addition of large and complex numbers (units or pesos, for example), or certain operations of multiplication (such as numbers of units by unit prices). Second, once the substantive calculations were made and knotted down on the top string, the declaration of the information involved the ritual reactivation of the actions of calculation that had already been performed. In this case, the actions in court with the stones could have involved skimming through the actions of calculation to reach a result already memorized and knotted down on the top strings by the *chinukamana*. Such a confirmatory, or authorizing, function[43] could also have served to cover up the occasional sly misstatement (as in the case discussed above of the numbers and prices of camelids delivered). After all, there was no appeal against a *chinu* reading except by retaking the *chinukamana*'s own evidence, and perhaps asking him some new questions, as in fact occurred during the *Revista* of 1578.[44]

The Ethnocategories of the Sakaka *Chinu*

The next point to be made on the Sakaka tributary *chinu* for 1548–1551 concerns the order of what John Murra termed the "ethnocategories." Murra suggested that the categories in the Jauja khipu followed a certain culturally determined order: people (men and women); camelids (with those formally "delivered" accounted apart from those taken as booty by Pizarro's band); weavings, wool, and blankets; maize, quinoa, and potatoes. . . . But in the Aymara *chinu* presented in 1572, the order is completely different: first come miners and the silver they delivered; then maize, followed by *chuño*; then camelids and derived products; then rope (*cabuya*) products and Charcas honey and wax; followed by birds and eggs. Right at the end we find quinoa, potatoes, and salt (see Table 10.2). Why do we find such differences?

Part of the answer may lie in the different places and historical circumstances in which the khipu were constructed. For example, although miners and "people" share first place in both regions, it is difficult to suppose that the reason miners came first in Sakaka was unconnected with the dominant role of silver in the tributary demands of the *encomendero*. Hence the number of miners is accompanied by the number of silver marks produced each week and their value in current coinage (*pesos corrientes*). Maize and *chuño* might also come next because of their importance, as storable food, for the subsistence of the mining camps; maize was also the raw material for several derivatives, from popcorn and *mote*[45] to corn beer. Camelids and their derivatives could follow for the same reason, with cloth coming before rope; and we would expect honey to enjoy a higher rank in Charcas than in Jauja. But why should such basic subsistence materials as quinoa and potatoes come at the end of the list, together with salt? Perhaps because of their perishability, and consequently a lower monetary value?

We should note that these are *chinu* kept by the *chinukamana* for their own ends, without interference from—indeed, despite—the *encomendero*. The only interference from Europeans in the order of the categories would occur if the order of effects was chosen by the court in putting the questions, obliging the *chinukamana* to jump around in their *chinu* in order to read out the answers in a different order from that in which they had originally been knotted down. But the only reason the court might have had for doing so would be if it wished to follow the order of effects given by the *tasa*, which is demonstrably not the case. I think we must assume that the order given is the one chosen by the *chinukamana* for keeping their records.

This leads us to ask a different set of questions. Perhaps the reason the order in Sakaka was different from the order given in Jauja is due to the differences in the relative valuations of different forms of wealth that existed in different regions prior to the European invasion. We should remember that the Charka were one of the four nations whose men served as Inka soldiers,[46] and there was a close relationship between mining and warfare through the cult of the silver *huaca* at Porco.[47] Apart from their role in the maize production of Cochabamba, the Charka's only labor service was that of providing military service. Hence, their own status as a warrior people with maize agriculture was contrasted with that of the altiplanic "nations" such as the Karanqa or the Killaqa, who were sneeringly referred to as "herders."[48] Maize was a product the Charka could be proud of producing in their own nuclear territory, as well as in Cochabamba; and their own Kuysara had been chosen by the Inka to command the maize producers of Cochabamba. Equally, *chuño* for warriors was a high-status product, since without it, their campaigns would be impossible. Camelids would come next because of their role, not as transporters of produce for Cusco's warehouses, but as carriers of provisions for the Charka's own armies, which traveled as far as Ecuador in the service of the state. Cloth and rope products would be relatively low because of the Charka disdain for the "shepherds" of the altiplano; and the importance of honey in the Province of Charcas would explain its relatively high position. In this range of values, it is perhaps less surprising, then, that quinoa and potatoes should come at the end, in spite of their importance as staples, since both were associated with the high Andean agriculture practiced as an adjunct to herding by the altiplanic "pastoral nations." Neither product could be conserved easily for long-distance travel during campaigns. Salt is another product that comes low on both the Sakaka and the Jauja khipu, and it is also associated with the high Andean ecology, where its abundance may explain its relative valuation.

Such considerations offer a partial explanation of the different scale of values visible in the Sakaka *chinu*. This difference would be translated into a difference in the order and coding of the knotted cords, and would thus offer a clear example of that difference in the "logic" of different regional khipu alluded to by Cobo, Murúa, and Capoche. After all, if a khipukamayuq from a different region was confronted with categories ordered differently from his expectations, or perhaps color-coded in a regional style that was foreign to him, what possible chance would he have had of reading it?

The *Chinu* of the Prices

I comment next on the second type of *chinu* presented in the Sakaka restitution document, which was used by the same three *chinukamana* together with the tributary chinu we have been examining so far. This is the *chinu* on which were knotted down all the prices at which the effects delivered to Montemayor and his stewards were sold in La Plata and Potosí during the four years under consideration. The mere existence of such *chinu* illustrates the extraordinary rapidity with which the Aymara "nations" of Charcas assimilated the "market mechanism," participating from the very beginning in the vast market articulated by the silver production of Potosí. However, this participation was initially "forced," in the sense that the *chinukamana* were obliged to take the tribute from the *encomendero*'s house to the marketplace for sale. Here they could observe the process of price formation as part of the process of circulation while exchanging species for silver coins and bars of differing degrees of purity.

The prices given by these *chinu* are shown in Table 10.4, and the first thing that strikes us is that they register no price fluctuations at all between 1548 and 1551. We should remember that the tributary goods were taken to market several times in any one year, yet in the *chinu* of the prices a single price is assigned for each product each year. Some price change may be expected during this period, and at least one witness, Antonio Quixada, said they did change "a little." Where differences in the prices are given in some testimonies (e.g., 10 versus 12 pesos per *fanega* of *chuño*), the *chinu* shows the higher of the two prices in all of the four years. This meant, of course, that the value of the restitution sought in 1572 also came out higher.

Equally striking is the precision with which some Sakaka witnesses could cite, in 1578, the exact difference between the relatively small percentage of monetary depreciation in 1548-1551, when the silver in circulation (*pesos corrientes*) was worth, according to some, only 12 percent less than the *pesos ensayados* of 450 *maravedís* expected in monetary accounting,[49] and the far greater depreciation in the 1570s when up to 57 percent of each silver coin in circulation was tin, copper, or lead. It is significant that the comparative rates of depreciation were recalled and declared by the Andean leaders and *chinukamana*, showing the precision with which European means of exchange had been analyzed by Andean accountants. The situation described for 1548-1551 is one of relatively good quality coin and silver bars in circulation, together with an abundance of tributary species in need of conversion, combined with intense demand for both silver and species, and high prices—a typical boom situation.

The constancy of the prices throughout the four years reminds us, too, that at this time the amounts to be delivered may have been communicated to the Sakaka Indians by Montemayor or his stewards, not simply as a quantity of units, but rather as a quantity of money, whose acquisition would require the sale of a certain number of units at a fixed price. This was the practice among the Macha in 1553 (Platt 1978). Here, the *chinukamana* had knotted down the rate at which units had to be sold to acquire a specific sum of money. Money was therefore being used *metrologically*, in the sense described by Witold Kula (1980): rather than serving simply to express exchange values, it also served to *measure quantities of tributary units* according to the price they would fetch at a fixed rate (compare today's "twenty pounds of petrol, please" or "twenty dollars of gas, please" at a service station). In this system, a fall in real prices without a corresponding fall in the official rate of exchange would mean that more tributary goods would have to be provided to reach the same monetary total. In 1553, the Macha Indians responded by asking for a reassessment (*retasa*), not in the quantity of goods, but in the rate at which the goods were officially valued. By lowering official prices till they coincided approximately with real-market prices, the amounts of kind demanded could be kept relatively constant.

The high prices on the *chinu* may have been stable between 1548 and 1551, therefore, because they represented the constant rate at which tributary quantities were officially calculated. These prices, if maintained after real prices had gone down, would have implied the delivery of a larger quantity of goods. But was the difference in official and real values really made up in this way, to the Indians' disadvantage? In the Macha case, the *encomendero* or royal tax officials had managed to demand more goods to make up the difference: hence the Macha Indians' need to get the official price lowered. But the Sakaka *chinukamana* could equally well have retained the metrological function of the stable, higher prices, which meant the delivery of fewer tributary units while simultaneously paying less money to Montemayor on the pretext of a fall in real prices. This would certainly have been handy when calculating the value of all tribute extorted in each of the four years under review, for it represented a way of maximizing the value of the restitution. Once again, the *chinukamana* may have found a way of pitching their claims beyond what was strictly owing to them.

The *Chinu* of the Coca

In his (1975) article on the Jauja khipu, Murra asked why there was no reference to coca or red peppers, suggesting that they could have been included as dried food under the category of *cestillos de toda fruta*. Neither is there any mention of peppers or coca in the Sakaka tributary *chinu*. Peppers do not appear either in the *chinu* or in the *tasa;* possibly, neither Montemayor nor the tribute committee saw any reason to demand such an "unpalatable" object with a relatively low commercial value, although it must have been consumed by the Indian miners in Potosí. But coca was a different matter, and in Sakaka, coca was absent for good reason. It was knotted down on a completely different set of *chinu*, kept by a different group of *chinukamana*, who were resident down in the coca plantations of Tiraque, and therefore not present when the main set of tributary *chinu* were read out in 1572. Only later did these lowland *chinukamana* arrive at court to put the record straight. It is possible, then, that the absence of coca in the Jauja khipu read out in 1561 is also due to the fact that it was knotted down separately by a different group of khipukamayuq. How many other kinds of produce or labor service might have been accounted for on khipu kept separate from the main set of accounts?[50]

The "Memorial of the Coca," which presents the declarations of the three *chinukamana* of the coca,[51] is not a direct reading of the *chinu*, as is the case with the declarations of Achakata, Kumba, and Hururu. It reaches us with the statements of the different *chinukamana* already collated and reduced to a single narrative, and it is signed by Juan de Arévalo and Joan de Baños, both Spanish lawyers acting for the Sakaka Indians. However, the three *chinukamana* who declared the information also appeared to give evidence in answer to a new Sakaka questionnaire. Don Alonso Yawri, don Hernando Kaysa, and don Pedro Yana were all from Sakaka, but all three resided in the valleys and were accompanied in the court by the lords of the Charka colonists in Cochabamba: don Gerónimo Kuyu of Santiago del Paso and don Martín Champi and don Francisco Awatiri of Tiquipaya.

The "Memorial of the Coca" is not, then, the product of a court interrogation. However, the basis of the text is said to be a *relación* made by the "*quipocamayos* of the *chácaras* of coca . . . and all the *quipocamayos* that reside in the said valleys of the *yungas* declare it according to their *quipos*." The text does not allow us to detect variations between the *chinu*, their readings, their translation, and their transcription in Spanish, as in the case of the tributary *chinu* just analyzed. Nevertheless, the form of the text, which comes divided into the same four years from 1548 to 1551, with each year subdivided into three annual *mita*, or coca harvests, probably reflects the structuring of the information on the *chinu*, as it was read off by the three *chinukamana* for the lawyers to summarize. I have therefore risked schematizing the information in a hypothetical *chinu* structure (Table 10.5), which may at least have the value of clarifying some of the issues under discussion.

The text is headed by an explanation of why this information had not been given before (because of the absence of the *chinukamana* resident in "the said valleys of the *yungas*"), and by a list of the eleven fields where the coca is grown (one of them, Chuquioma, now inhabited by Spaniards). In my reconstruction, I have assumed the existence of a top string where the *mitas* for each year, and perhaps their values, were summed up. The main cord would identify the theme of the *chinu*—in this case, "coca given [in the first year of] Alonso's lordship." For ease of reference I have given the year (1548) in Christian reckoning, although one tributary *chinukamana*, don Luis Kumba, stated that he didn't know how to declare "the names of the years."[52] Then the three secondary cords classify the numerical information between three groups of strings corresponding to the three *mitas* of 1548. This is the least problematical part of the reconstruction.

The main problems arise when we reach the level of the pendant strings (third level). In the text we are given well-formed Spanish sentences, which are particularly detailed for the first *mita;* thereafter, much of this detail is omitted. This implies that all the Spanish narrative, except the categories and their numbers, corresponds to oral "fill-in," first elicited from the *chinukamana* in Aymara, then translated (though there is no reference to the interpreters), and finally rephrased and synthesized in Spanish by the lawyers.

In each of the three *mita*, the number of *cestos* harvested is given first, and it seems reasonable to assign these to a separate string coded in some way as *cestos de coca* with the numbers of *cestos* knotted onto the string. The next string gives the number of Indians who carried the harvest on their backs from the plantations to Totora, where they were unloaded in a storehouse. During this stage, the *cestos* were under the supervision of a steward, whose name is given for *mitas* 1 and 3 as Antón Gómez (the name of the steward is omitted in *mita* 2).

Then the *cestos* are transported on Indians or llamas from Totora to Montemayor's houses in La Plata (*mitas* 1 and 3) or Potosí (*mita* 2), under the direction of another of Montemayor's stewards, whose name is given on its first occurrence as "Quintero or Tintero." The hesitation about the first phoneme of the steward's name may be significant, since it suggests reliance on oral memory rather than an appeal to a phonetic coding in the cords, which would probably not have allowed this type of ambiguity. I have therefore omitted both stewards' names from the *chinu* reconstruction, leaving them in italics along with the rest of the narrative, which I suggest was supplied as oral gloss by the *chinukamana*.

However, there is more than one way of coding the information within the limits of the structure of the *chinu*. I have therefore proposed, for a single *mita*—simply by way of illustration—an alternative way of structuring the information in the bottom line, which places the harvest of *cestos* in the first position, and then places on two subsidiary strings the distinction between the two journeys made from the plantations to Totora and from Totora to Chuquisaca (as the *chinukamana* will have called La Plata) or Potosí. The actual numbers of Indians and llamas involved will then have been placed on two sub-subsidiary strings. Since Indians and llamas are interchangeable as regards carrying capacity (together they add up to approximately half the *cestos* to be transported, that is, two *cestos* per Indian/llama), it seems reasonable to keep them as neighboring alternatives at the bottom of the branching structure.

The possibility of selecting between different ways of structuring and coding the information returns us to the problem of the degree of "idiosyncrasy" involved in khipu design. What remains to be discovered is whether, at the level discussed, different ways of structuring data would have been equally intelligible to different *chinukamana* who shared the same overall tradition of *chinu* making. My feeling is that Achakata, for example, would have had little difficulty in detecting such minor differences in Kumba's *chinu*, given that he knew what the theme was and could infer from his own knowledge of the data how Kumba had chosen to proceed. For those coming from a different regional tradition, however, these low-level differences would have functioned to obfuscate still further any unauthorized attempt to read the Sakaka *chinu*.

CONCLUSIONS

What does this discussion imply for our understanding of Cusco's efforts to unify the administration of its realm with decimally organized khipu in line with a decimally organized system of social segmentation? First, we should not expect Aymara (or other regional) traditions of *chinu* construction necessarily to have followed all Inka conventions of structure or code. The relation between Inka khipu and Aymara *chinu* is an aspect of the relations between Cusco and regional structures of authority and organization, even if, in some cases, Cusco-sponsored elements may have been adopted into late

Aymara *chinu* construction. From a regional perspective, therefore, no significant "patterns" could necessarily be derived from a merely formal comparison of the distribution of design elements across an indiscriminately wide "universe" of khipu.

The process of consolidation of the Tawantinsuyu passed through the gradual, though incomplete, replacement of Aymara and other regional traditions of "numerical *chinu*" by the new "esoteric knowledge" of the imperial khipu stored in the self-declared "world-navel" at Cusco. But the fascination of imperial ideology and religion should not distract us from the wider historical task: the Tawantinsuyu must be situated in relation to other regional developments in the Andes, not all of which chose the path of pan-Andean centralization, standardization, and the subordination of all labor to the reproductive needs of an imperial theocracy. Part of this task consists, precisely, in leaving open the appropriate theoretical space for the study of non-Inka khipu.

Variability of design includes variability of construction materials. Can we associate the evolution of khipu with those hunting and herding societies of the high southern Andes who were responsible for the domestication of the llama and the alpaca? The notion of information being "trapped" or "imprisoned" in the cords is suggestive, particularly when taken together with the Spanish idea that khipu information is "declared," rather than "witnessed," by their keepers. The idea seems to be that of "revealing" or "releasing" information that has been knotted into the khipu by its keeper. Here, it may be useful to compare and contrast the actions of *giving evidence* for witnessed events or states of affairs, *declaring* stored or secret information, *describing* a coded khipu, and *reading* a Spanish written document.

My reconstruction of the *chinu* of the coca has distinguished between "bits" of information "trapped" in the cords and the oral gloss supplied by the keeper when bringing forth his hidden nuggets. If we remember Verónica Cereceda's suggestion that the khipu are to be thought of as living beings, it may be appropriate to compare khipu declarations with the procedures of Andean shamans. The distinction between the transmission of secret knowledge and the oral gloss may be comparable to the way the shaman combines transmission of a living being's "voice" with oral exegesis.[53]

I have tried to reconstruct the complex way in which tributary khipu were formed in relation to the *encomendero*'s repeated tributary demands and the sale of successive consignments of effects in the marketplaces of La Plata and Potosí. Although we do not yet know how the stones would have been used to make substantive calculations, their deft manipulation in formal situations might also have functioned as rituals of authorization. However, the idea of ritually reactivating the logical steps by which arithmetical conclusions are reached may remind us of the "desedimentation" process proposed by Edmund Husserl in his analysis of the epistemological requirements of any mathematical system.[54] This process requires the reactivation of the truth perceptions involved at each stage in the construction of a mathematical argument. From this perspective, then, we would have to distinguish between actually "re-living" the truth perceptions involved at different stages of the *chinu*-construction process (for which our glib phrase "checking the results" would be a very inadequate description), and a process of symbolically skimming through well-"sedimented" sums for more "theatrical" reasons of authorization, without actually recovering their original self-evidence.

In both cases, however, the procedures would bridge the gap between a mere number-crunching approach to numerical khipu and the deeper symbolic universe of Andean mathematics (Urton 1997). And it is at this point where the very distinction between numerical and narrative khipu begins to break down. As we recover, with the help of the stones, the constructional premises shared by each khipu, we also approach the symbolic bases of numerical operations. At this level, elementary concepts are brought into play that combine to express fundamental cosmological ideas. Color ideas such as the black/white opposition, or the choice between left/right in both twist directionality and positional ordering, are all part of the symbolic construction of the Andean universe. Ideas like "summation" or "balancing the accounts" are not purely referential: they are also dynamic metaphors that propitiate the social reproduction of the cosmos by ensuring equitable flows through reciprocal channels of exchange. This form of accountancy is a matter of ritual concern to all forms of Andean government, whatever sort of khipu may be involved.

Such elements may be incorporated within a future *theory of khipu declarations*. In constructing this theory, it will be useful to observe not only how and what the *chinukamana* declared, but also what they did not declare. As the first three Sakaka *chinukamana* explained in 1578, the reason they had not mentioned certain items during their first interrogation was that they had not been asked. As with modern fieldwork (and shamanic conversations), it was important to know how to put the appropriate questions. There are indications, for example, that in 1572 the court was not always clear about how best to interrogate the *chinukamana*, whereas in 1578 certain questions were put that had been omitted the first time round. Something had been learned in the interim. Thus the competence of the *chinukamana* cannot be separated from the competence of their audience: their declarations emerge from the thematic prompting they receive from those listening to them. This suggests that, with narrative khipu too, a dialogical emphasis should be placed on the way the receivers of information elicit the answers they seek, as well as on the skills and knowledge of the khipukamayuq themselves.

Let us return, finally, to the problem of the "historical" or "narrative" *khipu.* Cieza suggested that these functioned by storing and ordering the elements of different "plots," which could later be realized through narrative and song. It is tempting to compare such "plots" with Claude Lévi-Strauss's mythemes, which were abstracted by the mythographer from the source-narrative in which they were embedded. Lévi-Strauss's procedure attracted criticism from performance theorists and ethnographers of speaking, who wished to regard the thematic elements as emergent from the telling of the tale. But with "narrative khipu," it appears, the process was inverted. Themes were identified, and their interrelations were embodied in the khipu structure, before being communicated sequentially to verbal artists for transformation into oral performance. From this perspective, Andean khipu should not be regarded as "literal transcriptions" of specific oral performances; instead, they may have provided the "graphic" structures that underlay the production of many possible oral performances. The logical ordering of the fibers could, perhaps, be compared to structuralist diagrams, capable of generating many tales according to the skills of the singer. In this sense, it may be asked whether Lévi-Strauss was not unconsciously working from a rather Andean premise in approaching and ordering his Amazonian source material: he was, so to speak, "looking for the khipu" behind the different narratives.

The reconstruction of early colonial *chinu* by careful readings of their colonial transcriptions is a research tactic still in its infancy. Many other such transcriptions await detailed examination. Their analysis would allow us to create a typology of khipu in relation to their external political contexts, their social and ritual functions, and their internal sensibility and categorical organization. Their realistic reconstruction will demand collaboration between those familiar with the archaeological record, and ethnohistorians working on the sixteenth-century transition to the colonial system. It may not be too much to hope that, one day, a khipu will turn up which can be recognized as the original of a colonial transcription, and can therefore provide a partial test for the reconstructions that our ingenuity can devise today.

ACKNOWLEDGMENTS

I am grateful to Carlos Sempat Assadourian and Gary Urton for their helpful suggestions. All translations are mine.

NOTES

1. *Chinu* (Aymara) = "knot"; the Aymara equivalent of *khipu* (Quechua). I use the words *khipu* and *khipukamayuq*, respectively, to refer generally to the "knotted cords" employed at different times in the Andean region and their "keepers," and *chinu* and *chinukamana* to refer specifically to the pre-Inka tradition of "knotted cords" used by the Aymara diarchies of the southern Andes. "*Quipocamayo*" is reserved for citations.

2. Cobo 1964, 1: 368; cf. Tristan Platt 1987: 90–91.

3. Bertonio 1956, 2: 83. Tying a knot in one's handkerchief to remember something is an obvious example of cultural parallelism.

4. I assume here, if only as a "thought experiment," that the Naples document contains a proposal made by Jesuits in the early seventeenth century for understanding the nature of the legendary "narrative khipu." The document's authenticity is doubtful, but the rebus principle invoked is widely found in ancient civilizations, as well as in Jesuit syllabaries employed in the colonial Andes. See Roswith Hartmann 1989: 169–188.

5. Laurencich Minelli 1996: 63–64.

6. Following Cieza and Murúa, among other sources, I distinguish the lakeside kingdoms of the Collao from the several "nations" of the Province of Charcas, only one of which is called the Charka "nation" in the sixteenth-century sources. In this text, I use the spelling "Charcas" to refer to the province and "Charka" to refer to a specific "nation," or "federation," within that province.

7. Archivo General de Indias (hereafter AGI), Justicia 653: f. 8v. The committee was made up of Archbishop Loayza, Hernando de Santillán, and Domingo de Santo Tomás, and the *tasa* was brought to Sakaka in 1551 by Lorenzo de Estupiñán, who then became Corregidor of La Paz. As usual, it was based on prior inspections (*visitas*) ordered by the committee, as well as on consultations with knowledgeable informants (see f. 4r–v).

8. Urton 1994: 293–294.

9. Cobo 1964, 2: 143.

10. Murúa 1986: 374.

11. See Sampson 1985 for this typology of writing systems. For the combination of different systems within a single text, see, for example, the reading of the Egyptian Narmer Palette given in Layton 1991: 131–137.

12. When the Inka died, "they ordered the great *quipocamayos* to be called . . . so that they might communicate with others among them who, being chosen for their rhetorical skills and flowing words, know how to tell everything that has happened in good order, as we tell romances and carols [*romances y villancicos*] . . ." (Cieza de León 1985, Ch. 11: 27).

13. So I understand the discovery of Inka *unkus* (tunics) painted on or bricked into

the walls of Carangas *chullpas* (funerary towers) (Gisbert 1994; cf. Pärssinen 1993), together with the lavish gifts of *kumpi* cloth (design unspecified) given to the Charka lord Kuysara by Inka Wayna Qhapaq or Waskar (AGI, Justicia 653: ff. 68r, 75r).

14. Published in Espinoza Soriano 1969.

15. AGI, Charcas 56: ff. 41v–46v.

16. AGI, Patronato 115. I thank Thomas Abercrombie for this reference.

17. Published in Espinoza Soriano 1969: ff. 17v, 18r.

18. AGI, Justicia 653: f. 50v. Evidence of Juan Ortiz Picón (question 12).

19. AGI, Justicia 653: ff. 4r, 7v.

20. AGI, Justicia 653: f. 82r.

21. AGI, Justicia 449, no. 1: ff. 53r–55v.

22. These were also the names of the two parishes, with two altars and two priests, that coexisted within the jurisdiction of the single church of Chayanta (Cañete y Domínguez 1952; cf. Harris 1986).

23. Espinoza Soriano 1969.

24. AGI, Justicia 653. Various authors have referred to this document, including Carlos Sempat Assadourian, Thomas Abercrombie, Silvia Arce, Ximena Medinaceli, John Murra, Martti Pärssinen, and Gary Urton. A new selection and transcription, on which the present analysis is based, will be published in Tristan Platt, Thérèse Bouysse-Cassayne, Olivia Harris, and Thierry Saignes, eds., *Qaraqara/Charka* (in press).

25. Cf. Joan de Baños's defense of the Macha in 1579 against Spanish territorial encroachment (ANB, Tierras e Indios, Exp. Año 1579, no. 46).

26. Since the work of Paul Bohannan among the Tiv (1957), it has been commonplace to distinguish European legal practice from "non-Western" procedures by pointing, for example, to the African emphasis on solution by agreement and consensus as opposed to the "Western" emphasis on the proof of crime followed by fitting punishment. In the present case, it is worth examining an inverse hypothesis, which contrasts the exactitude of pre-Hispanic Andean systems of reckoning with a European preference for compromise (at least when dealing with Indian claims for restitution).

27. Murúa 1986: 375.

28. After Montemayor's death, Francisco Lobato was commissioned in the 1560s by Viceroy Conde de Nieva to inspect (*visitar*) the Sakaka in their impoverished state (AGI, Justicia 653: f. 22v). Montemayor's heirs alleged that Lobato invited the Sakaka Indians to claim against Montemayor but that they had said they had nothing to claim (AGI, Justicia 653: f. 205r).

29. Unlike Francisco Lobato, Núñez Bazán had actually consulted the Sakaka *chinu* while carrying out his inspection (AGI, Justicia 653: ff. 163r–165v) and so may have been better placed than Lobato to suggest filing a suit against Montemayor's heirs.

30. AGI, Justicia 653: f. 163r.

31. AGI, Justicia 653: f. 14r. Benino was author of the *Verdadera relación de lo sussedido en los Reinos e provincias del Peru desde la yda a ellos del Virrey Blasco Nunez Vela hasta el desbarato y muerte de Gonçalo Piçarro* (Sevilla, 1549). A facsimile reproduction with an introduction by José Toribio Medina was published by the Institut d'Ethnologie, Paris, in 1930.

32. AGI, Lima 118. I thank Concepción Gavira for sending me a photocopy of this letter.

33. For details of this valuable *encomienda* in the coca plantations below La Paz, see Murra 1991.

34. The date of Montemayor's death in 1556 is asserted by Joan de Baños; one witness, Diego Hernández de Castro, said that Montemayor had previously left for Spain "very rich" (AGI, Justicia 653: ff. 13r, question 10, and 28v, question 3).

35. The *tasa* in fact left open what proportion of the 80 loads should be in potatoes or *chuño;* see Table 10.1.

36. Only in 1578 were the *chinukamana* prompted by new questions to say that they would claim "in due course" for these *agravios, molestias y vejaciones* (AGI, Justicia 653: f. 278r). Montemayor's behavior, like that of other *encomenderos* in this period, seems to imitate Pizarro's in Cajamarca: the "natural lords" are imprisoned, tortured, and given mock hangings until they can produce their "ransom" in the form of ever more tributary goods.

37. One of the *chinukamana,* don Luis Cumba, in fact stated that he didn't know the names of either the months or the years (see AGI, Justicia 653: ff. 64r, question 2, and 68v, question 10). This would suggest that an Aymara or Inka time-reckoning system was incorporated into the structure of each *chinu.* But was Cumba also covering himself against detection?

38. These sums are expressed in the assayed silver pesos of 450 *maravedís* each (*pesos ensayados*), the notional standard to which real coins and bars (generally mixed with lead, copper, or tin) were reduced in Spanish accounting.

39. See AGI, Justicia 653: f. 312v, with reference to transport costs from the coca plantations to Potosí.

40. It is worth noting that the *chinukamana* are rarely referred to as "witnesses" (*testigos*); more generally they are called the *declarante* (declarer), or *él que declara* (the one who declares). This indicates that the relation between the *chinukamana* and their cords was considered by the court to differ from the relation between a "witness" and his evidence, and it may suggest an almost shamanic dimension to khipu reading: rather than establishing the empirical relation of a witness with ocular or hearsay evidence, the *chinukamana* brings us the "voice" of the living *chinu,* as if through its keeper it articulates the secret knowledge "imprisoned" within it to the waiting audience.

41. Compare a discussion in Murra 1975 of a similar problem in the interpretation of the Wanka khipu presented in 1561 by the lords of Hatun Jauja.

42. Compare Urton (1997) on Quechua concepts of number and the "mathematics of rectification." The notion of "fairness" administered from above, as in Julien's (1988) version of the Inka decimal system, should be counterweighed by notions of rectification "from below," such as is implied in the notion of "paring excesses" imposed by an overweening partner (Platt 1986, 1987). For a fuller analysis of the symbolism of black and white stones, see Platt 1987; and for the Aymara concept of *allqa* ("opposition," as between black and white), see Cereceda 1990.

43. I have previously indicated the importance of seeking the ritual dimensions of the act of "summation" (Platt 1987: 122).

44. In October 1578, the accountants of the two parties also attempted, by presenting a questionnaire and calling witnesses, to establish some values not given by the *chinukamana.* See the *Probanza en la liquidación* in AGI, Justicia 653: ff. 279r–283v.

45. Quechua, *mut'i* = soaked maize grains.

46. Espinoza Soriano 1969; Murra 1986.

47. See Abercrombie 1998, especially pp. 267–268.

48. See AGI, Justicia 432, no. 1. For a fuller treatment of the political opposition between "farmers" and "shepherds," see Platt et al., in press.

49. Gerónimo Cuyo, lord of Santiago del Paso, said that "each peso circulated with one *tomín* of interest, which comes out at 12 1/2 pesos percent"; and according to don Martín Chambi of Tiquipaya, silver bars were circulating at the time at only 10–11 percent beneath the official silver standard (answers to question 5; AGI, Justicia 653: ff. 398r–412v).

50. For example, it can be assumed that, under the Inka, a separate set of *chinu* would have registered the military services provided for the state by each social group within the Charka and Qaraqara federations.

51. AGI, Justicia 653: ff. 370r–372v.

52. AGI, Justicia 653: f. 68v, question 10. This was probably true for all the Sakaka *chinukamana*. I have suggested above that the year of each *chinu* was counted from the year each native lord assumed power (e.g., "Alonso").

53. This shamanic procedure is analyzed for the modern Macha in Platt 1997.

54. See Husserl 1970. See also the stimulating discussion of mythopoeia and sedimentation in Mimica 1992.

BIBLIOGRAPHY

Abercrombie, Thomas. 1998. *Pathways of Memory and Power: Ethnography and History among an Andean People*. Madison: University of Wisconsin Press.

Archivo General de Indias (Seville), Charcas 56.

Archivo General de Indias (Seville), Justicia 449.

Archivo General de Indias (Seville), Justicia 653. "Los caciques e indios de Sacaca contra los herederos de Alonso de Montemayor." First document of the second case in the file *Autos entre Partes, años 1576–79*.

Archivo General de Indias (Seville), Patronato 115.

Archivo Nacional de Bolivia (Sucre), Tierras e Indios. Expediente Año 1579, no. 46.

Arnold, Denise, Domingo Jiménez, and Juan de Dios Yapita. 1992. *Hacia un orden andino de las cosas*. La Paz: HISBOL/ILCA.

Ascher, Marcia, and Robert Ascher. 1975. "The Quipu as a Visible Language." *Visible Language* 9: 329–356.

Bertonio, Ludovico. 1956 [1612]. *Vocabulario de la Lengua Aymara*. La Paz: Don Bosco.

Bohannan, Paul. 1957. *Justice and Judgement among the Tiv*. Oxford: Oxford University Press.

Cañete y Domínguez, Pedro Vicente. 1952 [1789]. *Guía histórica, geográfica . . . del Gobierno e Intendencia de la Provincia de Potosí*. Potosí, Bolivia: Editorial Potosí.

Capoche, Luis. 1959 [1585]. *Relación general de la Villa Imperial de Potosí*. Edited by Luis Hanke and Gunnar Mendoza. Madrid: Biblioteca de Autores Españoles 122.

Cereceda, Verónica. 1986. "The Semiology of Andean Textiles." In *Anthropological History of Andean Polities*, edited by J. V. Murra, N. Wachtel, and J. Revel, 149–173. Cambridge: Cambridge University Press.

———. 1990. "A partir de los colores de un pájaro . . ." *Boletín del Museo Chileno de Arte Precolombino* 4: 57–104.

Cieza de León, Pedro. 1985 [1880/1553?]. *Crónica del Perú, Segunda Parte*. Lima: Pontificia Universidad Católica del Perú, Fondo Editorial, Academia Nacional de la Historia.

Cobo, Bernabé. 1964 [1653]. *Historia del Nuevo Mundo.* 2 vols. Biblioteca de Autores Españoles 91–92. Madrid: Ediciones Atlas.

Conklin, William. 1982. "The Information System of the Middle Horizon Quipus." In *Ethnoastronomy and Archaeoastronomy in the American Tropics,* edited by Anthony F. Aveni and Gary Urton. Annals of the New York Academy of Sciences, vol. 385. New York: New York Academy of Sciences.

Espinoza Soriano, Waldemar. 1969. "El 'Memorial' de Charcas: 'Chronicas' inédita de 1582." *Cantuta: Revista de la Universidad de la Educación* (Lima) 4: 117–152.

Gisbert, Teresa. 1994. "El señorío de los Carangas y los chullpares del Río Lauca." *Revista Andina* (Cusco) 24 (Año 12), no. 2: 427–485.

Harris, Olivia. 1986. "From Asymmetry to Triangle: Symbolic Transformations in Northern Potosí." In *Anthropological History of Andean Polities,* edited by J. V. Murra, N. Wachtel, and J. Revel, 260–279. Cambridge: Cambridge University Press.

Hartmann, Roswith. 1989. "Pictografías de tipo religioso-cristiano del área andina: Dos ejemplos." In *Iglesia, religión y sociedad en la historia latinoamericana, 1492–1945.* Congreso VIII de la Asociación de Historiadores Latinoamericanistas de Europa (AHILA), vol. 2. Szeged, Hungary: N.p.

Husserl, Edmund. 1970. "The Origin of Geometry." Appendix VI of *The Crisis of European Science and Transcendental Phenomenology.* Translated by David Carr. Evanston: Northwestern University Press.

Julien, Catherine. 1988. "How Inca Decimal Administration Worked." *Ethnohistory* 35, no. 3: 357–379.

Kula, Witold. 1980. *Las medidas y los hombres.* Mexico City: Siglo Veintiuno.

Laurencich Minelli, Laura. 1996. *La scrittura dell' antico Perù: Un mondo da scoprire.* Bologna: Cooperativa Libraria Editrice Bologna.

Layton, Robert. 1991. *The Anthropology of Art.* Cambridge: Cambridge University Press.

Lechtman, Heather. 1980. "The Central Andes: Metallurgy without Iron." In *The Coming of the Age of Iron,* edited by T. A. Wertime and J. D. Muhly, 267–334. New Haven: Yale University Press.

Locke, L. Leland. 1912. "The Ancient Quipo: A Peruvian Knot Record." *American Anthropologist* 14, no. 2: 325–332.

———. 1923. *The Ancient Quipu or Peruvian Knot Record.* New York: American Museum of Natural History.

Mimica, Jadran. 1992. *Intimations of Infinity: The Cultural Meanings of the Iqwaye Counting and Number System.* Oxford: Berg.

Murra, John V. 1975. "Las etnocategorías de un quipo estatal." In *Formaciones económicas y políticas del mundo andino.* Lima: Instituto de Estudios Peruanos.

———. 1986. "The Expansion of the Inka State: Armies, War, and Rebellions." In *Anthropological History of Andean Polities,* edited by J. Murra, N. Wachtel, and J. Revel, 49–58. Cambridge: Cambridge University Press.

———, ed. 1991. *Visita de los valles de Sonqo en los yunka de coca de La Paz [1568–1570].* Monografías Economía Quinto Centenario. Madrid: Antoni Bosch.

Murúa, Martín de. 1986 [1613]. *Historia General del Perú.* Edited by Manuel Ballesteros. Madrid: Historia 16.

Ong, Walter J. 1982. *Orality and Literacy: The Technologizing of the Word*. London and New York: Routledge.

Pärssinen, Martti. 1992. *Tawantinsuyu: The Inca State and Its Political Organization*. Studia Historica 43. Helsinki: Societas Historica Finlandiae.

———. 1993. "Torres funerarias decoradas en Caquiaviri." *Puma Punku* (La Paz) 2, nos. 5–6 (nueva época).

Platt, Tristan. 1978. "Acerca del sistema tributario pre-toledano en el Alto Peru." *Avances: Revista Boliviana de Estudios Históricos y Sociales* (La Paz) 1: 33–46.

———. 1986. "Mirrors and Maize: The Concept of Yanantin among the Macha of Potosí (Bolivia)." In *Anthropological History of Andean Polities*, edited by J. V. Murra, N. Wachtel, and J. Revel, 228–259. Cambridge: Cambridge University Press.

———. 1987. "Entre ch'axwa y mukhsa: para una historia del pensamiento político aymara." In *Tres reflexiones sobre el pensamiento andino*, by T. Bouysse-Cassayne, O. Harris, T. Platt, and V. Cereceda. La Paz: HISBOL.

———. 1997. "The Sound of Light: Emergent Communication through Quechua Shamanic Dialogue." In *Creating Context in Andean Cultures*, edited by Rosaleen Howard-Malverde, 196–226. Oxford Studies in Anthropological Linguistics. New York and Oxford: Oxford University Press.

Platt, Tristan, Thérèse Bouysse-Cassayne, Olivia Harris, and Thierry Saignes, eds. In press. *Qaraqara/Charka*. La Paz: Plural Editores.

Radicati di Primeglio, Carlos. 1979. *El sistema contable de los Incas: Yupana y quipu*. Lima: Librería Studium.

Sampson, Geoffrey. 1985. *Writing Systems*. London: Routledge.

Urton, Gary. 1994. "A New Twist in an Old Yarn: Variation in Knot Directionality in the Inka *Khipus*." *Baessler-Archiv*, Neue Folge, Band 42: 271–305.

——— (with Primitivo Nina Llanos). 1997. *The Social Life of Numbers: A Quechua Ontology of Numbers and Philosophy of Arithmetic*. Austin: University of Texas Press.

———. 1998. "From Knots to Narratives: Reconstructing the Art of Historical Record-Keeping in the Andes from Spanish Transcriptions of Inka *Khipus*." *Ethnohistory* 45, no. 3: 409–438.

Wachtel, Nathan. 1982. "The Mitimaes of the Cochabamba Valley: The Colonization Policy of Huayna Capac." In *The Inca and Aztec States, 1400–1800*, edited by G. Collier, R. Rosaldo, and J. Wirth, 199–235. New York: Academic Press.

Pérez Bocanegra's
Ritual formulario

ELEVEN   *Khipu Knots and Confession*

Regina Harrison

In this age of electronic memory devices—telephone message machines with personal "reminders" built in, caller ID gadgets that remember who just called (even though we didn't pick up the phone and even though they didn't say a word), e-mail that's stored forever in bottomless computer pits (retrieved in cases of harassment or to increase severance pay in layoffs), digital radio settings remembering the spot where we tune in during our commute, computers that remember how many "hits" a Web site receives—it is difficult to imagine a time when discussion of memory was theological, resulting in threats of hellfire and eternal damnation if the penitent forgot a single sin. The khipu, a sophisticated pre-electronic record-keeping device as important in the Viceroyalty of Peru as our modern gadgets are to us today, became an object of theological inquiry commented upon by priests and Indians alike in the parishes of the Viceroyalty of Peru.

Joyce Marcus, in her substantial study of Mesoamerican writing systems (1992: 27), characterizes the function of the Peruvian khipu as "record keeping to keep track of economic transactions." In other definitions, the khipu is also described for its accounting function and is frequently identified as a *nudo* (knot) or an account done by means of knots, *cuenta por nudo*. The verb is glossed as *leer nudos* (to read knots) or *contar por nudos* (to count using knots; Durán 1990: 773–774). However, translated from the Spanish, *contar* means not only "to count," but also signifies "to tell a story, to narrate." That meaning is implied in the Inca Garcilaso de la Vega's description of the khipu in which he attests to the use of the knots to yield histories, poems, legislation, and religious systems, in addition to numerical function.

Colonial khipu were useful in eliciting all sorts of information; Cristóbal Vaca de Castro used four older khipukamayuq, official Inka historians, in 1542 to gather information on genealogies and history (Urton 1990: 43). We know from Juan Polo de Ondegardo that he gathered 465 men and women, some of them khipu specialists, to recover Inkan history in 1559 (Duviols 1977: 116). Two other instances of historical renderings from khipu are mentioned in Pedro Sarmiento de Gamboa's *Historia de los Incas* (1942), for which more than one hundred khipu specialists were consulted; these historical accounts were later verified by forty-two descendants of Inkan nobility (Urton 1990: 19). Cristóbal de Molina ("el Cuzqueño"), in his "Relación de las fábulas y ritos de los Ingas," is one of the first to link the reading of the strings with Spanish Catholic practices: ". . . estos quipos que cassi son a modo de pavilos con que las biejas re[z]an en nuestra España salvo ser ramales" [these khipu that are very much like the candle wick strings with which the old women pray in our Spain, except that they are strings which twisted together come apart] (1988: 58).

El Cuzqueño's observation of similarities between the khipu and the Christian prayer rituals of the rosary are supplemented by other statements regarding the role of khipu in conversion. In a letter written in 1576, José de Acosta narrates a scene in which old men, crying, show him the knots and strings that help them accurately remember the teachings of the Christian doctrine: ". . . algunos viejos de ochenta y noventa años acudían a mí llorando y mostrándome unos cordeles, los nudos con que tenían señaladas las cosas que van aprendiendo de la doctrina en aquellos días" [some old men about eighty and ninety years old came over to me crying and showing me the strings, the knots of which indicated the matters that they are learning about the doctrine in those days] (1954b: 280). In the mission of Juli (1577), Acosta writes that men and women, seated separately in a little plaza, communally recited prayers and the doctrine each Sunday. With the aid of a native teacher, they prayed, "pasando unos quipos o registros que tienen, hechos de cordeles con nudos, por donde se acuerdan de lo que aprenden como nosotros por escrito" [passing around some khipu or registers that they have, made of strings and knots, in order to remember what they learn, as we do with writing] (1954b: 287).

Acosta was one of several persons chosen to work on the monumental *Doctrina christiana* in 1584, and the *Confessionario* and the *Tercero cathecismo . . .* in 1585. His observations on the usefulness of the khipu as a memory device (like writing) may have contributed to mention of khipu in the *Tercero cathecismo . . .* of 1585. Specifically, in Sermon Twelve, on the theme of confession, the narrative voice tells the Indian parishioners that they do not confess well because they do not enumerate all their sins, and therefore they will be condemned. However, according to this sermon, there is a way for the Andean penitents to correct these errors:

> Lo primero, hijo mío, has de pensar bien tus peccados, y hazer quipo dellos: como hazes quipo, quando eres tambocamayo, de lo q(ue) das ydelo q(ue) deuen: assi haz quipo delo que has hecho, contra Dios y contra tu proximo, y qua(n)tas vezes: si muchas, o si pocas. Y no solo has de dezir tus obras: sino tambien tus pensamientos malos . . . Despues de auer te pe(n)sado, y hecho quippo de tus peccados por los diez mandamientos, o como mejor supieres, has de pedir a Dios perdon . . .   (*TERCERO CATHECISMO* . . . 1985: 482–483)

> [The first thing you have to do, my son, is that you have to think a lot about your sins, and make a khipu out of them: make a khipu like when you are a *tambocamayoc*, of what you give out and what they owe you: just like that make a khipu of what you have done against God and against your neighbor, and how many times, a lot or a little. And you can't just say your actions [*obras*] but also your unclean thoughts [*pensamientos malos*] . . . and after you've thought about it by yourself, and made a khipu based on the Ten Commandments, or as best you can, you must ask God for forgiveness.]

According to Sermon Twelve, then and only then does the penitent go before the priest: "Hecho esto muy bien, hincado las rodillas ante el Padre di todos tus peccados quantos vinieron a tu memoria, que lo ayas confessado, y todos quantos te preguntare el Padre, sin callar ninguno" [Carrying this out well, on your knees before the priest just say all the sins that come into your memory, those that you have confessed, and all those that the Priest asks you, without hushing up one of them] (1985: 483).

Although Acosta and the other writers of the colonial sermons comment on the pious use of the khipu in 1576 and 1577, several years later a change in attitude had occurred. The Third Lima Council proclaims in the proceedings of 1583, article 37, that khipu are to be taken away from the Indians:

> y porque en lugar de libros los indios han usado y usan unos como registros hechos de diferentes hilos que ellos llaman quipos, y con estos conservan la memoria de su antigua superstición y ritos ceremonias y costumbres perversas, procuren con diligencia los

obispos que todos los memoriales o quipos que sirven para su
superstición, se les quiten totalmente a los yndios.

(BARTRA 1982: 103)

[and because instead of books the Indians have used and use some
registers made of different cords that they call khipu, and with these
they preserve the memories of their ancient superstitions and rites
and ceremonies and perverse traditions, let all bishops diligently look
for them, so that all these memory devices or khipu that serve their
superstition be taken away from the Indians.]

Despite this decision and strong wording against khipu use in 1583, the Sermon of 1585 (quoted above) recommends the listing of sins by khipu, and as
late as 1600 we still have a report in the *Crónica anónima* of Indians in the
Cusco region confessing by khipu: "haciendo memoria por unos cordeles y
ñudos de diferentes colores para confesarse generalmente" [remembering by
means of strings and knots of different colors in order to confess] (Mateos
1944, 2: 101).

THE ACT OF CONFESSION: COUNTS AND CONSCIENCE

In Europe, where Christian confession originated, aids to memory were similarly recommended. For instance, Saint Augustine mentions the use of a
memory device that some found useful. The word *SALIGIA* is an acronym
that was fashioned from the first letter of each sin: *superbia* (arrogance), *ava-
ritia* (avarice), *luxuria* (lust), *ira* (anger), *gula* (gluttony), *invidia* (envy), *acedia*
(slothfulness) (Lea 1896, 2:236). In *La confession coupée* (Paris, 1751), we learn
of the practice of listing each sin on a separate slip of paper (similar to index
cards); the penitent was to prepare for confession by turning over each card
before appearing in the confessional (cited by Lea 1896, 2:414). Although
some priests admitted written texts in the sacrament, by 1602 the pope declared that no written texts were to be consulted in the act of confession. The
call for uninterrupted dialogue is essential, as the sincerity and truthfulness of
the penitent is discerned by a series of cross questions in which the confessor
"probes the conscience of the sinner to the bottom" (Lea 1896, 2:367).

The act of confession was not an entirely new ceremony for the Andean
natives. The pages of an "Instrucción," written by Polo de Ondegardo in 1561–
1571, warned the Spanish priests that in the sierra and on the coast, the natives
traditionally confessed to male and female shamans. Confession was spoken,

and the penitent was aided in uncovering all the sins by the use of a stone rubbed on the body or the grasping of short and long straws (1985: 260–268). Although auricular confession and absolution may have seemed similar in their outward forms, the nature of sin differed in the two cultures. *Hucha* and *cama* were the Quechua words used to denote "sin"; both words imply debt and obligation to society, yet *hucha* became the preferred lexeme of the Spanish priests. In the context of Inkan society, R. T. Zuidema (1982, 1989) points out that it was a "sin" (*hucha*) to act against a lord, or to think badly of him, or to neglect one's duties in the ritual calendar, and Gerald Taylor (1987: 30) notes that *hucha* involves a linking of sin, law, and transactions with an all-encompassing concern for morality as well as the maintenance of ritual obligations.[1]

In the early seventeenth century, one priest, Juan Pérez Bocanegra, dwells at length on the persistent use of the khipu in the Andes as Indians enact the sacrament of Christian confession. A renowned master of the Quechua language, Pérez Bocanegra served as the general examiner of Quechua and Aymara in the diocese of Cusco, as a parish priest of Belén district in Cusco, and as a *presbítero* (priest) in the parish of Andahuaylillas, Province of Quispicanchi (see Mannheim 1991: 146). Pérez Bocanegra's *Ritual formulario*, a confession manual completed in 1622 but not published until 1631, richly describes the use of khipu, giving examples drawn from the writer's experiences in the region of Cusco. Pérez Bocanegra's exhortation against the khipu may highlight his active dedication to the conversion of the Indians in his parish.

As Diane Hopkins has noted, the date of his writing of the confession manual was a time of turmoil: the king of Spain had decreed that the Jesuits be given charge of Andahuaylillas (1621), but the ecclesiastic *cabildo* protested this decision, charging that the Jesuits had economic motives for wanting to be in the parish. Nevertheless, in 1628 the Jesuits did take control, relieving Pérez Bocanegra of his duties. It was only in 1636 that Pérez Bocanegra was returned to the parish (Hopkins 1983: 186–187). Even in such years of dispute regarding the parish (1621–1628), Pérez Bocanegra secured support for the printing of his manual. Proper authorities from the secular and regular orders issued the licensing approvals for the *Ritual formulario*, including the bishop of Cusco (1622), the general visitor and treasurer of the Cathedral of Cusco (1626), the Jesuit head of the Colegio in Cusco (1627), the archdeacon of Cusco (1628), and a Dominican friar in Lima (1628).

With missionary zeal, Pérez Bocanegra pens many observations of Andean customs in the vicinity of his parish. Special attention is paid to the khipu; he vehemently protests the use of the knots in several pages *ad longum*, as he himself notes, where he addresses his fellow priests in Spanish and does not translate to Quechua (1631: 103–126):

> Advierta tambien mucho el Confessor, que en esta ciudad, y fuera della haze(n) una cosa algunos Indios, è Indias (que se llama(n) hermanos mayores, y hermanas mayores entre ellos mismos:) y se les puede(n) poner nombre de alu(m)brados, y aturdidos, acerca de ciertos quipos, ñudos, y memorias, que traen para confessarse, como escrituras, y memoriales dellos. Porque estos tales Indios, y particularmente las Indias, enseñan a otras a se confessar por estos ñudos y señales; que los tiene(n) de muchos colores, para hazer diuision de los peccados, y el numero de los que an cometido, ò no, en esta manera.   (PÉREZ BOCANEGRA 1631: 111)

> [Let the Confessor be very aware that in this city and in its environs, the male Indians and the females (who are called older brothers and older sisters, referring to themselves that way) and you could call them the Illuminati (*alumbrados*) and confused ones do something with certain things called khipu, knots, and codicils (*memorias*), that they bring to confess themselves, like written materials, and their *memoriales*. Because these aforementioned Indians, and specifically the female Indians, teach the others to confess by means of these knots and signs, which they have in many colors, in order to separate their list of sins, and the number of sins that they have committed, or not, in this manner.]

With the native priest-shamans, prior to an interrogation from the Catholic priest, the Indians learn how to comment on their past sins, their own or those of other people:

> . . . los [pecados] que an cometido, ó los agenos que nunca cometieron. Porque les preguntan, que tanto tiempo à que no se confiessan: y si ocultaro(n) algun pecado en las confessiones passadas, que pecados eran; las vezes, y numero dellos: y particularmente, que les diga(n) los nombres de las mugeres, ò varones con quien ofendaron a Dios: y luego les mandan dezir al Padre.   (PÉREZ BOCANEGRA 1631: 111–112)

> [. . . the sins that they have committed, or those others that they didn't commit [but admitted] because they were never asked about them: how long since they last confessed, if they hid sins in their past

confessions, and what sins they were, the circumstances and the number of times: and especially that they state the names of the women or of the men with whom they offended God: and later tell all of this to the Priest.]

Now instructed in the rules of confession, as codified by the village elders, the Indians were then to show up for face-to-face encounters with the priest. Yet the elders often used the khipu for their own purposes as an instrument to help them remember exactly which sins to tell about and which ones to hide in the Christian confession:

> Y les manda uayan atando ñudos en sus hilos, que llama(n) *Caitu*,
> y son los pecados que les enseñan (los maestros, y maestras desta
> manera de confessar) los quales parecen: añadiendo, y poniendo sus
> ñudos otros que jamas cometiero(n) mandoles, y ensenandoles, a que
> digan es pecado el que no lo es, y al co(n)trario.
>
> (PÉREZ BOCANEGRA 1631: 112)

[And they tell them to tie certain knots on their strings, that they call *caitu*, and put on it the sins that they teach them (these male and female teachers who know how to deal with this kind of pagan confession) just as they should appear: adding and putting knots for sins they never committed they tell them to do, and telling them to claim as a sin what isn't a sin, and vice versa.]

Some of the confessions were entirely inappropriate, causing the priests to become suspicious:

> Enredandose en millares de errores, con estos quipos, y memo-
> rias. Demas de que no confiessan los pecados que an hecho: porque
> estos no los dizen al Confessor, sino solos los que les an enseñado
> estos tales Indios, è Indias; que los tienen por pecados, y los que an
> cometido no.   (PÉREZ BOCANEGRA 1631: 113)

[Tangling themselves up in thousands of errors, with these khipu and remembrances. Thus they do not confess those sins that they have committed to the Confessor Priest, only those that these male and female Teachers have taught them, what they think of as sins and that the sins they have committed are not sins.]

What exactly was it that Indians were told to confess by the "false" teachers? Luckily, to help us tally the particular sins we have the testimonies of extirpation confessed by the shaman men and women and written down by witnesses as they were brought before the church to testify. In a text gathered in Acas (1656), near Cajatambo, this statement by the indigenous Hernando Hacaspoma was recorded:

> que tan sola(men)te comfesasen a sus curas que comian carne los dias de cuaresma o vijilias faltaban de missa y juraban por dios que estos no eran pecados para comfesarlos con sus echiseros porque no los tenian por pecados y que los pecados de sensualidad y tratar con solteras los solteros tanpoco era pecado entre ellos y estos podian comfesar al cura ni los pecados de pensamiento lo eran tanpoco.
>
> (DUVIOLS 1986: 152)

> [that they should only confess to their priests that they ate meat the days of Lent or during vigils that they didn't go to mass and that they swore using the Lord's name these were the sins they should tell them because they weren't the sins that one should confess to the shaman-confessors, because the shaman-confessors didn't hold them to be sins. Sins of sensuality and the sin of single women and single men getting together were not sins among the indigenous, and these they could confess to the priest, sins of thought were not sins according to the Indian shaman-confessors.]

These transcripts often revealed what actions were considered "sinful" by Indians, as is evident in the transcript from Acas (1656):

> no guardar sus ayunos el bolber a mugeres que les abian ofendido el no haser sus ofrendas y sachrificios a sus malquis el entrar en las yglesias cuando los hasian el jurar falso segun el rito antiguo dellos que era cojer la tierra en la mano y besarla y desir: *caimi alpai caimi marcai* porque si desian algun pecado destos a los sacerdotes y curas bernian en conosimiento de sus ydolatrias.   (DUVIOLS 1986: 152)

> [(What do we confess to our own confessors?) not fasting, returning to former women friends, offending the *malquis* (ancestors) by not offering them sacrifices and also for going into the churches, swearing falsely according to an old rite where one grasped a handful of dirt

and kissed it saying: *caimi alpai caimi marcai* (here my land, here my village) because if they said any of these sins to the priests and pastors they would find out about their idolatry.]

Under no circumstances were the penitents to mention the idols and idolatry for fear of persecution, as seen in a text of 1586: "que quando se fuesen a comfesar por tiempo de quaresma con sus curas no descubriesen ni comfesasen estas ydolatrias porque no se supiesen y descubiertas las afrentasen" [that when they (the Indians) went to confess during Lent with the priests, don't let them find out nor confess acts of idol worship because they (the Catholic priests) don't know about the idols and once found out they will persecute them] (Duviols 1986: 152). This admonition is carefully penned in a drawing by Guaman Poma of an outdoor scene of confession in which the Indian begs for absolution with this revealing statement: "Have me confess all my sins, Father, but don't ask me about the *huaca*s and the idols" (Guaman Poma 1980: 603). The Indian's horror of confession alluded to the campaigns of extirpation in the early colonial period, when church officials delved into the Christian and pagan practices carried out in indigenous parishes in an attempt to abolish them. Many sacred objects (*huaca*s) were destroyed or taken away and many nonbeliever Indians were punished (see A. Acosta 1987; Duviols 1977).

In Andean confessions reported to us in the *Ritual formulario*, the ever watchful Pérez Bocanegra said that the priests interrogated the Indians so thoroughly that they often admitted that the elders had instructed them as to how to use the khipu to produce an "acceptable" confession for the priests:

> Assi me lo mandaron, y dixero(n) los hermanos, y hermanas, lo
> dixesse por estos ñudos: y dizen, que son confessiones generales.
> (PÉREZ BOCANEGRA 1631: 112)

[That's what the elder brothers and the elder sisters told me to do, to say a general confession by means of these knots.]

Pérez Bocanegra also tells us that some sins were reported and others were hidden, and that the size of the khipu often created such a mess that even the priest confessor was confused:

> De manera, que no saben lo que se confiessan, ni dizen, y ponen al
> Confessor en confusion, assi juzgando, como absolvie(n)do: . . .
> (PÉREZ BOCANEGRA 1631: 112)

[So they don't know what they are confessing, or saying, and they get the Confessor all confused, judging their sins and absolving them: . . .]

. . . muchos Indios y Indias . . . traen un orillo destos ñudos, mayores que el grandor de vna bola de bolos. . . . (Pérez Bocanegra 1631: 114, corrected from erroneous numbering of page 134)

[. . . many Indian men and women . . . bring with them a fabric selvage of these knots, bigger than the size of a ball in ninepins.]

And, says Pérez Bocanegra, he has further discovered that this incommunication is perpetuated in future years and with other persons, as these same khipu are passed on to others who come to confess:

. . . y è hallado, que guardan semejantes ñudos, para otra confession, aunque la hagan dentro de breue tiempo, ò para otro año. Y que los presta(n), y dan a los que se an de confessar de nueuo, ora sean moços o moças, viejos ò viejas: aduirtiendoles, que pecados an de dezir en cada color, ò ñudo: y mudan uno, y otro Confessor, porque no los çonozcan.   (PÉREZ BOCANEGRA 1631: 112)

[. . . and I have found out that they carefully save those khipu for another confession, even though they go to confession pretty soon after that, or even if it's a year later. And they loan them out, and they hand them off to those who come to confess another time, whether it's young boys or young girls, old men or old women: warning them exactly which sins they were to say for each color, or knot, and they carry them to another confessor, because he doesn't know them.]

Thus, in Pérez Bocanegra's experience, it is better to discourage the use of these memory aids and forbid the visitation with these elders who do "confession" sessions: "El remedio que yo hallo es, mandarles no se junten a semejantes consejos, castigandoles si los hizieren, que no se confiessen por estos ñudos, quitandoselos, sin dexarles de dezir por ellos palabra" [The remedy that I find is to forbid them to go to these confession sessions, punishing them if they go, telling them not to confess by means of these knots, seizing the knots, without letting them say one word using these things] (Pérez Bocanegra 1631: 112–113). A better solution, he proposes, is to use the very confession manual he has written and to burn those bundles of knots: "enseñarles a confessar conforme a este confessionario quitandoles aquellas cuentas, y ñudos, y quemandolos en su presencia. Y no darles el Sacramento de la Eucaristia, hasta tenerlos reduzidos, al buen orden de se confessar sin semejantes enredos, y defetos" [teach them to confess as is outlined in my confession manual, snatching away from them those accounts and knots and burning them in their presence. And don't give them the Sacrament of Eucharist, until you have them in compliance, orderly, confessing without such a mess and without errors] (Pérez Bocanegra 1631: 113).

With or without khipu, the matter of counting the number of sins was difficult for the Indians. Generally, according to Christian doctrine, an examination of conscience prior to confession allowed the penitent to sum up the venial and the mortal sins committed since the last confession. Similarly, Pérez Bocanegra reminds us that a numerical summary was required practice in the Andes: "es necessario declarar el numero de los pecados para que la confession sea entera. Y quando al penitente no se le acuerda determinadamente, enseñele a dezir cuantos pecados le pareces" [it is necessary to declare the number of occasions of sin so that the confession is complete. And if the penitent cannot remember accurately, teach him/her to say how many sins it seems like to him/her] (Pérez Bocanegra 1631: 106–107). But he tells in later pages what actually happens:

> Ni tampoco declara el numero de los pecados (poco mas, ò menos) que a cometido, que es necesario para la integridad de la confession. Antes si dize jurò diez vezes, otras diez, se emborrachò, fornicò, hurtò: sin añidir, ni quitar en quantos pecados confiessan este numero.   (PÉREZ BOCANEGRA 1631: 137 [117])

> [And neither do they (the Indians) declare the number of their sins, more or less, that they have committed, which is necessary for the integrity of the confession. If they say previously that they swore ten times, it's also ten times they got drunk, fornicated, robbed: without adding or subtracting, whatever sin it is, they say this number, ten.]

Twenty years later, Bishop Alonso Peña Montenegro still bemoans the lack of precision in the Andean Indian confession. Again the magic number is ten:

> . . . por ser tan torpes, y rudos, no saben averiguar el numero: y si el Confesor los obliga à que digan quantas veces dejaron de oír Misa? dicen que diez veces: y si les pregunta quántas veces se embriagaron?

responden, que diez veces: y si quiere saber quántas veces juraron
con mentira, ò creyeron en sueños, ò quebrantaron las fiestas, à todo
responden que diez veces. . . . Y si el Confesor les arguye, y pregunta,
que cómo es posible que en todos los pecados llegó al numero de
diez; sin que sean unos mas, y otros menos? Responden, que à diez
llegaron, que no mienten, y que dicen la verdad: . . .

[PEÑA MONTENEGRO 1985: 297)

[. . . because they are so dense and unformed they don't know how to
tally up the number of sins: and if the Confessor asks them to say how
many times they didn't hear mass, they say ten times; if they are asked
how many times they got drunk, it was ten times; and if asked how
many times they swore and lied, or if they believed in their dreams, or
they didn't keep the saints' days, they say ten to all of them, and if the
confessor argues with them and asks how it is possible that all of your
sins always come to ten, without some being a few more or a few less,
they say that they counted ten, that they are not lying and that they
are telling the truth: . . .]

However, the astute Confessor Priest can easily ferret out the truth, according to the bishop:

. . . dice que embriagó diez veces aquel año: aprietale el Confesor
y preguntale, quántas veces se havrá embriagado cada semana? y
responde, que cada semana una ù dos veces; y todo es mentira. . . .
Finalmente, como ellos no saben de Arithmetica, todas sus quentas
son erradas.   (PEÑA MONTENEGRO 1985: 297)

[. . . if he says that he got drunk ten times that year, close in on
him/her and ask him/her how many times would you have gotten
drunk each week? and she/he responds that each week one or two
times, and it's all a lie. In the end, because they don't understand
Arithmetic, all of their tallies are wrong.]

His practical advice concludes this section: "Don't let them tally their sins.
They cannot do it and it leads them into graver offenses against God" (Peña
Montenegro 1985: 297).

With much miscommunication, priests and Indians acted out culturally
inscribed roles. The Spaniards, on the whole, disparaged their shaman coun-

terparts as unlearned and diabolical in their adaptation of the khipu to the colonial situation. The Indians, meanwhile, continued to carry out the performance of their identity, culturally marked with their own instruments of tally, which outwardly conformed to the colonizers' code of confession but also subverted that very system of codification.

RITUAL AND PERFORMANCE

The use of the khipu in the sacrament of confession is presented as a scene of multilayered performance between two persons in several domains: interactions employing speech, body language, and the physical handling of the knots and strings. Performance studies emphasize the acts, gestures, and the very enactment of spectacle that often require an audience for interpretation. These performative acts may be subject to normative or regulatory discourses, which the performer subverts or supplements.

Foremost in providing graphic presentation of khipu performance are the black-and-white drawings of Felipe Guaman Poma de Ayala, especially the well-known illustration in which the prestigious khipukamayuq (khipu specialist) prominently displays the information-laden "archival" object, the khipu. The top cord is held conspicuously and the attached cords dangle (see Figure 11.1). Although Guaman Poma did not draw a khipu in the scene of confession, in his prose text of an idealized "good" confession (Figure 11.2), he encourages the use of the khipu *to remember sins:* "Que los dichos padres del santo sacramento de la confición mande exsaminar su ánima y consencia una semana el dicho penetente, aunque sea español. Y el yndio haga quipo de sus pecados" [The priests of the blessed sacrament of confession should make the penitent examine his soul and conscience for a week, even if he is a Spaniard. And the Indian should make a khipu of his sins] (Guaman Poma 1980: 585).

Our knowledge of the performative aspects of the khipu depend on Pérez Bocanegra's vivid and elaborate Spanish instructions to priests. His comments highlight the teaching process involved in "computing" sins on a khipu; the male and female elders, usually *hechiceros* (shamans), were skilled in khipu interpretation and instructed persons of all ages in the community. This teaching was further disseminated when nonspecialists, in turn, trained others in khipu performance. We know, again from Pérez Bocanegra, that khipu were stored and pulled out in future years to be used again, and also that khipu were loaned to others by the "owner." In the passing around of the khipu, and as community members taught each other, the same sins were consistently

FIGURE 11.1 Guaman Poma's drawing of a khipukamayuq (khipu specialist) prominently displaying a khipu.

FIGURE 11.2 Guaman Poma's drawing of an Indian at confession.

offered up to the priests. Thus, Pérez Bocanegra complains that small children were rattling off sins inappropriate to their age group, but which had been "written" for recitation on the knots of the khipu.

The representation of sins as depicted by knots and colors implies instruction by means of a standardized codification. In the early seventeenth century, when Pérez Bocanegra was actively confessing people in his parish, the Indians tallied up not only the numbers of sins but also the Christian categories of sin, in compliance with or in defiance of the clergy. One of the questions in Pérez Bocanegra's manual for confessors specifically asks about khipu in relation to the Eighth Commandment: "Thou shall not bear false witness." Penitents are interrogated about whether they have seen confession khipu belonging to others and then talked about these sins and sinners with other members of the community. As written in Pérez Bocanegra's manual, question number sixty-three regarding the Eighth Commandment, one of a long list of questions regarding the sin of "false witness," documents the fact that colors were closely identified with specific sins in a manner that made them readable by others:

Hallando quipos, do(n)de algun indio o india que tu conoces, auia
añudado sus pecados, para memoria de su confession, as lo mirado,
y por las colores de los ñudos, as sabido los pecados que hizieron, y
divulgastelos, u dixiste a alguna persona? y dime por averlo tu dicho
siguiosele al indio, o india, infame notable?

(PÉREZ BOCANEGRA 1631: 341)

[Finding khipu, in the dwelling of some Indian man or woman that
you know, who had made his/her knots, in order to remember the
confession, did you look at them, and by means of the colors of the
knots did you know of the sins that they committed and did you
spread it around and did you tell someone? And tell me, because you
spoke of this (to others), did significant shame fall upon the Indian
man or woman?][2]

Although Pérez Bocanegra teases us with the possibility of color coding in
khipu, he never writes a detailed description of such a meaning system. Disconcerting is the Quechua passage of the quote cited above, in which color is
not mentioned at all by Pérez Bocanegra, who instead (in his Quechua translation) merely emphasizes the knots of the khipu as the means of obtaining
knowledge of the sins of the other person.

Of course, there are many other references to khipu colors among the
pages of the early colonial writers of the Andes. Raúl Porras Barrenechea's
Fuentes históricas peruanas (1955) lists many valuable references and specifically mentions color categories. Cristóbal de Molina mentions colors, as does
José de Acosta, in the sources we have examined previously. Furthermore,
the Inca Garcilaso and Friar Antonio de la Calancha write extensive lists of
the meaning of each color category (starting with gold and silver), as Porras
Barrenechea summarizes. In this book, Carol Mackey's research with contemporary herders' khipu (Chapter 13), Frank Salomon's study on the coast
(Chapter 12), and William Conklin's description of elements of khipu construction (Chapter 3) all attest to the use of color, as does the register of a
wide range of color categories in camelid fibers in research by Jorge A. Flores
Ochoa (1986). Marcia and Robert Ascher (1981) have well represented the
variance in color patterning in solid colors, colors twisted together, and the
importance of overall patterning.

In research that I carried out in Cusco some years ago, I spoke with one
priest, Father Juan Antonio Manya, who told me of seeing a khipu used for
confession about forty years ago. A bilingual Spanish-Quechua speaker, he

dictated to me the attributions of a color-coded khipu he remembers from Chinchero:

red = sexual sin
black = killing someone
vivid orangeish red = thievery
green = the external kiss (*sunkha*) on the chin and side of the face
yellow = hypocrisy (*ishqui uhya*)
white = venial sins
gray = lie   (PERSONAL COMMUNICATION 1992)

In this recent manifestation of khipu recording, the influences of Christian symbolism and color are salient, as is the particular Quechua inventory of sins, elaborated from their own sense of infractions before God and their community.

Although the presence of color may figure prominently in the performative display of khipu, there is also reference to blind khipu readers and confessional practice. Pérez Bocanegra, in casting aspersions on the *hechiceros*, notes that many are often blind, yet despite that handicap they instruct the community on khipu in the confessional. A most splendid example is taken from the Jesuit letters from the region of Cusco (1602), where a blind man brought in an eighteen-foot khipu that had certain objects (stones, bones, feathers) enmeshed in it that represented various sins, "conforme a la materia de peccado que avía de confessar" [in accordance with the material of the sin that he had to confess] (Cabredo 1986: 214).[3] So intricate was the accounting of sins by this old man that he needed four days to render up his tally, crying all the while.

Marcia and Robert Ascher write of the complexity of the sense of touch inherent in the workings of the khipu, noting that in the act of making the khipu, where the recording is carried out:

use had to be learned, and the learning involved a sense of touch. . . .
[T]he quipumaker's way of recording—direct construction—required tactile sensitivity to a much greater degree [than that required by the Sumerian clay tablet writer]. In fact, the overall aesthetic of the quipu is related to the tactile: the manner of recording and the recording itself are decidedly rhythmic; the first in the activity, the second in the effect. We seldom realize the potential of our sense of touch, and we are usually unaware of its association with rhythm. Yet any-

one familiar with the activity of caressing will immediately see the
connection between touch and rhythm.   (1981: 61)

Similarly, in the act of reading a khipu, a tactile sense is primary, whether
in the simple full display where the khipu ends are held, or in wrapping it
around the body in ritual, or in the actual fingering of the knots and objects
held in the cords.

The calming effect of touch is well documented in numerous clinical examples—infants grow faster with tactile stimulation, blood pressure is lowered when petting domestic animals, worry beads relieve stress—as is apparent in popular newspaper accounts and scholarly medical treatises. Given the
circumstances of confession in the colonies, the Indian who arrived for the
sacrament may have reaped such a benefit by touching the soothing knots and
strings in moments of extreme anxiety regarding the recitation of their sins
before the priest. Indians were rounded up by the clergy to confess their sins
or coerced by the *kuraka* (who were in turn pressured by the priests). Indians
did not seek out confession on their own; it was mandatory that the Indians
be present for confession. The priests wrote out a *padrón*, or census, recording that the parishioner had indeed confessed, in compliance with the yearly
ritual.

Apparently, Pérez Bocanegra understood the kinesics of the confession as
well as the theology of the ritual. He alternates between advising kindness
and understanding in the rite of confession and encouraging some aggressive
probing of conscience. Ever vigilant, he comments on behavior characteristics that mark a less-than-truthful accounting of sins:

> Y si le pareciere al Sacerdote, que el Indio, ò India calla, ò oculta
> algun pecado, halaguele dulcemente, con palabras amorosas, y
> blandas, ayudandole, y animandole, a q(ue) diga todas sus culpas:
> especialmente aquellas, que (por sus razones) quiere ocultar, que
> facilmente se echara de vèr; por el tragar amenudo la saliua, y no
> sosegar de rodillas, toser, mirar a vna, y otra parte, y otras señales,
> que Dios quiere que muestre, quando quiere cometer este sacrilegio.
> (PÉREZ BOCANEGRA 1631: 109–110)

[And if it seems to the Priest, that the male Indian, or female Indian,
gets quiet or hides whatever sin, cajole him or her with loving, non-
threatening words, helping them and encouraging them to say all
their sins: especially those which (for their reasons) they want to hide,

sins that are easily seen by the frequent swallowing of saliva, and not kneeling calmly, coughing, looking at one spot and then another, and other signs, which God has them show, when they want to commit this sacrilege.]

Recently, Oswaldo Pardo has summarized the importance of European sources that define interpretation of gesture and enunciation in the context of the contrition in New Spain. For the confession to be valid, demonstration of real sincerity and repentance must be evidenced in word and in bodily demeanor at the time of confession (Pardo 1996: 33). Similarly, Pérez Bocanegra insists that the priest had certain performance principles to fulfill: no looking at the face of the penitent, no seating of the penitent to one side of the priest, no humorous utterances or anything which would incite laughter, and no gestures (*ademanes*) or shaking (*meneos*) of the head, eyes, feet, or hands (1631: 109). The priest, as well, must be cautious in his behavior and voice: "mandele dezir sus pecados, . . . sin irle a la mano, ni por gesto, ni palabra afearselos: no le sea ocasion de hazerle desmayar" [have the penitent mention his/her sins, . . . without threatening him/her, by gesture, nor by words: it should not be an occasion to cause them to faint] (Pérez Bocanegra 1631: 108–109).

The site of ritual performance was dictated by the environs appropriate for the priest to hear confession. Pérez Bocanegra defines the optimal performance space as a place above reproach, where one can be seen and yet where no one else can hear what is said; that is where the priest must be seated to hear confessions. He cautiously adds that in confessing women, a priest should not go to their chambers (*aposentos*) or their bedrooms, or near their beds, or the hearth of their houses (Pérez Bocanegra 1631: 109).

In addition to use with the Catholic priests, the khipu may have already served in a context of ritual atonement traditional in the Andes. A khipu ritual noted by Pérez Bocanegra took place not in town but in the fields. Question number seventy-three on the First Commandment, listed in his *Formulario ritual*, mentions the other khipu performance that was troublesome to him: "Assi mismo en tus chacras de papas, yocas, sueles atar la paja co(n) muchos ñudos, y atadixos, ayunando tu, y diziendo a aquellos atados que ayunen por ti? Que sueles hazer con esto? dimelo todo? [*sic*]" [So in your planting fields of potatoes, of *oca*s, did you often tie up straw with a lot of knots and strung-together things, and fasting, did you tell those knots to fast for you also? Do you often do this? Tell me everything] (Pérez Bocanegra 1631: 133).[4] Here, no cotton or camelid wool is used; there is mention only of straw, a substance

FIGURE 11.3 Guaman Poma's drawing of an Indian confessing.

that has often been linked with confessional practices in the highland Andes. The awesome significance of the twisting of straw, seen in this passage, is complemented by a similar action in a Qollor Riti pilgrimage. According to Catherine Allen (1988: 195), several persons left the pilgrimage group to knot the tall grass along the path. In twisting the straw to the left, with their left hands, behind their backs so they did not look at it, the sinners deposited their sins.

Though the khipu is identified with the reckoning of sins in the annual confession, the rosary, a Catholic tallying device, should figure prominently in the post-confessional instructions when penance is meted out.[5] Fasting, praying by means of the rosary, and attending mass would all pertain to the performance of future events. However, Pérez Bocanegra cautions the clergy to assign a small penance to be enacted immediately, while the Indian remains in the presence of the priest (1631: 384).

Yet the rosary has its purpose and is culturally dominant in the drawings of Guaman Poma. Particularly in the sketch describing the pious Jesuits (Figure 11.3), the rosary provides the central focus, linking the priest and the penitent. The circle of beads is slipped over the Indian's extended left hand to overlie the coiled handmade rope on that hand, with assurance that the Christian practice would be enacted by the indigenous peoples. Certainly, that is the intent of José de Acosta's advice:

> En vez de los ritos perniciosos se introduzcan otros saludables, . . . [e]l agua bendita, las imágenes, los rosarios, las cuentas benditas, y las demás cosas que aprueba.   (ACOSTA 1954A: 565)

> [Instead of these pernicious rites, others more beneficial should be introduced, . . . such as holy water, religious images, rosaries, sacred explanations, and other approved items.]

However, in times of great cultural stress, the indigenous communities also disposed of many Christian items, including the rosary, in fear of the *huaca*'s reprisal:

> Diose un pregón en aquella provincia [de los Vilcas] que todos los yndios que adorasen lo que los xpnos. adoraban, y tubiesen cruzes, rozarios o ymágenes y vestidos de los españoles, auían de perecer en la enfermedad de pestilencia que la guaca enbiaba en castigo que se hauían hecho xpnos, . . . echaron de sí todo lo sobredicho, arrojando en todos los caminos y quebradas todas las cruzes y rozarios e ymágenes, sonbreros, [z]apatos y calsones y todas las demás cosas con los vestidos que de los españoles tenían.   (MATEOS 1944: 116)

> [It was circulated in the province (of Vilcas) that Indians who worshipped what the Spanish worshipped, and who had crosses, rosaries, images, and Spanish clothing, would die in the illness that the *huaca* sent as punishment for their conversion to Christianity . . . they got rid of all that stuff, throwing in the roads and off the cliffs crosses, rosaries, images, hats, shoes, underwear, and all the rest of the Spanish clothing that they had.]

FIGURE 11.4 Guaman Poma's drawing of a native official carrying a khipu and a book.

CONCLUSION

The khipu, an instrument of high prestige in Inkan knowledge systems, also served as a tool for calculation of more practical matters in the hands of shepherds. In confession rituals after the invasion of the Spaniards, the khipu enabled the *doctrina* (parish) Indian to fulfill the demands of an annual accounting of sins in the presence of the priest. Systematically, by means of colors and knots, the Indian penitents participated in a ritual reckoning of sins and the counting of offenses.

From Pérez Bocanegra's *Ritual formulario*, we glean an account of khipu technique and khipu transmission of knowledge. In the beginning of the seventeenth century, elderly male and female shamans (especially the women) actively encouraged the use of the device to record which sins to confess and which sins *not* to confess. In this annual ritual, and by means of the khipu, the community contradicted the imposed theological patterns. Although some khipu, especially those in Juli, were dutifully used to recite Christian prayers and doctrine as recorded in the Jesuit letters, Pérez Bocanegra's commentary reveals the existence of an alternative system of khipu use that serves to dilute Catholic authority.

Khipu are not a "writing system" in the pen-and-paper sense of literacy, but certainly the knots and strings performed the essential function of recording communal beliefs and strategies in the colonial period. Negotiated with recourse to the khipu tradition, a system of shared memory sustained indigenous values long before the indigenous populations claimed access to native scribes trained in European writing systems. Pérez Bocanegra privileges Western writing when he emphasizes the truth contained in the Book. He has a revealing phrase in which he tells his Indian parishioners that "the priests are your books [ellos son vuestros libros]" (1631: 421), and thus he denies Indians' agency in recording their own truths.

There are other options, of course. Indigenous people can author their own texts. Guaman Poma's "escribir es llorar" (to write is to cry) is a resonant and resilient comment on the colonial literacy project. Similar to the *regidor* found in the *Nueva corónica* (Figure 11.4), Guaman Poma sought information from both books and khipu. In putting an inked pen to paper, he made use of the European lettered alphabet to outline considerable injustice meted out by those in power. Equally as important was Guaman Poma's access to the content of the khipu, whereby he preserved indigenous knowledge. With recourse to *both* memory systems—lettered ciphers and knotted yarns— he (eventually) managed to turn the world upside down.

NOTES

1. See Harrison 1992, 1993, 1994, 1995a, and 1995b for a full description of confessional practice, native Andean categories of sin, and the process of conversion in the Andes.

2. The Quechua passage given on page 351 in Pérez Bocanegra 1631 differs from the Spanish version of the same passage: "Reccescaiqui carip, huarmip huchanta confessacunacampac; quipunta tarispa, ricocchu canqui, chai quipup ricchainimpiri, hucha rurascanta yachacchu canqui? hinaspa pimampas, sutincahpocchu canqui villacocchu canqui? Villahaui, chai huchacta sutinchacaiqui raicuca; chai cari, huarmiman, hattun manalli caccuna, chayarcanchu?" [Finding a khipu of sins, used in order to confess, of a man or a woman acquaintance known to you, did you look at it, from that khipu, did

you know the sins committed? Then to whomever, did you inform them of the names of the one who sinned? Tell me all; after naming the sinful persons, did some horrible evil thing come upon that man, that woman?]

3. I would like to thank Joanne Rappaport for calling this document to my attention. See her 1998 article, co-authored with Tom Cummins, in *CLAR* 7.

4. The Quechua is given on page 153 in Pérez Bocanegra 1631, and it differs slightly from the Spanish passage: "Papa chacraipi, Oca chacraiquipihuanipas, ichucta quipurcayaspaçaçecchu canqui, rantij çacinca ñispa, cairi I manam? Villahuai, tucui ima rurascai quictapas" [In your potato fields, also in your *oca* fields, did you make knots of *ichu* grass, fasting, saying, they fast for me? For what purpose? Tell me everything that you did].

5. Dana Leibsohn's paper "Quipus, Knotted Ropes, and Rosaries: Cultural Entanglement in Spanish America" questions an apparent similarity among these devices and cautions that "visual, formal parallels are not the primary ways that objects garner their trans-historical, trans-cultural power" (1997: 9).

REFERENCES CITED

Acosta, Antonio de. 1987. "La extirpación de las idolatrías en el Perú: Orígen y desarrollo de las campañas." *Revista Andina* 5, no. 1: 171–195.

Acosta, José de. 1954a [1580]. "De procuranda indorum salute o predicación del evangelio en las Indias." In *Obras del P. José de Acosta*, edited by F. Mateos, 389–609. Biblioteca de Autores Españoles, vol. 73. Madrid: Ediciones Atlas.

———. 1954b. "Escritos menores." In *Obras del P. José de Acosta*, edited by F. Mateos, 251–389. Biblioteca de Autores Españoles, vol. 73. Madrid: Ediciones Atlas.

Adorno, Rolena. 1988. "Writing about Reading: An Andean View of Literacy in the Early Spanish Colonial Period." *Yale Journal of Criticism* 2, no. 1: 197–203.

Allen, Catherine J. 1988. *The Hold Life Has: Coca and Cultural Identity in an Andean Community*. Washington, D.C.: Smithsonian Institution Press.

Ascher, Marcia, and Robert Ascher. 1997. *Mathematics of the Incas: Code of the Quipu*. Mineola, N.Y.: Dover.

Bartra, E. T., ed. 1982. *Tercer Concilio Limense (1582–1583)*. Lima: Facultad Pontificia y Civil de Teología de Lima.

Cabredo, P. R. 1986 [1602]. "Anua de 1602. Monumenta Peruana VIII (1603–1604)." In *Monumenta Historica Societatis Iesu*, vol. 128, edited by E. Fernández. Rome: Apud "Institutum Historicum Societatis Iesu."

Durán, J. G. 1990. *Monumenta catechetica hispanoamericana (siglos XVI–XVII)*. Vol. 2. Buenos Aires: Facultad de Teología de la Pontificia Universidad Católica Argentina.

Duviols, Pierre. 1977. *La destrucción de las religiones andinas (durante la conquista y la colonia)*. Mexico City: Universidad Nacional Autónoma de México.

———. 1986. *Cultura andina y represión: Procesos y visitas de idolatrías y hechicerías Cajatambo, siglo XVII*. Cusco: Centro de Estudios Rurales Andinos Bartolomé de Las Casas.

Flores Ochoa, Jorge A. 1986. "The Classification and Naming of South American Camelids." In *Anthropological History of Andean Polities*, edited by John V. Murra,

Nathan Wachtel, and Jacques Revel, 137–148. Cambridge: Cambridge University Press.

Guaman Poma de Ayala, Felipe. 1936 [1615]. *Nueva corónica y buen gobierno (Codex péruvien ilustré)*. Traveaux et Mémoires de l'Institut d'Ethnologie, vol. 23. Paris: Institut d'Ethnologie.

———. 1980 [1615]. *El primer nueva corónica y buen gobierno*, edited by J. V. Murra and Rolena Adorno. 3 vols. Mexico City: Siglo Veintiuno.

Harrison, Regina. 1992. *True Confessions: Quechua and Spanish Cultural Encounters in the Viceroyalty of Peru*. Latin American Studies Center Rockefeller Fellow Series, no. 5. College Park: University of Maryland.

———. 1993. "Confesando el pecado en los Andes: Del siglo XVI hacia nuestros días." *Revista Crítica de Literatura Latinoamericana* 19, no. 37: 169–185.

———. 1994. "The Theology of Concupiscence: Spanish-Quechua Confessional Manuals in the Andes." In *Encoded Encounters: Race, Gender, and Ethnicity in Colonial Latin America*, edited by Francisco Javier Cevallos, Jeffrey A. Cole, Nina M. Scott, and Nicomedes Suárez-Araúz, 135–153. Amherst: University of Massachusetts Press.

———. 1995a. "The Case of the Pregnant Penitent: Translating Quechua in the Andes." *Latin American Indian Literatures Journal* 11, no. 2 (fall): 108–128.

———. 1995b. "The Language and Rhetoric of Conversion in the Viceroyalty of Peru." *Poetics Today* 16, no. 1 (spring): 1–29.

Hopkins, Diane E. 1983. "The Colonial History of the Hacienda System in a Southern Peruvian Highland District." Ph.D. dissertation, Cornell University. Ann Arbor: University Microfilms.

Lea, H. C. 1896. *A History of Auricular Confession and Indulgences in the Latin Church*. 3 vols. Philadelphia: Lea Brothers.

Liebsohn, Dana. 1997. "Quipus, Knotted Ropes, and Rosaries: Cultural Entanglement in Spanish America." Paper read at the CUNY Renaissance Studies Conference, March.

Mannheim, Bruce. 1991. *The Language of the Inka since the European Invasion*. Austin: University of Texas Press.

Marcus, Joyce. 1992. *Mesoamerican Writing Systems: Propaganda, Myth, and History in Four Ancient Civilizations*. Princeton: Princeton University Press.

Mateos, F., ed. 1944 [1600]. "Crónica anónima de 1600 que se trata del establecimiento y misiones de la Compañía de Jesús en los países de habla española en la América Meridional." In *Historia general de la Compañía de Jesús en la provincia del Perú*, vol. 2. Madrid: Consejo Superior de Investigaciones Científicas/Instituto González Fernández de Oviedo.

Molina, Cristóbal de ("el Cuzqueño"). 1988 [1573]. "Relación de las fábulas y ritos de los Ingas." In *Fábulas y mitos de los Incas*, edited by Henrique Urbano and Pierre Duviols, 9–135. Madrid: Historia 16.

Pardo, Oswaldo F. 1996. "Bárbaros y mudos: Comunicación verbal y gestual en la confesión de los nahuas." *Colonial Latin American Review* 5, no. 1: 25–55.

Peña Montenegro, Alonso. 1985 [1661]. *Itinerario para parrochos de indios*. Guayaquil, Ecuador: N.p.

Pérez Bocanegra, Juan. 1631. *Ritual formulario e institucion de Curas para administrar a los naturales de este Reyno los Santos Sacramentos* . . . Lima: Geronymo de Contreras.

Polo de Ondegardo, Juan. 1985 [1585]. "Instrucción contra las cerimonias, y ritos que usan los Indios conforme el tiempo de su infidelidad." In *Confessionario para los Curas de Indios*. Corpus Hispanorum de Pace, vol. 26, no. 2: 253–263. Madrid: Consejo Superior de Investigaciones Científicas.

Porras Barrenechea, Raúl. 1955. *Fuentes históricas peruanas*. Lima: Juan Mejía Baca.

Rappaport, Joanne, and Tom Cummins. 1998. "Between Images and Writing: The Ritual of the King's Quillca." *Colonial Latin American Review* 7, no. 1: 7–32.

Sarmiento de Gamboa, Pedro. 1942 [1572]. *Historia de los Incas*. Buenos Aires: Emecé Editores.

Taylor, Gerald, ed. 1987. *Ritos y tradiciones de Huarochirí*. Lima: Instituto de Estudios Peruanos and the Instituto Francés de Estudios Andinos.

Tercero cathecismo y exposición de la doctrina christiana, por sermones. 1985 [1585]. Corpus Hispanorum de Pace, vol. 26, no. 2: 333–777. Madrid: Consejo Superior de Investigaciones Científicas.

Urton, Gary. 1990. *The History of a Myth: Pacariqtambo and the Origin of the Incas*. Austin: University of Texas Press.

Vaca de Castro, Cristóbal. 1929 [1608]. *Discurso sobre la descendencia y gobierno de los Incas*. Colección de Libros y Documentos Referentes a la Historia del Perú, 2d series, vol. 3. Lima: Sanmartí.

Zuidema, R. T. 1982. "Bureaucracy and Systematic Knowledge in Andean Civilization." In *The Inca and Aztec States: 1400–1800: Anthropology and History*, edited by George A. Collier, Renato A. Rosaldo, and John D. Wirth, 419–495. New York: Academic Press.

———. 1989. "At the King's Table: Inca Concepts of Sacred Kingship in Cuzco." *History and Anthropology* 4: 249–274.

PART FIVE

CONTEMPORARY KHIPU TRADITIONS

Patrimonial Khipu in a Modern Peruvian Village

TWELVE

An Introduction to the "Quipocamayos" *of Tupicocha, Huarochirí*

Frank Salomon

This chapter concerns a central Peruvian community that owns and ceremonially uses inherited cord records in perpetuating kinship corporations directly continuous with those of Inka and perhaps pre-Inka times. We know of these corporations because the village in question, San Andrés de Tupicocha in Huarochirí Province, Peru, is self-described in the only known early-colonial source that explains an Andean religious system in an Andean language, namely, the Quechua Huarochirí Manuscript (ca. 1608; translations include Salomon and Urioste 1991 and Taylor 1987). The cord records, though not themselves of pre-Hispanic antiquity, form a material link in a chain of institutional continuity extending farther back than the written record. Modern Tupicochans call their cord records *quipocamayos*,[1] *equipos*, or *caytus* (the last being a Quechua term meaning "wool thread, spool of wool, ball of wool, piece of cloth, string, cord," according to Lira 1944: 400).[2]

Here I first briefly summarize the *quipocamayos'* social context, which largely conserves the ideal structure stated in the 1608 Quechua text. It is this structure that the cord records are today taken to symbolize. Then I discuss the material form of the *quipocamayos* themselves, emphasizing local terms that may conserve elements of the premodern khipu maker's technical lexicon. I close by questioning, on the basis of Tupicochan observations, some common theoretical assumptions concerning the writing-like and text-like properties of cord records. These pages are intended as a preface to fuller explorations of the artifacts and their context, now in progress.

Khipu are mentioned twice in the 1608 Quechua source. In a chapter about the ritual reproduction of water rights, we learn that when the people of Concha Village went to visit the lake deities that owned their water, they "took a quipu[3] account of all the people who were absent and began to worship" (Salomon and Urioste 1991: 142). And in a chapter about the regimen that Checa villagers established, first by conquering aborigines and then by articulating their conquered domains with those of the Inka state, we learn that the Inka kept a cord account of his subsidies to the superhuman powers called *huacas*: ". . . the Inka would have offerings of his gold and silver given according to his *quipu* account, to all the *huacas*" (Salomon and Urioste 1991: 112). This remark occurs in the same chapter that deals with Tupicocha's territory and ritual regimen and may relate to the local prestige of cord records. Comparing these two passages, one may note that in the Inka era, as the oral authors remembered it, the khipu art was not exclusively the domain of Inka specialists, but was rather an informational common ground to which both local non-Inka ayllu, like Concha, and imperial authorities contributed.

In colonial times (Huertas Vallejos 1992; Spalding 1984), when Spaniards ill versed in the khipu art monopolized the higher administrative levels, indigenous polities (themselves having multilevel formations, consisting of ayllu, or localized descent groups, collected into *llacta*, or village-level settlements, and in some areas grouped into larger regional *curacazgos* or *cacicazgos mayores*) not only continued to record their own affairs on cords, but used them to manage articulation with the church and state for at least the first seven decades or so of Spanish rule (Pease 1990). In Huarochirí, we now know, such articulation lasted much longer. At the end of the first colonial lifetime, when Father Francisco de Avila was engaged in the skirmishes with his parishioners whose upshot would eventually be the creation of the Quechua Huarochirí Manuscript itself (Acosta 1987), khipu still counted for a great deal. When the villagers wrote charges against Father Avila, they mentioned annual cord records, kept by each village's *contador* (accountant), as the proof that Avila had illegally taken fodder and horses (AA/L Capítulos Leg. 1, Exp. 9: f. 3r). They also charged that he had impermissibly busied four of these "accountants" with minding animals (f. 3v), a charge implying that the khipu-keeping role had special dignity, which he had affronted. Villagers of Santiago de Tuna (adjacent to Tupicocha) adduced their knot records as proof of how many boys he had dragooned as swineherds and how many pitchers of maize beer he had extorted (ff. 10r, 11v). Other villages backed their complaints similarly. A hundred years later, at a time when khipu-based testimony was no longer common practice, a different priest accused of similar abuses in the same region adduced "*quipo[s] de paja*" (straw khipu)[4] as receipts proving parish officers had consented to the questioned transactions (AA/L Capítulos Leg. 27, Exp. VIII: ff. 36–39). In records of colonial khipu use for conducting village affairs, the villages that protagonized the Huarochirí myths—those of the "Checa thousand" (as the Inka, and later the Spanish administrations, labeled this group of settlements)—crop up frequently. San Andrés de Tupicocha, immediately north of San Damián, whence the 1608 Quechua source originates, figures centrally in the above-mentioned litigations, although until 1935 it was a minor and dependent component of the "thousand." Asked why their village alone has retained the cord records, Tupicochans say that when Chileans attacked neighboring Tuna and set it afire (a documented incident in the War of the Pacific [1879–1884]; Sotelo 1942: 69–77), Tupicocha safeguarded its regalia in a cave. Huarochirí is not mentioned in works on modern khipu (Mackey 1970, 1990a, 1990b; and works by Núñez del Prado, Uhle, and Soto collected in Mackey et al. 1990) nor in the one publication on a patrimonial khipu held as civic insignia (Ruiz Estrada 1981). Tupicocha today may be unique in displaying its khipu as currently functioning documents of civil legitimacy.

THE ROLE OF KHIPU IN THE CEREMONIAL REPRODUCTION OF MODERN AYLLU

As a modern *distrito* (district), Tupicocha holds lands from about 2,500 meters above sea level (masl) to about 4,800 meters on the westward flank of the Andes just south of Lima, at the headwaters of the Lurín River. Of the village's 1,543 people (according to the 1993 census; INEI 1994: 200), at most, half live exclusively in the community nucleus, located on a difficult secondary road at about 3,321 masl (Martínez Chuquizana 1996: 14, 21–24; Stiglich 1922: 1084). Of these, most but not all belonged to the 143 households registered for 1997 as *comuneros*. The remainder live in the outlying "annex" villages, or have double domicile in Tupicocha and Lima, or live full-time in Lima. Despite its location less than a day's journey from the capital and despite some residents' semiproletarian or mercantile ways of life, Tupicocha in 1997 lacked electricity or other industrial infrastructures, and relied for subsistence as well as commercial production on an intricate system of canals, terraces, and walled pastures, begun in pre-Hispanic antiquity and continued by the Peasant Community as a perpetual work in progress. To coordinate labor in improving and maintaining the system, the community relies on ten ayllu, or *parcialidades* (the former term is used in intra-ayllu context, the latter in context of village-wide integration).

These are lineal continuations of the ayllu of Checa as described in the 1608 Quechua Huarochirí Manuscript (Astete 1997). In its account, the Checa were the fifth of seven groups descended from the "children" of the great regional deity Paria Caca. This group's hero, Tutay Quiri, as he led his conquering protégés northward through the Lurín and Rímac basins, allotted formerly Yunca lands to Checa ayllu. The ayllu mentioned in Chapter 24 of the Quechua source are:

1. Allauca
2. Sat Pasca
3. P[a?]sa Quine
4. Muxica
5. Caca Sica
6. Sulc Pahca (Yasapa)
7. Chauti (of Yunca, i.e., coastal origin)
8. Huanri (of Yunca, i.e., coastal origin)

Two of these, P[a?]sa Quine and Sulc Pahca, are either extinct or remembered under other names. Chauti has apparently given rise to the independent village of Chaute (or perhaps a newer polity occupies lands that once bore its name). Caca Sica persists as an ayllu in neighboring Santiago de Tuna. The rest still exist in Tupicocha, whose current *parcialidades* or ayllu are:[5]

1. Primera Allauca
2. Primera Satafasca
3. Primer Huangre
4. Unión Chaucacolca
5. Mújica
6. Cacarima
7. Segunda Allauca
8. Segunda Satafasca
9. Centro Huangre
10. Huangre Boys[6]

To understand the prominence of patrimonial khipu one must appreciate these groups' role as the core of civic labor organization. From an intra-ayllu viewpoint, ayllu are understood as preexisting constituents of the *comunidad*. From a community viewpoint, they are "sectors" (*parcialidades*) of the village totality. All collective labor—a considerable part of the yearly productive

cycle—is planned by the Community, constituted as the joint meeting of the
ayllu presidents (traditionally called *camachicos*) with the Community's Junta
Directiva (elected board of directors). The order of ritual precedence of the
ayllu, as given above, never varies. The work quotas assigned to each are made
proportional to unequal numbers of members and are adjusted for difficul-
ties of terrain in the respective "stretches" of work by the system known in
Quechua-speaking areas as *chuta* (Urton 1984). Ayllu as corporations today
control only a small share of productive resources. Each ayllu, although it is
an intimate *Gemeinschaft* (annual meetings are sometimes called "family re-
unions"), is also a political and administrative unit endowed with a complete
board of directors of its own, and a complex ritual apparatus that serves for
fund-raising. Every child of an ayllu member patrilineally inherits an eligi-
bility to petition for *socio*, or member, status in the father's ayllu on reach-
ing adulthood. Membership is conferred by consensus of members. Married
women are said to belong "body and soul" to their husbands' ayllu, but un-
married women, especially if they are single parents, can become full members of their natal ayllu. People of both sexes who opt not to become *socios*,
usually the same people who migrate to Lima or elsewhere, are known as
"children of the ayllu" and are expected—though they cannot be compelled—
to continue attending their kinship group's festivals and to support it with
monetary or in-kind pledges. In a limited fashion, they maintain the corporate presence of the ayllu in Lima. The content of *quipocamayos*, today unde-
ciphered, is likely to have concerned some of the above facets of ayllu self-
management, or perhaps additional functions they have since relinquished,
such as landholding and the provision of credit. No unit higher than the
ayllu/*parcialidad* traditionally claimed ownership of *quipocamayos* or authority
over them.[7]

The present system of ayllu arose by fission from six "historic" ayllu. Oral
tradition and ayllu books concur that five of these held, up to the early twentieth century, two khipu. The sixth, Cacarima, did not begin inventorying
its single *quipocamayo* until 1926, so we do not know if an earlier mate had
been lost. When Allauca divided into two segments, each received one *quipocamayo*, and Satafasca bifurcated the same way. Huangre divided into three,
but only one Huangre *quipocamayo* still exists, held by the "Primer" (First) of
the Huangre corporations. Chaucacolca remained united and retains both its
quipocamayos. (Chaucacolca's epithet "Unión" reflects pride in having over-
come divisive tendencies.) The conservation history of Mújica's *quipocamayos*
is complex. Ayllu books reported the loss of one member of its pair, and in
its absence, Mújica displayed a fragment of the counterpart, appended to a

quipocamayo of unusual design. The fragment was lost due to rough handling in ritual context between 1995 and 1997. In 1998, the lost Mújica *quipocamayo* was recovered.

Each year, on the second and third days of January, Tupicocha holds a general civic meeting at which the village's multiple governing bodies (Gobernación, Municipalidad/Distrito, and Comunidad Campesina) renew their mandates. This meeting is called the Huayrona, and the meeting place, a civic center consisting of a large plaza with adjacent buildings, is called the Collca.[8] The Huayrona, together with certain moments in the January 5–8 Pascua Reyes ritual cycle, is the only time when the patrimonial khipu come into public view. Attendance is compulsory for *socios* (but, in practice, only on the second day). Government officials such as the Subprefecto of the province or NGO personnel may be invited. Among external observers, Dr. Hilda Araujo of the Universidad Nacional de La Molina was probably the first anthropological witness of this event, which has also been viewed by various students from Lima's Catholic University. The present writer viewed the 1995, 1997, and 2000 cycles.

On the second day of the Huayrona, each ayllu readies its *quipocamayo* for display. When taken from its storage bag and arrayed with all pendants hanging parallel, the khipu is said to be *peinado* (combed). It is then twisted into a single cable, and the cable is tied into a single large knot, with the one extreme of the main cord protruding at the top. This positioning is called *cerro* (mountain) or *culebra* (snake) or *peaña*. A *peaña* is the two-step pyramid that forms the base of the cross, a key symbol (in Ortner's 1973 term) also used in many other contexts, usually as a sacred boundary marker. The *quipocamayo* is placed on a colorful cushion or pad of folded cloth and carried along by the ayllu when it parades to the civic meeting as a group. During the meeting, each *quipocamayo* rests at a spot designated with an X (*aspa*) of fresh straw, at a specific place along the perimeter delimiting the sacred precinct (see Figure 12.1). At the end of the meeting, each outgoing president of a *parcialidad* installs his successor by tying the *quipocamayo* onto the new officer's body, from left shoulder to right hip "like the presidential sash." The presidents are then saluted together and parade past the other authorities (see Figure 12.2), thereby finishing the Huayrona.

No living person in Tupicocha claims ability to read or make *quipocamayos*. If one asks what *quipocamayos* mean, common answers are, for example, "They contain the laws, they say what the *camachico* must do"; "They're like an almanac: the days, the harvests are in there, everything. Whether it will be a good year or not"; "They're writings. Every knot is a letter. They have an

FIGURE 12.1 *Quipocamayos* of eight ayllu or *parcialidades* on display during the second day of the general civic meeting (Huayrona), January 3, 1995. At the end of the meeting, presidents-elect of ayllu don them as they assume office.

alphabet"; "They're our Magna Carta, the foundation, the constitution." Although Tupicochans are aware of the Inka past and know that the Inka made cord records, they do not regard the *quipocamayos* as Inka artifacts. Far from recalling the glories of Cusco, these objects symbolize local autochthony, and the fact that nobody can read them is the source of some disquiet. Everyone treats them as sacred. No one is to alter them (except for a few obvious repairs made to conserve fallen or broken cords).

We do not know whether Tupicochans learned the khipu art from the Inka or whether Inka khipu practice, like most Inka technology, rather represented a system of coordination among smaller, older, regionally variant systems. What we do know is that the Tupicochan examples—unlike the majority of extant museum specimens, which appear to have imperial associations—are records of the minimal corporate constituents[9] of a society. They therefore provide some clues to the role of khipu making as a general social competence in grassroots organization and as an ingredient in the intellectual life of base-level society. (The khipu that colonial native lords used in organizing lawsuits, *visitas*, and the like were perhaps of similar character.) Tupicochan specimens *grosso modo* match some Inka conventions and techniques—certainly much more so than do the ethnographic specimens studied by Carol

FIGURE 12.2 Celso Alberco, 1995 president of Ayllu Unión Chaucacolca, wears Quipocamayo UCh-01 as he is inducted.

Mackey in Chapter 13 of this book—but they also include other techniques not found in the (known) Inka specimens. As I suggest below, they allow one to speculate that the work of collecting and recording social self-knowledge had a local lore of its own, separable from Inka or Spanish statecraft.

CHRONOLOGY AND MATERIALS OF TUPICOCHA'S *QUIPOCAMAYOS*

An analysis of fibers found in the storage bag of Chaucacolca's second *quipo-camayo* (UCh-02 [10]), which is not displayed in the January cycle because of its poor condition, was performed by the fiber microscopist Richard Bisbing at McCrone Associates laboratories (Westmont, Illinois). It shows that the fiber is almost entirely alpaca wool. Cordage of varied color consists of naturally different-colored wool, but the samples also contain dyed fibers of a slightly bluish red and of a bright blue. Dyes have not been chemically identified; the blue is said by local *hilanderas*[11] (women experienced in wool technology) to be a now disused flower dye called *azul tiñi-tiñi*.

Although most Inka khipu are cotton, ancient or historic woolen khipu do exist in small numbers (Urton 1994: 275). Mackey (1970: 26) thinks woolen cord records may once have been prevalent in the highlands. Certainly wool would be the logical material for local (as opposed to imperial) khipu technology, since highlanders could procure it from their own resources even if they lacked control over lower-valley enclaves. (Many such enclaves were lost in the colonial era.)

Four portions of this same fiber, taken from separate, differently colored bits of cordage and therefore likely to represent four different khipu pendants, were submitted to accelerator radiocarbon dating at the University of Arizona Radiocarbon Laboratory. Three yielded dates in the range from 1650 to the republican era, possibly up to 1950.[12] (From 1650 to 1950 various environmental factors conspired to produce organic carbon that is inherently ambiguous in chronology, hence the wide bracketing.) The fourth yielded a modern date, that is, posterior to the advent of "bomb carbon," and is assigned to 1954 or 1955.[13] At least one man who was reputedly a *quipocamayo* expert was still alive at that date, but it is likelier that the fiber comes from a repair or from one of the cords attached at the extremes of the main cord today to facilitate the wearing of the artifact as a sash.

Historico-cultural data help somewhat in narrowing the range of possible dates. First of all, Tupicocha had abandoned the herding of alpacas and the processing of alpaca fiber long before 1950. No villager consulted can remember having heard any Tupicochan say that the village ever had such animals or produced its own alpaca garments. Given the constant, acute focus on agropastoral knowledge in village discussion, I consider it unlikely that such a fundamental fact as camelid herding would be forgotten in less than the lifetime of the oldest living people. The end of camelid herding is therefore not likely to be much later than the turn of the twentieth century. Of course, after it ended, villagers could conceivably have acquired unspun fiber from the *hualachos*, or llama caravaners, who annually descend from the high cordillera. But caravaners do not generally sell unspun wool. For value-added and logistical reasons, they prefer to trade in finished products. Also, the very large variety of colors and fibers used seems easier to explain if one posits direct herd access.

When did cords cease to be official media? About a century ago, ayllu began to keep written inventories of corporately owned goods. Mújica's oldest book (APM/SAT s/n.: f. 13r) already in 1898 mentions the *quipocamayos* as artifacts "*de anterior*" (of former [times]). This phrase suggests they were then going out of use or even disused.

So the *quipocamayos* were seemingly obsolescent by the early twentieth century. How much earlier their florescence occurred is hard to tell. A late-colonial or early-republican chronology cannot be foreclosed. The fact that the specimens closely match the drawings in Felipe Guaman Poma de Ayala's book (1980: 335, 348, 358, 360, and 800 in the manuscript pagination) allows speculation on a long conservation of the design tradition Guaman Poma saw around 1600. It may be relevant that Guaman Poma passed through Huaro-chirí and met Avila's parishioners (Mejía Xesspe 1942: 7).

As we will see below, there is reason to think that any given *quipocamayo* contains components with disparate dates, so it makes more sense to target the idea of a *quipocamayo*'s use-life, rather than its manufacture. At present, the best guess is that these specimens' use-life included the later nineteenth century, and in some ayllu may have begun before then or continued after that time.

Although important ethnohistorical writings focus on colonial khipu that underpinned native testimony in litigation and administration (Murra 1974; Rostworowski 1990), specimens of certifiably post-Pizarran cord-record technology are rare, or perhaps rarely identified. As we approach these, interpretation should be framed in relation not just to the Inka khipu tradition but to colonial norms of documentation and bookkeeping, which may have modified it.

SOME PHYSICAL CHARACTERISTICS OF THE PATRIMONIAL *QUIPOCAMAYOS*

Relative to all known khipu, the Tupicochan specimens are of medium to fairly large size. Unlike the modern woolen specimens described by Mackey (1970), they all follow the basic Inka system in construction of main cord, cord attachments, pendants, and subsidiaries; in cord construction from thread to ply to cordage; and, with important exceptions noted below, in knotting. Their main cords vary from 35 to 189 cm, but much of the varia-tion is due to long "tails" and in one case a long "neck" rather than to the number of pendants. Pendants number from 69 to 125 and average 98 (if one includes the atypical specimen M-01) or 101 (if one leaves it out).[14] Wool arti-sans today call the main cord *tronco* (trunk), and pendants, *hilos*, or "threads." Subsidiaries are not numerous on most specimens and are totally absent on

FIGURE 12.3 *Pachacamanta*, or end ornament, of
Quipocamayo 1G-01, belonging to Ayllu Primer Huangre.
Note metal-wound threads making up the "Turk's head"
ornamentation.

two (Mújica's M-01 and Cacarima's). They are usually attached at cm 0 but
sometimes farther down pendants. Artisans call them the *compañías* (accom-
paniments) of pendants.

At the time of the symposium that generated this book, nine specimens
had been studied. Since then, one more, namely M-02, has come to light.
Most specimens bear "markers" (as they are called by the Aschers [1978])
of striking complexity, clearly indicating that the designers intended these
quipocamayos to be precious objects, and also perhaps that they meant them to
be identifiable when viewed from a distance, as in public ceremony. Markers
utilize a completely different palette of colors from data cords: crimsons, yellows, greens, and blues, none of which are found in the structural fiber of
main cords or pendants.

The most striking markers are ornamented knobs marking one extreme of
main cords. An elder with a long-standing enthusiasm for ritual (such persons
are called *costumbreros*) identified these as *pachacamantas* (see Figure 12.3).
If this word is, as it seems, a Hispano-Quechuism, its etymological sense is
"about the hundred." This is an important clue to the organizational significance of *quipocamayos*, suggesting as it does that the ayllu formerly counted
as the "hundreds" (*pachaka*) of which the Inkaic "Checa thousand" was composed. The *pachacamanta* of Primer Huangre's *quipocamayo*, shown in Figure
12.3, is decorated with two 6-bight, 7-strand Turk's heads made of cordage
wrapped in flat wire of copper or a copper alloy or compound.[15] This material
seems to imitate European designs, but the wrapping wire appears cut from
a flat sheet, suggesting native Andean manufacture.[16]

The smaller ornaments, which are similar in color scheme and occur along the main cord, are known today as *motas*, a term also applied to tufts and pompoms on church banners and altar cloths. Perhaps more significantly, they are also called *hitos*, which means "landmarks," such as boundary stones, milestones, or named natural features. This usage suggests that a *quipocamayo* is seen as having a geography of its own. In what sense the domain of land and the domain of cords are linked is still an open question. One villager hazarded the hypothesis that they are linked iconically: the khipu in its coiled display position might represent a "mountain," on whose flanks the protruding tufts could be taken as boundary markers, canal junctions, or delimiters of pasture. But others say the tufts might be "landmarks" in a metaphorical sense, that is, markers that guide the beholder along the main cord, just as milestones and boundary stones guide a traveler along a road, by signaling extensions and discontinuities in space. If that guess is correct, one might further guess that the extension of the main cord is correlated to time, and the markers to extensions or discontinuities such as planting periods or holidays.

The pendant cords are of varied diameter (about 1 mm to slightly over 3 mm) and include two of the three kinds of bichrome design that the Aschers described from museum specimens. The more common kind of two-color construction is the sort called *moteado*, or "mottled," in the literature (Ascher and Ascher 1978: 18; 1981: 21), which results from including threads of dissimilar color in each of two or more plies. A rare bichromy, found in only one *quipocamayo*, is the "candy cane" design, in which plies themselves are of dissimilar color. Bicolor cords are called *pallari* or *pallarado* or *pallaradito*. Tricolors of complex structure also occur. Most of the cordage has hard and even glossy surfaces, but some cords have a nap (whether from wear or by design is not known). Nappy bichromes or trichromes appear tweedy and are called *jerga* (tweed) by local artisans. Another form of multicolor design occurs when one or more threads (not plies) of blue, red, or yellow—the same hues found on *pachacamantas* and *hitos*, but never in cordage—are run through part or all of the pendant parallel to one or more plies. This gives the effect of a bright "underlining." Artisans say of such a cord that it is made *con su hilo* or *con hilo* (with its thread), or that it has a *cantito*[17] (little edging). A form of accentuation or annotation that must have been added at a later stage of construction consists of small tufts of unspun fiber tied inside data knots. Such tufts' colors contrast with those of their cord.

It has long been noted that khipu include both S-twisted and Z-twisted (or S-plied and Z-plied) cords. This is also true of Tupicochan examples. Modern Tupicochans say that working in either an S or Z direction is only a personal idiosyncrasy, but in the case of the Tupicochan specimens, it is likely to have been a conventionally meaningful design feature. The reason for this thinking is that the originally paired set consisting of specimen 1SF-01 and 2SF-01, that is, the pair that belonged to undivided Ayllu Satafasca until the 1920s, contrasts in cord directionality. Quipocamayo 2SF-01, which belongs to the junior segment, is overwhelmingly Z-plied, and its counterpart, 1SF-01, of the senior segment, is overwhelmingly S-plied.

The knotting of Tupicochan khipu includes all the common Inka types, but there are also knots unknown in the Inka typology of Locke (1923, 1929), which has been used with some variation by most later authors (Ascher and Ascher 1978, 1981; Day 1967; Nordenskiöld 1979; Urton 1994). What might be called classical khipu knots are the simple overhand knot, coded "s" in the Ascher database, the figure-eight knot, or "e," and the Inka long knot, or "L." In addition to these, Tupicochans used three other knots, all long knots. We do not yet know whether they are significant features rather than errors or allomorphs of the Inka L knot. But considering that they are harder to make than Inka L knots, it is difficult to see why anyone would introduce the extra mechanical and visual complexity unless it carried some significance. One of the less familiar kinds occurs in denominations over nine (notably in Mújica's Quipocamayo M-01), which suggests that decimal arithmetic does not exhaust their meanings.

The first of these noncanonical knots is what I will call the Tupicocha knot. It is the commonest long knot in the nine studied specimens. It loosely resembles a hangman's knot but is actually more closely related to an unnamed hitch that the incomparable knot expert Clifford W. Ashley registered for attaching fishhooks, as well as to one variant of the monkey's tail stopper knot (1944: 53, illus. 324; 88, illus. 535, left). Modern Tupicochans remark that it is puzzling, because no actual knot is visible. When perfectly executed, it looks as if the vertical pendant were encased by an unsecured cylinder of cord circling it in a tight spiral (see Figure 12.4). Actually, the knot is a close relative of the Inka long knot. Both are begun by bending the free, or working, end of the cord upward in a ∪, but, whereas one makes an Inka L by passing the descending spiral turns that signify integers only around the descending axis of the knot (let us say, the left vertical of the ∪), leaving the ascending axis visible, one makes a Tupicocha knot by binding the turns tightly around both axes.

This knot is very difficult to distinguish without destructive manipulation from the "monkey's fist" (Ashley 1944: 354, illus. 2203). Some of the Tupicochan long knots are probably in fact monkey's fists. The two differ in the

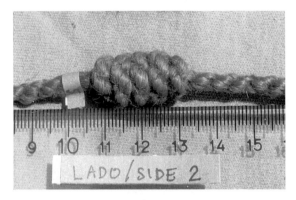

FIGURE 12.4 Pendant 5 of Segunda Satafasca's
Quipocamayo 2SF-01 contains a "Tupicocha" long knot.

following way. While the Tupicocha knot is made by constructing a U with
two axes first, then winding turns downward from the top around both, the
more difficult monkey's fist begins with a downward axis only, then makes the
turns around it going upward, and finally constructs the second axis by a second downward pass, running the working end through the turns and parallel
to the first axis.[18]

However, there is another and perhaps more significant way to make a
Tupicocha knot, namely, by modifying an extant Inka long knot. One must
slacken its exposed or ascending vertical axis, and, by winding it around the
extant turns in a contrary direction, exhaust them. The effect of this surprising "rope trick" is to replace the turns with a series of oppositely spiraled
turns lacking an exposed axis (Ashley 1944: 94, illus. 566). Such a transformation might have expressed a transvaluation of the long knot's value (such
as, postulating a speculative example, negative to positive).

In the majority of examples, the Tupicocha knot (or monkey's fist) is difficult to interpret (as R. Ascher, who has probably "read" more knots than any
living person, confirms[19]). The reason is that the bend forming the bottom of
the U is visible from one side but not from the other, so, for example, a knot
that looks like a "4" from one side will look like a "5" from the other. Assuming turns do encode integers, "4" is probably a better gloss, because the bottom of the U is not topologically similar to the turns. This attribute seems to
have bothered the makers of the *quipocamayos* too, for they took pains to hide
the bottom of the U as much as possible, and some acquired a knack (which
I have not been able to duplicate) for making it virtually disappear inside the
"cylinder" of turns.

Two other long knots outside the Lockean typology occur. One is identical to Ashley's "multiple figure-eight knot" (1944: 85, illus. 523, center; 94, illus. 568), also identified by Graumont and Hensel (1952: plate 48, illus. 340). It occurs only in Ayllu Mújica's Quipocamayo M-01. It is made by weaving the successive descending turns around both of the axes of the U that begins the knot, while crossing over back and forth between them in a figure-eight movement. A finished Mújica knot (see Figure 12.5) looks like two separate stacks of turns. We do not know whether they are to be counted separately, summed, or read as a tens and a units place.

The last of the noncanonical knots might be called a reversing knot, be-

FIGURE 12.5 Ayllu Mújicas's Quipocamayo M-01, Pendant 5, shows the multiple figure-eight long knot.

cause it is made like the Tupicocha knot but reverses directionality in mid descent. That is, the first few turns spiral counterclockwise and the last few clockwise, or vice versa. A few other types occur rarely or only once, and it is not clear whether they are errors, allomorphs, or meaningful variants.

Finally, at the whole-khipu level of construction, one observes that nine Tupicochan specimens are color banded. That is, cords are grouped together by approximate color, including groups of *pallaris*, or bicolors. There are also groups of pendants of a given color all having subsidiaries of the same contrasting color (for example, 1SF-01 Pendants 11 through 14s1, which are off-white with brown subsidiaries). The single exception to the otherwise strong banding rule, M-01 of Ayllu Mújica, presents cords in a different and very interesting pattern: they are grouped in sets of four, each set being initiated by a pendant of the color called *chumpi* (light to mid-reddish brown) and having as its third member a light gray (*oque*)[20] pendant. The pendants that make up the second member of each set, if taken as a series, form a secondary pattern: a gradient running from pale to dark colors and back again. The pendants in fourth position vary widely without apparent pattern. It is as if the khipu expresses sixteen iterations of a social agenda, or sixteen items of a given class, each of which was recorded in a syntactically standardized form (filling in a form, as it were). Each iteration or item has four attributes (pendants) about which statements (knots) are made. Two of the attributes (first and third cords) are qualitatively constant and apparently bear varying quantitative or paradigmatic statements. The second attribute passes through one cycle of intensification or disintensification during sixteen iterations, or else it is a continuously varying attribute of simultaneous items, used to sort the items in a pattern something like a bell curve. The fourth attribute may be a comment, or a variable not systematically related to the first three.[21]

QUIPOCAMAYOS AND OPERATIONAL DEVICES: IN WHAT SENSE ARE CORD RECORDS TEXTS?

Since conclusions about this data set are still premature, I will end with a frankly speculative invitation to rethink some aspects of the general khipu problem. To begin with, let us consider two facts about the Tupicocha set which escape the paradigm established by Locke—one because it lies above the levels of analysis that interested him, and one because it falls below.

The overlying fact in the Lockean model is the pairing of khipu. Pairing of complementary artifacts, for example drinking goblets (Guaman Poma 1980: 246), is a general expression of Andean people's frequent recurrence to dualism in ideology and in schematic reasoning (Gelles 1995). Until the twentieth century, each ayllu's publicly displayed records were normally two, and only two, *quipocamayos*. What was the functional relationship between paired specimens?

An oral tradition from Ayllu Chaucacolca holds that one belonged to the incoming, and one to the outgoing, ayllu president (*camachico*), both of whom were (and still are) present at the Huayrona investiture ceremony.

The intravillage written record provides a slightly different explanation of pairing: Ayllu Mújica's oldest book (APM/SAT s/n.: 16v–19r, entries for 1900) and still-undivided Satafasca's second book (AP1SF/SAT No. 2: 1–2, 1913) both say the ayllu had a double leadership, consisting of a *camachico* and a *mayor*;[22] each holding one *quipocamayo*. In the 1930s, when the hierarchy had changed to a presidential system, the president and his vice president held them (APCh/SAT No. 3: 226). The now extinct *mayor* office is said in oral tradition to have been one of moral authority, held by a man who had already held the presidency and was therefore able to advise the president as well as act as his ambassador.

The two models are not mutually exclusive, provided one is willing to interpret the oral tradition as meaning that one khipu was *at any given time* the insignia of the incoming, and the other of the outgoing, ayllu head. The cited Satafasca book provides a clarifying detail to the effect that the *mayor*'s political powers were to be exercised only in the first semester of each year. Combining this datum with the information that *mayores* should be ex-presidents, one can envision an oscillating and hierarchical plan. If Khipu A were held by Individual X in his presidential year (year 1900, let us say), he would take it with him as he became outgoing president and *mayor* for 1901. Meanwhile, Khipu B would be held by the 1901 president, Individual Y, who would in turn carry it into his *mayoral* year, 1902. Since X would have finished his *mayorazgo* during 1901 (ideally by midyear), Khipu A would again be available to the 1902 president, Individual Z. Comparable alternating structures are quite commonly used in Huarochirí ceremonial systems; Tupicocha, for example, fêtes its patron saint and its main Virgin image in alternate years, much as (during the time that Chapter 24 of the 1608 Quechua manuscript describes) the Checa ritual cycle oscillated in two-year periods between celebrating the Machua Yunca (a ritual cycle associated with aboriginal tradition) and the Chuta Cara (one associated with the traditions of invading highlanders).

If paired khipu once formed a closed set, and if the pair moved through time in alternation while expressing changing politico-ritual realities, then one may assume that the actual data registered on each one in some way corresponded to the ongoing tasks of office. The data would have changed as the holders updated their information or executed their administrative duties. Current information would have overwritten older information. In other words, khipu of this sort would not have been, like today's intra-ayllu books of record, unchanging arrays of encoded information that accumulated over time—that is, texts—but rather schemata of a short-term planned future, a present, and/or a recent past. Though I do not dispute the possibility that the Inka or perhaps others held accumulating "archives" of administrative or historical khipu text, this seems an unrealistic model for Tupicocha khipu.

An accumulating history can hardly consist of two, and only two, volumes. A likelier analogy than one with bookish history is that khipu served as *simulation tools*, whose data changed parallel to the relationship between politico-ritual agenda and actual performance. One might think of such records as engaged with unique facts of action over time, and to that degree they were historical, but within a finite, recurrent retrospective and prospective horizon.

This line of thought leads one toward conflict with one of the basic conventions of khipu study, namely, the assumption that they are recording devices and not operational devices. This assumption is an overgeneralization from Leland Locke's justified comment in his pathbreaking numerical decipherment that "the quipu was not adapted for calculations" (1923: 32). That is, unlike the *yupana* (Andean counting board), called "Andean abacus" by Wassén, which seems to have been its counterpart (Aitken 1990; Ansión 1990; Guaman Poma 1980: 360; Pereyra 1990; Radicati di Primeglio 1990; Wassén 1990), the knot-cord technology does not allow one to make and move the signs representing numbers with anything like the speed at which one can calculate them. Inka specimens do indeed seem to reflect the final inscription of calculations made separately and presented *ex post facto* to a khipukamayuq working at a craftsman's deliberate pace. Most museum specimens do indeed show impressive uniformity of technique and format, and William Conklin, who has inspected the material culture of khipu more carefully than anyone else, confirms[23] that Inka specimens were probably not operational devices. Any observer of fine Inka examples can readily accept the existence of cord records made with the purpose of textlike fixity. But this does not close the question of whether other examples could or did have "operational" use.

Let us first ask under what conditions khipu might have been useful simulators for working toward social rationality, and then ask whether Tupicochan specimens actually have physical properties compatible with use as simulation tools, "game boards" (Gelles [1995: 722] suggested this promising simile apropos of dual models), or "emblematic frames" (Harris 1995: 168–169). This will require study of "micro" features that fall below the Lockean frame of study.

The calculation of sums and other numerical relationships among the elements of a system only becomes meaningful *after* one has arranged the data. First one must formulate a problem in terms of discrete signs, then acquire sign pieces that match the elements of the problem, and next place the signs into patterns that simulate the problem. Only then does calculation enter in. Viewing khipu as records of calculation entails a misleading concentration on only the *last* stages of their actual employ, and covers only a *part* of their functional gamut. Before calculation begins, symbols must be deployed so as to represent reality and possibility usefully, and this may be the harder part of the task. Solutions must be reached anew as reality changes. For example, in distributing irrigation turns in a climate where the arrival and duration of rains is only marginally predictable, the number of irrigators must be brought into relation with a shifting set of irrigable fields and irrigation turns. The tokens that represent each must therefore be rearranged. To allow for precise discussion among decision makers, the array of items and options needs in some way to be made public. If the decision chain is complex, visible means of doing so may well be superior to verbal ones (as anybody who has tried to discuss a timetable without a blackboard knows). Such functionality may underlie the remarkably long duration and versatility of cord-based information technology, even when in competition with alphanumerical systems.

In order to test the hypothesis that Tupicochan khipu functioned as operative devices, one must pay attention to detailed physical features below the level of what is usually considered to be the data-bearing structure. I will argue that the Tupicochan specimens do have features compatible with use as simulation devices.

First, if a khipu served as an operative device over various cycles, it is likely to show heterogeneity of manufacture. The number of households entitled to a turn of group labor, for example, will have varied, and some cords will have been lost or worn out. The personnel making the record will have changed, leaving differences of "handwriting" in the product. The stock of fiber will also have varied somewhat, so that renderings of an "emically" significant color (*chumpi*, etc.) will differ somewhat in their "etic" performance (actual chroma). This "retrodiction" is confirmed many times over. I asked modern woolworkers in Tupicocha to group khipu cords by color and found that "emic" colors each comprise Munsell color taxa that vary by two or more

FIGURE 12.6 In Pendants 29–31 of Unión Chaucacolca's *Quipocamayo* UCh-01, *pallaris* (bicolors) of "mottled" structure vary in diameter by a ratio of 1 to 3.

grades of saturation and of hue. There are disparities in the "handwriting" of similar knots (i.e., equivalent number and knot type) on single khipu or even within single color bands. Cords that belong to a single band and color vary in diameter by ratios of up to 3:1, and are unlikely to have been made as parts of a uniform batch (see Figure 12.6). They also vary in texture, tightness, and degree of wear.

Second, an operational khipu would have technical characteristics allowing easy movement, removal, and attachment of elements. It has not been noted in the literature, but the fact is that the standard attachment of pendants allows one either to remove and reattach a pendant individually or to reposition it by sliding, without disturbing the rest of the khipu. In fact, the khipu half-hitch is the optimal design for mobility. One can slide a pendant by loosening its attachment loop and carrying it past adjacent pendants, pulling the extremes of pendants through the moving loop until the desired position is reached, then retightening. Although this might be difficult in the tightly tied cotton Inka khipu, it would be easier with Tupicochan specimens. Some Tupicochan specimens show stretches of bare main cord. Of course, cords may have been lost, but they may also have been removed. Other specimens, notably Chaucacolca's UCh-01, have jammed main cords; they may be bearing more pendants than they were originally designed for. It is equally easy to create immobile pendants by inserting them between plies of the main cord, but nobody did so in Tupicocha, and in museum specimens such insertion is exceedingly rare.

Third, if the default of an operational device is movability of sign-bearing parts, those parts that are not to be moved, or are to be moved jointly if at all, should bear signs or mechanical devices that impede mobility. Several such devices are in evidence. One is an irregular attachment in which the attachment loop of one pendant is tightened over that of an adjacent one, apparently signaling that the two are to be taken together; the latter cannot be loosened and moved without also loosening the former. Another device that falls outside the conventional canon of khipu literature is the tying of pendants to each other by attachments at midcord, so as to allow them to be readily moved but only if moved together. In Tupicocha, only pairs (not necessarily adjacent) are tied to each other, but at least one case of multiple bundled pendants occurs in other collections.[24] A third device, indicating the highest level of immobilization, is the binding of a group of pendants to each other with stitches right through their attachment loops. This makes it impossible to move the group at all, because the affected cords cannot be loosened from the main cord or from each other (see Figure 12.7).

Fourth, if *quipocamayos* used cords made on separate occasions by separate hands, and perhaps used pendants modified while unattached to the main cord, one could expect a low degree of positional standardization of knots relative to the main cord. Unlike Inka specimens, they would not exhibit knots readily identifiable as belonging to tens or units places. Tupicochans themselves notice the poor alignment of knots in most of their specimens. Figure 12.8 shows a representative example.

In sum, there are *prima facie* reasons to entertain the notions that the Tupicochan khipu were (1) operational devices, (2) the work of multiple makers,

FIGURE 12.7 On Ayllu Segunda Satafasca's Quipocamayo 2SF-01, a series of pendants are bound to each other and to the main cord with sewing thread.

and (3) altered on multiple occasions. Unlike inscriptions or books, the Tupicochan specimens seem made for only conditional fixity.

The basic structures of these khipu—*pachacamantas*, main cords, and markers—were in my view not intended as archival records but as simulation tools or "game boards," cycled over and over, handed on to successive officeholders, and presumably "rewritten" in successive uses. As for the data cords, perhaps a closer simile would be a deck, as of cards. Pendants may have represented a finite set of categorized entities, such as male/female/underage/overage workers, which had to be distributed among a planned set of occasions, such as collective work days keyed to the irrigation cycle. The users of the artifact, probably the ayllu members in meetings coordinated by officers, would have "played" the deck, deploying it so as to bring out a workable pattern for the leaders to administer. Much of the intellectual effort of modern ayllu and community affairs concerns deploying the "deck" of available resources in just such a way. The khipu medium is well suited to the task.

Discussion of khipu has for many years been constrained by the question of whether ancient Peruvians did or did not have "writing" in the sense defined by grammatologists (Animato et al. 1994; Laurencich Minelli 1996; Pärssinen 1992: 31–50), that is, encoded representations of utterances in a specific language. We have not been ready enough to ask what other products of social interaction and reason can be encoded, or how the process of making coded artifacts other than writing "proper" fits into the conduct of social life. Perhaps we can best appreciate the powers of the Tupicocha code by thinking of it as an achievement of an unfamiliar sort: a medium for collective, multivariate reasoning in which the attributes of the record are the direct precipitate of many decisions and performances within a corporation. A Tupicochan khipu was, perhaps, an act of social totalization, with the society itself as author. At any given moment, by studying the deployment of tokens (Schmandt-Besserat 1988) representing the "knowns" of social life on a one-to-one scale, it was possible to reach reasoned and consensual options for a future that also contained unknowns.

ACKNOWLEDGMENTS

The author gratefully acknowledges the help of many persons and agencies: first and foremost, the 1995, 1997, and 2000 presidents of the *parcialidades* of Tupicocha and the authorities of Comunidad Campesina San Andrés de Tupicocha, and also the National Science Foundation, the Wenner Gren Foundation, the School of American Research, and the Instituto de Estudios Peruanos. Among individuals, León Modesto Rojas, Celso Alberco, Sebastián Alberco Ramírez, Alberto Vilcayauri and Elba Vilcayauri, David McJunkin, and Melania Alvarez-Adem have my special gratitude.

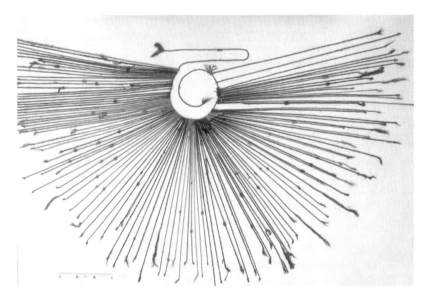

FIGURE 12.8 Seen in radial array, Ayllu Primera Allauca's Quipocamayo 1A-01 shows unstandardized placement of knots on pendants.

NOTES

1. Since modern Tupicochans do not know Quechua (or the Kauki-like language that formerly underlay it), I treat non-Spanish words as Hispano-Quechuisms and spell them with the same Spanish orthography villagers use for their own records.

2. The term *equipo* may be motivated by folk-etymological likening to the Spanish word for "team," because ayllu do in fact function as work teams and even have their own soccer teams.

3. Colonial Quechua terms are reproduced as spelled in their sources.

4. The use of such humble material as straw suggests that, in addition to the well-made khipu that survive by interment or curation, the cord technology also served to make temporary jottings or single-item memoranda.

5. There is some inconsistency in local applications of Spanish gender to these names, both in speech and in written records.

6. The English word "Boys" entered by analogy with a popular soccer team of the 1920s, the "Sport Boys" of Callao.

7. In 1998 the Municipality of Tupicocha took on itself a nontraditional stewardship of the newly recovered tenth *quipocamayo*.

8. The Collca, recently built, replaces the older "Collca de Santa Rosa." The term "Collca" derives from the Quechua term for "storehouse," and both structures indeed had storage rooms alongside their central ceremonial plazas. The storage capacity was formerly used for harvests held as communal property.

9. Ayllu are minimal for political purposes, but in discussing kinship and genealogy, members sometimes refer to the still smaller unit *familia*, which is implicitly defined as the set of people sharing a surname by patrilineal inheritance from a putative focal ancestor.

10. This and similar identifiers were devised by the present author in making the descriptive register of Tupicochan *quipocamayos*.

11. Dominga Antiporta and Vicenta Javier Medina.

12. Samples AA22422, AA22423, and AA22425.

13. AA22426.

14. Using 1995 data; rough handling of the khipu in ritual contexts apparently caused loss of certain cords in the interval 1995–1997.

15. For identification of the construction, thanks go to Patricia Hilts.

16. Elena Phipps, personal communication 1998.

17. Meanings of *canto* in standard Spanish include the edge of a book opposite the spine, the unsharpened edge of a knife, etc.

18. Thanks are due to Patricia Hilts for pointing out this likeness.

19. Robert Ascher, personal communication, April 13, 1997.

20. The main elements of this reading of M-01 were reached independently by Justo Rueda, a Tupicochan artisan specializing in wool.

21. The full cord-by-cord catalogue of the *quipocamayos* and studies of ethnographic analogies will be published in the near future.

22. The replacement of these titles of office dates from the 1920s onward and probably relates to the terms on which national authorities of the Leguía *"oncenio"* allowed indigenous institutions to officialize themselves.

23. Conklin, personal communication as commentary in discussion of the present chapter, 1997.

24. An example was exhibited by Urton at the meeting whose studies are published herein.

REFERENCES CITED

Unpublished Archival Manuscripts

AA/L (Archivo Arzobispal/Lima) Capítulos Leg. 1, Exp. 9. 1607. Proceso remitido por el señor dean y provisor al doctor padilla vicario general de capitulos contra el doctor francisco de avila cura y beneficiado de el [*sic*] doctrina de san damian y sus anejos.

AA/L (Archivo Arzobispal/Lima) Capítulos Leg. 27, Exp. VIII. 1705–1719. Causa de Capítulos seguida por los caciques principales de las doctrinas de Pampas, Cochas, Cañete, San Damián, Conchucos, Atabillos, Chincha, Cotaparaco, Canta, Chancay, Sobre los agravios que cometen los curas en la administración de los Sacramentos, llevándoles crecidos derechos parroquiales. Ambrosio de Medina, notario.

APCh/SAT (Archivo de la Parcialidad de Chaucacolca/San Andrés de Tupicocha) No. 3. *Libro No. 3: Libro de Acta de Instalación de la Parcialidad de Chaucacolca*. 1936–1952.

APM/SAT (Archivo de la Parcialidad de Mújica/San Andrés de Tupicocha) s/n. 1898–1916. [Libro fragmentario sin título. Actas de la Parcialidad Mújica.]

AP1SF/SAT (Archivo de la Parcialidad de Primera Satafasca/San Andrés de Tupicocha) No. 2. [Libro sin título. Actas de Satafasca indivisa desde 1913 y de Primera Satafasca hasta 1945.]

Nonarchival Sources

Acosta, Antonio. 1987. "Francisco de Avila. Cusco 1573(?)–Lima 1647." In *Ritos y tradiciones de Huarochirí del siglo XVII*, edited and translated by Gerald Taylor, 551–616. Historia Andina, no. 12. Lima: Instituto de Estudios Peruanos and Instituto Francés de Estudios Andinos.

Aitken-Soux, Percy, and Faustino Ccama. 1990. "Abaco andino, instrumento ancestral de cómputo." In *Quipu y yupana*, edited by Carol Mackey et al., 267–272. Lima: Consejo Nacional de Ciencia y Tecnología.

Animato, Carlo, Paolo A. Rossi, and Clara Miccinelli. 1994. *Quipu: Il nodo parlante dei misteriosi Incas*. Genova: Ediczioni Culturali Internazionali.

Ansión, Juan. 1990. "Cómo calculaban los incas." In *Quipu y yupana*, edited by Carol Mackey et al., 257–266. Lima: Consejo Nacional de Ciencia y Tecnología.

Ascher, Marcia, and Robert Ascher. 1978. *Code of the Quipu: Databook*. Ann Arbor: University of Michigan Press. Now available only on microfiche from Cornell University Archives, Ithaca, N.Y.

———. 1981. *Code of the Quipu: A Study in Media, Mathematics, and Culture*. Ann Arbor: University of Michigan Press.

Ashley, Clifford W. 1944. *The Ashley Book of Knots*. Garden City, N.Y.: Doubleday.

Astete, Guillermo. 1997. "Anotaciones sobre los checa del alto Pachacámac." Thesis in progress, Departamento de Antropología, Pontificia Universidad Católica del Perú, Lima.

Day, Cyrus Lawrence. 1967. *Quipus and Witches' Knots: The Role of the Knot in Primitive and Ancient Cultures.* Lawrence: University of Kansas Press.

Gelles, Paul H. 1995. "Equilibrium and Extraction: Dual Organization in the Andes." *American Ethnologist* 22, no. 4: 710–742.

Graumont, Raoul, and John Hensel. 1952. *Encyclopedia of Knots and Fancy Rope Work.* 4th ed. Cambridge, Md.: Cornell Maritime Press.

Guaman Poma de Ayala, Felipe. 1980 [1615]. *Nueva corónica y buen gobierno.* Edited by John V. Murra and Rolena Adorno, with translations by Jorge L. Urioste. 3 vols. Mexico City: Siglo Veintiuno.

Harris, Roy. 1995. *Signs of Writing.* London: Routledge.

Huertas Vallejos, Lorenzo. 1992. "Aspectos de la historia de Huarochirí en los siglos XVI y XVII." In *Huarochirí: Ocho mil años de historia,* Tomo 1, edited by Vladimiro Thatar Alvarez et al., 241–270. Santa Eulalia (Huarochirí, Perú): Municipalidad de Santa Eulalia de Acopaya.

INEI (Instituto Nacional de Estadística e Informática, Dirección Nacional de Censos y Encuestas). 1994. *Censo Nacional 1993: Resultados Definitivos. Tomo 1. No. 2. Departamento de Lima.* Lima: Instituto Nacional de Estadistica e Informática.

Laurencich Minelli, Laura. 1996. *La scrittura dell'antico Perù: Un modo da scoprire.* Bologna: CLUEB.

Lira, Jorge A. 1944. *Diccionario Kkechuwa-Español.* Tucumán, Argentina: Universidad Nacional de Tucumán, Instituto de Historia, Lingüística y Folklor, Departamento de Investigaciones Regionales.

Locke, L. Leland. 1923. *The Ancient Quipu or Peruvian Knot Record.* New York: American Museum of Natural History.

———. 1929. "Supplementary Notes on the Quipus in the American Museum of Natural History." Anthropological Papers of the American Museum of Natural History 33: 30–73. New York: American Museum of Natural History.

Mackey, Carol J. 1970. "Knot Records in Ancient and Modern Peru." Ph.D. dissertation, Department of Anthropology, University of California, Berkeley.

———. 1990a. "Comparación entre quipu inca y quipus modernos." In *Quipu y yupana,* edited by Carol Mackey et al., 135–156. Lima: Consejo Nacional de Ciencia y Tecnología.

———. 1990b. "Nieves Yucra Huatta y la continuidad en la tradición del uso del quipu." In *Quipu y yupana,* edited by Carol Mackey et al., 157–164. Lima: Consejo Nacional de Ciencia y Tecnología.

Mackey, Carol, Hugo Pereyra, Carlos Radicati di Primeglio, Humberto Rodríguez, and Oscar Valverde, eds. 1990. *Quipu y yupana: Colección de escritos.* Lima: Consejo Nacional de Ciencia y Tecnología.

Martínez Chuquizana, T. Alejandro. 1996. "Descripción geográfica del Distrito de San Andrés de Tupicocha." Manuscript. Tupicocha and Lima.

Mejía Xesspe, M. Toribio. 1942. *Historia de la antigua provincia de Anan Yauyo.* Lima: N.p.

Murra, John V. 1974. "Las etno-categorías de un *khipu* estatal." In *Formaciones económicas y políticas en el mundo andino,* edited by John V. Murra, 243–254. Lima: Instituto de Estudios Peruanos.

Nordenskiöld, Erland von. 1979 [1925]. *The Secret of the Peruvian Quipus.* New York: AMS Press.

Ortner, Sherry B. 1973. "On Key Symbols." *American Anthropologist* 75, no. 5: 1338–1346.

Pärssinen, Martti. 1992. *Tawantinsuyu: The Inca State and Its Political Organization.* Helsinki: Societas Historica Finlandiae.

Pease, Franklin. 1990. "Utilización de quipus en los primeros tiempos coloniales." In *Quipu y yupana,* edited by Carol Mackey et al., 67–72. Lima: Consejo Nacional de Ciencia y Tecnología.

Pereyra Sánchez, Hugo. 1990. "La yupana, complemento operacional del quipu." In *Quipu y yupana,* edited by Carol Mackey et al., 235–255. Lima: Consejo Nacional de Ciencia y Tecnología.

Radicati di Primeglio, Carlos. 1990. "Tableros de escaques en el antiguo Perú." In *Quipu y yupana,* edited by Carol Mackey et al., 219–234. Lima: Consejo Nacional de Ciencia y Tecnología.

Rostworowski de Díez Canseco, María. 1990. "La visita de Urcos de 1652: Un kipu pueblerino." *Historia y Cultura* 20: 295–317.

Ruiz Estrada, Arturo. 1981. *Los quipus de Rapaz.* Huacho, Peru: Universidad Nacional "José Faustino Sánchez Carrión," Centro de Investigación de Ciencia y Tecnología de Huacho.

Salomon, Frank, and George Urioste, eds. and trans. 1991. *The Huarochirí Manuscript: A Testament of Ancient and Colonial Andean Religion.* Austin: University of Texas Press.

Schmandt-Besserat, Denise. 1988. "From Accounting to Written Language: The Role of Abstract Counting in the Invention of Writing." In *The Social Construction of Written Communication,* edited by Bennett A. Rafoth and Donald L. Rubin, 119–130. Norwood, N.J.: Ablex Publishing.

Sotelo, Hildebrando R. 1942. *Las insurrecciones y levantamientos en Huarochirí y sus factores determinantes.* Ph.D. dissertation, Facultad de Letras de la Universidad Nacional Mayor de San Marcos. Lima: Empresa Periodística S.A. "La Prensa."

Spalding, Karen. 1984. *Huarochirí: An Andean Society under Inca and Spanish Rule.* Stanford: Stanford University Press.

Stiglich, Germán. 1922. *Diccionario geográfico del Perú.* Vol. 2. Lima: Imprenta Torres Aguirre.

Taylor, Gerald. 1983. "Lengua general y lenguas particulares en la antigua provincia de Yauyos (Perú)." *Revista de Indias* 43, no. 171: 265–289.

———, ed. and trans., with Antonio Acosta. 1987. *Ritos y tradiciones de Huarochirí del siglo XVII.* Historia Andina, no. 12. Lima: Instituto de Estudios Peruanos and Instituto Francés de Estudios Andinos.

Urton, Gary. 1984. "*Chuta:* El espacio de la práctica social en Pacariqtambo, Perú." *Revista Andina* 2, no. 1: 7–56.

———. 1994. "A New Twist in an Old Yarn: Variation in Knot Directionality in the Inka *Khipus.*" *Baessler-Archiv,* Neue Folge, Band 42: 271–305.

Wassén, Henry. 1990 [1931]. "El antiguo ábaco peruano según el manuscrito de Guaman Poma." In *Quipu y yupana,* edited by Carol Mackey et al., 205–218. Lima: Consejo Nacional de Ciencia y Tecnología.

The Continuing Khipu Traditions

THIRTEEN   *Principles and Practices*

Carol Mackey

INTRODUCTION

Few people realize that khipu—knotted cords used to record data—are still used in the highlands of Peru. Khipu were the principal devices used in the pre-Hispanic Andes to process information. Although khipu predate the Inka by at least four hundred years (Conklin 1982), they are associated chiefly with the Inka, who flourished from ca. A.D. 1400 until 1532, when the Spanish conquistadores toppled their empire. Although the Spanish chroniclers noted that the Inka recorded at least two kinds of information on khipu—statistical and nonstatistical—the primary function of khipu was to record statistical data. The kinds of data that were encoded on statistical khipu included information on astronomy (Guaman Poma de Ayala 1956); weapons (Calancha 1976; Cieza de León 1959); foodstuffs (Cieza 1959); manufactured goods (Cieza 1959; Guaman Poma 1956); and census data (Betanzos 1987; Cieza 1959). The Spaniards, however, also remarked that nonstatistical khipu existed. These were used for recording historical events and oral literature (cf. Cieza 1959). The Spaniards continued to refer to khipu as recording devices during the colonial period (1532 to 1821), while the earliest documented "modern" khipu dates to William Stevenson's work in 1825. Over the centuries it has been the form rather than the function of khipu that has changed. Modern khipu are still composed of knots placed mainly on camelid fiber, but modern khipu are not standardized as they were in Inka times.

The processing of large amounts of data is a complex operation that includes the collection, storage, encoding, and retrieval of information. All khipu, whether Inka, colonial, or modern, could accomplish these tasks. Nonetheless, over the centuries, khipu have undergone changes in all of these facets.

THE ROLE OF THE KHIPU AND THEIR MAKERS

Though khipu predate the Inka, the majority of archaeological examples come from that time period. Some 600 years have passed since the Inka rose to power, and during that time khipu have changed in their social role and their structure. This chapter examines the role of modern khipu, the individuals who recorded the data, and the objects they counted.

Information about the use of khipu into colonial times comes to us from the Spanish *visitas*, or inspections (Julien 1991; Murra 1975, 1982; Pease 1990; Rostworowski 1990). We know, for instance, that the Visita General of 1549 followed a standard questionnaire issued from Lima, whose answers were often taken from data extracted from khipu by khipukamayuq, or khipu makers. The Spanish documents, however, do not always mention the use of khipu; but because statistical information was recorded as separate items, just as if counts were being "read" from individual strings on a khipu, it is thought that khipu were indeed being used. As John Murra, writing about the Visita General of 1549, notes, "they [the Spanish teams sent to evaluate population figures and resources] consulted the local lords and their khipukamayuq, who had continued knotting down the demographic and other quantitative data through almost a decade of armed resistance [to the Spaniards] plus seven years of colonial rule" (1982: 239).

It appears that well into the sixteenth century men trained as khipuka-mayuq continued to record data much as they had during Inka times. Khipu users in colonial times were still men of responsibility and position, but it was a marginal position within the new Spanish regime. As Joanne Rappaport (1994) points out, status was accorded to those who had learned to read and to write in Spanish. In 1988 I interviewed Nieves Yucra (Mackey 1990b), one of the last of his generation to use khipu on the island of Taquile, Lake Titicaca. Several young men on the island asked me why I chose to interview Yucra when it was they who knew how to read and write.

No special word exists in Spanish for either khipu or for the khipu user — the khipukamayuq. Khipu today are generally referred to by descriptive terms, such as "*hilos de lana*" (wool strings) or "*hilos con nudos*" (strings with knots). In the late 1960s, I interviewed eighteen men and one woman who

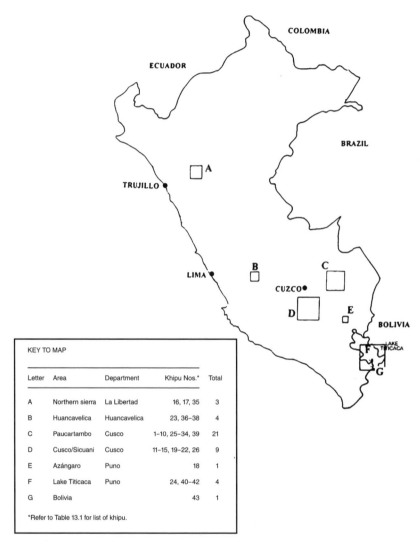

KEY TO MAP

Letter	Area	Department	Khipu Nos.*	Total
A	Northern sierra	La Libertad	16, 17, 35	3
B	Huancavelica	Huancavelica	23, 36–38	4
C	Paucartambo	Cusco	1–10, 25–34, 39	21
D	Cusco/Sicuani	Cusco	11–15, 19–22, 26	9
E	Azángaro	Puno	18	1
F	Lake Titicaca	Puno	24, 40–42	4
G	Bolivia		43	1

*Refer to Table 13.1 for list of khipu.

FIGURE 13.1 Location of modern khipu in Peru and Bolivia.

used khipu. My research took me into the sierra of La Libertad, in northern Peru, and as far south as the Department of Puno. Most of my work, however, focused on the northeastern portion of the Department of Cusco, around the area of Paucartambo (see Figure 13.1).

Modern khipu are associated with conservative indigenous customs and indicate that the khipu users are illiterate. In spite of this, modern users are generally men of responsibility and position within their community, although not within the larger society. Khipu are found in two distinct settings: the hacienda and the autonomous community. In the first instance, khipu users were directly responsible for recording the resources of the hacienda, while in the second case, men who lived in communities not associated with an hacienda, and who had knowledge of khipu use, kept records of their personal holdings to pass on to their children.

The men who used khipu generally had high status, though their status did not result from their use of khipu, as in Inka times, but from the fact that they were often village headmen who, because of their position, were chosen by the *mayordomo* (majordomo) of the hacienda to keep records (Mackey 1970). In the autonomous communities, men who had knowledge of khipu used them for their personal accounts, such as in the community of Ccotane (Department of Cusco). In this community, the khipu users were above average in wealth, suggesting that the need to record holdings was often an indication of affluence. Unlike the formal education accorded to Inka bureaucrats, modern khipu users had only informal training. With the exception of one woman in the region of Lake Langui (Area D, Figure 13.1), all of the people I interviewed were males, and all of them said that they learned the recording system from their fathers.

The majority of modern khipu examples come from haciendas. These estates were not concerned with reporting how many people lived on their lands, but rather with the results of their labor. This included the amount of produce that was grown and the number of animals under their care. Several of the men I interviewed said that they worked six days for the hacienda and one day for themselves, so that the majority of what they produced belonged to the hacienda. Other men divided the year in halves. For example, one man on the Hacienda Ccachupata, in the region of Paucartambo, spent half the year living in an isolated house high above his village tending potatoes. These potatoes dehydrate (becoming *chuño*) during six months of exposure to freezing night air and to warm days. It was his task to count all the potatoes as he placed them in bags in preparation for market. This count, he said, "was only for the hacienda" (Mackey 1970).

We also find examples of modern khipu used to count noncomestibles. One of the most interesting examples is a khipu that kept account of money held in the town treasury. This khipu belonged to a man who was a khipu maker at the Hacienda Viluyu, in the Sicuani area. His account recorded the money in the treasury that was held by the mestizo *alcalde* (mayor) of the nearby town of Descanso. Although the amount was entered in a ledgerbook kept in the town, a separate count was also entered on a khipu to show other native Quechua-speaking residents of the area (Mackey 1970).

The time of year when the data were retrieved from the khipu depended on whether the maker of the khipu lived in a village tied to an hacienda or in a community. For those living in communities who kept track of their own goods, the khipu served as a continuous account that did not stop at the end of a year. The hacienda, on the other hand, generally required one count per year, which was reported to the majordomo or to the owner in August or October. Just as hacienda khipu are specific for one year, they are also generally specific to one class of objects. The man who reports on livestock is not the same person who records produce, no doubt because on an hacienda these two economic pursuits are carried out in different areas or at different elevations. Llamas are generally herded in the puna (over 3,800 m), while other livestock are raised at lower elevations but apart from the agricultural area.

Modern khipu makers store their khipu either inside or outside their houses. Khipu from the Inka site of Puruchuco, near Lima, and the modern khipu from the Hacienda Ccachupata, near Paucartambo, were both stored in small, ceramic cooking vessels (*ollas*) and buried outside the house (Mackey 1970). Even though the men had to report the information recorded on the khipu to the hacienda administrators, they still kept their khipu as permanent records. Several men told me that they saved their khipu for their entire life, while others said they held them for just a year. One man told me that he untied the khipu cords and reused them, and another said that the majordomo of the hacienda retained possession of his khipu. But most men agreed that it was necessary to hold on to khipu, even after losing their position as headmen, since this was the only record they had. Over the course of my fieldwork I purchased twenty-two examples of modern khipu. Interestingly, before the khipu were sold to me, copies of each were made. Since most archaeological khipu are found in tombs, one wonders if Inka khipu found in tombs were copies of originals passed on by Inka khipukamayuq to their superiors.

Although khipu survived into the modern period, today they are used only sporadically throughout the central Andes. The scattered distribution and marginal position in society of modern-day khipu have prevented the emergence of a single modern khipu tradition. Instead, post-colonial khipu show great variability in morphology and in numerical notation.

RECORDING THE NUMERICAL MESSAGE

Khipu, whether Inka or modern, record two types of information: how many items were counted and the nature of the items counted. Each type of information has its own set of codes. The knots themselves, their position, and their spatial relations on a cord record numerical information. The other sets of data, the objects themselves, have numerous mnemonic codes that represent them. All of these variables, however, are "read" together and, as Elizabeth Boone notes, "these two parallel sets of information [on a khipu] are assimilated at one time and it is instantaneous" (1994: 21).

General Khipu Characteristics

In this section I focus on the symbols used to encode numbers, and I explore how modern khipu operate without the standardized Inka numerical system. Although the emphasis here is on modern khipu, I will first describe an Inka statistical khipu to compare its features to those of modern khipu. Further analysis of Inka khipu, however, will not be presented in this chapter, since that is the subject of other chapters in this book (see Conklin, Chapter 3, and Urton, Chapter 8).

The majority of Inka khipu used for statistical records have a standardized form that consists of a horizontal main or transverse cord, to which vertical pendant cords are attached. The main cord is generally thicker than the pendant cords, and the latter are all attached to the main cord with a half-hitch knot. Knots tied on the pendant cords receive their numerical value by their position, spacing, and type of knot, so that each cord carries a numerical total of an item. Pendant cords may have other cords appended to them. These are called subsidiary cords, and they alter the number found on the principal pendant cord either by adding or subtracting from the total on the pendant to which they are attached. Were it not for the existence on some, but not all, khipu of a pendant cord that generally goes in the opposite direction from the other pendants and carries a total of the knots on the khipu, scholars would never have been able to decipher the knotted system (Locke 1923).

The standard Inka system used as many as three types (and subtypes) of knots to denote numbers (see Conklin, Chapter 3, this book). These knot types are: (1) an overhand knot for denominations of 10, 100, and 1,000; (2) the long knot for units 2 through 9; and (3) the figure-eight knot used to denote the number 1 (Ascher and Ascher 1969; Locke 1923; Nordenskiöld 1925; Radicati di Primeglio 1950; Uhle 1897). Modern khipu generally use only overhand knots, although exceptions can be found. Two examples of long knots occur on Khipu No. 16 from the Hacienda Angasmarca in the northern sierra (Area A, Figure 13.1). This khipu used the long knot to signify two different things: (1) in the first example, the knot does not have a numerical value but acts only to separate two totals; (2) on another pendant on the same khipu the long knot represents the count of four. It is important to remember that in modern khipu it is not only the knots that symbolize numerical value but also a range of symbols, used in conjunction with the knots, that communicate the numerical message. One concept that has remained constant since Inka times is the rule of knot position, that is, knots valued as lower numbers occur toward the bottom of the pendant cord, and knots with greater values occur in clusters higher on the pendant.

Modern khipu also preserve the notion of subsidiary cords, although their location on the khipu is very different from that on Inka examples. The majority of modern khipu have cords or pieces of yarn that function as subsidiaries even though they are not located on the pendant itself. Instead, these cords are often located on the main cord close to the pendant or pendants whose numbers they alter.

One interesting aspect of colonial and modern khipu is that they are so much smaller than their Inka counterparts, although there are some exceptions to this rule. For example, the khipu described by Arturo Ruiz Estrada (1990) and Frank Salomon (1997 and Chapter 12, this book) are probably colonial in date, but they are within the size range of Inka khipu. Most modern khipu, however, have fewer than ten pendants. Decreasing the number of pendants is accomplished by making one pendant do the work of many, or creating what I will refer to below as "accounting zones." These zones are created when modern khipu users, rather than adding new pendants, divide one pendant into several zones composed of clusters of knots, with each zone representing a separate category and total.

The Modern Khipu Sample

The modern khipu sample used in this chapter is drawn from my own research (Mackey 1970; 1990) and from other studies (Bastian 1895; Cohen 1957; Guimaraes 1907; Núñez del Prado 1950; Prochaska 1988; Soto Flores 1951; Uhle 1897; see Table 13.1).

In order to discuss the various aspects of modern khipu, I have used the same type designations, A–C, as in a previous study (Mackey 1970); however, only Type B could be more finely divided into subtypes. My sample consists of forty-three modern khipu, twenty-four of which I collected. The criteria for these types are based on khipu morphology and the number of mnemonic symbols used to signify numerical value.

Khipu Types

Based on the results of this study, I isolated six principles used by khipu makers to denote numerical values. These principles served as the basis for establishing the types and subtypes. As can be seen in Table 13.2, each type employs a unique combination of the six principles. The khipu types, and their variants when they exist, will be discussed in relation to the principles shown in Table 13.2.

TYPE A KHIPU.   The Type A khipu mimics standard Inka khipu in form because it is composed of a horizontal element with vertical cords appended to it. This is the second most common type and makes up 21 percent of the sample. Leland Locke (1923) first noted that modern khipu do not have pendant cords attached to the main cord in the same manner as Inka khipu. Often, the cords are simply draped over the main cord. Type A khipu have main cords that range in length from 36 to 56 centimeters, while their pendants average 30 centimeters in length. The exception is the khipu that Nieves Yucra, on the island of Taquile, keeps as a "backup" to the khipu he uses every day. The backup khipu is the largest modern khipu I encountered. Its rope pendants measure 1.20 meters in length (Mackey 1990b). There is no correlation between Type A khipu and a specific geographical area, as khipu of this type are found from the northern sierra to Lake Titicaca (see Table 13.1).

To illustrate this type I have chosen Khipu No. 9 (see Table 13.1 and Figure 13.2), which was used to count sheep raised at the Hacienda Hucapunca in the Department of Cusco. Most of the cords carry numerical symbols that use the concept of hierarchical position; that is, the symbol denoting a higher number is always placed above the lower numbers. However, Cord III is an exception to this rule (Figure 13.2).

On Cord III, a count of forty (four overhand knots) occurs at the top left under the two subsidiary cords. The groups of ten knots denoting hundreds follow in consecutive order. Since khipu were always read from left to right, this reverses the principle of the order of knot hierarchy since the lower count of forty is read first.

Although using cord thickness to denote a higher numerical value is frequently found in Type B khipu, it is not a common feature of Type A khipu.

TABLE 13.1.   Provenience of Modern Khipu Samples

Modern Khipu Collected by the Author			
No.	Provenience	Department	Type
1	Hda. Ccachupata	Cusco	B2
2	Hda. Ccachupata	Cusco	B1-c
3	Hda. Huattocto	Cusco	C
4	Micapata	Cusco	B1-b
5	Micapata	Cusco	C
6	Micapata	Cusco	A
7	Micapata	Cusco	C
8	Micapata	Cusco	B1-a
9	Hda. Hucapunca	Cusco	A
10	Ccotane	Cusco	A
11	Descanso	Cusco	B1-a
12	Sicuani	Cusco	B2
13	Descanso	Cusco	B1-a
14	Quellabamba	Cusco	B1-a
15	Quellabamba	Cusco	B1-a
16	Hda. Angasmarca	La Libertad	A
17	Hda. Angasmarca	La Libertad	C
18	Azángaro	Puno	A
19	Hda. Parque	Cusco	B2
20	Hda. Parque	Cusco	B1-a
21	Hda. Parque	Cusco	B2
22	Hda. Parque	Cusco	B2
23	Laramarca	Huancavelica	B2
24	Taquile	Puno	A
Published Khipu			
25	Núñez del Prado 1950	Cusco	B1-c
26	Núñez del Prado 1950	Cusco	B2
27	Núñez del Prado 1950	Cusco	B1-a
28	Núñez del Prado 1950	Cusco	B2
29	Núñez del Prado 1950	Cusco	B1-c
30	Núñez del Prado 1950	Cusco	B1-c
31	Núñez del Prado 1950	Cusco	B1-b
32	Núñez del Prado 1950	Cusco	B1-c
33	Núñez del Prado 1950	Cusco	B2
34	Núñez del Prado 1950	Cusco	B1-b
35	Guimaraes 1907	La Libertad	?

TABLE 13.1.   Continued

No.	Provenience	Department	Type
36	Soto Flores 1951	Huancavelica	B2
37	Soto Flores 1951	Huancavelica	B2
38	Soto Flores 1951	Huancavelica	B2
39	Cohen 1957	Cusco	B2
40	Bastian 1895	Puno	A
41	Bastian 1895	Puno	A
42	Bastian 1895	Puno	A
43	Uhle 1987	Cutusuma, Bolivia	B2

However, one cord, VI, on Khipu No. 9 (see Figure 13.2) does employ this principle. The thickest part of the cord, which is four-ply, has a knot valued at one hundred. The lower portion of this same cord is untwisted to create two thinner cords, which carry knots that have a lower numerical value.

As can be seen in Cord III (see Figure 13.2), this khipu uses a technique common to Type A: clustering ten overhand knots to represent one hundred. A colored string of either green or yellow cotton separates each group of ten knots. The man who made Khipu No. 9, Sr. Sánchez, said that clusters of tens are "easier to read." Even though he used clusters of knots, the basic concept of hierarchical numerical values is maintained except, as mentioned above, on Cord III. It is interesting to note that Cord VII shows more than ten knots in a row (cf. Salomon, Chapter 12, and Urton, Chapter 8, this book). When asked the reason for this, Sr. Sánchez said that he did not put these knots into groups of ten because each knot represented the number one. So, in his mnemonic device, overhand knots representing the number ten were clustered into groups of ten knots while overhand knots representing one were not.

Another technique was used to denote the number ten on Khipu No. 9 (see Figure 13.2). On Cord I, a loop rather than a knot is employed to indicate ten. In this case, loops act just as knots do: the higher positions of the loops on the cord correspond to a higher value (ten), while the knots below represent ones. The khipu maker said that the loops had an additional function other than their use to denote the number ten. He used loops to signal the first cord, or the starting position, of the khipu. By knowing which was the beginning cord, he remembered the number values of the knots.

This example of a Type A khipu has a feature shared with its Inka counterparts and with other modern khipu: the use of subsidiaries to change the total

330   Carol Mackey

TABLE 13.2.   Six Principles of Modern Khipu Making

Principles	A	B1-a	B1-b	B1-c	B2	C
(1) The relative position of knots on the cord	X	X	X	X	X	X
(2) The thickness of the knot to establish numerical value		X	X	X	X	X
(3) The use of clusters of ten knots to denote the numerical value of 100	X					
(4) The use of loops in place of knots	X				X	
(5) The establishment of the first cord, or beginning, of the khipu	X	X	X	X	X	X
(6) The use of accounting zones		X	X	X		

of a completed cord by addition or subtraction. Rather than untying the cord, the khipu maker adds strings with knots that will alter the total of a cord. In example No. 9 (see Figure 13.2), these small subsidiaries are made of horse hair, are attached to the main cord, and are intended to alter the totals of Cords II, III, IV, VI, and VII. The subsidiaries on Khipu No. 9 all contain one or two overhand knots, each of which is read as ten. Each subsidiary cord represents animals—in this case sheep—that have died during the year. For example, Cord IV shows a total of 208 sheep for which the shepherd had initially assumed responsibility. The subsidiary string IVa, tied onto the main cord to the left of Cord IV, indicates that twenty sheep, of the total indicated on Cord IV, died, altering the count of Cord IV to 188. The shepherd had to account to the hacienda for all the sheep that were in his care, both living and dead.

TYPE B KHIPU.   Though the Type B khipu appears to be very simple in its form, its symbolism is very complex. It is also the most common form of modern khipu, consisting of 70 percent of the sample. Type B, which I divided into two subtypes, B1 with three variants (a, b, and c) and B2, is formed by using one length of two-ply yarn, which is then doubled. When the yarn is doubled, the thicker portion at the top, composed of four plies, is knotted. This leaves the bottom portion as two loose pendant cords of two plies each (see Figure 13.3, B1-a–c).

Since Type B khipu consist of a folded length of yarn, the longest side was measured to gain some idea of pendant length. These lengths range from 12 to 58 centimeters. Type B khipu are widespread in the central Andean region and are especially popular in the Paucartambo and Sicuani areas (see Figure 13.1).

Subtype Bl-a Khipu.   The B1-a subtype adheres to the first principle shown in Table 13.2, that is, the highest number is found in the highest position on the khipu cord. Used in conjunction with this principle is the second principle: the thicker the knot, the higher the value. In Subtype B1-a khipu, the top, thicker portion carries the highest numbers. Oscar Núñez del Prado (1950: 14) first noted this feature of knot thickness on khipu he collected in the Paucartambo area, and it was later verified by the khipu I collected in the same area (Mackey 1970). This principle, however, is also found in other regions, as will be noted below.

Two other principles are used in tandem with those described above. Modern khipu makers repeatedly stated that they "read" their khipu from left

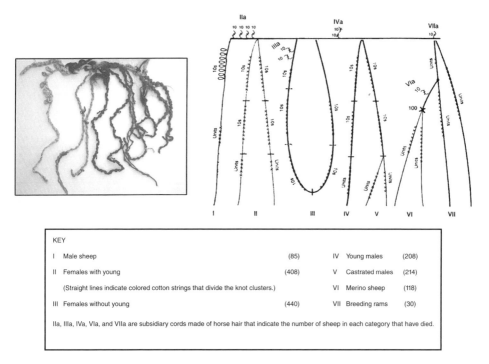

FIGURE 13.2 Example of Type A modern khipu: Khipu No. 9, count of sheep.

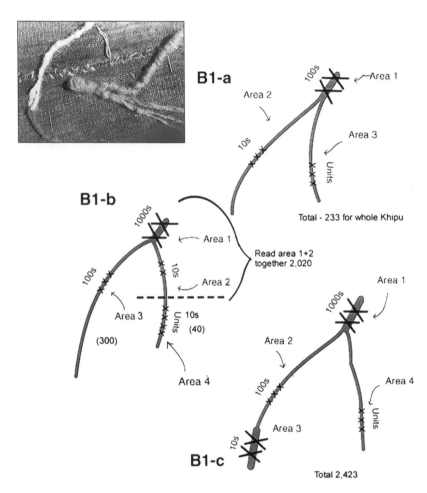

FIGURE 13.3 Example of Subtype B1 modern khipu. This type exhibits the most variation in recording and reading numbers.

to right. It is thus very important to know which is the left-hand, or starting, cord. A variety of mnemonic techniques are used to signal this cord. In Type B khipu, when the yarn is doubled, it is not doubled exactly in half, but one side is purposely kept longer than the other. The majority of khipu makers designate the longer cord as the "left" side, or starting point, of the khipu. If the khipu maker did not know the starting point, he would not be able to remember the value of the knots on either of the two pendant cords.

Subtype B1-b Khipu.   The B1-b Subtype exhibits small differences in form, but significant differences in mnemonic function from either Subtype B1-a or B1-c. Subtype B1-b registers as many as three clusters of knots on the same cord. This in itself is not notable. What *is* notable is that each cluster relates to a *separate* count of items, so that each knot cluster acts as its own pendant cord. This is an example of principle six (see Table 13.2), or what I have termed accounting zones. In this way, several items may be counted on one cord; for example, two varieties of maize are counted on a single khipu — 2,020 yellow and 340 white ears of maize (see Figure 13.3, B1-b). The khipu maker had to remember the order of the items counted and the totals for each. Although this Subtype B1-b is not common, it does illustrate a main function of modern khipu: as aids to memory. The knots and the sums they represent help the khipu maker remember the numerical value, and the order of the numerical clusters helps him remember what was being counted.

Subtype B1-c Khipu.   Subtype B1-c also carries a high number of knot clusters. This Subtype B1-c, however, is a count for a single item, such as sheep or maize. The dilemma facing the modern khipu maker is how to represent the different decimal values (units, tens, hundreds, and thousands) using only an overhand knot. The Inka khipukamayuq could at least distinguish between units and higher numbers by using the long knot for the units and the overhand knots for the higher numbers. In this modern subtype (B1-c), the khipu maker used the first principle of relative position of the knot on the cord, as well as the second principle of thickness. In the sample collected by Núñez del Prado (1950) in the Paucartambo area, thickness of the knot is used *two* times on the same cord. The Subtype B1-c khipu shown in Figure 13.3 indicates that the thick portion at the top carries the knots denoting the highest numbers (thousands), while the thick portion at the bottom of the cord denotes tens. The second cord, on the right-hand side, only records the units. Therefore, these khipu have two portions of the cord that are thicker, and they are used for the highest and second highest numbers on the khipu.

Khipu makers from other regions indicated that they knew at a glance that this subtype (B1-c) would carry a total in the thousands in spite of the fact that the principle of thickness had been violated. Their visual cue was the proliferation of knot clusters. When there were four knot clusters, one at the top as well as three other clusters on other portions of the cord, they knew automatically that the top number was in the thousands. Obviously, this works only if all decimal values are represented. This observation is noteworthy because, aside from using a cluster of ten knots to represent one hundred, this

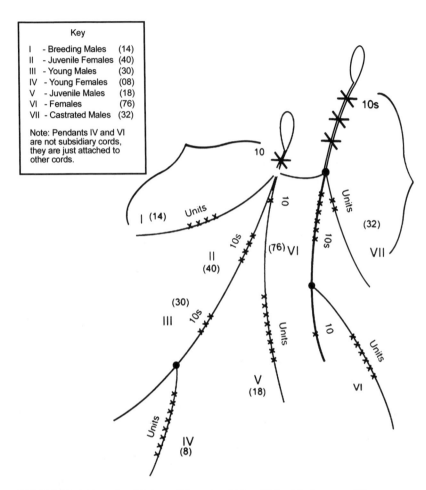

Key

	- Breeding Males	(14)
II	- Juvenile Females	(40)
III	- Young Males	(30)
IV	- Young Females	(08)
V	- Juvenile Males	(18)
VI	- Females	(76)
VII	- Castrated Males	(32)

Note: Pendants IV and VI are not subsidiary cords, they are just attached to other cords.

FIGURE 13.4 Example of Subtype B2 modern khipu: Khipu No. 1, count of llamas.

is the only other instance where the khipu maker can distinguish the values of the numbers at a glance.

Subtype B2 Khipu.   Subtype B2 refers to a khipu that is composed of two Subtype B1 khipu tied together at the top. An example of this subtype is illustrated by Khipu No. 1 (see Figure 13.4) and comes from the village of Ccollpata, Hacienda Ccachupata, in the Paucartambo area. The khipu is made of llama fiber, in both natural and dyed colors, and carries a count for llamas.

In this example, the principles of relative knot position and knot thickness are generally used to indicate higher numbers (see Table 13.2). The other distinguishing feature of this subtype is the proliferation of knot clusters on the khipu (indicated in Figure 13.4 by roman numerals). The two principles of position and thickness can be seen on Cords I and VII, on the left and right side of the khipu. The knots numbered II, III, and IV, however, illustrate the principle of accounting zones, and each cluster of knots represents a separate total of a different subclass of llamas such as young females, infant males, etc. (see key to Figure 13.4).

Although accounting zone IV resembles a subsidiary cord such as those found on Inka khipu, it does not function as such. Instead, it was meant to function as an independent pendant, with its own count. Similarly, both cords numbered VI (see Figure 13.4) are read together as one cord and represent a total of seventy-six female llamas. The reason for adding on these cords, according to the khipu maker, is that they helped him distinguish the various subclasses of llamas being counted.

In this example, cord length did not play a role in establishing the start of the khipu, because the cords on the left and right side are the same lengths. To identify the starting cord, the khipu maker focused on three features. First, he remembered that the total of the first pendant was fourteen. Second, he remembered the color of the "first" cord: brown. Finally, he recalled that the top left loop, made by doubling the cord, was at a lower position than the "right" loop. The combination of these three features—starting number, color, and relative location of a loop—provided him with a complex yet effective mnemonic device for determining the beginning of his khipu. This is an excellent example of the number of mnemonic attributes necessary to recall one fact. The khipu maker stressed that the beginning of the khipu is so important that he felt more secure with three attributes to remind him. This is also one of the few khipu that used cord color to jog the memory.

TYPE C KHIPU.   Type C is the least complex of the modern khipu, consisting of just one length of two-ply yarn that has been knotted, with no pendant cords (see Figure 13.5).

This type is found mainly in the Sicuani and Paucartambo areas and is represented by 9 percent of the sample. Only the principles of position and starting point are used in this type (see Table 13.2). As in Inka khipu, this type uses the position of the knots on the cord to indicate the knots' numerical value. Knots representing one hundred are placed closer to the beginning of the pendant and separated by a space from the knots with lower numerical numbers (see Table 13.2). Since the knots are all overhand knots, in order

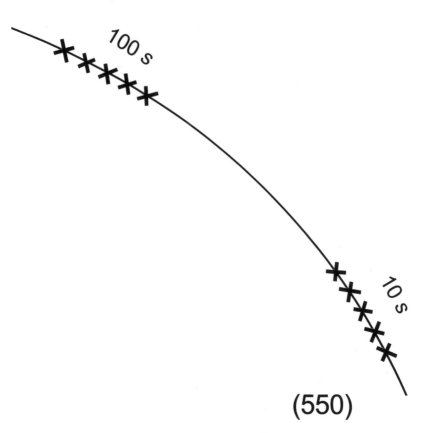

FIGURE 13.5 Example of Type C modern khipu.

to know which knot is higher, it is also necessary to determine which end of the khipu is the beginning. The makers of Type C khipu used a variety of mnemonic devices to do this. One khipu maker told me that he placed a knot with no numerical value at one end of the khipu, well away from the other knot clusters, which acted like a period at the end of a sentence. Another man commented that he always started the higher knots closer to one end and left a large space at the other end (i.e., the "bottom"). Yet another khipu maker expressed frustration with this type of khipu, saying it was impossible to remember which end to start with, so he just remembered the total number on the khipu. Why use a khipu, then, if the number is to be remembered? One possible explanation is the reason offered by so many khipu makers: that the khipu provides an enduring record of a task's performance and is tangible evidence of the khipu maker's prior position on the hacienda.

Counting to Ten and Beyond

Most modern khipu register totals of animals or produce from counts that reach well into the thousands; however, the actual counting process itself is not represented on the khipu. The objects must first be counted one by one and only then can the total be noted on the khipu. How do these khipu users keep track of the count during that process? The answer lies in some very clever innovations carried out by the khipu makers.

It should be noted that when dealing with very large herds, the herds and the responsibility to count them were often divided among several men on an hacienda. The men reported totals from their khipu to the headman, who recorded their totals on his "master," or summary, khipu. The headman then turned over his khipu to the majordomo, who wrote down the information (Mackey 1970).

Oscar Núñez del Prado (1950: 17) observed another method in the Paucartambo area that was used to count *chuño* (dehydrated potatoes). There the khipu maker had to present to the hacienda the total number of potatoes in each sack. He said that first a sack was filled, then emptied. The men counted the *chuño* that had filled the sack by taking five potatoes in each hand (ten potatoes) and putting these into groups of one hundred. Next they put the groups of one hundred into groups of one thousand. According to Núñez, this way of counting is called *layqa* in Quechua. The ethnographic reports also highlight the existence of another intermediate step carried out by the khipu makers but not recorded on the khipu in which khipu makers used grains of quinoa, kernels of maize, or pellets of dung to represent ten or one hundred. These items were then tallied and the sum was entered on the khipu cord (Mackey 1970; Núñez 1950; Wassén 1990).

Summary

Since modern khipu appear to be so idiosyncratic, it is amazing that only six principles are used, alone or in combination, to record numerical data on khipu. Although at first glance it appears that the six principles are all equally weighted, this is not the case. For example, the second principle—that knot thickness is equated with the numerical value of the knot—is mostly seen in the Type B khipu; although it is mentioned for Type A, it occurs on only one of the nine Type A khipu in the sample of forty-three.

The overriding principle that survives from Inka khipu is that knot position on the cord determines its value. Exceptions to this rule occur when modern users place the totals for separate counts on one cord, ignoring the principle of knot position. Even when the principle of position is followed, there are many modern innovations not seen in earlier khipu, such as the use of thickness to show higher value, or the clustering of ten knots to be "read" as one hundred. Many of the innovations are attempts by the modern khipu maker to distinguish one cluster of knots from another, since, unlike the Inka, modern users generally employ only the overhand knot. One of the interesting findings of this study is the complexity of the mnemonic cues for "first cord" or "left side" of a khipu; as many as three features were used to remember this cord. This was a problem also faced by ancient users, although they solved it differently. The Inka khipukamayuq used visual cues such as colored tassels to determine the beginning of the khipu or a blank space (or "tail") to denote the end of the khipu (Mackey 1970).

ENCODING THE CATEGORIES

In this final section I address one of the most difficult problems concerning the interpretation of ancient khipu. We know that each khipu cord carries a number, represented by knots, of a certain item or object. Although the encoding of the category to which the object belongs is just as important as the number, we still do not have a complete understanding of how information identifying different categories or classes of objects was encoded on Inka khipu. We can get a clearer understanding of these issues by studying modern khipu.

Counts of Produce

Most khipu that deal with produce represent totals of one kind of item, although khipu concerned with two or more items do exist. I collected three khipu from Sr. Quispe—from the Hacienda Micapata in the province of Paucartambo—that illustrate one man's use of categories. Sr. Quispe informed me that on Khipu No. 7 (a Type C khipu) he placed items within his hierarchical scheme. *Habas* (beans) were on the left side, and quinoa (grain) was on the right side. To distinguish between the two categories he used the color of the two cords. On the left side, on a cord of brown llama fiber, were eleven knots representing the eleven sacks of *habas*, and on the right side, on a cord of white llama fiber, were three knots denoting the sacks of quinoa. The second khipu, No. 8 (a Subtype B1-a khipu), was made entirely of white llama fiber. The objects counted were sacks of yellow maize on the longer, left string and sacks of white maize on the shorter, right cord. As we have seen before, length played an important role in determining the starting point, and, in this case, it also provided a mnemonic cue for distinguishing between subcategories.

Sr. Quispe's third khipu, No. 6 (Type A), is also of llama fiber and is important because it shows a number of commodities that he placed in hierarchical order. The order is as follows:

(1) The first cord is red llama fiber and represents a count of 140 sacks of potatoes.
(2) The second cord is yellow camelid fiber and represents 120 sacks of *chuño* (dehydrated potatoes).
(3) The third cord is orange llama fiber and has knots that stand for 10 sacks of *chuño* made from another kind of potato.
(4) The fourth, also of llama fiber, is green and has fourteen knots representing 14 sacks of white maize.
(5) The fifth cord is purple and has knots that stand for 30 sacks of yellow maize.

I found these three khipu to be very interesting because their maker was so emphatic about always using the same order whenever he counted. Yet he was not consistent in his hierarchy, since in Khipu No. 8 he recalled that he had placed yellow maize first, while on Khipu No. 6 he placed white maize first, followed by yellow maize. In order to determine the ranking of categories, it would have been helpful to have a larger number of khipu with counts of multiple items, but these khipu were in a minority in the sample.

Counts of Animals

In the khipu that I collected, most animal counts are of sheep rather than of llamas. This may reflect the location of my fieldwork; the khipu users that I interviewed did not live in the puna, where camelids are generally herded. The villages I visited were located between 3,000 m and 3,800 m, which tends to be more of a sheep-raising area. Several individuals on the haciendas that I visited mentioned a full-time llama "guardian," who kept his own khipu and lived at a higher elevation. My discussion in this section focuses on two examples from my collection that make use of categories for animal counts.

LLAMAS.   The two khipu that recorded camelids are Khipu No. 1 from an hacienda in the Paucartambo area (see Figure 13.4) and No. 18 from a community in Azángaro. As can be seen in Table 13.3, these two counts reflect their ranking of the ethnocategories. In spite of their different geographic

TABLE 13.3. Ethnocategories of Llamas as Represented on the Cords of
Modern Khipu

Khipu #1—Cusco (Hda. Ccachupata)		Khipu #18—Puno (Azángaro)	
Toros	Breeding bulls	*Toros*	Breeding bulls
Vaquillonas	Juvenile females	*Castrados*	Castrated bulls
Crías machos	Young males	*Crías hembras*	Young females
Crías hembras	Young females	*Madres*	Females who have given birth
Torillos	Juvenile males	*Crías machos*	Young males
Madres	Females who have given birth		
Castrados	Castrated bulls		

locations, the general ethnocategories of the two herders were similar in that
both named sires, young of both sexes, females, and gelded males. They differed in that the khipu maker in Paucartambo had another age category, that
of juveniles of both sexes.

In his 1986 study, Jorge Flores Ochoa commented on the complexity with
which some herders view the age of their animals. The life history of the animal is much more complex than its simple chronological age. As Flores points
out: "One should note that the actual number of years the animal has lived is
not thought to be decisive for determining its age. The considerations taken
into account have more to do with the quality of the range used for graz-
ing, the altitude, the number of offspring produced, illnesses, state of teeth,
quality and quantity of fleece produced, load-carrying capacity, and other
factors that may differ from one area to another. These factors are taken into
account when the time comes to separate the flocks of males from females,
to castrate the males considered unsuitable for breeding, and also to shear or
slaughter the old animals" (140).

According to Flores, the gender of the animal is based more on its reproductive history than on its sex. For example, some of the herders interviewed
by Flores (1986: 139) indicated that they did not consider a female who did
not reproduce to be in the same "gender" as a fertile female. Nevertheless,
the two examples shown in Table 13.3 do not indicate this separation.

The two khipu show a subclass of castrated male llamas. This consistency
is probably based on the behavior of the male, since llamas fight for possession of females (Flannery, Marcus, and Reynolds 1989; Flores Ochoa 1986).
Herds are not generally separated by gender, therefore one herding strategy
is to castrate a large number of the males when they are between three and

four years of age (Flannery, Marcus, and Reynolds 1989). This helps herders in several ways because the castrated animals produce better meat, produce better fiber, and can be used to haul cargo (Flores Ochoa 1986). Even though the sample of khipu is small, the responses of the khipu makers, combined with recent ethnographic studies, indicate that the criteria for age and sex among herders is very complex and does vary. Both khipu examples reflect the gelding of the males and the separation, on cords, by some age and sex criteria.

SHEEP.   Sheep were introduced to Peru in the sixteenth century. As Benjamin Orlove (1977) points out, sheep, unlike llamas, are not aggressive and the males do not fight over females, so the sexes are not separated. Even so, the khipu belonging to the shepherds that I interviewed showed the same subclasses as were noted for llamas, including castrated males. Perhaps sheep are separated for ease in counting or because this was a familiar way to keep track of herd animals, since it helps the shepherd to be aware of the flock's age and sex categories. Orlove notes that the managers of the most productive flocks are concerned with the selection of stud rams and the culling of ewes. If this selection is not done, the flock will revert to feral characteristics, resulting in a change in the quality, quantity, and color of the fleece (Orlove 1977: 209). Thus, the more detailed counts represented in the khipu could summarize these characteristics for the shepherd and the hacienda. It appears that cultural norms regarding the fertility of the females, as noted by Flores Ochoa (1986), were applied by the shepherds in my sample; females with young are recorded on a separate cord from females without lambs (Table 13.4). The llama herders I interviewed did not differentiate according to the fiber of their animals, but that distinction was made among shepherds. Of the two breeds introduced by the Spaniards in the sixteenth century—merino and churra—merino is noted for its "fine, crimpy wool" (Orlove 1977; Romero, personal communication 1997). Since this breed has a strong tendency to flock, they are easy to herd, but they are also subject to disease and have a high mortality rate. These characteristics of age, sex, reproductive capacity, and wool are demonstrated by the khipu categories shown in Table 13.4 (see also Figure 13.2).

The information contained on colonial and modern khipu demonstrates that not all khipu recorded numerical data in the same way. There were three systems of recording data: (1) some records were totals of one category, for example, 423 llamas; (2) other counts were totals of several categories, often ranked in importance, such as llamas, alpacas, and sheep; and (3) yet other

TABLE 13.4.   Ethnocategories of Sheep

Khipu #9—Cusco (Hda. Hucapunca)		Khipu #11—Cusco (Descanso)	
Machos	Males	*Madres*	Females who have given birth
Madres	Females who have given birth		
Machorras	Females without young	*Borregos*	Young males
Borregos	Young males	*Machos*	Males
Capones	Castrated males	*Crías*	Young females
Merinos	Sheep with fine wool		
Padrillos	Breeding rams	**Khipu #12—Cusco (Sicuani)**	
		Borregos	Young males
		Maltones	Young females
		Madres	Females who have given birth

counts divided a single category—llamas—into demographic classes and sub-classes, such as males, females, females with young, and so forth. The choice and order of categories within a class appear to vary by region and by individual. It is interesting, however, that some of the same categories are used by khipu makers for both llamas and sheep.

We have no direct evidence for the system used by the Inka—they may have used all three systems or just one—but colonial and modern khipu employ all three systems, and often on the same khipu (cf. Murra 1975, 1982). Modern users frequently tie or join two associated khipu together. In these instances, one khipu represents the total of a category and the other records the breakdown of the category into subclasses. Inka khipu are also found tied together, perhaps signifying the same concept.

DISCUSSION

One of the aims of this study is to use the results of modern khipu analysis to shed light on many of the unanswered problems concerning Inka khipu. Although it is obvious that there is not an unbroken continuity in the khipu tradition, nevertheless certain modern khipu practices may prove useful in interpreting the knot records of the past.

I agree with the Aschers (Ascher and Ascher 1981) and William Conklin (Chapter 3, this book) that the knots were one of the last symbols to be encoded on khipu, whether Inka, colonial, or modern. Khipu users first had to decide whether the knots would represent a total count or a finer breakdown of a category. In Inka khipu, this was accomplished by adding pendant cords to the horizontal or main cord. As we have seen, modern khipu makers did not use a large number of pendants, but often designated one pendant cord to carry several distinct totals or accounting zones, sometimes violating the principle of placing the highest number at the top of the cord.

The number of pendant cords attached to the main cord is a striking difference between ancient and modern khipu. Modern khipu rarely have more than 12 pendant cords, while ancient khipu generally have many more than this. For example, the number of cords found on the twenty-three khipu from Puruchuco ranged from 4 to 115 pendants, with the average being 40 (Mackey 1970). Why do Inka khipu have more cords? Perhaps the answer lies in the number of times per year a count was taken. On modern haciendas, counts were taken once a year, but one chronicler reports that during Inka rule, counts were made every four months (Cieza 1959). With few exceptions (Murra 1975; Ruiz Estrada 1990; Salomon 1997), colonial khipu also appear to be small, having fewer than 20 cords, perhaps because they, like modern khipu, represent fewer than three counts per year. Another reason modern khipu may be smaller than their Inka counterparts is their specificity with regard to category. Modern khipu often record the total of one category on a few cords, such as the number of sacks of maize for an entire year. On the other hand, colonial khipu include the totals of all categories of tribute, both in kind and in labor, on one khipu, so that animals, produce, and manufactured goods are all recorded together. Either of these explanations—the number of counts per year or the way numerical counts were recorded—could be plausible explanations for differences in the number of pendants used in Inka, colonial, and modern khipu.

Questions remain concerning the manner in which objects were recorded on the khipu. To the majority of modern khipu makers, color did not appear to represent the category being counted. Rather, color was more often used to signal the "first," or "left," cord of a modern khipu. The men I interviewed all agreed that a ranking of classes or subclasses took place within a category, but this ranking varied idiosyncratically, a characteristic that also applies to khipu from the colonial period.

CONCLUSION

Knotted strings or records are known from other areas of the New World where they were used to record rites of passage, such as births or deaths (Leechman and Harrington 1921); however, no other tradition of knotted records reached the complexity of Inka khipu. Although they had other functions, khipu were the primary bureaucratic tool of Inka administration for keeping accounts of human and natural resources. Khipu may have survived the turmoil of the Spanish invasion because they were transferred from an Inka bureaucracy to a similar colonial one. In the colonial period, khipu continued to be used to record tribute, mainly in labor or in kind, given by the indigenous people to the representatives of the Spanish Crown. Modern khipu were also bureaucratic in nature, but they were linked not to the state but to another hierarchical institution: the hacienda. Since 1968, and the onset of agrarian reform in Peru, the use of the khipu has slowly disappeared.

Modern khipu differ as much from one another as they do from Inka examples. The high number of idiosyncratic, mnemonic devices used to register numerical value in modern khipu is directly related to the fact that no standard numerical system exists for them. In contrast, khipu in Inka times were much more standardized.

In this chapter I have analyzed modern khipu according to their morphological traits and placed them into three types. Only Type A mimics the form of Inka khipu; the other two modern types are not found in the archaeological record. Since modern khipu generally use just one knot type—the overhand knot—six mnemonic principles are employed to give numerical value to the knots. These are: (1) the relative position of knots on the cord; (2) the thickness of the knot to establish numerical value; (3) the use of clusters of ten knots to denote one hundred; (4) the use of loops in place of knots; (5) the establishment of the first cord, or beginning, of the khipu; and (6) accounting zones. These principles are used to varying degrees and in different combinations, generally dyads or triads, on the three khipu types. For example, the second principle, the use of a thicker knot to establish numerical value, is most characteristic of Type B khipu, especially those from the Paucartambo area. The third principle, the use of clusters of ten knots to denote one hundred, is found only on Types A and C. The most important principle employed in Inka as well as on all types of modern khipu is the relative position of the knot on the cord as an indicator of value; that is, knots placed higher on the cord have a higher numerical value. Another surviving feature of Inka khipu is the use of subsidiary cords. These appendages follow the Inka concept of altering the numerical count of a pendant cord by indicating values to be added to or subtracted from the total count. Modern subsidiaries, however, do not resemble their Inka counterparts in form, as they are often attached to the main or horizontal cord and rarely to the cord they alter.

Although knots and their numerical value receive the most attention in khipu discussions, it is just as important to consider the symbols used to encode the identity of the items being counted. It has been suggested that the color of the khipu cord symbolized the objects or categories counted on Inka khipu; in modern khipu, however, although cords are dyed, cord color is rarely used to denote the categories that are counted. In modern khipu, classes and subclasses of a category are represented by other mnemonic means—such as the use of loops rather than knots, cord length, and an individual's hierarchical order of classes and subclasses. Both colonial and modern khipu demonstrate a hierarchical ranking of items, but the extant documents referring to colonial khipu and the modern examples in my sample do not reveal a universal hierarchical order. This study aims to clarify the principles and practices of khipu record keeping in the modern Andes as a basis for rethinking earlier—colonial and pre-Columbian—principles and practices.

BIBLIOGRAPHY

Ascher, Marcia, and Robert Ascher. 1969. "Cords (Quipus)." *Nature* 222: 529–533.
———. 1981. *Code of the Quipu.* Ann Arbor: University of Michigan Press.
Bastian, Adolph. 1895. "Aus Briefen Herrn Dr. Uhle's." *Ethnologisches Notizblatt* (Berlin) 1: 80–83.
Betanzos, Juan de. 1987 [1551]. *Suma y narración de los Incas.* Transcription, notes, and prologue by María del Carmen Martín Rubio. Madrid: Ediciones Atlas.
Boone, Elizabeth H. 1994. "Introduction: Writing and Recording Knowledge." In *Writing without Words: Alternative Literacies in Mesoamerica and the Andes,* edited by E. H. Boone and W. D. Mignolo, 3–26. Durham: Duke University Press.
Calancha, Antonio de la. 1976 [1638]. *Crónica moralizada del orden de San Agustín en el Perú con sucesos ejemplares en esta monarquía.* Barcelona: N.p.
Cieza de León, Pedro de. 1959 [1553]. *The Incas.* Translated by Harriet de Onis; edited by Victor W. Von Hagen. Norman: University of Oklahoma Press.
Cohen, John. 1957. "Q'eros: A Study in Survival." *Natural History* 66, no. 9: 482–493.
Conklin, William J. 1982. "The Information System of Middle Horizon Quipus." In *The Annals of the New York Academy of Sciences,* edited by Anthony Aveni and Gary Urton, 261–282. New York: New York Academy of Sciences.
Flannery, Kent V., Joyce Marcus, and Robert Reynolds. 1989. *The Flocks of the Wamani: A Study of Llama Herders on the Punas of Ayacucho, Peru.* New York: Academic Press.
Flores Ochoa, Jorge A. 1979. *Pastoralists of the Andes.* Translated by Ralph Bolton. Philadelphia: Ishi.
———. 1986. "The Classification and Naming of South American Camelids." In *Anthropological History of Andean Polities,* edited by John V. Murra, Nathan Wachtel, and Jacques Revel, 137–148. Cambridge: Cambridge University Press.
Guaman Poma de Ayala, Felipe. 1956 [1587–1615]. *El primer nueva corónica y buen gobierno.* Lima: Editorial Cultural.
Guimaraes, Enrique. 1907. "Algo sobre los quipus." *Revista Histórica* (Lima) 2: 55–62.
Julien, Catherine J. 1991. *Condesuyo: The Political Division of Territory under Inca and Spanish Rule.* Bonn: BAS 19.

Leechman, J. D., and M. R. Harrington. 1921. *String Records of the Northwest.* New York: Museum of the American Indian, Heye Foundation.

Locke, L. Leland. 1923. *The Ancient Quipu or Peruvian Knot Record.* New York: American Museum of Natural History.

Mackey, Carol J. 1970. "Knot Records in Ancient and Modern Peru." Ph.D. dissertation, Department of Anthropology, University of California, Berkeley.

———. 1990a. "Comparación entre quipu inca y quipus modernos." In *Quipu y yupana: Colección de escritos,* edited by Carol Mackey et al., 135–156. Lima: Consejo Nacional de Ciencia y Tecnología.

———. 1990b. "Nieves Yucra Huatta y la continuidad en la tradición del uso del quipu." In *Quipu y yupana: Colección de escritos,* edited by Carol Mackey et al., 157–164. Lima: Consejo Nacional de Ciencia y Tecnología.

Murra, John V. 1965. "Herds and Herders in the Inca State." In *Man, Culture, and Animals: The Role of Animals in Human Ecological Adjustments,* edited by Anthony Leeds and Andrew Veyada, 185–215. Washington, D.C.: American Association for the Advancement of Science.

———. 1975. "Las etno-categorías de un *khipu* estatal." In *Formaciones económicas y políticas del mundo andino,* by John Murra, 243–254. Lima: Instituto de Estudios Peruanos.

———. 1982. "The Mit'a Obligation of Ethnic Groups to the Inca State." In *The Inca and Aztec States: 1400–1800: Anthropology and History,* edited by George Collier, Renato Rosaldo, and John Wirth. New York: Academic Press.

Nordenskiöld, Erland von. 1925. "The Secret of the Peruvian Quipus." *Comparative Ethnographical Studies* (Goteburg) 6, pt. 1: 3–37, pt. 2: 3–36.

Núñez del Prado, Oscar. 1950. "El *kipu* moderno." *Tradición,* Revista Peruana de Cultura (Cusco) 1, vol. 2, nos. 3–6.

Orlove, Benjamin S. 1977. *Alpacas, Sheep, and Men: The Wool Export Economy and Regional Society in Southern Peru.* New York: Academic Press.

Pease, Franklin. 1990. "Utilización de quipus en los primeros tiempos coloniales." In *Quipu y yupana: Colección de escritos,* edited by Carol Mackey et al., 67–72. Lima: Consejo Nacional de Ciencia y Tecnología.

Prochaska, Rita G. 1988. *Taquile: Tejiendo un mundo mágico.* Lima: Arius.

Radicati di Primeglio, Carlos. 1950. "Introducción al estudio de los quipus." *Documenta* (Lima), no. 2: 244–339.

Rappaport, Joanne. 1994. "Object and Alphabet: Andean Indians and Documents in the Colonial Period." In *Writing without Words: Alternative Literacies in Mesoamerica and the Andes,* edited by E. H. Boone and W. D. Mignolo, 271–291. Durham: Duke University Press.

Rostworowski, Maria. 1990. "Los *kipu* en la planificación inca." In *Quipu y yupana: Colección de escritos,* edited by Carol Mackey et al., 59–66. Lima: Consejo Nacional de Ciencia y Tecnología.

Ruiz Estrada, Arturo. 1990. "Notas sobre un quipu de la costa nor-central del Perú." In *Quipu y yupana: Colección de escritos,* edited by Carol Mackey et al., 191–194. Lima: Consejo Nacional de Ciencia y Tecnología.

Salomon, Frank. 1997. "Los quipus y libros de la Tupicocha de hoy: Un informe preliminar." In *Arqueología, antropología e historia en los Andes: Homenaje a Maria Rost-*

worowski, edited by Rafael Varon Gabai and Javier Flores Espinoza, 241–258. Lima: Instituto de Estudios Peruanos.

Soto Flores, Froilán. 1950–1951. "Los kipus modernos de la comunidad de Laramarca." *Revista del Museo Nacional* (Lima) 19–20: 299–306.

Stevenson, William Bennett. 1825. *Twenty Years Residence in South America.* Vol. 2. London: Hurst, Robinson.

Uhle, Max. 1897. "A Modern Quipu from Cutusuma, Bolivia." *Bulletin of the Museum of Science and Art of Pennsylvania* (Philadelphia) 1, no. 2: 51–63.

Wassén, Henry. 1990. "El antiguo ábaco peruano según el manuscrito de Guaman Poma." In *Quipu y yupana: Colección de escritos,* edited by Carol Mackey et al., 205–234. Lima: Consejo Nacional de Ciencia y Tecnología.

CONTRIBUTORS

Marcia Ascher, Emerita Professor of Mathematics, Department of Mathematics & Computer Science, Ithaca College

Robert Ascher, Professor of Anthropology, Department of Anthropology, Cornell University

William J Conklin, Research Associate, The Textile Museum, Washington, D.C.

Regina Harrison, Professor of Comparative Literature, Professor of Latin American Literatures, and Affiliate Professor of Anthropology, University of Maryland

Rosaleen Howard, Senior Lecturer, Institute of Latin American Studies, University of Liverpool

Sabine P. Hyland, Assistant Professor of Anthropology, Department of Anthropology, St. Norbert College, De Pere, Wisconsin

Carol Mackey, Professor Emerita in Anthropology, Department of Anthropology, California State University Northridge

Tristan Platt, Reader in Anthropology and Amerindian Studies, School of Philosophical and Anthropological Studies, University of St. Andrews, Fife, Scotland

Jeffrey Quilter, Director of Pre-Columbian Studies and Curator, Pre-Columbian Collection, Dumbarton Oaks, Washington, D.C.

Frank Salomon, Professor of Anthropology, Department of Anthropology, University of Wisconsin–Madison

Carlos Sempat Assadourian, Professor, Centro de Estudios Históricos, El Colegio de México

Gary Urton, Dumbarton Oaks Professor of Pre-Columbian Studies, Harvard University

ceque, 30, 46, 126–127
Cera, R., 152
Cereceda, V., 230
ceremonies, 133, 140n.6, 163; khipu
    records of, 16
cesto, 236, 242, 255
Chachapoyas, 153, 157, 176, 194n.9
Charcas, 227, 231, 232, 260n.6. *See also*
    Charka
Charka, 231, 232, 239, 251, 260n.6
chasqui, 55, 142n.32, 210, 211
Chayanta, 161n.22
Chayantaka, 234
Checa, 294, 295, 296, 309
Chichas, 232
chinu, 3, 226, 228, 231, 260n.1; of coca,
    244–245, 254–256, 257; code of, 246;
    numerical, 257; Sakaka, 235–238;
    types, 243. *See also* khipu
chinukamana, 228, 234, 235, 237, 240,
    244, 250–251. *See also* khipukamayuq
Christ, 163
Christianity, 12, 136, 137, 155, 164, 267,
    285
chronology, 4, 68, 78; of khipu use,
    198–199, 202, 300–302
Chuis, 232
chullpa, 261n.13
chuño, 238, 337
Chupaycho, 231
chuta, 297
Chuta Cara, 309
Cieza de León, P. de, 7, 120, 121, 126,
    140n.4, 230, 259, 343
cipher, 192n.2
Cipriani, L., 152
coast: of Peru, 60
Cobo, Bernabé, 16, 135–136; on khipu
    reading, 17, 201, 202, 229, 231
coca, 228, 236, 237, 240, 242; khipu of
    deliveries of, 244–245; Memorial of,
    254. *See also chinu*
Cochabamba, 232, 233, 234
code, 128, 138; numeric, 131; transmis-
    sion of, in telegraphy, 205–206
Coe, M. D., xixn.1, 13, 198

Cohen, J., 326, 329
Collao, 260n.6
Collca, 298, 316n.8
color, 14, 15, 70; of accounting stones,
    247; bands, 308, 312, 329; of ele-
    ments of the universe, 162; of fleece,
    341; loss of meaning of, 136; of ma-
    terial, 60, 63; as mnemonic, 335; of
    Moro-urco, 64; paired with number,
    109–110; organization of strings by,
    95, 97, 101, 108; relation to ply, 75;
    in signing sins, 271, 275, 279–281; in
    signs, 128; of strings and herd ani-
    mals, 146n.85; symbolism of, 124,
    128, 129–130, 280–281, 339, 343, 345;
    symbolism of, in Chinchero, 281;
    in Tupicocha khipu, 303–304, 308,
    311–312; variegated, 72, 73, 131
communication: by telegraphy, 206;
    theory of, 80
computer, 81–82, 221n.2, 278; languages,
    207
Concha, 294
Condori Mamani, G., 30
confession: use of khipu in, 12–13, 138,
    139, 268–269, 271–278, 282–284;
    sacrament of, 278
Conklin, H., 161, 168n.15
Conklin, W., 198, 225, 280, 310, 320, 342
construction: chronology of, 66; of
    khipu, 59, 110; sequence of, 57
corn, 140n.7; used in accounting, 124
cotton: color of, 60, 63; khipu of, 60–62
Coulmas, F., 106
counting, 337; in Andean hunting, 226;
    and Near-East, 214; of produce, 338–
    339; related to pictographs, 217; sins,
    276
Covarrubias, S. de, 193n.3
cue, 131, 134, 190
cult: Pachacamac, 162
culture hero, 168n.16
cumbi, 240, 261n.13
Cumis, J. A., 152, 226
Cummins, T., 11, 17, 27, 106, 167n.13,
    184, 288n.3

prayer: use of khipu in, 137
price, 216, 242, 243, 247, 249; *chinu* of, 252–253
priest, 271–272, 277, 282, 287, 294; role of, in confession, 277. *See also amauta*
primary cord, 63, 66, 71, 122, 131, 302, 325
Prochaska, R. G., 326
province, 120, 129; khipu of, 123
puna, 136
Purua, 166n.9
Puruchuco, 324, 343
pyramid, 298

Qaraqara, 231, 232–233
Quechua, 26–27, 172, 175, 182; catechism, 145n.73, 153; documents written in, 190; examiner of, 270; Huamalíes, 27, 42, 47n.2; as lingua franca, 203; numbers, 83; numerical ontology, 191; as sacred language, 162, 176; Southern Peruvian, 56; structure of, 82–83
quillca, 143n.44
Quilter, J., 11, 199
quipo. *See* khipu
quipu de canuto, 62
Quipocamayos, 145n.66, 146n.76, 156, 254; display of, 298–300; in Tupicocha, 293. *See also* khipukamayuq
Quito, 155, 157, 158, 165, 240; history of, 146n.76; khipu in, 159; observation of equinox in, 162

Radicati di Primeglio, C., 11, 62, 142n.31, 143n.44, 228, 310
radiocarbon dating, 301
rank, 64, 339, 341, 343, 345; signed by *tocapu*, 221n.3
Rappaport, J., 17, 28, 288n.3, 321
rationalization, 28, 45
reading, 133; khipu, 59, 83, 228, 331–332; relation to speech, 182–183
rebus, 132, 226, 230
reciprocity, 80–81
recollection, 27, 41

redundancy, 110
registers, 192n.2
religion: Inka, 165; and khipu records, 136
remembering, 120; in Quechua narrative, 27, 29–30, 46; sins, with khipu, 278
repartimiento, 233
re-ply, 70, 71
rhythm. *See* structure, rhythmic
Ricoeur, Paul, 28
ritual of ayllu, 297
Rivero, M., 147n.94
Rivero y Ustáriz, M., 136
Rivet, P., 152
road, 62
Rodríguez, G., 7
rosary, 54, 267, 284–285; in Guaman Poma drawings, 285
Rosenblat, A., 192n.1
Rosetta Stone, 106
Rosny, Leon de, 18, 152, 166n.1
Rossi, P., 152
Rostworowski, M., 7, 8, 302, 321
Roussakis, V., 63
Rowe, A. P., 221n.3
Rowe, J. H., 8, 107, 126, 168n.16, 221n.3
royalty, 135
Ruiz Estrada, A., 295, 326, 343

Sacaca, 7, 227, 233, 234
sacrifice, 67
Salomon, F., 18, 48n.12, 83, 194n.12, 293, 326, 343
Sampson, G., 105, 179
Sangro, Raimondo di, 18, 151–152, 160–161
Santa Cruz Pachacuti, J. de, 133, 143n.40
Santo Tomás, D. de, 134, 140n.7, 143n.44
Sarmiento de Gamboa, P., 8, 267
Schmandt-Besserat, D., 213–215, 217–218, 315
script, 203; in khipu, 227
secondary cord, 66–67, 73–74, 78. *See also* subsidiary
secretaries, khipukamayuq as, 200